FOREIGN INVESTMENTS IN INDIA

FOREIGN
INVESTMENTS
IN INDIA

MICHAEL KIDRON

LONDON
OXFORD UNIVERSITY PRESS
NEW YORK   BOMBAY
1965

Oxford University Press, Amen House, London E.C.4

GLASGOW NEW YORK TORONTO MELBOURNE WELLINGTON
BOMBAY CALCUTTA MADRAS KARACHI LAHORE DACCA
CAPE TOWN SALISBURY NAIROBI IBADAN
KUALA LUMPUR HONG KONG

Printed in Great Britain
by Ebenezer Baylis and Son, Limited
The Trinity Press, Worcester, and London

PREFACE

THE nature of foreign private business investment in India has altered radically since Independence. Its volume, its fields of interest, its typical organizational forms have all changed, sometimes beyond recognition. It is the direction and outcome of these changes that constitute the substance of this book.

Part I presents a rough profile of foreign business investment about the time of Independence and some of the factors which made change necessary. Part II deals with the changing relations between the three wings of the modern sector—foreign private, domestic private, and domestic state capital—since then; Part III with foreign private capital as it is evolving; and Part IV outlines, briefly, some of the economic and social corollaries for India.

Dealing with concepts and relationships that enjoy, at best, a twilight existence in the world of official statistics, and with a topic not often subjected to disinterested scrutiny, this book has had to range widely for its detail. If violence to the truth in this or that particular has ensued, let me apologize now. The larger features have escaped unharmed, I trust. This I owe to the knowledge and generosity of the many friends and colleagues in India and at home who have helped at every stage of the work. Some may not be recalled from the anonymity of their official positions—in the United Kingdom Board of Trade, the UK Trade Commissions in India, the very many Government of India Ministries, Agencies, Commissions, and other bodies, the foreign missions in New Delhi, or wherever. Others have spoken in the name of their firms, for which thanks are due especially to Associated Electrical Industries, Birla Brothers, Booker Brothers McConnell and Co., British American Tobacco Co., Burmah Oil Co., Burmah Shell Oil Storage and Distributing Co. of India, Carborundum Universal, Chartered Bank, The Commonwealth Development Finance Co., Dastur and Co., General Electric Co., Imperial Chemical Industries, Industrial Credit and Investment Corporation of India, Investment Corporation of India, James Warren and Co., Joseph Lucas, Lloyds Bank, Mahindra and Mahindra, Metal Box Co., Paterson and Co., Place, Siddons and Gough, Premier Tyres, Shell International Petroleum Co., the Shri Ram group, Tata and Sons, Tata Iron and Steel Co., TI and M

v

Sales, the TVS group, Tube Investments, Vickers, Unilever, and West Coast Paper. Yet others have spoken in the name of their associations, of which the Bengal Chamber of Commerce, the Bombay Chamber of Commerce, the Employers' Federation of India, the Federation of Indian Chambers of Commerce and Industry, the India, Pakistan and Burma Association, and the Indian Tea Association proved to be especially valuable. And there are many that have helped in a personal capacity, amongst whom Vera Anstey, Charles Bettelheim, Ygael Gluckstein, Nigel Harris, R. K. Hazari, A. S. B. Olver, K. N. Raj, K. S. Shelvankar, Daniel Thorner, and Maurice Zinkin have read the manuscript in its entirety and commented at length and persuasively; and George Carvelho has commented on parts of it. I am grateful also to Richard Kempshall who kindly checked the Tables. I owe an especial debt to A. S. B. Olver not only for criticizing the manuscript firmly but for sustaining the project in innumerable ways from its inception, and to Sachin Chaudhuri who never faltered as an introduction to both the economy and the economists of India. Much of what is new in the book is due to the efforts of library staffs, particularly those of The Royal Institute of International Affairs and the Indian High Commission in London, and more particularly to the indefatigable Winifred Thorne, Chief Librarian at the High Commission, without whose efforts Indian studies would be very much leaner than they are.

The study was undertaken at the instance of The Royal Institute of International Affairs whose patience and generosity never flagged even when the writing overran its allotted span, and who made possible a lengthy and fruitful visit to India. Thanks are also due to the Bank of England's Houblon-Norman Fund for a timely grant, and to the British Council, the Indian University Grants Commission, and the Centre of Advanced Study, University of Bombay, for jointly financing a further trip.

Throughout, I have used *state* to denote the Central administration and *State* to denote Provincial administration; minister to denote Union Minister unless otherwise stated; and *foreign* and *foreign-controlled*, *Indian* and *Indian-controlled* interchangeably. I have used the Indian numeration *lakh* (one hundred thousand) and *crore* (ten million).

London, 1965　　　　　　　　　　　　　MICHAEL KIDRON

ABBREVIATIONS

ACCI	Associated Chambers of Commerce and Industry
A-IMO	All-India Manufacturers' Organization
CSO	Central Statistical Organization
FICCI	Federation of Indian Chambers of Commerce and Industry
IBRD	International Bank for Reconstruction and Development
IFC	Industrial Finance Corporation
INC	Indian National Congress
NIDC	National Industrial Development Corporation
[N]PC	[National] Planning Commission
STC	State Trading Corporation

Abbreviations of newspapers and periodicals may be found in the list of References, pp. 333–49.

CONTENTS

PART II—INDIAN AND FOREIGN CAPITAL

3. HOSTILITY

PART III—THE FOREIGN SECTOR TODAY

5. SCOPE AND IMPORTANCE OF FOREIGN INVESTMENT

6. BEHAVIOUR OF FOREIGN CAPITAL

PART IV—CONCLUSIONS

7. THE COST TO INDIA

LIST OF TABLES

PART I

EMPIRE AND DECLINE

CHAPTER ONE

EMPIRE

I FOREIGN CAPITAL

(a) *Distribution and domination:* With Independence, India became host to a large body of foreign capital. It was three-quarters British, almost entirely privately-owned, and still fairly typical of business investment in a colonial economy. Characteristically, it concentrated on extractive industries and processing for export, on international trade, and on ancillary services. At the first official count, less than a year after Independence, a little over one quarter was in tea and jute which together made up half India's exports; 17 per cent in trading; finance and management accounted for about 8 per cent; and utilities (electricity mainly) and transport (shipping mainly) for about 6 per cent each. No more than one-fifth was invested in manufacturing other than jute.[1]

Although much of the detail changed, the over-all distribution of foreign investment remained remarkably constant through two world wars and the intervening depression. An estimate for 1914–15 allocated 35 per cent of foreign-owned paid-up capital operating wholly in India to tea and jute exports.[2] Were all foreign capital included, particularly shipping and trading, the proportion would have been more like the later one. In 1930, the bulk of British investment was thought to be in 'tea, jute, cotton, mining, timber, leather, shipping, railways, agriculture, engineering, insurance, banking, and in general all forms of export and import trade'.[3]

Characteristically, foreign capital dominated its chosen fields. It is not easy to unscramble foreign and domestic capital and even more difficult to determine when ownership becomes control.[4] Yet the

[1] From sources as in Table 11, p. 243 below.
[2] D. H. Buchanan, *The Development of Capitalistic Enterprise in India*, p. 154. References are given in full, pp. 333 ff. below.
[3] Associated Chambers of Commerce of India and Ceylon, Memorandum to the Indian Statutory (Simon) Commission, Vol. XVII, Part II of the *Evidence*, p. 108.
[4] The Associated Chambers thought the first 'almost impossible' since 'foreign companies floated and managed by British managing agencies are frequently

3

broad outlines are reasonably clear—and agreed. Foreign units were invariably—and quite naturally—the largest and most influential in any industry. In 1926–7 companies registered abroad averaged eighteen times the paid-up capital of companies registered in India.[1] As late as 1944 and taking Indian-dominated industries only, the average foreign cotton mill employed 3,300 workers as against 1,800 for an Indian mill; the average foreign leather works 3,800 as against 110; the average paper mill 1,900 as against 600; and the average sugar press 690 as against 550.[2]

More conclusive was the fact that foreign investments in shared industries far outweighed anything the Indian investor could put up for a very long time. In 1949–50, 85 per cent of the area planted to tea was still foreign-controlled as was more than half the paid-up capital in plantation industries generally;[3] foreign control in jute was variously estimated at between 70 and 95 per cent.[4] Wool and hides were 80 per cent foreign in 1945;[5] coal, 71 per cent in 1944[6] or 65–75 per cent in an official estimate for 1948;[7] other mining, 73 per cent in the late forties;[8] and gold and magnesium mining entirely so.[9] The service industries were as tightly held: inland steamer services were 85 per cent British in 1945[10] and overseas shipping a complete foreign monopoly until the end of 1946.[11] As late as 1951–2, 34–39 per cent of imports and 37–44 per cent of exports were handled by foreign firms; and more than two-thirds of import and export trade financing by the foreign 'exchange' banks,[12] while very nearly half (47 per cent)

---

owned to a very large extent by Indians. Similarly, in many companies generally regarded as Indian, a considerable number of the shareholders may be British.' (ibid.) The second is discussed in Chapter 6 (pp. 285 ff. below).

[1] From Buchanan, *Capitalistic Enterprise in India*, p. 153.

[2] From Gokhale Institute, *Notes on the Rise of the Business Communities in India*, Table 8, p. 21.

[3] ibid., Table 7, p. 20; p. 45.

[4] ibid., Tables 5 and 7, pp. 10 and 20; H. V. Kamath, MP, cited in *Economic Weekly*, 1 September 1951, p. 843; *The Times*, 9 October 1958; S. Sarma, *Foreign Investments in India*, p. 28.

[5] Sarma, loc. cit.   [6] Gokhale Institute, op. cit., p. 22.

[7] *Capital*, 29 April 1948, cited in D. K. Rangnekar, *Poverty and Capital Development in India*, p. 89n.

[8] H. V. Kamath, loc. cit.   [9] Gokhale Institute, op. cit., p. 6.

[10] Sarma, op. cit., p. 28.

[11] M. A. Master, 'The Merchant Shipping Bill', *Transport*, April 1958, reprinted in *Indian Ship*, p. 93.

[12] 'Survey of Distribution of Imports and Exports Between Indian and non-Indian Firms in 1951 and 1952', (Reserve Bank of India, *Bulletin*, February 1954, p. 101).

of non-life insurance business written direct in the country was in foreign hands.[1]

These sectors were interrelated and mutually complementary. Indeed they grew out of one another. While this alone would have strengthened foreign dominance in each, the whole was substantially reinforced by the unique system of business organization that evolved in the country and became its most characteristic form—the managing agency.[2]

(b) *Managing agency:* Management contracts between British companies and Anglo-Indian merchants—as resident British traders were then called—first became known in the eighteen-thirties when the East India Company's monopoly of trade ended. In the forties the sea passage between the two countries was regularized and speeded up, and in the fifties India began to attract a flood of British capital for her first railway boom. The merchants had a unique opportunity to branch out from export *trading* into *production* for exports if only they could acquire new funds; for their part, London and Liverpool houses would supply capital if only they could find reliable management able to cope with alien conditions at the end of what was still, despite improvement, a long and erratic line of communication.

As they grew popular, these Agreements assumed a form which outlasted the flow of outside capital. They generally provided for the managing agency to be represented on the board of directors of a joint firm, no matter what proportion of the capital it held; and for one of its partners to act, *ex officio*, as chairman of the board. The agency would receive a percentage of turnover or of profits, a commission on purchases or sales, and a 'head office allowance' for its services; it would normally expect to receive interest on loans advanced and various other fees. In practice, it became the decisive partner, so much so that companies managed by foreign-controlled managing agencies are officially considered to be foreign-controlled whatever the ownership.[3]

Since their remuneration and representation were not specifically related to the amount of money they had put up, and since Agreements were entered into for a score or so years at a time, were often

[1] United Nations Conference on Trade and Development, *Insurance Costs in the Balance of Payments of Developing Countries*, Appendix II, p. 12.

[2] For the importance of the system in the mid-fifties, see Raj K. Nigam, *Managing Agencies in India*, pp. 3–5, 14, 35–48.

[3] See below, p. 274 n. 2.

irrevocable, normally inherited, and always alienable, the agencies had every incentive to accumulate them, withdrawing funds from established ventures to do so. On the eve of the Second World War the sixty-one foreign agencies were managing more than 600 rupee companies in addition to a number of sterling ones. Some were well above average: of the ten major British houses or groups, Andrew Yule managed 59, Bird-Heilger 37, Martin Burn 34, Begg Sutherland 27, Duncan and Octavius Steel 25 each, McLeod, Gillanders Arbuthnot, and Shaw Wallace 22 each, and Jardine Henderson 20.[1] These were not large accumulations of small companies. On the contrary, they were all among the seventeen 'top' managing agencies active in 1954–5;[2] they accounted for two-fifths of the number of large companies (with paid-up capital of Rs 50 lakhs and above) managed by public managing agencies.[3] Andrew Yule, Bird-Heilger, and Martin Burn were among the ten largest groups in the country in 1951,[4] and so on.

Given the narrowness of markets, sizes of this order implied an amazing diversity of interests: of the ten houses mentioned, only Duncan was managing companies in under three industries on the eve of the Second World War; Andrew Yule, at the other extreme, had eighteen companies in tea, fifteen in coal mining, eleven in jute, two in jute-pressing, three in shipping, and one each in electricity, engineering, soft drinks, paper, finance, flour-milling and a number of other spheres. The average number of industries straddled by the ten was seven, the median number five.[5]

Diversification was not a random process. From the start the lack of modern industry encouraged the agencies to seek self-sufficiency, each developing its own sources of raw materials, its own services, and a substantial market within its own operations. Martin Burn's steel output went largely into their railway engineering workshop which serviced their large railway interests, alternatively into their constructional engineering activities which found further support in their cement interests, and so on. Andrew Yule's jute mills required

---

[1] From A. K. Banerji, *India's Balance of Payments*, Appendixes B and C, pp. 210–25.

[2] Nigam, op. cit., Statement 13, pp. 50–55. By then three or four had become Indian-controlled (see Appendix I, p. 323, below).

[3] ibid., Statement 19, pp. 65–66.

[4] R. K. Hazari, *The Structure of the Corporate Private Sector*, Table 4.3, pp. 23–25. By 1951 Martin Burn was probably Indian-controlled.

[5] from Banerji, loc. cit.

electricity and coal supplies which in turn required engineering facilities, transport, and the host of ancillary materials and services to be found within that complex. Parry's went from bonemeal to phosphates, and then through sulphuric acid to super-phosphates; to plain jars to hold the acid and from there to pottery, sanitary ware, and crockery. To some degree they all showed a similar pattern.[1]

For much the same reasons they were as diversified in function. Since their companies developed ahead of modern banking, as was the case in cotton, jute, tea, and coal, for example, the managing agency turned banker providing short, medium, and long-term credit with a minimum of fuss.[2] They acted as underwriters, brokers, and guarantors, relying on closely associated finance and insurance companies to do so; they were technical and investment consultants to their companies, recruiting agents and much else. In short, by using their own resources flexibly and without too much regard for form they managed to compensate to some extent for the dearth of economic and social overheads and institutions, and for the scarcity of capital and skills, which hampered early investments in India. In doing so they contributed a great deal to the self-sufficiency and interlocking character of the foreign sector as a whole.

(c) *Interlocking character:* Two further contributions were made by the widespread interpenetration of personnel and interests within the foreign sector and the formation of exclusive foreign trade associations.

The first is well documented. M. M. Mehta shows that 55 top directors shared 809 directorships in foreign-controlled companies at the beginning of the fifties. Of these 171 were in jute, 125 in coal, 34 in cotton, 33 in sugar, 16 in banking, 14 in insurance, 31 in investment houses, 88 in power and electricity, and 297 in other industries. At the apex there were ten men with 300 directorships between them.[3] These multiple directorships crossed managing agency lines and provided some of the links between them: the eight leading foreign

[1] S. K. Basu, *The Managing Agency System, in Prospect and Retrospect*, pp. 33–36 gives a number of examples. Hilton Brown traces the diversification of Parry in some detail: *Parry's of Madras*, pp. 139 ff.

[2] As late as 1935, the senior partner in Andrew Yule affirmed his own and other companies' independence of banks for financing their widespread operations (P. S. Lokanathan, *Industrial Organization in India*, pp. 217–18).

[3] M. M. Mehta, *Combination Movement in Indian Industry*, Table IX, pp. 30–32.

directors with a total of 233 directorships, held 58 in the Martin Burn group of companies, 36 in the Bird group, 18 in Heilger's, 14 in Andrew Yule's, 11 in McLeod's, 10 in Jardine Henderson's, 9 in Octavius Steel's, 7 each in Shaw Wallace's and Macneill and Barry's, 5 in Gillanders Arbuthnot's, and 58 in companies managed by smaller agencies.[1]

Though less well documented the exclusiveness of foreign trade and commercial associations was as pronounced in practice. It started early:

> To return to Madras in 1836 [writes Parry's chronicler]; in that year, on the 29th of September, at a 'largely attended meeting' at Binny's in Armenian Street, the Madras Chamber of Commerce was founded. . . . The Governor Sir Frederick Adam, while giving the new Chamber his blessing, expressed dissatisfaction at the absence of the 'principal native merchants'; the Chamber was able to reply that only two of these gentlemen had expressed a wish to be admitted and these had been admitted. In 1936 in the year of the Chamber's centenary there were still, by a curious coincidence, only two Indian members. . . .[2]

The absence of Indians was not, in fact, coincidental. While not debarred from membership in so many words, the workings and atmosphere of the foreign business organizations were such as to encourage them to set up bodies of their own. Ultimately, almost every foreign organization in shared industries had an Indian mirror image. The Indian Tea Association, founded by British planters in 1881, was followed by the Indian Tea Planters' Association; the Indian Mining Association (1892) by the Indian Mining Federation (1913) and the Indian Colliery Owners' Association (1933) representing Indian interests large and small; the Indian Paper Makers' Association by the Indian Paper Mills Association. The Indian Jute Mills Association (1884), the Indian Central Cotton Committee, and the Exchange Banks' Association, all originally British, had each an Indian counterpart. Even the smallest were paired: for example, the [British] Cycle Manufacturers' Association with the [Indian] All-India Cycle Manufacturers' Association.

Commercial organizations were no different. The 1830's generation of British Chambers which followed the demise of the East India Company as a trader was matched in the 1880's by an Indian generation. The provincial organizations which came later continued the

---

[1] M. M. Mehta, *Combination Movement in Indian Industry*, Table XV, p. 48.
[2] Hilton Brown, op. cit., p. 66.

segregation and finally the national organizations—the [British] Associated Chambers of Commerce and Industry (1920) and the [Indian] Federation of Indian Chambers of Commerce and Industry (1927)—did the same.

The picture of mutual exclusiveness can be overdrawn: large firms, particularly the new-type international giants which began to take an interest in India in the inter-war years, often held dual membership; as many as thirty of FICCI's 102 affiliated chambers and associations were thought to be foreign-dominated at the time of Independence.[1] None the less, it is substantially true.

Many of the foreign associations were entrusted with considerable powers by the Government; some—notably the Indian Tea Association—were assisted financially. Yet they remained organizations of British business. At best they showed indifference to the special needs of Indian capital, at worst they obstructed.

Banking is a case in point. Many of the difficulties of which Indian business complained throughout the first half of the century—the inaccessibility of banks, and of credit where banks were to be found, the high cost of loans, the privileges granted to foreign borrowers, and much else[2]—were a perfectly normal response by British banks to business conditions at the time. If they concentrated in the large towns, it was because the business was there; if they dealt, by preference, with British clients and on easier terms, it was because they had surer knowledge of their credit-worthiness, because they had close links with them at home, because many of their clients were directors of the Presidency Banks (later Imperial Bank) which acted as a rudimentary Central Bank, or for any one of a host of similar reasons. Yet there was substance in the charge of conscious and active discrimination. The Exchange Banks opposed the Presidency Banks' move to open London offices, refused to admit the Tata Industrial Bank to the list of eligible purchasers of Council Bills, opposed the establishment of a Central Bank and, as late as 1940, the introduction of banking legislation. During the Second World War the Exchange Banks' Association effectively annulled the gains Indian banks had made (in association with one or two American

[1] Gokhale Institute, *Business Communities in India*, Table 12, p. 32.

[2] See, for example, Indian Central Banking Enquiry Committee, 1931, Vol. I, Part II—*Minority Report*, particularly Chapter XIII, 'Foreign Banks: Complaints Against Them' (pp. 193–216), and the Evidence of the Indian Chambers of Commerce, Vol. II, *Evidence* (Written); Indian Industrial Commission, *Report*, 1918, Chapter XX, 'Industrial Finance' (pp. 176–86).

banks) in handling foreign transactions.[1] It was not until the end of the war that they began to come to terms with the Indian sector.[2]

(*d*) *The use of indigenous capital:* As long as British funds were available, the managing agencies had little cause to look elsewhere. Now and again one came across Indian shareholdings in a British-managed company but they were of no consequence in aggregate.[3]

The First World War initiated a fundamental change. The agency houses were virtually cut off from their financial sources when they needed them most. Although the flow resumed after the war it was much reduced, averaging about half the reverse flow of interest and dividends throughout the twenties. It dried up completely the following decade when a substantial volume of repatriated capital—Rs 2 crores a year perhaps, between 1931–2 and 1936–7—joined the stream of investment earnings.[4]

The heroic age of expansion had passed for the agency houses too; but if they were to exploit the marginal opportunities for growth, to keep up the stream of remittances and meet new Indian competition; if, further, the traditional policy of administering other people's funds was to be maintained, Indian capital had to be taken in, and that in substantial quantities. By the nineteen-twenties majority ownership, as distinct from control, of the largest organized industry, jute, had passed into Indian hands although only two mills had Indian managing agencies in 1922;[5] by 1950 it was three-quarters Indian[6] (although still foreign-controlled).[7] Indian ownership in the coal industry was unofficially estimated at 78 per cent in 1949[8] and officially at 85 per cent six years later; it was 71 per cent in mining other than coal.[9] Tea was an exception until the

---

[1] J. J. Pardiwalla, *Exchange Banks in India* (Ph.D. thesis), pp. 181–2, 244.

[2] See Chintaman Deshmukh, *Central Banking in India—A Retrospect.* Deshmukh was Governor of the Reserve Bank of India from 1943 to 1949.

[3] See Basu, *The Managing Agency System*, p. 70.

[4] D. H. N. Gurtoo, *India's Balance of Payments 1920–1960*, Chapter 6.

[5] Gokhale Institute, *Business Communities in India*, p. 3, citing evidence given to the Indian Fiscal Commission, 1922. See also V. Anstey, *The Economic Development of India*, p. 281; Basu, op. cit., p. 70.

[6] Parliamentary answer cited in UK Board of Trade, *India, Economic and Commercial Conditions in India*, 1952, p. 112.

[7] See above, p. 4.

[8] Kumud Basu, President, Indian Mining Association, (*Capital*, 24 March 1949, p. 454).

[9] Parliamentary answer, March 1954, cited in G. Tyson, 'Foreign Investment in India', *International Affairs*, April 1955, p. 175.

Second World War when a large switch—thought to have involved an eighth of the tea area in South India alone[1]—reduced the foreign share to three-fifths of the total investment.[2]

There is no way of following the process as it unfolded, yet the results are clear. By mid-1948, foreign managing agencies held, on average, under 15 per cent of the paid-up share capital of their managed companies. A fraction of the rest was held directly abroad. But the bulk—85 per cent—was owned by Indians.[3] The methods of ensuring continued control were naturally complex, involving holding companies, interlocking ownership and direction, held together under a shroud of secrecy. They were largely effective until well into the period of Independence.

(e) *The sources of power:* One broad conclusion emerges from this sketch of the foreign sector in British times. Its power did not rest primarily on ownership, although a virtual monopoly of a few key industries naturally helped. Had it done so, the heart of the system, the managing agencies, would have been lost well before the Second World War. Similarly, while its ability to provide certain technical and managerial skills was important, these were neither so complex nor so scarce after the First World War as to constitute an impregnable monopoly. This Indian capital was soon to demonstrate. The essence of its power lay rather in organization—its self-sufficiency, its integrated and articulated character, its flexibility—and in its being able to draft in outside resources in men, money, markets, or whatever, when necessary. In a larger context this power rested on a sympathetic government and a specific form of international economy both of which lay beyond its own area of control.

II FOREIGN RULE

Relations between Government and foreign business before Independence were complex. While state aid in shipping and railway construction, in making land and labour available to tea planters, and so on, provided the scaffolding without which foreign private enterprise might never have risen off the ground, it was one which they had lobbied for and planned in both Britain and India for years[4] and

[1] *EW*, 3 September 1949, p. 14.

[2] Parliamentary answer, March 1954, cited in Tyson, loc. cit.

[3] RBI, *Census*, Table III–20, pp. 73–74. It ranged from 1·4 per cent in finance to one-third in trading.

[4] See, for example, D. Thorner, *Investment in Empire*.

which, however largely conceived, never seemed adequate. As Lord Rothschild assured the Currency Commission in the last year of the century, 'any amount of capital could be found in England for Indian enterprise if the Indian Government had given facilities and had been more liberal to private enterprise'.[1]

So it was that although British business enjoyed almost sole access to the Government in the early years and a disproportionate weight in the legislatures from 1909, and while there was considerable interchange in personnel at the upper reaches of Government and business, the value of all this was impaired by the technically irresponsible and despotic character of British political rule. Conflict between them was continuous; yet in the large issues of economic policy as they arose this century, the Government's views normally coincided with those of foreign as against Indian capital.

(a) *Tariff policy:* The last vestiges of tariff protection were dropped in the 1870's. By then *laissez faire* had been elevated into the 'secular religion of the British middle class'.[2] It was an exacting religion: if a grain ship bound for Calcutta foundered off the coast of famine-stricken Orissa, the natural laws of political economy, reinforced by instructions from the Lieutenant-Governor, decreed that it continue on its way. If natural decay rendered it useless before transhipment could be effected, so be it. 'By the time relief came', wrote Philip Woodruff in a celebrated work, 'a quarter of the population were dead'.[3]

The creed had its catechismal aspect. Witness Lord Hardinge:

Lord Morley came up to us, and taking me aside asked if I would like to succeed Lord Minto as Viceroy of India. . . . What struck me as curious at the time was that the only question he put to me was whether I was a free-trader, and I was honestly able to say that I was then and always had been a free-trader. He told me that I might regard the matter as settled. . . .[4]

The First World War shocked the British Government into an appreciation of the Empire's lag in economic and military power.[5]

[1] Quoted in *Capital*, 9 February 1899, reprinted in ibid., 12 February 1959, p. 185.

[2] The phrase is Strachey's, from *The End of Empire*, p. 55.

[3] *The Guardians*, quoted in ibid., p. 56.

[4] *My Indian Years: 1910–1916*, pp. 3–4.

[5] In India the first intimation of change came, ironically, from Lord Hardinge, now Viceroy: 'It is becoming increasingly clear [he wrote in a dispatch to the Secretary of State for India, November 1915] that a definite and self-conscious policy of improving the industrial capabilities of India will have to be pursued

An Indian Industrial Commission was appointed in 1916. It recommended (1918) that 'in future Government must play an active part in the industrial development of the country with the aim of making India more self contained in respect of men and materials.'[1]

A year later the Joint Select Committee examining the Government of India Bill suggested a convention on 'fiscal autonomy' for India. This—and the dusty answer given a Lancashire delegation by the Secretary of State—proved to be a turning point. General import duties were raised in 1921 and again in 1925; the excise on Indian cotton textiles was dropped. Discriminating protection recommended by the Fiscal Commission of 1921 became official policy and a Tariff Board was set up (1923) to review applications. In 1924 the iron and steel industry was granted protection at $33\frac{1}{3}$ per cent as well as a number of subsidies.

The memory of war receded and with it the promise of change. Although fiscal autonomy was never renounced, after 1924 it assumed an increasingly discriminatory, pro-British bias. The Tariff Board interpreted their terms of reference more narrowly with every application. Sixteen out of fifty-five were rejected and many others changed beyond hope of effectiveness. The original recommendation to establish a permanent Board with a full-time staff was modified in favour of *ad hoc* Boards with narrower horizons. Decisions took an interminable time to come through: an application from the cotton textiles industry in April 1932 waited thirty-one months—seven with the Board, twenty-four with the Government—before receiving an answer; it took twenty-three months for the match industry's application of October 1926, eleven for iron and steel (August 1933), fifteen for paper (December 1937), twenty-four for sugar (March 1937). Purely Indian industries fared worse than foreign ones: cement and glass were denied protection; import duties on iron and steel were lowered in 1927 and the subsidy to Tata abolished. On the other hand, the foreign-dominated match industry was given the protection it requested. When on one occasion the Tariff Board

---

after the war, unless she is to become the dumping ground for the manufacture of foreign nations who will be competing the more keenly for markets, the more it becomes apparent that the political future of the large nations depends on their economic position. . . . After the war India will consider herself entitled to demand the utmost help which her Government can afford, to enable her to take her place, so far as circumstances permit, as a manufacturing country.' (Quoted in A. R. Desai, *Social Background of Indian Nationalism*, p. 98.)

[1] Quoted in Fiscal Commission (1949–50), *Report*, p. 45.

recommended protection for a section of the woollen industry, the Government refused endorsement on the grounds that an important part of it, viz., two British-controlled units that had neither supported the application nor tendered evidence, was not considered.[1]

While individual British-controlled ventures suffered from some aspects of Government tariff policy, the brunt of it obviously bore down on Indian capital. It was less geared to foreign trade; it had to make do to a larger extent with the market, techniques, and funds it could find locally. Without protection and without removing the special privileges granted to British imports throughout the thirties[2] these were bound to be limited.

(b) *Industrial policy:* Official policy on industrialization was naturally related, and subject to the same rhythm. From the 1850's public works were financed out of current revenues—sparingly; requests for subsidies for heavy industry were repeatedly denied; several attempts to set up investment banks were blocked and the field left clear for orthodox British banking which was then, as now, totally unsuited for the purpose. Railways converged on the ports with little regard for internal economic logic and none for uniformity of gauges and rates. Railway building had little 'spread effect': permission to buy government stores in India came only in 1928 and preference for local manufactures in 1931. Recommendations of the Famine Enquiry Commission, 1880, to encourage industry and sponsor technical training officially were ignored for nearly forty years.

Early this century the Government of Madras attempted to break the pattern: with the Viceroy, Lord Curzon's support, a Provincial Department of Industries was set up.[3] Its activities 'aroused the opposition of the local European commercial community, who interpreted them as a serious menace to private enterprise and an unwarrantable intervention on the part of the State in matters beyond the sphere of Government. . . .'[4]

Lord Morley, Secretary of State for India, disapproved, the Department was disbanded, the leather tannery which had provoked

[1] Fiscal Commission (1949–50), *Report*, pp. 51–58.

[2] These privileges were embodied, *inter alia*, in the Ottawa Agreement, 1932; The Tariff Amendment Act, 1934; and the Supplementary Trade Agreement, 1935.

[3] A history of the Department is to be found as Appendix J of the Indian Industrial Commission, *Report*, 1918, pp. 402–24.

[4] Indian Industrial Commission, *Report*, p. 70.

the largest outcry sold, the experimental handloom shops abandoned, and Sir Alfred Chatterton, Director of Industrial and Technical Enquiries, allowed to leave for Mysore. Similar experiments elsewhere—notably the United Provinces—were similarly quashed.[1]

Wartime encouragement to industry proved even more ephemeral than the new tariff policy. Under the Reforms Act, 1919, industry became a Provincial subject while fiscal, tariff, transport, and general economic policy remained with the Centre. As an experienced observer of the day wrote:

Unfortunately since the funds available have been wholly inadequate, no very important policies could be initiated. Furthermore, the encouragement of industry requires a far-reaching unified government policy concerning not only raw materials and methods of production, but markets as well. . . . It is doubtful whether the mere provincial offices set up in India will have any considerable effect.[2]

An Imperial Department of Industries was founded in 1921, but it never amounted to much.[3] Individual industries were blighted in the prevailing wind. An early attempt at locomotive production foundered when the Government and the Railway Board decided to continue their patronage of British manufacturers after the First World War.[4] Plans for ship-building and motor-car production took the same course.

For a time it looked as if the Second World War would also bring little material change. One foreign observer wrote:

British policy in the first two years of the war continued to be dominated by commercial motives, and was therefore opposed to any rapid or extensive growth of Indian-controlled heavy industries. . . . Only the smallest beginnings had been made in the development of the metallurgical, chemical and other heavy industries for which India possessed all the necessary raw materials, and nothing effective had been done to eliminate the twin bottlenecks of lack of machinery and a skilled labour shortage which continued to cripple India's efforts toward industrial expansion.[5]

---

[1] Anstey, *The Economic Development of India*, pp. 210–12.

[2] Buchanan, *Capitalistic Enterprise in India*, p. 464.

[3] Writing a decade later, Vera Anstey observed: '. . . it has not yet undertaken any fargoing constructive functions.' (*Economic Development of India*, 1st ed. p. 220.)

[4] See Nehru, *Discovery of India*, pp. 416–17.

[5] K. L. Mitchell, *Industrialization of the Western Pacific*, p. 295. See also H. Mendershausen, 'The Pattern of Overseas Economic Development in World War II', *Economia Internazionale*, August 1951, p. 752 *passim*; Lokanathan, *Industrialization*, 3rd ed., pp. 14–15; G. D. Birla, 'India's War Prosperity—A Myth', speech of 15 April 1941, in *The Path to Prosperity*, pp. 437 ff.

And as late as May 1945, J. R. D. Tata insisted to a London audience:

There might have been isolated cases of expansion, but on the whole, when armament factories and other specialised industries connected with the war have been excluded, there has been none.[1]

(c) *Transport policy:* Even after the major *railways* had been taken over by the state, many were still run by British managing agencies. Indian interests were unanimous—in the Legislative Council throughout the First World War, before the Industrial Commission of 1916–18, the Railway Committee of 1920–1, the Fiscal Commission of 1921–2, and subsequently throughout the period of British rule—that the rate structure, agreed by British capital and the state, encouraged foreign at the expense of domestic trade, and favoured foreign over domestic business interests.[2]

The conflict over *shipping* was, if possible, even fiercer. 'It is hardly possible to write with restraint on the treatment which Indian shipping has received from its own Government', wrote Walchand Hirachand, the pioneer of India's merchant marine:

British shipping interests have often claimed that they have built up the Indian trade at considerable sacrifice. It is, however, well-known how Mackinnon obtained at the breakfast table a subsidy from Sir Bartle Frere, the then Governor of Bombay, in 1863, and turned the Burma Steam Navigation Co. Ltd. into the British India Company of today. Not only did the British India not undergo any sacrifice but it minted tons of money by its virtual monopoly of the coastal trade in India. . . . Moreover, it was almost a scandal when the presence of Lord Inchcape as the Chairman of the Retrenchment Committee in India secured for his company, the British India, a contract for the carriage of coal to Burma for a long period of ten years on very favourable terms—which the Government refused to disclose—without even giving an opportunity to an Indian company to put in the tender despite the assurances given by the Government. . . . I need not mention the large sums of money which have been paid to the British shipping companies under the Mail Contracts and the exclusive privileges given to them for carrying practically the entire requirements of Government stores and other materials on the coast. Under the guise of helping the so-called 'Empire Shipping' which meant in practice British Shipping only, the Civil and Military Officers enjoying the benefit of Lee passage were practically compelled to travel by the ships of the British Lines. And

---

[1] Quoted in J. B. Cohen, *The Role of the Government in Economic Development in India*, pp. I 11–12.
[2] See, for example, Fiscal Commission (1921–22), *Report*, pp. 72–74.

even today when they want to appoint a Controller of Indian Shipping who is expected to look after the interests of ships owned, controlled and managed by Indians, the Government of India cannot find a responsible Indian to fulfil that office but has appointed a Britisher who in his life-time has done everything possible to stifle the growth and development of Indian shipping in this country.[1]

(*d*) *Monetary policy:* Indian currency history has been studded with battles over the rupee exchange rate. As the Jathars explain, 'the bias of the British Government and British business interests was towards a high rather than a low ratio for the rupee; in other words, towards making a certain number of rupees earned in India worth more and more in terms of pounds, shillings and pence in England.'[2] Naturally Indian interests were opposed.

There was a similar struggle over the constitution of the Reserve Bank—in the Legislative Assembly in 1927, the Round Table Conference in 1931, and then again in the Legislative Assembly in 1933–4. Indian interests fought for an official central bank controlled by the Legislature against a combined front of British private capital in India and at home and a Government that clung to the idea of a shareholders' bank, 'independent of political pressures', on the model of the Bank of England.[3]

(*e*) *Staffing policy:* In a despotic régime, even in one committed to *laissez faire*, staffing policy assumes a special importance. The official attitude was expressed forcibly by the Viceroy, Sir John Lawrence, in a letter to the Secretary of State, 17 August 1867:

The chief objection to a change [in the manner of recruitment to the Indian Civil Service] is that of policy. We conquered India mainly by force of arms, though policy and good government have largely aided us. In like manner we must hold it. The Englishmen must always be in the front rank, holding the post of honour and of power as the condition of our retaining our rule.[4]

To this end, competitive entrance examinations were held exclusively in England until 1928; a distinction between the covenanted

---

[1] 'Why Indian Shipping Does Not Grow', *Bombay Investors' Year Book*, 1940, p. 4. of offprint. Substantially the same charges, and others, are set out more formally in *Indian Ship*.
[2] G. B. and K. G. Jathar, *Indian Economics*, p. 303.
[3] See K. N. Raj, *Monetary Policy of the Reserve Bank of India*, pp. 95–98.
[4] Quoted in B. B. Misra, *The Indian Middle Classes*, p. 372.

and uncovenanted branches of the service was maintained; the recommendations of the Royal Commission on Public Services (1912) were deferred until after the First World War; and subsequent recommendations—those of the Montford Commission (1919) to open up one-third of ICS posts to Indians and of the Lee Commission (1924) to allocate one half *by 1939*—were accepted with more deliberation than speed.[1]

Although conditions changed radically during the Second World War, the conflict remained. At its close, Indians in authority and in business were apprehensive of an influx from Britain into the higher reaches of the Government. They did their best to hold it off, primarily by using the powers vested in the Government of India and the Secretary of State to ration sea passages. The British Trade Commissioner in India, backed enthusiastically by local British business, mounted a campaign to win official sponsorship of sea passages for the Trade Commission and the British Board of Trade. He won, and although the influx failed to materialize it was through no lack of opportunity.[2]

(*f*) *The Second World War:* The war affected many of the policies at issue. Indianization of the bureaucracy and armed services grew rapidly. 'The land was scoured, and scoured again,' writes Maurice Zinkin, 'to find army officers, purchase officers, officers of a hundred and one different sorts. The arcana of power were made public, and Government gave itself over to what was in effect one of the greatest training programmes in history.'[3]

On the specific problems of economic development, policy outran practice. The need to outflank Congress and its National Planning Committee, the obvious inadequacies of India's war economy, new ideas gaining currency in the West, were among the factors in the change. Essential industries were assured of protection after the war. A number of 'reconstruction committees' were set up to plan postwar developments; a consultative committee of economists was formed under the chairmanship of the Commerce Member; in July 1944, a Department of Planning and Development was created under

[1] M. R. Palande, *Introduction to Indian Administration*, revised ed., p. 460. See also ibid., pp. 180–1 and refs.

[2] Information supplied in confidence.

[3] 'Some Aspects of Change in Indian Society', in N. V. Sovani and V. M. Dandekar, *Changing India*, p. 336.

Sir Ardeshir Dalal, a signatory to the Bombay Plan;[1] and in October 1946 an Advisory Planning Board appointed.

Many of the measures adopted after Independence were foreshadowed during this period. The *Reports on the Progress of Reconstruction Planning*, 1944, recommended that power development and arms production be undertaken by the state, that such other industries as could not attract private capital be supported financially, and advocated policies whereby the 'profit motive' would be 'harnessed to social needs'.[2] A *Statement on Government Industrial Policy*, dated 21 April 1945, went further. It envisaged outright nationalization of industry 'in the interests of co-ordinated development'; where private capital remained shy; where the tax element predominated in the price of a product; or simply 'if required in the national interest'. (Among the twenty industries listed were textiles, sugar, and rubber.) The Government was to be responsible for 'certain prerequisites of industrial progress' such as transport; for assistance to key industries such as electrical machinery, machine tools, and motor vehicles; and would exercise a substantial degree of control over management, expenditure, appointments, profit levels, and so on in assisted industries.[3] The Advisory Planning Board's recommendations were equally forthright.[4] The promise was large. In a way it derived from another, future system, and was soon overtaken by events.

III INDIAN CAPITAL

For years after Independence, Indian capital bore the marks of having grown in the shadows of a powerful, tightly-knit foreign competitor, and an unsympathetic, frequently hostile state.

(*a*) *Spasmodic growth:* It developed slowly, too slowly to absorb

[1] *A Plan of Economic Development for India*, Part I published in January 1944, Part II in January 1945. Its signatories were central figures in Indian business; Sir Purshotamdas Thakurdas, J. R. D. Tata, G. D. Birla, Sir Ardeshir Dalal, Sir Shri Ram, Kasturbhai Lalbhai, A. D. Shroff, and John Matthai.

[2] *First Report*, p. 29; *Second Report*, p. 9; cited in M. H. Gopal, 'Indian Industrial Policy', *IEJ*, Vol. IV, No. 4, April 1957, p. 317.

[3] Cited in Gopal, loc. cit., pp. 319–20.

[4] 'Apart from Defence Industries and any industry or branch of any industry which it might be found desirable to start as a state enterprise due to the reluctance of private capital to undertake it, the nationalization of the following should be considered: coal, mineral oils, iron and steel, motor-, air-, and river-transport.' (Quoted in P. Prasad, *Some Economic Problems of Public Enterprises in India*, p. 95.)

more than a small proportion of the growing labour force.[1] It grew in spurts, wherever and whenever it found shelter from competition and gained some sustenance from the state. There were three such periods: during the First and Second World Wars and in the 1930's.

The First World War had little lasting effect. Although paid-up capital of joint-stock companies increased nearly three and a half times between 1913 and 1921–2[2] and domestic production of manufactures rose from 23 to 29 per cent of offtake in the same period,[3] the impetus was quickly lost when government policy shifted from 'discriminating protection' to 'discriminating free trade'[4] and the industrial base proved too narrow to sustain it. Except perhaps in initiating the process of Indianizing the bureaucracy and providing a glimpse of what was possible in the way of industrial expansion under suitable conditions, it was an episode.

The second period left a larger residue. As a by-product of Imperial Preference some protection was granted Indian industry; at the same time foreign markets, and with them the foreign sector, stagnated. It was now that many of the major Indian groups, particularly the Marwari ones, first made their mark: the Birlas went into sugar and cotton on a large scale, and into paper, cycles, textile machinery; Dalmia-Jain went into sugar and cement and started or took over large companies like Rohtas Industries, National Safe Deposit and Cold Storage, and Dalmia Cement.

Production of Indian-dominated industries went up considerably. Between 1922–3 and 1938–9, cement output increased sixfold to 1·2 million tons a year, cotton piece goods two and a half times to 4·3 billion yards, paper more than double to 60,000 tons, sugar twelvefold to over a million tons, pig iron over threefold to 1·6

[1] Using Indian Census data, Schwartzberg shows an over-all decline in employment in processing and manufacture from 10·3 to 8·8 per cent of the labour force between 1901 and 1951 (*Occupational Structure and Level of Economic Development in India*, Table 5, p. 127). Absolute industrial employment increased from 254,000 to 2,434,000 between 1892 and 1949 (C. A. Myers, *Labour Problems in the Industrialization of India*, Table 6, p. 17) compared with an increase in the Labour force, crudely estimated, from 94 million (1891) to 142 million (1951) (from A. J. Coale and E. K. Hoover, *Population Growth and Economic Development*, pp. 30, 231.)

[2] N. Islam, *Foreign Capital and Economic Development: Japan, India, and Canada*, p. 85.

[3] *Annual Statistical Abstract of British India* an *Annual Review of India's Foreign Trade*, cited ibid., p. 99.

[4] See above, p. 13. The phrase is G. D. Birla's, in 'Solvency through Production', 14 February 1930, *Path to Prosperity*, p. 141.

million tons, and steel ingots more than sevenfold to a million tons.[1] By the end of the period 39 per cent of the offtake of manufactures was 'made in India'.[2]

The greatest expansion came during the Second World War. Investment increased by some seven or eight per cent of the national income over the war years, Government outlay more than fourfold between 1939–40 and 1944–5.[3] Most established Indian-controlled industries expanded; cotton by a fifth, steel by two-fifths, cement and paper doubled. The minute chemical industry grew and others were begun—ferro-alloys; non-ferrous metals; diesel engines, machine tools, sewing machines; a few items of tea, textile, and oil-processing machinery, railway equipment and so on.[4] By 1943–4, three-fifths of the offtake of manufactures came from local plants.[5] Industries developed—but not a self-sustaining industrial system. As in the First World War, the absence of a capital-goods sector made itself felt: 'established industries . . . worked multiple shifts but the difficulties of imports of essential requirements led to tremendous wear and tear.'[6]

(b) *Unbalanced growth:* The lopsidedness of Indian industrial growth was pronounced. In 1946, despite wartime developments, cotton and jute textiles accounted for 45 per cent of the fixed capital in 29 major industries.[7]

A comparison of factory employment in India and Britain at the close of the forties shows that textiles accounted for 40 per cent of workers in India (cotton and jute) and 6·5 per cent in Britain (cotton, woollen, worsted); engineering, iron and steel, and related industries, for 15·9 and 47·3 per cent respectively; and chemicals for 0·7 and 5·6 per cent.[8]

---

[1] P. A. Wadia and K. T. Merchant, *Our Economic Problem*, 5th ed., p. 430.

[2] Islam, loc. cit.

[3] Datar and Patel, 'Employment During the Second World War', *IER*, February 1956, pp. 14–16. These magnitudes are greater in real terms than those targeted for—and attained—during the Second Plan, 1956–61.

[4] Wadia and Merchant, op. cit., pp. 430, 431; Fiscal Commission (1949–50), *Report*, Vol. I, p. 22; Vol. IV, Table XX, pp. 18–19.

[5] Islam, loc. cit.   [6] Wadia and Merchant, p. 431.

[7] Census of Manufacturers, 1946, Vol. I, cited in Rangnekar, *Poverty and Capital Development*, p. 105.

[8] Figures for India (1949) from Myers, *Labour Problems*, Table 6, p. 17; for Britain (1950) from Mutual Security Agency Mission, *Economic Development in the United Kingdom*, Chart 5A, pp. 21–22.

(*c*) *Concentration:* If foreign business was concentrated and tightly held, merely to exist Indian capital needed to be, if possible, even more concentrated and tightly held: in 1958 the eight largest Indian groups controlled 23 per cent of net capital stock in the private sector, including foreign firms; two of them—Tata and Birla—held over 14 per cent between them.[1] Indian-dominated industries showed as much concentration as foreign ones: fifteen groups controlled one-fifth of the number of cotton-mills in 1949;[2] two groups have controlled all but a minute fraction of cement-making capacity since the late thirties.[3] Examples could be multiplied.[4]

(*d*) *Diversification:* Where foreign capital found flexibility in its wealth of institutions, its common culture, and a sympathetic govern-ment, Indian capital sought it in tightly-knit family groups, re-inforced by caste and community ties. The personal nature of this control, as well as the example of the foreign sector, its exclusiveness and self-sufficiency, and general factors such as the narrowness of Indian markets, resulted in an even greater diversity of interests within each group than obtained in the British houses, although with little sign of the internal coherence noted in their case. The Birla group is an outstanding example. In 1951 it controlled 245 companies and was substantially interested in another eleven. Of the 195 *public* companies in the complex (eight of which were among the fifty largest in the country by the end of the decade), seventy-one were in investment financing, thirty-four in trade, twelve in cotton, eleven in engineering, nine each in sugar and tea, six in property, five each in jute, publishing, and managing agencies, four each in food and in-surance, three in plastics and glass, two each in coal mining, power, non-ferrous metals, and transport, and one each in mining other than coal, rayon, chemicals, paper, construction, fireclay, and banking. Two were unclassified.[5]

While the Birla complex is by far the largest in terms of the number of companies it contains, it is by no means exceptional in its

---

[1] From Hazari, *Structure of the Corporate Private Sector*, Table 4.3, pp. 23–25. One of the eight—Martin Burn—was originally British; by 1951 control had in all probability passed into the hands of the Mukerji and Banerji families.

[2] Mehta, *Combination Movement in Indian Industry*, p. 10.

[3] D. L. Spencer, *India, Mixed Enterprise and Western Business*, p. 27.

[4] Mehta's *Combination Movement in Indian Industry*, and *Structure of Indian Industries* are useful guides to the period.

[5] Hazari, *Structure of the Corporate Private Sector*, pp. 36, 66.

spread of interests: Tata's 68 *public* companies ranged over at least twenty industries in 1951; the Dalmia-Sahu-Jain group's 63 *public* companies over eighteen industries; the Bangurs' 44 over fifteen industries; the Thapars' 30 over twelve industries;[1] and so on.

(e) *Technological backwardness:* No family group, however extended, could provide the resources for empires of this size and diversity, the more so as hired management was even less plentiful than it is today. 'Cheque book capitalism' took root, the managing agency system was made to reveal an incredible capacity for financial manipulation and malfeasance,[2] 'selection and promotion . . . by favour' became the rule, 'sufficient regard . . . not [being] paid to efficiency',[3] and technological backwardness fed on itself. Add to this the lack of a machine-making industry, the need therefore to carry large stocks at the end of a long foreign-dominated supply line, the difficulties of adapting foreign machinery, and a multitude of associated factors—and the general inefficiency of Indian industry can begin to be grasped. Paper manufacturing might serve as an example, if only because it was closely scrutinized as late as 1954. Eddison writes,

Most foreign-made equipment was planned and constructed for use under contrasting climatic conditions, and with dissimilar raw materials, differing grades of chemicals, and more highly trained workers than are to be found in India. In consequence, this equipment often gives unexpected difficulties and generally operates at lower efficiency than it would in its native land.

Additional problems arise from the fact that many imported units have designed into them automatic devices and mechanical conveyors which are economically justified only in countries where labour cost are much higher than they are in India.[4]

[1] From Hazari, op. cit., Tables 6.1, 6.52, 8.18; pp. 56, 84, 140. Actual diversification was wider than would appear from Hazari's admittedly rudimentary classification.

[2] The literature on this—mostly concerned with Indian-controlled managing agencies—is enormous, and absorbing. Reference to official sources only would include the *Reports* and volumes of *Evidence* of the Indian Industrial Commission, 1918, the Fiscal Commission 1921–2, the Tariff Board on the cotton textiles industry, 1926 and 1932, the Banking Enquiry Committee, 1932. Two post-Independence classics are the *Report* and volumes of *Evidence* of the Company Law Committee, 1952, and the *Report of the [Vivian Bose] Commission of Enquiry on the Administration of Dalmia-Jain Companies,* 1963.

[3] All-India Manufacturers' Organization (A-IMO), *Rapid Development of Indian Industries,* p. 20.

[4] J. Eddison, *Industrial Development in the Growth of the Pulp and Paper Industry in India,* pp. 264–5.

The machines are not only unsuitable in many cases but equipment costs are 15 to 25 per cent higher in India than in the country of origin. . . .[1] . . . inflated, not only by freight, handling and duty charges but also by the monopolistic pricing policies of the suppliers. . . . Extended delivery times force the mills to carry excessively large and expensive inventories . . . and to fabricate, in so far as possible, their own substitutes for worn or damaged equipment fittings.[2]

There being no domestic machine production, the industry contained a jumble of machine types: twenty-seven of the forty-six were British, seven German, four Belgian, and the rest Swedish, American, Canadian, or Japanese. Nineteen were produced by one manufacturer; no more than five of the rest came from any one firm. There was, therefore, no sales and service organization in the country and paper producers were thrust back on their own inadequate resources.[3]

(f) *Political and economic programmes:* Inefficiency, dependence, lack of initiative, and the host of debilitating corollaries of late, unprotected industrialization combined to make Indian capital more self-conscious and programmatic than many of its counterparts abroad. Their first priority was to alter the situation whereby, as they saw it,

the investment of foreign capital in Indian agricultural, mineral and industrial concerns . . . has resulted in the acquisition by foreign interests of a measure of control over India's economic-political life which has both warped and retarded national development.[4]

This could only be done if the imbalances inherited from the colonial past were righted and the deficiency in heavy industry made good:

Till [basic] industries are developed, we shall naturally be at the mercy of foreign countries. To shorten this period of dependence it is necessary to give priority to basic industries over other industries and thus to speed up development.[5]

[1] J. Eddison, *Industrial Development in the Growth of the Pulp and Paper Industry in India*, p. 264.

[2] ibid., p. 87.

[3] ibid., pp. 54–55. See also Sir Norman Kipping on the 'international exhibition of machine tools and production machines' in some private sector factories (FBI, *India 1963*, p. 8).

[4] Resolution of Indian National Congress, National Planning Committee, under Nehru's chairmanship and including many prominent industrialists, 12 November 1945, quoted in L. Natarajan, *American Shadow over India*, 2nd ed., p. 48.

[5] *Bombay Plan*, 1944, Section 91, Penguin ed., p. 58. (See also below, pp. 72 f.) The All-India Manufacturers' Organization specified what these basic industries were: iron and steel, machinery and machine tools, mill machinery, electrical

The new balanced economy was not to be allowed to fall again into foreign hands.[1] Protection, exchange control, and a host of other regulations were to ensure that.

None of these was conceivable without state planning. As early as 1931, Congress had demanded that the 'state . . . own or control key industries and services, mineral resources, railways, waterways, shipping and other means of public transport'.[2]

The theme was to recur again and again, *forte* when the political arm of the nationalist movement was dealing with questions of marginal interest to Indian business,[3] *piano* when the general question of nationalization was raised. In the latter case, only 'foreign interests . . . particularly those involving the utilization of scarce natural resources' were to be affected and then only 'on payment of reasonable compensation'.[4]

Planning was inconceivable without political freedom. If anything, state power meant more to Indian than to foreign capital: very early on, at the time of the Swadeshi movement of 1905–8, it had learned the value to business of a frontal assault—the boycott—on foreign business. The campaign 'acted as a stimulant to all Indian business',[5] brought Indian insurance into being, and was long remembered for having given the first indication of what national unity and independence might mean to the rising Indian *bourgeoisie*. A head-on collision of this sort could not last however. For all its frustration, Indian capital was utterly and demonstrably dependent on foreign capital for supplies, services, and so on. Its attitude was necessarily ambivalent. On the one hand, it supported a nationalist movement dedicated to attacking foreign capital and added sallies of its own;[6]

machinery, coal and derivatives, automobiles and aircraft, internal combustion engines, shipping and ship-building, aluminium, heavy and fine chemicals and plastics, paper and pulp, and rayon (A–IMO, *Rapid Development*, p. 15).

[1] See below, pp. 72 f.

[2] All-India Congress Committee, resolution on 'Fundamental Rights and Duties and Economic Program', reprinted in Indian National Congress (INC), *Resolutions 1924–54*, p. 9.

[3] A National Planning Sub-Committee advocated '*a complete state monopoly*' in chemicals, and condemned the admission of 'foreign capital and enterprise, in alliance with Indian enterprise'. (NPC, *Chemical Industries*, Report of the Sub-Committee, p. 5. Italics in original.) See also INC, *Resolutions 1924–54*, p. 17.

[4] National Planning Committee resolution, quoted in Natarajan, *American Shadow over India*, 2nd ed., p. 48. See also the *National Planning Committee Hand-book*, p. 57, quoted in Arun Bose, *Indo-British Big Business Deals*, pp. 47–48.

[5] Gokhale Institute, *Business Communities in India*, p. 3.

[6] See below, Chapter 3, Section I, p. 65 ff.

on the other, it found itself in continuous contact with the enemy, often in the same firms, sometimes in the same organizations, the same delegations, and negotiating bodies. Some sections of Indian capital were less uncompromising than others.[1] But even the most intransigent vacillated now and again. While G. D. Birla, for long the outstanding spokesman of the nationalist wing, might demand the repatriation of all British investments in 1943,[2] he was not above seeking further British investments in 1945.[3] The dilemma was acute, and if it was insoluble in practice, at least it might be moderated by control of the state.

[1] Perhaps the most celebrated 'betrayal' was the series of agreements culminating in the 'Lees-Mody Pact' of October 1933, when the Bombay Millowners' Association were persuaded to exempt British textiles from a tariff increase aimed at the Japanese, in exchange for minor concessions in the Empire market. 'They have lost their nerves', declared G. D. Birla in the Legislative Assembly, '. . . it is the duty of this House to see that, in their impatience, they may not do something which is against their own interest and against the interests of this country.' (Speech on 'Imperial Preference', 25 March 1930, in *Path to Prosperity*, p. 193.) 'As a matter of fact', wrote Nehru later, 'the Bombay mill industry in a body, during the continuance of civil disobedience and when we were preaching the boycott of British goods, had the temerity to conclude a pact with Lancashire. From the point of view of the Congress, this was a gross betrayal of the national cause, and it was characterized as such. The representative of the Bombay millowners in the Assembly also consistently ran down the Congress as extremists while most of us were in gaol.' (*Autobiography*, p. 367.)

[2] See, for example, 'Guarantees India Must Have', March 1943, in *Path to Prosperity*, pp. 506–7.

[3] See below, p. 70.

CHAPTER TWO

DECLINE OF EMPIRE

THE First World War announced the end of an era; depression and the Second World War destroyed it utterly. With it went, in effect, old-type foreign capital of the sort described in Chapter 1.

I INTERNATIONAL FACTORS

(a) *Investment at home:* Next to the growth of state intervention perhaps the most important changes in developed economics this century have been the expansion of manufacturing and the emergence of giant industrial firms as the major custodians of society's savings. The picture is well known: war made special demands on industry, and international tensions still do so; demand of this type and on this scale is best met by big firms able to support research and development and to exploit the economies of large scale; their military importance and close contacts with government have lent them continued advantages with the result that they generally form the fastest-growing section of the economy.[1] Two interrelated developments have enabled them to finance this expansion. One is the effect of increased taxation on dividend policy: as the proportion of company income paid out in tax grew, dividend and interest payments fell[2] and industrial expansion took place predominantly through self-financing.[3] Second is the institutionalization of personal

---

[1] See S. J. Prais, 'Size, Growth and Concentration', in B. Tew and R. F. Henderson (eds.), *Studies in Company Finance*, Table 8.1, p. 109, for figures relating to post-war Britain.

[2] Taxes rose from 14 to 39 per cent of net company income in Britain between 1938 and 1956 at the same time as dividend and interest payments fell from 68 to 35 per cent (Prais, 'Dividend Policy and Income Appropriation', in Tew and Henderson, op. cit., Table 2.1, p. 27). Dividends alone averaged as little as 23 per cent between 1949 and 1956 (Treasury *Bulletin for Industry*, No. 119, April 1959) compared with 53 per cent in 1922 and 67 per cent in 1912 (J. Enoch Powell, *Saving in a Free Society*, Table II, p. 29); and their value in real terms fell absolutely between 1938 and 1956 (Prais, 'Dividend Policy . . .', Tew and Henderson, p. 26).

[3] Brian Tew, 'Self-Financing', in ibid., Table 3.1, p. 44.

savings—particularly in life assurance and pension funds—and their growing involvement in industrial financing.[1]

Developments in merchant banking, once an institution of particular importance to countries like India, illustrate some of the impact of these changes. Traditionally oriented on foreign and colonial investment and trade, they have shown a dramatic shift in interest towards domestic industrial banking since the war. Close links have been forged with industrial groups as between Lazards and English Electric, or Schroder and Pressed Steel; more recently some have opened provincial offices;[2] and there have been a number of amalgamations between old-established houses 'disproportionately strong in foreign business' and younger firms concentrating on the 'home industrial financing which has been the mainstay of most firms which have expanded in recent years'.[3]

Although many of them were swept back into international operations in 1962 in preparation for Britain's entry into the Common Market, the new ventures could scarcely be farther from what they once were: industrial financing replaced commerce, utilities, and investment in Government; Europe took the place of Empire; and far from setting the pace and determining the locus of activity they acted very much as the specialist financial agents of big industry.

The flow of capital has been directly affected. In the past it migrated from industrial countries in response to their need for supplementary raw materials, food, and markets. As has been shown in the case of India, investment was typically in trade, in extractive and agricultural industries, and in the services, like transport, required to sustain them.[4] Something of this still remains today as can be seen from the

[1] Figures for Britain can be found in 'The Employment of Savings', *Midland Bank Review*, November 1960, Table, p. 10; *Radcliffe Report*, Tables 15, 16, pp. 84, 89, and p. 86.

[2] Singer and Friedlander in Leeds and Birmingham; Close Brothers in Liverpool; the Ionian Bank in Manchester and Birmingham; Edward Bates in Liverpool and Edinburgh; Rothschild in Birmingham.

[3] *The Times*, 10 February 1960. Examples of such amalgamations are Philip Hill, Higginson & Co., itself the product of a previous merger between a relatively young finance company and an old-established merchant bank, with Erlangers, one of the City's leading merchant banks, in 1959, and again with M. Samuel to form Hill, Samuel and Co. early in 1965; Lazards with Edward de Stein, early in 1960; Kleinworts with Robert, Benson, Lonsdale and Co. in November 1960; Schroder with Helbert, Wagg, in May that year; Keyser with Ullmann in March 1962. Some have linked up further with insurance funds; e.g. Philip Hill, Higginson, Erlangers, with Eagle Star; Samuel Montague with Pearl.

[4] See above, p. 3.

importance of petroleum investments—some two-fifths of the total in the first post-war decade.[1] But it is weakening. On a purely economic plane, growing industrial diversity in developed countries and the technological intensification it entails have done as much to lessen the need for primary materials as have secular boom and the growth of state purchasing to lessen the demand for auxiliary markets.

Little need be said on the latter. As a consumer of arms alone, the state provides a market within a developed economy far more stable and much larger in aggregate than anything to be found in backward countries. As for the supply of raw materials, three developments are particularly important, all three brought to rapid maturation this generation. One is the saving in the use of raw materials as a result of greater industrial efficiency and the shift from 'light' to 'heavy' industries.[2]

Second is the increasing use of manufacturing techniques in the production of industry's own raw materials and the growing popularity of 'natural' raw materials that lend themselves easily to industrial exploitation—like oil. Even excluding oil, consumption of raw materials in industrial countries is growing in the same direction as their manufactured content.[3] The third is closely related. It is the breakthrough of manufacturing techniques in agriculture in the developed west and its transition from a food-deficit to a food-surplus area.[4]

[1] W. B. Dale and R. N. Bale, *Private United States Venture Capital*, pp. 6–7.
[2] In the United States, gross national product increased from four to eight times the value of its raw materials input between 1900 and 1950. (US Department of Commerce, *Raw Materials in the United States Economy*, Washington DC, 1954, cited in UN, *World Economic Survey 1955*, p. 36.)
[3] While the consumption of cotton in industrial countries rose by 7 per cent between 1950/2 and 1955/7, wool by 12 per cent, rubber by 15 per cent, jute by 17 per cent, and copper by 20 per cent, consumption of substitute *processed* materials, largely synthetics, rose appreciably faster: steel 31 per cent, wood-pulp 33 per cent, synthetic rubber 44 per cent, aluminium 61 per cent, plastic materials 96 per cent, and synthetic fibres 211 per cent (National Institute of Economic and Social Research, cited in *Barclays Bank Review*, February 1961).
[4] Despite official dampers, agricultural yields in the United States have been growing at 3–4 per cent yearly since the Second World War, well above average for the economy as a whole (see *The Economist*, 30 December 1961, p. 1289; *Economic Report of the US President*, January 1960, cited in A. Shonfield, *The Attack on World Poverty*, p. 176); in France, with a four-year break, it has topped 4·5 per cent yearly (*The Economist*, 1 September 1962, p. 774); and within the Common Market countries as a group, nine-tenths of food intake is produced locally and self-sufficiency is within sight (*The Times*, 3 September 1963). Even in

While the first factor has affected all raw materials producers, the second and third have singled out the backward exporting countries with particular vehemence.

The flagging in both the traditional pull and push towards foreign investment has reduced the flow of private capital from Britain. Not that it is negligible. What with government encouragement and the accumulated business ties and habits of generations, recent capital exports have probably been larger than during any comparable period—some £300–400 million a year over the last decade.[1] None the less, they have been much less significant economically for both supplier and recipients than in their hey-day before the First World War: in the last decade or so, investment abroad has run at about 2 per cent of gross national product compared with 8 per cent in the earlier period; they have absorbed a tenth of savings compared with half before 1914;[2] and returns on foreign investment have been running at slightly over 2 per cent of national income[3] compared with 4 per cent in the 1880's, 7 per cent in 1903, and 10 per cent in 1914.[4] In the two decades before the First World War, 61 per cent of all new capital issues was on overseas account;[5] by 1938 these were

---

Britain, home production now accounts for about half the consumption by volume of a larger population compared with about one-third in 1939. ('Changes in Britain's Agriculture', *MBR*, August 1964, p. 19.)

[1] The lower figure is an official estimate for 1953–63, closely supported by another for 1946–57 (*Assistance from the United Kingdom for Overseas Development*, Cmd. 974, March 1960, p. 6; *Aid to Developing Countries*, Cmd. 2147, September 1963, p. 8; *Radcliffe Report*, Table 33, p. 264); the higher figure is Conan's for 1956–7 (*Capital Imports into Sterling Countries*, p. 84). Between 1885 and 1895, capital exports from Britain averaged some £30 million a year, and during the following decade, some £40 million a year (*Problems of International Investment*, p. 115) or, in today's prices, about £100 million annually over the whole period. They became massive only between 1905 and 1913— some £200 million a year—but even then did not reach the £150 million mark, roughly the current rate in real terms, until 1910 (C. K. Hobson, cited in Conan, op. cit., p. 82). Feis gives lower figures: £185 million annual average for 1910–13 (*Europe the World's Banker, 1870–1914*, pp. 14–15).

[2] Current proportion from estimates in the text and the Central Statistical Organization's 'Blue Books' on *National Income Statistics*; pre-First World War proportion—very rough estimates based on Feis, op. cit., pp. 5, 14–15.

[3] Annual average of 'net income from abroad' for 1953–6 as given in the Blue Books plus an estimated £200 million of earnings reinvested abroad as given in the *Radcliffe Report*, p. 264, and *The Times*, 24 April 1958.

[4] Feis, op. cit., p. 16; Jenks gives a figure of 20 per cent for 1914 (*The Migration of British Capital to 1875*, pp. 5–6).

[5] from A. R. Hall, 'A Note on the English Capital Market', in *Economica*, February 1957, p. 62.

down to 30 per cent and more recently accounted for no more than 20 per cent of the total.[1]

If private capital exports could cope more or less with the scale of industrialization abroad at the pre-1914 pace, today it manifestly cannot.

The direction of flow has also changed. While the overwhelming bulk of British investment overseas in 1914 was in the backward countries of the day, and almost half within the Empire,[2] since the Second World War the flow has increasingly been towards developed countries in and outside the Commonwealth, half or less than half going to backward countries.[3] The extent of change is obscured by the continued growth, largely out of ploughed-back profits, of inherited blocks of investment in backward Commonwealth countries; it is none the less becoming increasingly apparent.[4]

What with the new pattern of savings in developed western economies which has enabled the large industrial organization to marry financial near-independence to an increasingly strong position technologically and in production; the ruin of the traditional investing strata; the reduced emphasis on winning raw materials for industry; the increasing ease in communication and travel; and the decline in the flow to backward countries of skills, attitudes, and the societies that engendered them—the *identity of the international investor* has changed radically over the last two generations. Industrial firms—not merchant banks or trading companies—are now the majors.[5]

The typical *form of investment* has changed in a similar manner. Where investment in directly controlled branches and subsidiaries constituted under 10 per cent of total British foreign holdings before the First World War, in 1958 they accounted for 87 per cent of investments in the Commonwealth.[6]

Indian experience conforms to these trends. Between mid-1948 and

[1] UN, *The International Flow of Private Capital 1956–1958*, p. 57.

[2] from Feis, *Europe the World's Banker*, p. 23.

[3] Some £150 million a year in the 1960's as estimated in *Aid to Developing Countries*, Cmd. 2147, p. 8.

[4] 'There has been a tendency in recent years for the flow of private capital to the developing [backward] countries to level off or even decline. . . .' (ibid.)

[5] 'The outstanding feature of post-war years', writes an authority on British capital flows, 'has perhaps been the investment of private capital in industry [abroad]' (Conan, *Capital Imports*, p. 48), and 90 per cent of the more easily traced American gross private investment overseas went into industry and oil production in the 1950–7 period. (From UN, *Private Capital 1956–1958*, Table 7, p. 27.)

[6] From Conan, op. cit., pp. 49, 64, 85.

the end of 1961, some Rs 438 crores gross—Rs 307 crores net—of foreign, non-banking, private business investment flowed into the country,[1] more than doubling the original total of Rs 256 crores.[2] Most of this, and almost all the fresh capital, went into manufacturing and petroleum, the latter heavily biased towards its manufacturing—or refining—end. Old-type spheres of investment—plantations, mining, trade, managing agencies—either declined absolutely or grew slowly. Within manufacturing, the traditional textile industries lost capital on balance, while technologically intensive branches such as chemicals or electrical goods grew greatly.[3] And the ratio of direct to portfolio investments rose from about 1:6 to 10:1 between 1910 and 1960.[4]

Old-type foreign capital has been hard hit by these changes in investment. It deploys too few resources and is committed to too narrow a range of products to adapt easily by 'bringing in new skills, new techniques, new trades and industries: and at the same time, reducing or relinquishing activity in trades and crafts which were introduced many years ago', as have many of the large international firms.[5] Where it makes the attempt it finds difficulty in meeting the new generation of foreign capital on a competitive footing. Not only is it normally less efficient, more heavily committed to foreign operations and to one or two regions, but it is at a disadvantage in dealing with the government precisely when the increasing interpenetration of politics and capital flows puts a premium on such dealings.[6] Where it has succeeded in making the transition, it

---

[1] See below, p. 299.

[2] Revised Reserve Bank figure ('Foreign Investments in India: 1959 and 1960' RBI, *Bulletin*, May 1961, Statement IV, p. 684).

[3] See below, p. 243.

[4] From Sir George Paish's estimates of British investments in India and Ceylon, 1910, as given in RBI, *Census*, p. 152; and RBI, *Survey 1961*, Statement 10, pp. 72–3.

[5] E. J. Pedler, Director, United Africa Company, largest of the Unilever subsidiaries, in an address at Chatham House, reprinted in *International Affairs*, October 1955, p. 467.

[6] A senior British trade official with wide experience of India saw the key difference between the 'international firm' and the 'regional firm' in their scale of priorities. The former, in his view, places its country, its profits locally, and its host country in that order of importance, the same order that he, a British civil servant, was bound to adopt, while the latter's hierarchy of values started with profits and ended with the United Kingdom. Not surprisingly, he found the international firm always willing to consult him locally, and his superiors in London, before making an important move; while regional firms, less able to afford the time, more committed to adopting an attitude to local events, less able

has had to undertake far-reaching changes in internal organization.[1]

(b) *Trade:* A limited degree of industrialization in countries exporting primary products was as much a product of world wars and depression as was diversification in developed industrial ones. Resulting from both is the decline in the traditional exchange between them of food and raw materials for manufactured goods. Excluding oil—a special case—the export volume of primary products from non-industrial countries increased at less than half the rate of exports from industrial countries between 1928 and 1955; the share of non-industrial countries in world exports dropping from under one-third to under one-quarter in the period.[2]

India's foreign trade complies narrowly with these trends.[3] The volume of *exports*—four-fifths of which are based on agricultural products—dropped by about a third between the late nineteen-twenties and -fifties. Tea—21 per cent by value in the Second Plan— is static, faced with saturation in the major British market and with sharpening competition on the part of old producers (Ceylon, Japan) and new ones (East Africa, Argentina, Iran). Jute and jute products— 18 per cent—are now two-thirds the volume they were in the mid-twenties (from undivided India). A combination of circumstances, including the spread of substitutes, Pakistan competition, quota restrictions and price mark-ups in Western Europe, permit little hope of expansion. Exports of cotton textiles—10 per cent—are even less likely to grow in view of the rapid spread of the industry throughout the world, particularly to cheap modern producers like Hong Kong, and quota restrictions in developed countries. Much the same can be said of the rest of India's traditional agricultural exports —raw cotton, nuts, vegetable oils, spices, tobacco, fruit and vegetables, gums, resins, and hides, skins, and leather—which together made up another 30 per cent of foreign earnings.

New engineering and chemical exports have been able to find only

---

to influence their course, and possessing a distinct order of priorities, often by-passed his office and advice.

[1] See below, pp. 56 ff.

[2] GATT, *Trends in International Trade*, Geneva, 1958, cited in R. Nurkse, *Patterns of Trade and Development*, p. 20.

[3] Unless otherwise stated, the information in this and the following paragraphs is based on the Export Promotion Committee, *Report*, 1957; Import and Export Policy (Mudaliar) Committee, *Report*, 1962; *Statistical Abstracts*; PC, *Third Plan*, pp. 134–6, *passim*; GATT, *Trade of Less-Developed Countries*, 1962; UN, *A Study of Trade*; S. J. Patel, 'Export Prospects . . .', *EJ*, September 1959.

limited access to markets abroad. Where they are not restricted in entering developed markets by 'voluntary' export quotas agreed with foreign producers, they have to compete on equal terms with established producers in their home territories. Access has often been made more difficult by agreements between foreign producers and their Indian associates to limit sales to certain areas.[1] And entry into other developing markets is naturally complicated by protection. None the less, these exports nearly trebled during the last decade to form just under 4 per cent of the total at its end. The fastest-growing export item has been, and will probably continue to be, iron ore which is expected to have increased six or sevenfold in the decade ending with the Third Plan, and in 1960–1 accounted for over 3 per cent of the total.

Since before the war, the volume of *imports* has risen by about one-quarter and their composition radically altered. Industrial consumer goods have declined from about one-half to about one-eighth of the total; about one-fifth are food imports, two-fifths industrial raw materials, and under one-third capital goods. Except for the last these are relatively new items.

The direction of India's foreign trade has also changed a great deal following the world trend towards diversification and, more recently, in response to pressures from aid- and credit-giving countries. Before the First World War, Britain was still supplying more than three-fifths of imports and taking a quarter of exports in return.[2] In 1963–4, Britain supplied 15 per cent of imports and took 21 per cent of exports, compared with 34 and 17 per cent respectively for the United States, 12 and 7 per cent for the Common Market countries, 11 and 13 per cent for Eastern Bloc countries, and 8 and 13 per cent for Japan.[3] The growth of trade with the Eastern Bloc has been the most significant feature of recent years; in eleven years, 1952/3–1963/4, exports rose from 0·4 to 13 per cent of the total, and imports from almost nothing to one-ninth.[4]

There is little comfort in all this for the old import-export houses. Their traditional export lines are declining or stagnating. In the event of new ones attaining the volume and importance of the old, it is not the general exporter that would reap the benefit, but manu-

[1] See below, pp. 280, 283–4.
[2] K. S. Shelvankar, *The Problem of India*, p. 143; Islam, *Foreign Capital*, p. 87.
[3] RBI, *Bulletin*, November 1964, Table 44, pp. 1469–70.
[4] From H. M. Patel in *ET*, 6 March 1962; *The Economist*, 1 June 1963, p. 928; *India 1963*.

facturers trading on their own account or, to some extent, the official State Trading Corporation acting as agent in the growing trade with the eastern bloc.[1] Nor is the foreign house likely to flourish within the declining segment remaining to established exporters. Were it not for tea, two-thirds of which is still handled by old-type British firms, and, perhaps, jute yarns and manufacturers (about 30 per cent), their share of the export trade might well have declined to virtually nothing.[2]

The outlook for them in imports is even worse. The Government is now the major importer of food, some raw materials (notably steel), and capital goods to the extent of 45 per cent of the total in 1960–1. In the private sector, capital goods imports—one-sixth of the total in that year—are now almost always supplied directly to the ultimate user, more often than not as investment in kind by foreign firms; raw materials and intermediate goods, which together account for well over half and in which oil is an important element, also tend to bypass the general importer. The result is that 'established importers' accounted for little more than one-tenth of imports in 1959–60 compared with over three-fifths of all import licences by value in 1951, and 'actual users' for 56 per cent of imports compared with 23 per cent of licences in the earlier year.[3] As a group, importers are going through a lean season;[4] and foreign importers are doing worse than average.[5]

The increase in the number of India's trading partners has also dealt harshly with the old British firms. Many of the advantages that accrued from the close-knit web of British suppliers, shipping, finance, insurance, markets, and Government are less relevant than they were. At the same time many of the new suppliers prefer

[1] Within four years of being formed the STC was handling under 5 per cent of all India's exports and about one-fifth of exports to the eastern bloc. (Economist Intelligence Unit, *The State Trading Corporation*, pp. 13, 44.)

[2] External Transactions of Foreign-Controlled Companies in India—1958', RBI, *Bulletin*, January 1960, Table II, p. 14. Even in tea, the share of British exporters declined fairly rapidly during the three years spanned by the article, from 72·9 per cent in 1956 to 64·7 per cent in 1958.

[3] Bhagwati, 'Indian Balance of Payments Policy and Exchange Auctions', *OEP*, February 1962, p. 53; *Mudaliar Report*, Appendix H, p. 109.

[4] 'Of late', wrote the All-India Importers' Association, 'the word "import" is believed to connote some anti-national activity and the importer is maligned as the agent of a foreign manufacturer, an enemy of the indigenous industry and a total misfit in the present setup.' (*Memorandum on Import and Export Policy Committee Questionnaire*, 1961, p. 3.)

[5] See below, pp. 42–43.

not to use channels developed by and for their competitors. Early in the thirties, German interests formed links directly with Indian houses; they have continued to do so; Japanese and Americans follow suit; as do Eastern Bloc countries which in any case are encouraged to route their fast-growing trade with India more and more through the State Trading Corporation and other official agencies. In this way British houses were side-stepped by design at their most vital point—the link between India and the world economy—and denied access to a growing proportion of the country's trade just as this trade entered into secular decline on its export side and changed its character, to their detriment, on the import side.

(c) *Skills:* 'One reason why the managing agency system has continued is that there has not been a sufficient supply of managerial ability to meet the need.'[1] The same might be said of technical skills, at one time virtually the exclusive province of the British managing agencies. Much has happened to change matters.

A quarter-century of full employment has reduced to a trickle the flow of 'fortune seekers' who once preferred the uncertainty of work abroad to the certainties of unemployment and depression at home. In particular, the great Scottish emigration commemorated in many of the managing agency names in Calcutta is now barely more than a gentle spill over the border southwards. Prosperity has had an indirect effect in lowering the marrying age and so inhibiting the free movement of recruits overseas and in setting a more inflexible term to their stay.

Heavy personal taxation in developing countries reinforces these effects. Expatriate management and staff other than technicians receive no tax concessions in India. Rates have increased continuously in the years of Independence so that in the significant £5–10,000 a year bracket they have since 1957 been uniformly higher than in Britain, most Continental countries, the United States, and Japan.[2]

As important a deterrent since 1955 has been the taxation of all perquisites including severance grants. When it is remembered that these 'perks' could amount to half the basic salary, six months'

[1] NCAER (National Council of Applied Economic Research), *The Managing Agency System*, p. 126.

[2] NCAER, *Taxation and Foreign Investment*, pp. 14–16; IIPO, *Monthly*, March 1964, Blue Supplement, p. xi, Table I.

home leave every three years, including a round-trip passage to Britain for the entire family, a large well-furnished house ('bungalow'), up to four servants, and a chauffeur-driven car, as in a fairly typical paper mill;[1] that they frequently covered entertainment and club allowances, and a grant towards the education of children; that the sale of a partner's interest on retirement might have amounted, in a good year and in a large company, to as much as a couple of hundred thousand pounds or more, it is clear that the visions—more often than not groundless but none the less widespread—of quick enrichment and early retirement 'to have hunting in Scotland and fishing in Devonshire', in the wistful phrase of one old-timer, have lost much of their substance. As this same director concluded, 'none of these young chaps coming out here now will be able to do that'.

Where, notwithstanding, a small migration of managerial skills is induced, it is normally on terms that old-type British capital finds hard to meet. Experience shows that an after-tax income one-quarter to half as much again as the home income is needed to secure a recruit for an overseas posting.[2] In order to achieve this at the rates of personal taxation prevailing in the early sixties, a married man with two children would have had to receive between 30 and 60 per cent above the rupee equivalent of his English salary at £2,000 a year, rising to between double and quadruple at £6,000 a year, before falling off again at the higher levels. To meet American requirements, the disparities would need to be greater, rising from between 50 and 100 per cent more at $5,600 a year to a peak of between 180 and 360 per cent more at $28,000. The new industrial giants might be able to afford this level of payments; old-type firms cannot.

Tax considerations do not apply directly in the case of purely technical staff, at least not for their first three years in the country. Even here, however, the large international firm enjoys some advantage in that they have a greater proportion of such staff and often operate a system of shunting them from country to country. It can, further, be expected to choose its recruits more carefully, has the organization to do so and, having chosen, can afford, before sending

[1] Eddison, *Growth of the Pulp and Paper Industry in India*, p. 186. These, plus 'a suitable outfit allowance' are also recommended in an article otherwise devoted to the theme: 'a foreign technician is in many cases a white elephant to . . . Indian industry'. ('Employment of Foreign Technicians in India', *ET*, 7 June 1962.)

[2] Studies cited in NCAER, *Taxation and Foreign Investment*, p. 10; J. S. fforde, *An International Trade in Managerial Skills*, p. 35.

them abroad, to train them—and their wives—in the arts of 'over-seasmanship' either intramurally or, increasingly in Britain, in special institutions like the Oversea Service. The regional firm is necessarily less selective, hence more vulnerable.

There is more here than a problem of resources. The prospect of a career with an international firm is becoming progressively more attractive as they swing round to the view of '*jobs* abroad as an integral part of management training and promotion',[1] in contrast with the *expatriate career* that is within the provenance of the old-type regional firm. Where employment with the one offers a reasonably clear perspective of advancement with years and experience, promotion in the other is frequently and necessarily arbitrary and capricious—the more so as a substantial minority of these firms are still private companies. As one disenchanted employee of a large managing agency put it after complaining about the distribution of bonus between three directors and seventy staff in the proportion of 2 : 3— 'No one knows the declared profit or sees a statement. What one gets is what one's own boss or the management thinks one is worth.' In his case there was no promotion or incentive scheme; leave times depended on the firm. No wonder, as he said, 'the bright ones don't return for a second contract'. No wonder, too, that there has been throughout this sector 'a small but highly lethal trickle of wastage among the 30–35-year-old age group.'[2]

Taken together with the bunched retirements of senior management at the end of the Second World War, the shortage of foreign staff has clearly become a major problem for old-type foreign capital.

This might be thought an admirable background for rapid recruitment amongst the growing Indian middle class. The skills required are normally not too specialized; financially it would be attractive; and there is every encouragement from a government committed to Indianization in the upper reaches of foreign management. Yet, paradoxically, it is the international firm that has gone farthest in employing Indians in such positions while the regional firm which needs them most has been reluctant to undergo any dilution. Although Indians formed 78 per cent of all employees earning Rs 1,000 a month and above in foreign-controlled companies in January 1963, they accounted for 45 per cent in plantations at that date, 57 per cent

---

[1] PEP, *Management and Underdeveloped Countries*, June 1959, p. 126.
[2] fforde, *Managerial Skills*, p. 136.

in banking, 65 per cent in transit and transport. New industries, on the other hand, even technologically complex ones, show a consistently high rating: oil companies 91 per cent, chemicals 89 per cent, rubber 88, metals including iron and steel 87, printing, publishing, and paper 84, machinery 83 per cent, and so on.[1]

The marked difference in behaviour of the two foreign sectors is not surprising. Even if it were to approach Indianization of management with equal enthusiasm, old-type foreign capital is inherently less capable of putting it into effect. It is, on the whole, a contracting sector under pressure from such of the old, expatriate staff as cannot start afresh, to reserve them jobs and the avenues of promotion still available. The firms are generally too small to excise centres of opposition by posting, repatriation, training, or dismissal in the way large international firms have done.[2] Although all foreign capital is in theory subject to the same official pressure for Indianization, it is new firms seeking permission to start up, or firms wishing to undertake large-scale expansion that are most vulnerable in practice.

There is more to it. By reason of the scale and international character of its operations, the typical new investing company has found it necessary to build a system of control into the structure of the organization. If it appears tolerant of the national origins of high-level staff in its foreign subsidiaries, if as in India its encouragement of '-ization' often precedes and exceeds the requirements of law, this is due more to it being able to displace decisive authority upwards than to any other factor. This the old-type plantation or forestry enterprise, the relatively small cotton or jute mill cannot do so easily. They operate with individually recruited staff and an unsophisticated mechanical and technological apparatus which does not require more than rudimentary division of labour within the firm. Their regional concentration precludes a division between a controlling centre and an operational periphery and makes the displacement of authority difficult. Local infiltration of their top executive and technical strata is therefore tantamount to dilution of control and a step in the direction of losing it entirely.[3]

It is for this reason above all that the enduring lack of home recruits cannot be made good by enrolment in India without a fundamental change in the character of the old-type foreign sector, and that the

---

[1] GOI Press Note, 21 February 1964.
[2] See, for example, fforde, *Managerial Skills*, pp. 103–4.
[3] See discussion below, pp. 294 ff.

shortage of top-level staff has become a critical problem as becomes clear from even the briefest conversation with management.

II INDIAN COMPETITION

The isolation that flowed from war and depression and from the structural changes they wrought in developed economies gave Indian capital the opportunities denied foreign investors. Although both grew under the stimulus of what amounted to a protected market, Indian capital's expansion was relatively greater, more enduring, and, ultimately, inimical to foreign capital's pre-eminence.

Indian investment did not by and large upset foreign control in its traditional fields until after the Second World War,[1] and often not until the mid-fifties; but the control had become far from absolute. The insistence of Indian shareholders that ownership be converted into influence could not be denied entirely. As a result, the proportion of Indian directors in the major foreign jute firms rose from just above 5 to over 51 per cent between 1920 and 1950; from 5 to 54 per cent in the major foreign coal companies; and from 5 to 32 per cent in foreign tea firms during the slightly longer period, 1920–55.[2]

Changes in the distribution of directorships on the Boards of foreign managing agencies are perhaps a more accurate indication of the shifting relation of forces. Here Indian progress was slower but still considerable—from 17 out of 382 directorships in the thirteen top British houses (some 4 per cent) in 1911, to 316 out of 741, or 43 per cent in 1951.[3] The diffusion of control was not confined to a few companies: where 85 per cent of foreign tea companies had no Indians at all on the Boards in 1920, the proportion had dropped to 40 per cent by 1955; in other industries the drop was steeper, from 88 to 10 per cent in coal, and from 84 to 2 per cent in jute between 1920 and 1950.[4] By the mid-fifties when circumstances favoured the final heave towards full and explicit Indian hegemony in nearly all but the most technologically intensive fields, foreign capital had been sufficiently infiltrated for the transfer to be accomplished with a minimum of difficulty.

[1] See above, p. 3.
[2] From Basu, *Managing Agency System*, Table II prepared by Amitava Sen, p. 213.
[3] Mehta, *Structure of Indian Industries*, p. 316.
[4] Amitava Sen, Table I, in Basu, op. cit., p. 212.

Encroachment was one approach. Another was open assault. From earliest times Indian capital had nestled in the margins of foreign capital's favoured fields. Although it acquired thereby the smallest and least efficient units, it gained a stake and experience in modern production on which it could build in times of expansion. More important as it turned out was its adoption of new industries which foreign capital was reluctant to enter. It was in these that Indian capital often proved more enterprising than its British rivals. The Tata steel works, incorporated in 1907, long remained a symbol of Indian temerity and British timorousness in breaking new ground; and although both expanded in war and depression, it was Indian enterprise that took to the new industries with any enthusiasm.[1]

Strict comparison between the two is impossible, but where a list of companies founded by Indian managing agencies shows a heavy concentration of incorporations during the late thirties and the war, and then, after a hiatus, during the modern planning period,[2] a group of thirty-two of the largest foreign houses shows a steep decline in the number of newly incorporated managed companies from 79 in the 1910–19 decade, to 55 in the twenties, 28 in the thirties, 13 in the forties, and 5 between 1950 and 1956.[3] Between 1936–7 and 1942–3 non-Indian companies increased their paid-up capital by 1 per cent compared with 17 per cent for Indian companies.[4]

Studies of individual industries reveal the same picture. The inquiry into the paper industry already quoted found 'initiative and leadership passing more and more into the hands of Indian-controlled companies' from 1936 onwards, despite the fact that the industry has been 'overwhelmingly dominated by British-managed firms for the first three-quarters of a century of its existence'.[5] Although the British firms maintained higher and more consistent standards of quality,[6] Indian management was found to be

more energetic, aggressive, and willing to take financial risks. . . . [They] were prepared to gamble on the growing demand for paper both in the late 1930s and in the early 1950s to a much greater extent than were their

[1] See above, pp. 19 f.
[2] See Gokhale Institute, *Business Communities in India*, pp. 50–52.
[3] G. Tyson, *Managing Agency*, p. 42.
[4] *Recent Social and Economic Trends in India*, pp. 63–65, quoted in Bose, *Indo-British Big Business Deals*, p. 10.
[5] Eddison, *Growth of the Pulp and Paper Industry in India*, p. 215.
[6] ibid., p. 146.

Western-managed counterparts. They did not limit themselves to the expansion they could achieve out of their own resources but made much of their growth on borrowed money.[1]

After the war it was the Indian manufacturers that toured paper-making plants in North America;[2] and it was the Birla group, today the largest producers, that first undertook a major expansion at the end of the decade, by doubling capacity at their Orient Mills. Subsequent expansion has made this group the best equipped technically and the cheapest producer in the country.[3] Where British firms did grow—as has F. W. Heilger in Orissa—they did so piecemeal and reluctantly, in response to government pressure.[4]

The assault on foreign capital's dominating position scored some success even before Independence. Amongst industries that had achieved importance by the First World War, and disregarding cotton textiles which even then was four-fifths Indian-controlled, the foreign-controlled labour force fell from 45 to 11 per cent of the total in sugar refining by the Second World War and from 100 to 83 per cent in jute by 1937.[5] Between 1911 and 1921 the number of tea gardens run by foreign public companies in Bengal fell from 66 to 54 per cent of the total and the number run privately from 19 to 11 per cent.[6] The foreign share of coal production in that province fell from over four-fifths to two-thirds between 1904 and 1920.[7] Two relative newcomers show the same trend: more than nine-tenths of the labour employed in cement making was on indigenous capital's payroll by 1944;[8] and the foreign share of paper output fell from 86 to 34 per cent between 1913 and 1957.[9]

Finance was no exception: in 1914 foreign banks held well over 70 per cent of all deposits; by 1937 their share had dropped to 57 per cent,[10] and by 1947 to 17 per cent.[11]

International trade followed the same course: by 1951–2, 61–66 per cent of non-Government imports and 56–63 per cent of such

---

[1] Eddison, *Growth of the Pulp and Paper Industry in India*, p. 235.

[2] ibid., p. 130.   [3] ibid., p. 230.   [4] ibid., p. 223.

[5] Gokhale Institute, *Business Communities in India*, Tables 1, 5, 8; pp. 4–5, 10, 21.

[6] Buchanan, *Capitalistic Enterprise in India*, p. 68.   [7] ibid., pp. 267, 268.

[8] Gokhale Institute, op. cit., Table 8, p. 21.

[9] Eddison, *Growth of the Pulp and Paper Industry*, p. 225. These shifts in relative importance are the more impressive in view of the expansion of total production during the periods mentioned (see above, p. 21).

[10] Islam, *Foreign Capital*, p. 172.

[11] Pardiwalla, 'Exchange Banks in India', *EW*, 10 February 1951, p. 154.

exports were handled by Indian firms.[1] Five years later, slightly over 70 per cent of trade each way was handled by Indian firms. Were it not for the strong foreign hold on tea exports (amounting to more than two-thirds) and on mineral oil imports (nearly 100 per cent), Indian progress would have been even more marked.[2]

Indian capital naturally thrust towards trade and uncomplicated industries for which machinery, processes, and skills were freely available, abroad if not in India, and which required a relatively modest outlay; precisely the spheres in which old-type foreign capital was interested. Initially this did not matter too much. Foreign capital's pre-eminence was not seriously threatened so long as it had the use of Indian funds with which to compete against independent Indian capital, a facility it enjoyed until the transfer of power. But with Independence the balance of advantage for the Indian investor swung decisively towards 'national' capital: it was the leaders of the Indian business community who now possessed detailed knowledge of government intentions just when these intentions were becoming more and more relevant to business; in the aftermath of the anti-British campaign, purely Indian business enjoyed a freedom from scrutiny and criticism in politically sensitive areas such as tax avoidance and evasion, relations with licensing and enforcement authorities, with workers and trade unions which British houses could not claim; British business became even more cautious and unenterprising than before. In short, with Independence came the long-delayed unity of Indian capital and the final isolation of its old-type British counterpart.

The manner of the change showed how powerless the latter had become. Once the post-war flood of voluntary capital repatriations had largely abated, a second, albeit lesser wave of take-overs and attempted take-overs, began to gather momentum. It beat down with ruinous effect on the old foreign sector in the 1950's. The techniques were simple. Inflation had driven a substantial wedge between current and book values in the conservative foreign accounts, between potential and prevailing share prices. An easy money market and complaisant Indian shareholders allowed local investors to buy controlling ownership in British-managed companies at well above

[1] 'Survey of Distribution of Imports and Exports Between Indian and Non-Indian Firms—1951 and 1952', RBI, *Bulletin*, February 1954, p. 101.
[2] 'External Transactions of Foreign-Controlled Companies in India—1958', RBI, *Bulletin*, January 1960, Tables II, III, pp. 14, 15. However, see p. 219 n. 1.

market rates and to abrogate, or threaten to abrogate, their managing agency agreements. In the bilious, undoubtedly exaggerated tones of one principal of a large Calcutta house,

A chap in a Gandhi cap and a dhoti that's none too clean walks into your office one day and says, 'Mr. X, I own 51 per cent of your company.' And, by George, you find that he does too! Then he tells you he wants a seat on your Board. Well, you can't give a seat to a man whom you know ought to be in jail![1]

In the event, as more than one of them found to their surprise, you could and did.

The process started with jute soon after Independence. It spread to tea, light engineering, and insurance in the fifties, despite an Ordinance of July 1951 requiring official sanction for changes in control over any company, and reached a climax in the middle of the decade. By 1957 it had run its course. Some of the take-over campaigns were enormous in scope. Bangur, now among the eight largest Indian groups, emerged from relative obscurity at the end of the Second World War largely by this method.[2] Dalmia-Sahu-Jain, one of the top four at the end of the decade, also owed much to it. Haridas Mundhra, principal in the *affaire* which brought about the resignation of the Finance Minister, T. T. Krishnamachari, in 1958, looked for a time as if he might reach the same stature.[3] At every level, in both managed and managing companies the apathy and tacit co-operation of Indian shareholders on which British managing houses had built their system of control, was clearly on the way out.

They responded in two ways. Many felt compelled to take refuge in the secretiveness which was coming increasingly under public attack. To quote the British-dominated Bengal Chamber of Commerce:

. . . there is objection to the disclosure of Directors' and Managing Agents' shareholdings in the balance sheets [of managed companies]. . . .

[1] Reported in G. A. Wiggins, *Private Foreign Investment in the Development of India*, p. 34.

[2] Hazari, *Structure of the Corporate Private Sector*, p. 115.

[3] Since his conviction for fraud it has become fashionable to talk of Mundhra as just another wide-boy with, perhaps, more nerve than most. Before that, however, he was considered to be 'no mere speculator, such as we are familiar with on the kerb market . . . he works on a bigger canvas, and with more energy and shrewdness than that' (*Capital*, 17 February 1955, p. 223). He inspired sufficient confidence for a number of foreign banks to finance his operations (Evidence of Mr. James Esplen, Partner, Place, Siddons and Gough, cited in Chagla Commission, *Report*, p. 11).

This would, it is considered in cases where the holdings are low, merely draw the attention of unscrupulous speculators to the fact and encourage them to corner the shares with a view to gaining control and removing either the Directors or Managing Agents or both.[1]

As a result many houses clung to their partnership or private company structure long after taxation considerations and the need for more money and new recruits to management pointed to the advantages of going public. Not that it did them much good: their defensive stance prevented growth and often proved a major ingredient in the insecurity felt by expatriate staff, which fed back into a still greater defensiveness.

A more important response was for the managing agencies to try and beat 'cornerers' at their own game. In his authoritative study of thirty-two of the principal houses, Tyson states that

practically every one of the managing agents interrogated have, at some time or another in recent years, had to lay out considerable sums in order to add to their shareholding in managed companies to protect their management contracts . . . [since] every large managing agency concern has at one time or another suffered in greater or less degree from speculative raids upon the shareholding of its managed companies. . . .[2]

The broader effects of such investments will be taken up below; here it is sufficient to note the fact and to point out that nothing could be more injurious to an agency house and to old-type foreign capital as a whole. Its strength lay precisely in its freedom to move resources from plant to plant and between industries as occasion presented itself, and in the associated freedom to exercise control over large masses of capital with relatively slight investment of its own. Self-defence through immobilization is a burden it cannot bear.

III INDEPENDENCE AND THE STATE

(a) *Independence:* To suggest that Independence flowed directly from the changes in the international setting described in the first part of this chapter and from the associated strengthening of Indian capital's position is to oversimplify immeasurably a complex historical process. The rise of the nationalist movement, the sudden weakening of Britain during the war, the restiveness pervading her

[1] Memorandum on the 'Advantages of the Managing Agency System in the Case of a Group of Coal Companies', Company Law Committee, 1950–1, *Written Evidence*, Vol. I, Part I, p. 83.
[2] *Managing Agency*, pp. 21–22.

own and the Indian armed forces at its close, and many other factors need to be taken into account. Yet there is a sense in which these changes were decisive: they weakened the traditional forms of Indo-British complementarity and ensured that any inroads made into British power, whether from within the country or without, would not be made good. They gave, as it were, permissive authority for changes in British colonial policy.

After the First World War, the old foreign sector contributed little, if anything, to the solution of India's mounting unemployment problem.[1] Its stagnation and decline focused Indian labour's attacks on foreign rule, sharpening their demand for an expanding economy and for the political status that might engender it. In this they were at one with Indian capital that hastened to fill the partial vacuum created, but that found its further development hampered by foreign rule.[2]

In its turn, Indian capital drew strength from the new forms of foreign investment. These were geared to the domestic market, interested in its expansion, in finding workers with modern skills and partners versed in local conditions—interested in fact in economic growth and in the politics of growth. Even the falling off in recruitment to expatriate careers was a factor in hastening the transfer of power: it left gaps in the Indian administration, police, and army, that had to be filled by Indians or not at all. To complete the passage quoted from Maurice Zinkin:

In 1939, had the British gone overnight, India would have found itself desperately, perhaps fatally short of all the people needed to run a modern State. By 1946, there were enough. There were not any to spare, but there were enough. From then on, British rule was dead, for the British no longer had a function to perform.[3]

Abroad, the spread of an industrial economy beyond Britain, her decline as an exporter of cheap consumer staples together with her restrictive control of India's foreign trade and economic relations, subjected her to mounting international pressure to relinquish the advantages she held in the country. On the Allied side alone, it culminated during the Second World War in the promise to dismantle Imperial Preference as a condition of American Lend-Lease,[4]

[1] See Anstey, 'Economic Development', in O'Malley (ed.), *Modern India and the West*, p. 278.
[2] See above, pp. 11 ff.   [3] See above, p. 18.
[4] Article 7 of the 1942 Agreement.

and in recurrent American demands for colonial independence as part of the post-war settlement;[1] it was epitomized in Roosevelt's abortive attempt to meet Stalin *à deux* (without Churchill) to outline a post-war settlement early in 1943.[2]

Finally, the onset of Cold War made of Independence and economic development two great counters in a global confrontation which deals in political status as earnestly as in missiles.

These were some of the factors in India's independence—certainly not all. That they derived to some extent from the developments outlined above is clear. It is clear too that their influence reached beyond the act of Independence to define the tasks and policy of the new India, namely economic development and a reconstruction of the economy to implement it. In the nature of things, they also predetermined a greatly enhanced and active role in the economy for the new state.

The state confronts all foreign capital in three capacities—as competitor, regulator of the conditions of activity, and protector of Indian capital. But it is old-type foreign capital that bears the brunt of the first two which are dealt with in the following sections.[3]

(*b*) *State competition:* Since Independence, particularly since the mid-fifties when the switch towards rapid industrialization occurred, the state has been competing actively for Indian resources; providing capital and skills; and undertaking more and more direct production.

If, towards the end, the great strength of old-type British capital lay in its being able to deploy Indian savings on a large scale, increased *direct* taxation—by well over 250 per cent between 1948–9 and 1964–5[4]—has tended to limit its source at the same time as increased government borrowing—Rs 90–100 crores a year during the Second Plan and Rs 150–200 crores a year subsequently, compared with a small net repayment during 1935–40[5]—has diverted it to other channels. Given the background of increasingly large drafts on Indian savings by the new industrial sector, both Indian and

---

[1] See, for example, Cordell Hull, *Memoirs*, pp. 1477–78, 1496, 1600–1, *passim*: N. Mansergh, *Survey of British Commonwealth Affairs*, Vol. IV, pp. 146, 192, 193.

[2] US Department of State, *Foreign Relations of the United States, Conferences at Cairo and Teheran*, pp. 3–4, 10–12.

[3] See below, pp. 223, 317–9 ff. for discussion of the state's role in shielding Indian capital from foreign competition.

[4] See Appendix 4 below, p. 332.

[5] S. L. N. Simha, *The Capital Market of India*, Table 21, pp. 82–83.

foreign, and of its own pressing need for more funds to help make the transition to new activities or defend its position in the old, competition in this sphere becomes something of a problem. Roughly the same might be said of the *demand* for skills. Although the old foreign sector has proved reluctant to employ Indians in the higher managerial positions,[1] the dent made in the available supply by recruitment to government service[2] cannot fail to have added to their difficulties, particularly in view of the competition from new foreign business and the lessened flow from abroad.

Competition in the *supply* of finance, skill, and services has been more damaging, for here has occurred a straight substitution by the larger, more pervasive institution. During the Second Plan, 1956–61, the Government provided directly 56 per cent of investment in industry and minerals production, amounting to some Rs 175 crores a year.[3] Transfers to private industry were also far from negligible. Apart from Rs 12–16 lakhs a year during the Second Plan made available directly as loans and equity participation,[4] the special financial institutions, some of which are of very recent origin, were contributing up to Rs 22 crores a year towards the end of the fifties[5] and have become very much more important since.[6]

In a different class, the nationalized Life Insurance Corporation

[1] See above, pp. 38–39.

[2] In the eleven years following Independence, something of the order of a quarter of a million persons in 'professional, technical and related categories, and administrative, executive and managerial categories' were added to government and public authority payrolls. (Estimate supplied by courtesy of the Central Statistical Organization, Labour Statistics Division.)

[3] PC, *Third Plan*, p. 39.

[4] Simha, op. cit., Table 46, p. 203; *Budget 1960–61*, Annexure VII: Provisions for Plan Expenditure – Capital Budget, pp. 503–15.

[5] 'Loans disbursed' by the Industrial Finance Corporation, annual average 1957/8–1960/1—Rs 7·7 crores; 'loans disbursed' by the State Finance Corporations, annual average 1958/9–1960/1—Rs 4 crores; grants and loans by the National Industrial Development Corporation, 1958–9—Rs 2·05 crores; 'financial assistance' by the Industrial Credit and Investment Corporation of India Ltd., 1959—Rs 7 crores; the Refinance Corporation for Industry Private Ltd., annual average 1959/60–1960/1—Rs 1·5 crores. Total about Rs 22 crores (RBI, *Currency and Finance*).

[6] 'Financial Assistance' disbursed by the IFC, July 1962–June 1963, Rs 22·43 crores (RBI, *Bulletin*, November 1963, Table I, p. 1414); 'loans disbursed' by the NIDC, 1962–3, Rs 3·50 crores (ibid., p. 1420); 'loans and investments (gross)' disbursed by the ICICI, 1963, Rs 10·8 crores (ibid., May 1964, p. 649); 'disbursements' by the Refinance Corporation for Industry, 1962, Rs 13·25 crores (*EW*, 21 March 1964, p. 537). Total, not including the State Finance Corporation —Rs 49·98 crores. In addition, an Industrial Development Bank was established in the summer of 1964.

was investing more than Rs 7 crores in company shares and debentures in 1958, two years after being taken over by the state.[1] Altogether, the flow of state funds to modern industry in the private sector was of the order of Rs 43–45 crores *a year* towards the end of the decade compared with a total managing agency investment *outstanding* in the middle of the decade officially estimated at some Rs 50–60 crores.[2]

Naturally, not all private capital benefits from state financing in equal measure: the new large firm is especially favoured, and the managing agency still has some role at the lower reaches of business. Even there, however, it is a limited one.[3]

Similar in effect has been the provision of technical and managerial skills—once almost a monopoly of the British houses—by the state. Between Independence and the end of 1961, the number of students graduating from engineering colleges and polytechnics increased seven or eightfold; that of science graduates fourfold in the shorter period up to 1959–60 and of commerce graduates three to fourfold.[4] Management training has begun in a number of colleges; many of the statutory financial institutions make provision for assisting industry in technical and organizational matters; the Development Wing of the Ministry of Commerce and Industry places its technical staff at the service of the private sector, especially in engineering and chemicals; and training establishments are attached to most of the important state plants. Equally corrosive are the training provisions written into all agreements involving foreign technical collaboration in state projects and the requirement for progressive Indianization in the private foreign sector. Taken together, these measures have virtually eliminated old-type foreign capital as a source of skills.

Production in the public sector has added to their difficulties. The

---

[1] Simha, *Capital Market of India*, Table 15A, p. 68.

[2] *LS Debates*, 6 September 1955, Vol. VII, No. 32, Cols. 12405, 12406.

[3] A breakdown of liabilities of eighty-four large public companies with a paid-up capital of Rs 75 lakhs or more shows that official and quasi-official sources together accounted for 26·3 per cent of the total as against 1·3 per cent from managing agencies. In contrast, public funds formed only 6·4 per cent of the debt of smaller firms with paid-up capital of Rs 10–25 lakhs, as against 7 per cent from managing agencies (NCAER, *Managing Agency*, pp. 72, 74). Rosen shows very clearly the bias towards big established firms on the part of public financing institutions (see p. 231 n. 2, below).

[4] Figures supplied by courtesy of the Central Statistical Organization, Labour Statistics Division.

5

state now provides many of the services traditionally supplied by old-type foreign capital: electric power to the extent of three-fifths of the total in 1960–1, and growing fast;[1] transport—virtually all by air and rail, a considerable amount by road, and over a fourth in shipping.[2] The state now owns the largest bank in the country and the largest trading organization, holds a monopoly of life insurance, runs a number of industrial and service establishments, produces one-fifth of coal output and so on—all of these being fields which old-type foreign capital had dominated.

(c) *Regulation:* Implicit in economic planning and a growing state sector is a comprehensive apparatus of control over private capital. It embraces investment, modes of operation, prices, profits, labour relations, foreign trade and currency, banking—everything in fact that bears on the conduct of business.

The volume of paper-work can be immense. From a study undertaken jointly by the Ministry of Commerce and Industry and the Federation of Indian Chambers of Commerce and Industry in 1961, it appears that cotton textile firms submit on average 312 returns a year, more than one per working day.[3] The time taken can be staggering[4] and the cost for business commensurate. As one company chairman noted before the process really gathered momentum:

Practically every industrial concern of any consequence today feels obliged not only to employ extra staff to cope with the growing volume of inquiries from, and correspondence with, Government offices and officials,

---

[1] PC, *Third Plan*, Table 9, p. 402.   [2] See below, p. 221.

[3] Information received privately from the FICCI. Critics of the 'licence Raj' deal in even larger numbers: 8,228 returns per year per cotton mill according to A. D. Shroff (speech to the 'Democratic Group' of the Indian Merchants' Chamber, reported in *Capital*, 20 November 1952, p. 654).

[4] Interviews at the various economic Ministries in the winter of 1961–2 threw up a fair number of cases in which two years or more were spent in passing through the Industrial Licence, Capital Goods, Foreign Agreements, and Capital Issues Committees, although cases were also known of all four Committees having completed their labours in seven days. In mid-1963, the FICCI was moved to express 'grave concern' at the 'sharp fall' and 'declining trend' in official licensing productivity. They claimed it took an average of over three months for an application to be considered by the Industrial Licensing Committee for the first time, two to three months for a review, six weeks between approval and the issuing of a licence (or more if clarifications were required), and six to twelve months for a Capital Goods Licence (*ET*, 21 June 1963). A full description of the complexities of licensing may be found in 'Government Procedures and Industrial Development', *EW* Annual Number, February 1964, pp. 265–8.

but has, in addition, either to maintain a representation in New Delhi or arrange pilgrimages to that costly capital, or both.[1]

While all firms are affected by the fact of regulation, it is probably true that old-type foreign capital finds the burden heavier than most.

As to the content of regulations, foreign investment in financial or trading concerns is normally not allowed. Within manufacturing it is the heavy, technologically intensive, capital-using and capital-importing but import-saving project that is most likely to be favoured. Similarly, with Indian participation in ownership and control—the more of it the better from the point of view of obtaining required licences. Although not invested with the power of law and frequently ignored,[2] these criteria are clearly inimical to a body of investment biased towards trading, towards light, simple manufacturing, and towards exclusive foreign control.

So it is within the narrower compass of industrial licensing. Beyond issuing a list twice a year of industries in which applications will ordinarily be rejected and another in which they will be approved (from the capacity angle only), the licensing authorities avoid too explicit a statement of their requirements, reserving the right to deal with applicants on an *ad hoc* basis. In practice, old-type foreign firms are hit hardest by this. Of the three segments in a rough tripartite division of the private sector—domestic, and the two wings of foreign capital—they are least able to afford the talent, time, and money for presenting the minutiae of a project effectively, least able to make the 'proper approach' to officialdom, and most likely to suffer from its bias towards bigness.

They are also the hardest hit by the very existence of investment regulations: these strike at the heart of their former strength—the mobility and flexibility with which they could re-deploy resources in response to changing circumstances. Protective tariffs, import restrictions, currency control, and the requirement for 'progressive manufacture' have played havoc with their import-export trade, eliminating many of the greatest names in the business. Price controls have affected the traditional industries almost exclusively—textiles, mining, plantations.

Probably the most crippling of regulations from the old foreign sector's point of view are those embodied in the Companies Act,

[1] Mr. Sreenivasan, Chairman, Kolar Gold Field Mining Company, as reported in *EE*, 17 July 1953, p. 104.
[2] See below, pp. 100 ff.

1956, and its 1960 Amendment, particularly in the sections relating to managing agencies. Although aimed primarily at the more flamboyant excesses usually attributed to Indian houses, their effect has been to reinforce the economic changes sapping the roots of managing agency organization as such. The Government was empowered to prohibit the use of managing agencies in any industry; official sanction is required for their appointment or for renewal of an Agreement; Agreements are limited in time and renewals subject to rigorous safeguards; no managing agency is allowed to manage more than ten public companies or their subsidiaries; transfers of managing agency rights require official approval and are in no case hereditable; payment for managing agency services is limited as are commissions on sales and purchases where these are not abolished altogether; compensation for loss of office is discontinued or very much curtailed; loans by companies to their managing agencies are prohibited and a low ceiling set to current accounts held with them; inter-company loans are restricted; and managing agencies debarred from engaging on their own account in any business likely to compete with that of their managed companies. Opposition to the Act was vociferous throughout its preparation,[1] and many of its provisions were circumvented after it came into force.[2] None the less it

[1] Inside the Lok Sabha, see especially Mohanlal L. Shah, Note of Dissent, Company Law Committee *Report*, pp. 213–21; Tulsidas Kilachand and G. D. Somani, Note of Dissent on the Report of the Joint Committee on the Bill; observations on the Report by N. C. Karayalar (all of which are reprinted in *Extracts from Gazette of India, Extraordinary*, Part II, Section 2, 2 May 1955); speech by G. D. Somani, *LS Debates*, 31 August 1955 (col. 11623). Outside parliament see, especially, FICCI, *Memorandum on the Report of the Companies Law Committee*, 1952; *Views of the Federation of Indian Chambers of Commerce and Industry on the Companies Bill*, 1953; Employers' Association, *Achievements of [the] Managing Agency System*, Calcutta, 1954; ACCI, *Memorandum on the Companies Law Bill*, 1955.

[2] In order to continue as buying and selling agents, many managing agencies terminated their Agreements after having secured appointment of their nominees as managing directors of the companies before the Act reached the Statute Book (*Annual Report of the Working and Administration of the Companies Act, 1956–7*, pp. 10, 13, 77; *EW*, 18 April 1959, pp. 530–1); within two years of Enactment 227 public companies had been converted into private companies in order, presumably, to escape the restriction on the number of managed companies (*Annual Report . . . Companies Act*, 1956–7, p. 13); of the 54 public limited companies listed in the *Investor's India Yearbooks* of 1955–8 inclusive as having terminated their Agreements, 15 appointed their previous managing agencies as 'Secretaries and Treasurers', that is, to substantially the same controlling positions (Basu, *Managing Agency System*, Appendix to Chapter 7, pp. 183–5) and all but four of the remainder were reported as 'being managed

added greatly to the difficulties managing agencies were experiencing in any case in new economic circumstances, and hastened their decline, the number of managed companies falling from 5,055 to 1,440 in the eight years following enactment, from 18 to 6 per cent of the possible total.[1]

IV WITHDRAWAL AND CHANGE

Many of the developments outlined in this chapter have borne heavily on profits in the industries most favoured by old-type foreign capital. While all activities averaged 9·5 per cent between 1948 and 1955, profits in jute, cotton, and other textiles averaged 8·2 per cent, in trading 5·4, coal-mining 8·5, and electricity 8·5 per cent. Plantations were a major exception: tea averaging 17·2 per cent and coffee and rubber 15·6 per cent.[2] Under the circumstances, it is not surprising that the traditional foreign sector has undergone fundamental change since Independence, brought about both through voluntary withdrawal and structural adaptation.

(a) *Withdrawal:* Foreign capital began to leave India after the financial crisis of 1931.[3] Repatriations grew in volume during and immediately after the Second World War, particularly in the periods following the Quit India campaign in August 1942 and between the breakdown of the Cabinet Mission's plan, May 1946, and the final 'Mountbatten Plan' of June 1947. At a guess—necessarily a very

---

ostensibly by Boards of Directors, but their promotion and management remain in the same hands' (*EW*, 18 April 1959, p. 531); taking advantage of the Finance Minister's statement that the measure 'would not affect those who received only fixed salaries, whether they were called managers or technical experts or chief engineers' (*Times of India*, 1 September 1955), many directors have assumed other titles and so escaped the earnings ceiling; companies have been amalgamated at one extreme and others diversified at the other while 'nearly all leading Houses have multiplied the number of their managing agency concerns to avoid the legal limit of ten companies under the same managing agency' (*EW*, 18 April 1959, p. 531).

[1] Raj. K. Nigam, 'The Impact of the Companies Act on the Managing Agency System', *Company News and Notes*, Vol. I, No. 23, 2 September 1963, Table 1, p. 36.

[2] From H. K. Mazumdar, *Business Saving in India*, Table 42, p. 143, based on Reserve Bank and Taxation Enquiry Commission data. Profits are 'gross profits as a percentage of capital employed', and relate in all but textiles, electricity, and the total, to 1950–5 inclusive.

[3] See above, p. 10.

rough one—some Rs 1,350 crores of *British* capital was shipped out between August 1942 and July 1948.[1] More than Rs 720 crores of this was on account of the retirement of private loans and business investment.[2]

By mid-1948, when the Reserve Bank undertook its *Census* of foreign investment, the tide had turned. The position also became clearer: from then up to the end of 1961, capital repatriations totalled some Rs 123 crores.[3] A substantial part of this—Rs 41·1 crores in the three years 1958–60—was on account of the oil companies;[4] the rest, almost entirely from traditional investment.

The extent of withdrawal is best shown, and most significantly, in relation to the managing agencies. In 1938 there were 61 British-controlled houses; by 1962, no more than 25 (including the separate parts of amalgamations) remained British, 32 had passed into Indian control, and the rest had disappeared or were not known to be active or were difficult to allocate.[5] Of the Rs 15·84 crores of liquidations recorded between 15 July 1947 and 31 March 1953, more than one-third (Rs 5·31 crores) was on their account.[6]

A number of special factors affected the managing agencies. Their leverage over large masses of unowned capital made them a favourite target for Indian businessmen, and transfer prices were correspond-

---

[1] Reserve Bank officials consider the best pre-Independence estimates of British investment to be those of the Associated Chambers of Commerce of India and Ceylon (*Memorandum* to the Simon Commission) relating to 1930–1 and the later corroboratory estimate by *The Statist* in 1939 (RBI, *Census*, pp. 15, 16). Taking the later estimate of £1,071–1,120 million or some Rs 1,500 crores and subtracting the revised figure for *British* private long-term business investment for mid-1948 as given in the Reserve Bank's 1953 *Survey* (p. 75)—investment in government and similar securities being negligible—gives the figure in the text, thus: $1500 - 72/100 \times 210) = 1349$. No account is taken of differences in geographic coverage, definition, or valuation.

[2] Rs 930 crores (*The Statist's* £700 million) minus Rs 210 crores (RBI, *Survey 1953* figure). To some extent there is independent corroboration. *Capital* gives Rs 148 crores as the figure for all repatriations between July 1947 and December 1953 (21 October 1954, p. 525); the Reserve Bank an estimated Rs 50 crores for the period July 1948–December 1953 (*Survey 1953*, p. 82) which leaves the year July 1947–June 1948 with an outflow of about Rs 100 crores. Since it is not known to be a peak year for capital withdrawals (having followed the political settlement of 3 June 1947), a total of Rs 720 crores for British capital in the six years 1942–8 does not seem excessive.

[3] An estimated Rs 50 crores, July 1948–December 1953 (RBI, *Survey 1953*, p. 82); Rs 73·1 crores, 1954–61 (RBI, *Survey 1961*, Statement 22, p. 92).

[4] 'Foreign Investments . . . 1960', RBI, *Bulletin*, October 1962, p. 1534.

[5] See Appendix I, p. 323, below.

[6] *Capital*, 3 September 1953, p. 321, citing figures given to the Lok Sabha.

ingly high. Their dependence on Government favour made them particularly vulnerable to the official discrimination expected of, and to some extent obtained from, independent India.[1] Many 'old hands' retired in a body at the end of the war without being able to find replacements. And in the mid-fifties the sudden lurch towards state economic intervention, the Companies Act, and the rash of 'corners' and take-overs augmented the arguments to withdraw.

Business investments were seldom liquidated in their entirety. Between August 1947 and September 1952 only 66 foreign firms were sold outright to Indian interests, for a total of under Rs 15 crores;[2] in the overlapping period, mid-1948 to April 1959, 94 British concerns were sold and under Rs 18 crores transferred.[3] Except in periods of great political uncertainty such as followed the failure of the Cabinet Mission (when many Govan Bros. companies were acquired by the Dalmia group, and the big Swadeshi Cotton Mills at Kanpur were sold), the normal course was to sell a proportion of assets at the inflated prices at the time while retaining as much as might ensure control. Parry's and Co., largest of the three British managing agencies that dominated South Indian trade, illustrates one method: after trebling its share capital by a two-to-one bonus issue, the company went public early in 1948, selling one quarter of the larger equity at four times its face value, the directors thus recouping the entire new nominal value of the company's assets while retaining control.[4] The foreign tea companies illustrate another: on the one hand they forestalled unwelcome take-overs by writing up existing assets to the extent of Rs 20 crores in 1954 and 1955;[5] on the other,

the moment they earn surplus funds the tendency is to bring the funds

[1] See below, Chapter 3, p. 97.

[2] B. R. Bhagat, Parliamentary Secretary to the Minister of Finance, Lok Sabha, reported in *Hindu*, 9 November 1952.

[3] *Capital*, 17 September 1959, p. 404.

[4] Wiggins, *Private Foreign Investment*, p. 35. Premia on new managing agency issues were normally high although not always as high as in Parry's case. Sur instances four cases in this period: Martin Burn—75 per cent premium, Jardine Henderson—120 per cent, Shaw Wallace—80 per cent, Gillanders—87·5 per cent. ('Ownership of Calcutta Managing Agency Houses', *EW* Annual Number, February 1962, p. 281.)

[5] RBI, *Survey* 1955, p. 17. Tea companies accounted for nearly all the upward revaluation of assets between mid-1948 and the end of 1959, totalling some Rs 47 crores ('Post-war Foreign Investments in India', ECAFE, *Bulletin*, June 1962, p. 4).

back to this country [Britain], whatever the [Bank] rate. They do not invest them locally.[1]

What with withdrawals of old-type foreign capital and an even heavier influx of new capital, the character of the foreign sector as a whole changed rapidly.[2] It was a transformation both aided and recorded by changes in managing agencies.

(b) *Change—the managing agencies:* Writing of the atmosphere in British managing agency boardrooms at the time of the greatest out-cry against the Companies Bill, an American observer 'discovered very little panic over what appeared to be a veritable death sentence for these giant corporations.[3] While not welcoming the proposed legislation, spokesmen of the sector nevertheless found it possible to face the prospect publicly without alarm:

I do not expect any real harm will come to good managements as a result of this law, no matter what name they use to describe themselves [said K. G. Milne, President of the Bombay Chamber of Commerce]. Of course, there will be the usual extra and wasteful work which fresh govern-ment controls always bring to the hard-working and conscientious citizen.[4]

No doubt some of this equanimity stemmed from the managing agencies having already partly pulled out of the country; mostly, however, it reflected their having evolved towards a new type of operation in response to the environmental changes outlined in this chapter.

Their first major adaptation, largely completed within five years of the end of the war, was a rapid *concentration* of capital through amalgamation, purchase, and public flotation of shares. None of this was entirely new. Some of the best-known houses of the period were themselves the product of early mergers; some were already public companies; and all, since the thirties, had felt in one form or another the need to cope with the growing size of initial capital requirements, sharpening local competition, high personal taxation and death duties abroad. But with peace and Independence, the old reasons became more exigent and new ones—government regulation, the fear of anti-foreign discrimination, the rush of take-overs and 'corners',

[1] W. G. Pullen, General Manager, Chartered Bank, presenting evidence on behalf of the Eastern sector of the British Overseas Banks Association to the Radcliffe Committee, *Minutes*, para. 4751, p. 331.

[2] See below, Chapter 5.

[3] Wiggins, *Private Foreign Investment*, p. 157.

[4] *Times of India*, 4 May 1955.

the desire to repatriate part, at least, of their stake, an increase in taxation, and so on—were added. By 1950, eight of the fourteen largest British houses had become public companies, four of them had taken over or amalgamated with others.[1]

Paradoxically, this abrupt modernization in structure, undertaken partly through fear of an expected onslaught by Indian capital, accelerated the second major change—the *Indianization* of old-type British capital.

Its extent and something of the conflicts it occasionally engendered have already been noted.[2] More remarkable is the ease with which it took place, the degree to which it was a voluntary process agreed between Indian and British interests.[3] It had been foreshadowed for a long time. Behind the bald recital of facts about the diffusion of power amongst Indian shareholders in foreign firms, lay a process of interpenetration between Indian and British interests, a mutual acquaintanceship between Indian and British businessmen that began to assume the features of tradition. The Jatias were widely known as associates of Andrew Yule, the Kanorias for their connexions with McLeod, the Bangurs with Bird and Gillanders Arbuthnot, the Mookerjees and Bannerjees with Martin-Burn (while it was still British-controlled), the Tatas with Macneill and Barry, the Poddars with Shaw Wallace, and so on.[4]

---

[1] The eight, British at the end of the war, are: Duncan Bros., Gillanders Arbuthnot, Jardine Henderson, Macneill and Barry, Martin Burn, McLeod, Octavius Steel, and Shaw Wallace. Of these, Jardine Henderson, Macneill and Barry, Martin Burn, and McLeod had grown substantially through amalgamation and take-over.

[2] See above, pp. 43–44.

[3] The distinction between voluntary and involuntary Indianization of capital is highly artificial. Almost everything foreign companies were doing in the period was steeped in the fear of possible compulsion. Parry's chronicler gives an idea of the prevailing mood:

'Hodgson has been shown returning depressed from his meeting with Sir Stafford Cripps and full of misgivings as to the future of sterling Companies in India; he immediately proceeded to carry this beyond the realm of theory by proposing the conversion of EID (East India Distilleries) to a rupee company at the close of the war. . . . he pointed to attempts made in the past to fix a percentage of Indian Directors on the boards of Companies and a percentage of capital in Indian hands, and he envisaged a post-Independence Companies Act which might well make these claims compulsory. Even a rupee Company would have to conform to such an Act but would be in a better position than a sterling Company—supposing sterling Companies were allowed to trade at all. Time has shown that these fears were exaggerated but in 1942 they were very real.' (Hilton Brown, *Parry's of Madras*, pp. 298–9.)

[4] Mehta, *Structure of Indian Industries*, p. 318.

This drawing together went beyond the confines of individual companies. While the war perpetuated many of the old Indo-British conflicts and produced some new ones—the Empire dollar pool, the ultimate fate of India's sterling balances—it also injected new incentives to Indo-British collaboration. For virtually the first time, the two business communities had to deal with the state as purchaser, regulator, or patron on a vast scale, and this in a period of unprecedented boom. Some of their mutual exclusiveness was bound to be swept aside. In 1940, British and Indian interests reconstituted the Cement Marketing Company; the following year, foreign and Indian firms formed the Federation of Woollen Manufacturers in India; in 1943, the two paper industry associations combined to form the Indian Paper Control and Distributing Organization[1] and have continued to 'find themselves in close accord and appear to be quite effective in apprising officialdom of the problems and needs of the paper mills'.[2]

The onrush of Independence found British interests even more willing: by 1946, a form of collaboration between the tea planters' associations was being canvassed;[3] the following year the President of the Indian Chemical Manufacturers' Association could claim to represent the entire chemical and pharmaceutical industry.[4] In 1948 the three coal-mining associations combined in the Joint Coalfields Committee in order to 'co-ordinate the policy of the Associations on labour problems, to negotiate with the government on the controlled prices of coal, and to deal with the supply of wagons and matters of common interest'.[5] The following year an *ad hoc* committee was 'exploring the practical task of amalgamating the three bodies'.[6] The Exchange Banks' Association took in Indian members.[7] Later still, the Government added their plea for central associations 'with a view to ensuring that all common problems connected with price and quality, standards, market practices, rationalised distribution,

[1] Gokhale Institute, *Business Communities in India*, pp. 37, 38.

[2] Eddison, *Pulp and Paper Industry*, pp. 125–6.

[3] Chairman of the Indian Tea Association speaking to the Indian Tea Planters' Association, 1946, cited in Gokhale Institute, *Business Communities*, p. 45.

[4] Dr. K. A. Hamied, Presidential Address, quoted in Gokhale Institute, op. cit., p. 41.

[5] Indian Colliery Owners' Association, *Annual Report*, 1948, quoted in Gokhale Institute, op. cit., p. 47.

[6] Kumud Basu, President, Indian Mining Association, as reported in *Capital*, 24 March 1949, p. 454.

[7] Pardiwalla, *Exchange Banks in India*, p. 78.

negotiations with State and Central Governments etc., are dealt with from a common angle'.[1] As a direct consequence, the two bicycle manufacturers' organizations merged in 1958; the two paint producers' bodies came together in the Indian Paint Association in 1960;[2] and feelers were put out in a number of other industries. Perhaps the most pointed of recent examples was the transfer, in May 1963, of the *Statesman*, last of the British-owned newspapers, to a consortium of twelve groups, five British and seven Indian.[3]

This gradual drawing together of Indian and old-type foreign business was never completed and probably never will be. It has not yet brought the British-dominated Associated Chambers of Commerce and Industry and its Indian opposite number, the Federation of Indian Chambers of Commerce and Industry, into common harness. None the less it eased the crucial jump from British to Indian control in many spheres and helped the old foreign sector to draw in its extra-territorial horns to some extent and concentrate on the booming Indian market.

The resulting *diversification* is the third major change to have overtaken old-type foreign capital. It started with the smaller companies, but ultimately embraced them all.

There are a number of distinct strands here. Companies engaged exclusively in traditional occupations with low planning priority, such as jute, cotton textiles, or tea, have undertaken little beyond modernization and rationalization. Among the more notable of these is Bird-Heilger's reorganization of their jute mills at a cost of some Rs 5·5 crores up to 1960, Finlay's complete rehabilitation of their major cotton mills at a cost of nearly Rs 6 crores, and Duncan's opening of a tea-buying department in 1953.[4] In many cases renewals are not being made: in 1956 the Plantation Enquiry Commission found that 45 per cent of the foreign-held tea area was under pre-1910 bushes, compared with 19 per cent of the Indian-held area.[5]

---

[1] Tariff Commission, *Report on . . . Paper and Paper Boards*, 1959, p. 67.
[2] *Capital*, 14 July 1960, pp. 40–41.
[3] The British groups are: Andrew Yule; Bird-Heilger; Guest, Keen, Williams; Inchcape; and the Bombay Company. The Indians: Tata; Martin Burn; Mafatlal; C. H. Bhabha; Khatau Makanji; Visanji, Sons & Co.; Murugappa Chettiar.
[4] Unless otherwise stated, the illustrations in this and the following two paragraphs are drawn from Tyson, *Managing Agency*, Appendix, pp. 55–70, without, however, preserving their anonymity.
[5] From *Report*, Part I, Annexure XXVII, p. 480.

Companies active in fields with high planning priority—mining, cement, paper, engineering—have been encouraged by their managing agencies to expand fast: coal companies within the Bird-Heilger group have doubled their output to 3·5 million tons on a capital outlay of over Rs 5 crores, while some of the other companies in the group have expanded iron ore, limestone, and dolomite production. The group has put up a new Rs 3 crore paper mill in Orissa and expanded its old one. In engineering it has more than doubled output of finished steel castings and structurals and increased production in associated fields. Parry increased their output of sulphuric acid twentyfold between 1945–6 and 1958–9, and of chemical fertilizers more than fivefold. Balmer Lawrie has had its engineering interests increase production of heavy structurals nearly fourfold since the war. Andrew Yule's seven coal companies have spent over Rs 5 crores on re-equipment, expansion, and development since 1947. . . .

Finally, there is a new interest in, and a shift towards previously unexplored fields. In this the largest foreign groups have been less active, perhaps, than comparable Indian ones.[1] None the less they have made considerable progress. Finlay have set up two companies for the manufacture of chemicals used in the cotton textile industry; Duncan have established the first wool-combing plant in the country and a plan to manufacture carbon black; Balmer Lawrie have started two plants for the production of high-grade greases and expanded facilities for the production of railway wagons, blast furnace and gas cleaning plant; Gillanders have gone into electrolytic copper refining; and so on.

Probably the most significant feature of this shift to new fields is the large partnership role invariably assigned to new, technologically-specialized foreign firms, and the renewal of an old intermediary function of the managing agency as 'the nexus between the [foreign] investor and the new joint-stock enterprise'.[2] Not that the old British houses are the most popular of Indian partners with new foreign investors. They are normally too extensively committed and without liquid funds, still too tightly held as compared with director-

---

[1] While gross capital stock of public companies in the eight largest Indian groups increased from 23·66 to 30·56 per cent of the total in all non-Government public companies between 1951 and 1958, that of the two largest foreign groups —Andrew Yule and Bird-Heilger—fell from 4·29 to 2·55 per cent (from Hazari, *Structure of the Corporate Private Sector*, Table 4.2, p. 22).

[2] Bengal Chamber of Commerce, Memorandum, Company Law Committee, *Written Evidence*, Vol. I, Part I, p. 70.

run firms and, despite limitations on fees, still expensive.[1] None the less they are not bypassed completely. In the three years for which data exist, 1959–60 to 1961–2, British houses promoted eight of the 107 joint financial ventures authorized, forming links with manufacturing firms in five countries.[2]

These internal changes have very nearly completed the work begun in the economies of the developed world and actively pursued by Indian capital and the Government, namely, the effacement of the distinct forms of business associated with old-type foreign capital. In so far as it has chosen to remain in the country, and in all but such relatively stagnating, although still very important, fields as tea and jute, the traditional foreign sector has been persuaded and pummelled into forms of organization, types of activity, modes of collaboration, and, as important, a set of attitudes that are becoming less and less distinguishable from those of its new partners. With few exceptions, its specific preoccupations can be included, without too much straining, with those of foreign capital as a whole.

[1] Views expressed privately.   [2] Sources as on p. 239 n. 5.

PART II

INDIAN AND FOREIGN CAPITAL

CHAPTER THREE

HOSTILITY

I PREPARING FOR POWER

DURING the half-century before Independence Indian business had set into an attitude of hard hostility towards foreign capital. Towards the end of the war it assumed a definition that could not be misinterpreted. 'British investments in India should be repatriated with the help of our accumulated [sterling] balances', demanded Sir Rahimtoola M. Chinoy in the name of the Indian Merchants' Chamber;[1] let 'all British investments in India be repatriated,' echoed G. D. Birla for Indian capital as a whole.[2]

(a) *Ingredients of hostility*: There were a number of these. Indian business was smarting under what they thought to be *discriminatory restrictions* imposed in the name of the war effort precisely when they saw an unprecedented opportunity to expand. The Government were taken to task again and again for suppressing the recommendations of the American 'Grady' Mission which toured India in 1942 and was believed to have advocated rapid industrialization.[3] They were accused of having 'actively helped British shipping interests to entrench themselves in India's trade' 'while practically the whole of the Indian-controlled shipping has been requisitioned for war purposes', of having assigned shipping control in India to representatives of British shipping interests,[4] and of having allocated shipping space so as 'not only to foster but to cripple Indian industries'.[5] They were charged with ruining the Indian chemical industry to favour

---

[1] The occasion was a debate on 'commercial safeguards' for British interests at the Federation of Indian Chambers of Commerce and Industry Annual Meeting, Delhi, 27–28 March 1943, *Proceedings 1943*, Vol. III, p. 162.

[2] Article on 'Guarantees India Must Have', reprinted in *Path to Prosperity*, p. 507.

[3] See, for example, *Commerce*, 28 November 1942, cited in Cohen, *Economic Development in India*, pp. I 11–12.

[4] *EE*, 27 August 1943, p. 515. See also Walchand Hirachand as quoted above, pp. 16–17.

[5] B. C. Ghose, Indian Insurance Institute, Calcutta, at 17th Annual Meeting, FICCI, *Proceedings 1944*, Vol. III, p. 125.

ICI;[1] of discriminating against local production of textile mill stores, plywood, tobacco, paper, and other products to favour imports;[2] of importing consumer goods 'in the name of anti-inflation' in order to deny Indian industry shipping space for much-needed capital goods; of encouraging the United Kingdom Commercial Corporation to 'spread its tentacles' throughout the country while sitting on the proposed Indian Commercial Corporation and allowing the Export Advisory Council to stagnate;[3] of using controls over internal transport to hinder the distribution of Indian-made goods while allowing their imported equivalents to travel freely;[4] and so on. Capital issues control was seen as a device to link machinery imports to British suppliers and to favour British firms in India.[5] Despite the felt need for technical assistance from abroad, the bringing in of experts was thought to be 'a dangerous portent for the future reconstruction of India'. Similarly, 'scientific research is being organised to serve British interests. . . . The proposal to establish national physical and national chemical laboratories, in itself so urgent and desirable, has to be examined in the light of who is to control them and with what objectives.'[6]

Summing up at various periods, Indian publicists were unanimous in seeing a conspiracy against Indian growth: 'powerful interests are operating abroad for the purpose of throttling further industrialisation of this country', wrote *Commerce* after the Grady Mission Report was suppressed;[7] 'there was a plan—clearcut and thorough—to prevent the industrialisation of this country in the post-war period;'[8] and from the present Secretary of the Employers' Federa-

[1] *EE* editorial, 'The New Octopus', 7 April 1944, p. 525.

[2] See Morarji J. Vaidya, representing the Association of Indian Industries, Bombay, speech at 18th Annual Meeting, FICCI, *Proceedings 1945*, Vol. III, p. 123; Shanti Prasad Jain, representing the Bihar Industries Association, Patna, at the 19th Annual Meeting, FICCI, *Proceedings 1946*, Vol. III, pp. 30–31; G. D. Birla to 19th Annual Meeting, reported in *EE*, 5 April 1946, reprinted in *Path to Prosperity*, pp. 82 ff.

[3] Kumararajah Sir Muthiah Chettiar, Presidential speech to 17th Annual Meeting, FICCI, reported in *EE*, 10 March 1944, p. 362.

[4] G. D. Birla at the 19th Annual Meeting, FICCI, quoted in *EE*, 5 April 1946, p. 569.

[5] ibid.; also G. D. Birla, 'Preliminaries of Planning', speech of 20 April 1945, in *Path to Prosperity*, pp. 67–68.

[6] *EE*, 10 March 1944, p. 363.

[7] 28 November 1942, cited in Cohen, *Economic Development in India*, pp. I 11–12.

[8] *EE*, 31 August 1945, quoted in Desai, *Recent Trends in Indian Nationalism*, p. 29.

tion of India: 'British policy was opposed to any *rapid* growth of heavy industries *controlled and managed by Indians*'.[1]

Some of this suspicion was exaggerated; much of it justified: independent scholars have stressed the parsimony with which the strings of industrialization were loosened even at the height of the war.[2]

But this was not the only, nor the most important ingredient of hostility. Exhilaration at the thought of early delivery from British political control was tempered with a lively awareness of Indian capital's *weakness*—'Her [India's] industries', wrote the *Eastern Economist*, 'are pygmies in a world of giants'[3]—and with a fear that the gains made during the war would disappear with the renewal of competition afterwards. The fear centred on the activities—past and future—of foreign-controlled rupee companies: 'The resolution [on the Post-War Position of Industries Established During the War] as worded', said Dr. L. C. Jariwala for the Association of Indian Industries, Bombay, 'seeks tariff protection, but I take it that it implies protection from non-Indian industries established in this country. The manufacturer who is competing with you from without must not be allowed to compete with you from within. It will be a very dangerous thing and will be very detrimental to the interests of our industry.'[4] 'Assurance is . . . called for that the post-war industrial development of India especially in key industries will be the exclusive sphere of Indian enterprise both in respect of ownership and control', echoed the *Eastern Economist*.[5] The All-India Manufacturers' Organization was more explicit. Dealing specifically with the '(India) Ltds.', they wrote:

Given their much larger world connection and experience, these concerns are able to compete on more than equal terms with the corresponding Indian concerns in the same field. They obtain all the fiscal and financial advantages open to Indians; in addition, they have the silent sympathy from the mystic bond of racial affinity with the rulers of the land, which procures them invisible, but not the less effective, advantage in their competition with their indigenous rivals. This device cannot be too strongly opposed.[6]

---

[1] Nabagopal Das, *Industrial Enterprise in India*, p. 8. Italics in original.
[2] See above, pp. 15–16.   [3] 13 October 1944, p. 413.
[4] 17th Annual Meeting, FICCI, *Proceedings 1944*, Vol. III, p. 121.
[5] 12 May 1944, p. 727.
[6] Statement on the Agenda of the International Business Conference at Rye, New York, mid-November 1944, A-IMO, *India and International Economic Policies*, p. 41.

Delegates to the 18th Annual Meeting of FICCI were dismayed to learn that the number of new '(India) Ltds.' registered had risen from five in the *four years* ending on 31 March 1943 to 103 in the *single year* 1943–4,[1] and devoted practically the whole of the crucial debate on Government's Policy Regarding Post-War Industrial Development to the theme. After pointing out that

the so-called India Ltd. companies . . . are really foreign companies [that] have established themselves in this country . . . and . . . monopolised most of the larger industries which should otherwise have been in our hands,

Morarji J. Vaidya, representing the Association of Indian Industries and a considerable business figure in his own right, concluded:

the remedy against such corporations being set up in the future is a clear straight surgical operation, namely to delete the . . . sections in the Government of India Act [allowing their formation].[2]

From the other end of the country, N. N. Rakshit, representing the Bengal Industries Association, Calcutta:

With a view to checking them it would be essential that the Government should suitably revise the recommendations of the External Capital Committee with an eye to the protection of the Indian indigenous Industries.[3]

And soon afterwards, noting that no reference was made to '(India) Ltds.' in the Government's Industrial Policy Statement, M. A. Master, President of the Indian Merchants' Chamber warned:

India would prefer to go without industrial development rather than allow the creation of new East India Companies in this country, which would not only militate against her economic independence [but] would also effectively prevent her from acquiring her political freedom.[4]

These fears were not without effect. In its first statement on economic policy, the Congress-dominated Interim Government declared:

It seems to us preferable that the goods which the country cannot produce at present but would be in a position to produce later on, should continue to be imported from other countries rather than that their local manufacture should be started or expanded by foreign firms. In the course of

---

[1] *EE*, 6 April 1945, p. 424. The figures had been laid before the Legislative Assembly a few weeks prior to the meeting.
[2] *Proceedings 1945*, Vol. III, p. 122.   [3] ibid., p. 127.
[4] Reported in *EE*, 18 May 1945, p. 658.

time it will be possible to restrict or discontinue foreign imports but foreign vested interests once created would be difficult to dislodge.[1]

(b) *Some ingredients of collaboration:* It would be wrong to assume that the Indian business community was always and unanimously hostile to foreign capital. The necessity of doing business with foreign firms and the possibilities of profitable collaboration with them had given rise to a subsidiary, if normally muted, theme—the demand for a share of profits. As early as 1928 the Indian Merchants' Chamber had proposed that the Western Indian Match Company be registered in India with three-quarters of its capital held locally and three-quarters of its directors Indians.[2] The Lees-Mody Pact of 1933 split the indigenous textile industry into two on the issue.[3] Even during the Second World War, continued foreign investment appeared acceptable if the basic condition were satisfied. As expressed by the *Eastern Economist*:

It should . . . be a condition of the establishment of foreign companies in India that they should have . . . Indian capital and Indian representation on the board of management [and] arrangements for the training of technicians.[4]

The theme was taken up increasingly by a section of big Indian business as the war drew to a close,[5] reaching a crescendo in the summer of 1945 with the visit to Britain and the United States of an officially-sponsored Indian Industrial Mission, led by the heads of the two outstanding Indian groups, J. R. D. Tata and G. D. Birla.

When first mooted, the tour caused consternation amongst the smaller fry of Indian business.[6] It was condemned as the first step towards an 'illegitimate marriage' between foreign and domestic big business.[7] Gandhi too was concerned lest the Mission commit Independent India before a political settlement was in sight.[8] The cudgels

---

[1] Advisory Planning Board *Report*, December 1946, quoted in Sarma, *Foreign Investments in India*, p. 47.

[2] *Report of the Indian Merchants' Chamber, 1928*, Bombay, 1929, p. 14.

[3] See above, p. 26 n. 1.   [4] 9 July 1943, p. 254.

[5] Reports of discussions between British and American textile machinery manufacturers, local textile interests, and the Textile Control Board appeared in the *Eastern Economist*, 25 February 1944, p. 295. Other negotiations were reported on in the issue of 24 November 1944, p. 578; *passim*.

[6] Natarajan, *American Shadow over India*, 2nd ed., p. 27.

[7] Manu Subedar, Speech in the Legislative Assembly, quoted in ibid., p. 49.

[8] *EE*, 18 May 1945, p. 642.

were taken up by spokesmen for big Indian business. Ramakrishna Dalmia:

I . . . do not agree with those leaders who, without sound knowledge of trade and business, have been protesting against the import of foreign capital.[1]

The *Eastern Economist*:

We must expect alliances, agreements and contracts between foreign industrialists and ours. . . . There can be no objection, in principle, to these transactions. Indeed, they become natural and necessary once we grant . . . that our country should be industrialised and that the process would cost much less if we could enlist foreign technical and financial co-operation for the purpose. . . .[2]

The quarrel died down quickly. Although the 'Industrialists' Delegation . . . found . . . a definite change in the attitude of British industry towards Indian industrial development . . . [and] large British industrialists were not merely reconciling themselves to the inevitability of the industrialisation of India but in many cases seem to be in accord with India's political aspirations';[3] although agreement seems to have been reached on some aspects of technical collaboration, notably the assignment of shares in exchange for know-how in addition to royalties and fees;[4] and although, finally, a few Indo-foreign collaboration agreements were reached (among them the early motor-car agreements: Birla-Nuffield, Birla-Studebaker, Premier-Chrysler; some of the Kirloskar collaborations; and some deals in textile machinery and rayon) neither side was willing as yet to compromise on control. 'We made it clear to them', reported G. D. Birla, 'that under no circumstances would India allow the control of new industries to be exercised by non-Indians.'[5]

The dominant theme of hostility reasserted itself, less fervent per-

---

[1] Chairman's report to the annual meeting of Bharat Bank, in *EE*, 22 June 1945, quoted in Bose, *Indo-British Big Business Deals*, p. 46.

[2] *EE*, 18 May 1945, p. 642.

[3] *EE* editorial, 29 June 1945, p. 857. The journal's editor, P. S. Lokanathan, accompanied the delegation.

[4] See the lines of agreement in the Birla-Nuffield deal (Bose, op. cit., p. 31, and references). The form of agreement was foreshadowed in Birla's *Eastern Economist*: 'It would be possible to give a share of the profits to British industrialists without their investment or that in lieu of profits a certain number of shares may be allocated to them' (29 June 1945, p. 858).

[5] 'An Industrial Mission', in *Path to Prosperity*, p. 422. A more circumstantial account is given in *Free Press Journal*, Bombay, 25 June 1945, quoted in Bose, op. cit., pp. 24–28; see also P. S. Lokanathan, *EE*, 7 December 1945, p. 858.

haps, less unanimous, and more selective in its targets. The few working collaboration agreements were closely followed. When first announced, Kirloskar Bros.' 'arrangements' with Brush Electrical Engineering Co. and with the British Oil Engine (Export) Co. were greeted with a sense of outrage. 'It is surprising', commented the *Eastern Economist*, 'that even as the Indian Industrial Delegation in London is emphasising India's opposition to foreign control of Indian industry, these projects should hurriedly be brought to shape.'[1] When, in October, the terms were revealed—15 per cent of equity plus royalties in exchange for know-how and technical assistance— the journal refrained from comment. Nor did it comment when The Kirloskar Electric Co. and Kirloskar Oil Engines were registered in December.[2] By then, indeed, it was engaged on another front.

The National Planning Committee published a resolution on foreign capital on 12 November. The extreme position it took was now deeply disturbing to business and provoked an immediate reaction. Where the Committee pointed out that foreign investment had 'warped and retarded the nation's development', the *Eastern Economist* countered: 'it does not logically follow that the same inhibiting or warping effect would continue . . . when we have attained full political independence.' The Committee's conclusion that foreign capital should be retired from key industries and prevented from entering them in future was met by the arguments that

where the state is committed to encourage actively large-scale economic development, the resources of the state can always be brought to bear against the foreign companies . . . and that it would . . . be better to use the [resources devoted to compensation] to build up, as rapidly as possible, Indian industries which can compete with the foreign-owned or -managed concerns on an equal basis.

As for the Committee's wish to channel all borrowing abroad through the state, the journal broke its tradition of concurrence on this point to ask for clarification.[3]

(c) *Going it alone:* There was still, however, no question of relinquishing control nor any confidence that foreign capital would

---

[1] 8 June 1945, p. 756.

[2] *EE*, 19 October 1945, p. 597; 14 December 1945, p. 884.

[3] Editorial, 'The Future of Foreign Investments', *EE*, 23 November 1945, pp. 748–9.

comply. Here was an old theme. Demanding in the name of all borrowing countries that foreign capital does 'not seek to gain political control over the areas in which it is invested', that it limit its requirements of borrowers to maintaining 'stability and security in the most general sense of the term' and that 'foreign participation . . . be financial where necessary and only where necessary, otherwise . . . technical', the journal asked: 'Do these conditions stand a reasonable chance of fulfilment?', only to answer: 'Most assuredly not!'[1] Under the circumstances, Indian capital was prepared to go it alone.

One corollary was to underplay consistently the need for foreign resources. The *Eastern Economist* went on to assure readers that, provided India's sterling balances were made available, the need for funds from abroad 'may not be very large',[2] and the authors of the celebrated Bombay Plan, amongst whom were many of the leading business figures of the day, estimated the need for foreign loans at no more than Rs 700 crores or 7 per cent of the total investment,[3] compared with Rs 1,100 crores or 24 per cent in the Second Plan and Rs 2,200 crores or 29 per cent originally planned for the Third.[4] What little was contemplated was to take the form of loans, not equity and 'not accompanied by political influence or interference of foreign vested interests'.[5]

(*d*) *Support of state enterprise:* Given the weakness of Indian industry, another corollary was the wide acceptance of an enlarged and committed economic role for the future state. The *Eastern Economist* summed up the prevailing view: 'The real choice before the country is not between Government *versus* private enterprise but it is between Government-*cum*-British enterprise *versus* Government-*cum*-Indian enterprise.'[6]

Amongst themselves Indian businessmen were not prepared to go as far as many of the Resolutions they had supported in the past,[7] yet the Bombay planners were willing to concede a large degree of state ownership, control, and management, especially in 'entirely new industries or industries new to particular areas' and others which 'in

---

[1] *EE*, 25 August 1944, p. 202.   [2] ibid.
[3] Section 86, Penguin edition, pp. 55–56.   [4] PC, *Third Plan*, p. 95.
[5] *Bombay Plan*, section 82, p. 53.   [6] 7 July 1944, p. 2.
[7] See, for example, above, p. 25.

the public interest it is necessary for the state to control';[1] even the All-India Manufacturers' Organization, generally representative of smaller interests, was prepared to endorse (as a protective device) a 'system of *licencing* every concern operating in this country, so as to enable the licencing authority to test or judge if a concern . . . is a genuine Indian concern'.[2]

So far had they come in seeing the state as the sole protector against predatory foreign capital that they felt compelled to make far-reaching ideological concessions: 'we recognise that the existing economic organisation, based on private enterprise and ownership, has failed to bring about a satisfactory distribution of the national income,' wrote the Bombay planners in 1945.[3] And again, 'the distinction between capitalism and socialism has lost much of its significance from a practical standpoint'.[4]

Such sentiments were not to survive into Independence. By the time FICCI held its 19th Annual Meeting, March 1946, G. D. Birla had switched to an anti-controls policy which has come down in one form or another to this day. Moving a resolution on The Industrial Development of India, he said:

under the guise of planning and regionalization and in the name of targets, Government have adopted a policy of allocation under which they decide as to which party and at what place a certain factory should be erected. The result is that nepotism and corruption are encouraged. . . . A policy which creates a virtual monopoly for a certain individual or a firm cannot be in the best interests of the country. . . . I am therefore dead against Government deciding where and who should build up a certain industry.

His alternative, offered somewhat incongruously barely fifteen months after his signature had appeared on Part II of the *Bombay Plan*, lay in 'creating incentives and a certain kind of conditions' for private capital.[5]

It was, then, with these ideological impedimenta that Indian capital entered Independence: a renewed, though tempered, hostility towards foreign capital; a commitment to make do with its own resources—eked out, marginally, with foreign public loans; and support for state economic initiative as a likely vehicle of growth. As

---

[1] *Bombay Plan*, Part II, section 41, p. 95, and, for a discussion of state economic intervention, sections 39–46, pp. 94–100.
[2] A-IMO, *India*, p. 41. Italics in original.   [3] Part II, Section 2, p. 65.
[4] ibid., Section 37 ('Basic Principles'), p. 92.
[5] *Proceedings 1946*, Vol. III, pp. 23, 25.

Independence approached, some of the details appeared to lose their charm, but so momentous were the events of the first few years, that little was done to alter the picture as a whole.

II FROM INDEPENDENCE TO THE SECOND PLAN

(a) *Domestic background:* Independence dashed almost every hope entertained by Indian business. Within two months, *Partition* had claimed 300,000 dead; within six months, five or six million refugees had arrived. It took three years to resettle, semi-permanently, the bulk of the first wave from West Pakistan just as a fresh wave from the East began to break over Indian Bengal. It took longer for the loss of Pakistani raw materials to be made good: Indian raw cotton did not fully fill the gap until 1954–5; raw jute—not until 1961–2, and then not fully;[1] and the loss of former surplus areas aggravated India's alarming and growing food deficit. The fact that these areas were important buyers of manufactures and coal did not make matters any easier.

Administrative and political hastiness compounded the prevailing economic chaos. All controls were lifted in November 1947; by mid-1948 prices had risen by a third. Liberal imports of consumer goods mopped up some of the loose money but Rs 600 crores of reserves were spent in 1948–9. Devaluation in September 1949 set off a new inflationary trend and brought back controls. Stability was in sight when the Korean War set prices rising again.

Partition and its economic consequences helped to inflame the *industrial unrest* that accompanied Independence. Although organized labour as such took little part in the national movement,[2] it was receptive to the mood of impatience and expectancy that suffused the country, the more so as many labour leaders were individually prominent in the movement. Average real wages at the end of the Second World War, while beginning to rise, were between a tenth and a quarter below their 1940 peak;[3] registered employment went down

[1] From C. N. Vakil, *Economic Consequences of Divided India*, pp. 252, 264; Ministry of Food and Agriculture, *Forecast Crops 1949–50 to 1959–60*, pp. 109–10; *Indian Agriculture in Brief*, Table 4.1, pp. 67–68.

[2] See, for example, V. B. Karnik, *Indian Trade Unions*, pp. 105, 117.

[3] Myers, *Labour Problems*, Table 4, p. 10; Shreekant A. Palekar, 'Real Wages in India, 1939–1950', *EW*, January 1957, Table I, p. 157. Madras, with an increase of about one-third in the period, was the only important exception (*Indian Labour Gazette*, March 1949, cited in Harish Chandra, 'Wage Payments vis-a-vis Wage Incentives', *EW*, 12 November 1949).

by more than a tenth between 1945 and 1947 as military orders stopped and the level of industrial activity fell;[1] and the uncounted numbers of unemployed swelled as two-million-odd demobilized men were followed by millions of refugees.

Changes in the political leadership of the trade union movement added a cutting edge. With the formation of Congress Ministries in the Provinces in 1946, the Communist-led All-India Trade Union Congress abandoned the pro-Government, pro-production policies it had adopted in 1942 in favour of a more traditional stance. For the first time in five years strikes were condoned, even encouraged by the official leadership; within two years, under the Communist Party's new General Secretary, B. T. Ranadive, they became part of the world-wide insurrectionary strategy which heralded the Cold War. While almost all non-Communist labour leaders swung in the opposite direction, the clash over control of the trade union movement had consequences of its own. The non-Communist leadership came out of prison to find Communists installed in the only existing central organization. They set about forming rival federations: the Congress-led Indian National Trade Union Congress in May 1947, the Socialist-led Hind Mazdoor Sabha in December 1948, and the smaller, Revolutionary Socialist-led United Trade Union Congress in May 1949. Often enough, the formation of a new federation or its consolidation was attended by a struggle for recognition.[2]

Results were predictable: productivity took a plunge 'by about 20 to 30 per cent in certain lines' between 1939 and 1950;[3] by more than a third between 1939–40 and 1948–9 in the country's largest steelworks;[4] by more than a tenth over Indian industry as a whole in the decade 1938–48.[5] The number of registered unions jumped nearly

[1] Palekar, op. cit., Table 3, p. 159; H. Venkatasubbiah, *Indian Economy Since Independence*, p. 169.

[2] Probably the most famous was that conducted by Bombay's quarter-million textile workers, led by the Hind Mazdoor Sabha in August and September 1950. In this case the Communist/non-Communist rivalry was unimportant, and that between the new federations central to the issue: 'The INTUC opposed the strike from the start and INTUC volunteers have fully cooperated with the police right from the beginning for breaking the strike' (*EW*, 26 August 1950, p. 824).

[3] PC, *First Plan*, p. 441; see also Myers, *Labour Problems*, Table 4, p. 10.

[4] Average output per worker declined from 24·36 to 16·30 tons per year (Chairman's address to Tata Iron and Steel Co.'s annual meeting, August 1949, quoted in Fiscal Commission (1949–50), *Report*, Vol. I, pp. 231–2).

[5] R. Balakrishna, *Measurement of Productivity*, 2nd ed., pp. 26–27.

fourfold, from 865 to 3,150, between 1944–5 and 1948–9 and the membership of those submitting returns more than doubled, from 900,000 to two million.[1] And strike activity in the immediate post-war years reached a peak not seen for nearly a generation.[2]

The new *Government responded* with a mixture of concession and compulsion. With its Business Profits Tax, its Capital Gains Tax, and other measures, Liaquat Ali Khan's Budget, the last of the National Government, is remembered as a 'soak-the-rich' exercise. Early in 1947 a Five-Year Labour Programme was announced to implement the recommendations of the Royal Commission on Labour in India, 1931, and the Labour Investigation Committee, 1946.[3] Legislation followed hard on Independence: 1947—an amendment to the Trade Union Act, 1926, providing for compulsory recognition of unions, conferring bargaining rights on unions and protecting their right to organize; the Industrial Disputes Act providing for compulsory government adjudication and conciliation in disputes. 1948—a revised Factories Act which reduced the work week from 54 to 48 hours, introduced paid holidays, compulsory welfare services in large factories, and provision for licensing and inspection; the Employees' State Insurance Act covering all non-seasonal factories which provided for compulsory sickness, injury, and maternity insurance; the Minimum Wages Act, important primarily in plantation industries; the Dock Workers (Regulation and Employment) Act. These were only the more noteworthy. In addition, much of the important labour legislation of later years was initiated in this period: the Industrial Disputes (Appellate Tribunal) Act, 1950, the Plantations Labour Act, 1951, the Indian Mines Act, State Shops and Establishments Act, and the Employees' Provident Fund Act of 1952.

The Government did not stop at legislation. In December 1947, a Tripartite Industries Conference representing capital, labour, and the state met in New Delhi to discuss the economic chaos. Its final Industrial Truce Resolution while exhorting labour to recognize a

[1] Karnik, *Indian Trade Unions*, Appendix I, p. 259.

[2] See Appendix 2, p. 325, below.

[3] It promised, *inter alia*, improvements in security and recruitment for contract labour; welfare provisions and minimum wages; industrial housing and health schemes; apprenticeship; a 48-hour week, statutory rest periods, and paid holidays in mining; legislation to cover commercial undertakings, docks, transport, municipal employment; and to cover workmen's compensation (from précis in *Indian Labour Gazette*, March 1947, pp. 377–81).

'duty in contributing to the increase in the national income . . . to settle all disputes without recourse to interruption in or slowing down of production [and justifying] a fair return on capital employed . . . and reasonable reserves for . . . maintenance and expansion', also called on employers to 'recognise the proper role of labour in industry and the need to secure for labour fair wages and working conditions'.[1] To this end, machinery was to be established to determine, *in association with labour*, 'fair wages and conditions' as well as 'fair remuneration for capital'; works councils were to be set up in all plants; and a big industrial housing drive was to be mounted by business and the state.[2]

The Acts, the ordinances, and the activities were mostly unexceptional. Some were opposed *ab ovo* as not going far enough by labour spokesmen; others petered out or lost their teeth before reaching the statute book or the factory floor.[3] None the less, Indian business, schooled in the crudest forms of exploitation;[4] protected hitherto by the lightning rod of foreign rule; unused to the give and take of power; and generally ignorant, as much of India as of the wider world, was terrified, the more so as other measures affecting business seemed hostile and restrictive.[5] For the moment it looked to them as if labour had the ear of the Government.

The impression was strengthened by the pronounced populist tone

[1] Quoted in Karnik, *Indian Trade Unions*, p. 131.

[2] The Committee on Fair Wages was in fact set up the following year, and reported in 1949; and the housing drive was finally inaugurated in April 1949 'largely as a result of growing industrial unrest' (Rangnekar, *Poverty and Capital Development*, p. 189).

[3] The amendments to the Trade Union Act, 1936, have yet to be enforced; the Minimum Wages Act provided for State Governments to *publish* minima, without providing for enforcement. Also, see below, pp. 88–89.

[4] The Labour Investigation Committee had pointed some of the problems bluntly enough: 'On the whole [they wrote] it may be stated, that employers who take a most indifferent and nonchalant attitude towards welfare work and say that no rest shelters are provided as the whole premises belong to the workers themselves, no latrines are provided because workers prefer the open spaces, no canteens and sports are necessary because they are not likely to make use of such facilities, and so on, constitute the majority. It is apparent that unless the precise responsibilities of employers in regard to welfare work are defined *by law*, such employers are not likely to fall in line with their more enlightened and far-sighted confrères.' (*Report*, pp. 349–50. Italics in original.)

[5] Some of the main bogeys of the day were the recommendations of the Expert Committee on Profit Sharing, 1948; the decisions of the Governments of Madras, Uttar Pradesh, and Bombay to take over road transport or electricity or both; and the Industries (Development and Regulation) Bill which was enacted in 1951.

of *Congress propaganda and policy* statements. In their 'Objectives and Economic Program' of November 1947, the All-India Congress Committee addressed itself

to the next great task, namely, the establishment of real democracy in the country and a society based on social justice and equality . . . alternative to the acquisitive economy of private capitalism and the regimentation of a Totalitarian State.

The Program envisaged a ceiling for incomes and a periodic census of property to ensure enforcement, price control, co-operative enterprise in town and country, 'land to the tiller', and ceilings on land ownership. It held no comfort for big, modern business:

Industries producing articles of food and clothing and other consumer goods . . . should . . . for the most part be run on [a] cottage or small-scale basis. . . . In order to avoid competition between production so reserved for cottage industries and large-scale production, the state may bring under its control such competing large-scale industry.

In addition the state was to take over 'new undertakings in defense, key and public utility . . . [and] new undertakings which are in the nature of monopolies'. As for existing undertakings, 'the process of transfer from private to public ownership should commence after a period of five years' after prices had been forced down by, *inter alia*, 'legislation or administrative measures'. What remained of private enterprise in industry was to 'be subject to all such regulations and controls as are needed for the realisation of the objective of national policy in the matter of industrial development' including the abolition of the managing agency, a five per cent ceiling on dividends, controls over investment, allocation of 'surplus' profits to schemes of social welfare, and the settling of disputes through 'conciliation, arbitration and adjudication'.[1]

This accumulation of omens on top of the general shortage of raw materials and transport, and widespread labour unrest was too much for Indian capital. It underwent what was probably the severest crisis of confidence in its history. Industrial production fell off drastically from its wartime peak in most spheres as can be seen from the table on page 79. In many cases, long overdue renewals of plant and

[1] INC, *Resolutions 1924–54*, pp. 20–36. The Resolution was prepared by the Economic Program Committee of the All-India Congress Committee.

TABLE 1

India: Industrial production, war and immediate post-war period

	Wartime peak	*1947*	*1948*	*1949*
Finished steel (thousand tons)	1,000 (1941)	893	854	927
Cotton piece goods (million yds.)	4,852 (1944)	3,762	4,319	3,904
Jute manufactures (000 tons)	1,278 (1942)	1,052	1,091	946
Paint (000 cwt.)	1,141 (1944)	772	715	619
Sugar (000 tons)	1,210 (1941)	925	1,000	1,045
Cement (000 tons)	2,209 (1945)	1,448	1,553	2,102

Source: RBI, *Currency and Finance*, 1949–50, Statement 12, p. 150.

machinery were not made;[1] the capital market, particularly the new issues market, stagnated;[2] import licences for capital goods remained unutilized;[3] Government loans were not taken up;[4] and share prices fell steadily until 1952.[5]

Indian capital had little use for the broad optimism of pre-Independence. Broadcasting on All-India Radio, G. D. Birla turned his back on long-held views:

Though one of the authors of the Bombay Plan, I am afraid of uttering the word 'plan', because of late there has been an unhealthy craze for so-called planning, which at its best has meant only writing something on paper and putting all manner of obstruction in the way of increased production.[6]

Where the Bombay Planners had envisaged an expenditure of Rs 1,400 crores in the First Five-Year Plan, rising to Rs 5,700 crores in the Third (or something over twice as much in 1948 prices), Birla now spoke in terms of Rs 1,250 crores (two-fifths as much in real terms); where industry had been allocated nearly four times as much as agriculture (790: 200), it now claimed barely one-quarter more

---

[1] 'Even the old industries are not making proper allowances for depreciation and obsolescence. . . . In the cotton industries, 90 per cent of the machineries are nearly 40 years old; though renewals should have taken place after 25 years. In the jute, iron and steel industries, the conditions are not very different.' (K. N. Bhattacharya, 'Crisis in Incentives—A Problem in Indian Industries', *IJE*, April 1951, pp. 379–81.)

[2] See Appendixes 3(b) and 3(c) below, pp. 326 and 327.

[3] Only £14 million out of £83 million released from India's sterling balance for the purpose were used in the first year of Independence (*Capital*, 26 August 1948, p. 301).

[4] *EW*, 1 January 1949, p. 7.   [5] See below, Appendix 3(d), p. 328.

[6] Quoted in *Capital*, 8 April 1948, p. 613.

(428: 346).[1] The *Eastern Economist* had supported plans for a million-ton steel plant or two half-million ton plants; now it thought one half-million ton plant would suffice.[2]

In short, *capital was hesitant*, engaged in replacement investments but not probing beyond its wartime limits. The first three years of Independence were the worst. The Korean War boom then eased matters: export income in 1951 rose 35 per cent above the level of the previous year, the index of industrial production rose by a tenth, share prices rose, and corporate investment more than trebled between 1950–1 and 1951–2.[3] But it was short-lived. Industrial production slowed down again, no more than three-fifths of capacity being utilized in 1953,[4] corporate investment dropped to pre-Korean levels, share prices slumped badly, and unemployment became a major issue once again.

The break came with the *winter of 1953–4*. Supplies of raw materials became more plentiful just as the replacement investments had made some progress, and a record harvest both showed the outlines of the potentially vast domestic consumer market and shifted the terms of trade in favour of the industrial sector. The following year's crop was almost as good. At the same time, the Government's programme of public works, enshrined in the First Five-Year Plan, 1951–6, got off to a belated start inducing an expansion in related industries, notably iron and steel and cement; while the simultaneous re-emergence of unemployment as a political problem led the Government to expand the First Plan by some 15 per cent, effective from January 1954.[5] By then too, Indian capital had won its first policy battle with the state.[6]

Thereafter the private sector scarcely looked back. Industrial production increased rapidly, the output of capital goods growing at twice the rate of all others during the Second Plan period.[7] By the end of the Plan, idle capacity hardly existed in the major industries[8]

---

[1] *Bombay Plan*, Part I, Section 94, p. 59; *Capital*, loc. cit.; *EE*, 4 June 1948, pp. 1001–2.

[2] 6 May 1949, p. 730.

[3] See below, Appendixes 3(a), 3(d), and 3(e), pp. 326 and 328.

[4] G. Rosen, *Industrial Change in India*, Indian ed., p. 5.

[5] PC, *Review First Plan*, p. 10, table, pp. 19–20; W. Malenbaum, *Prospects for Indian Development*, p. 85.

[6] See below, pp. 83 ff.

[7] PC, *Review First Plan*, p. 182; Appendix 3(a), p. 326, below.

[8] Rosen, *Industrial Change*, Indian ed., p. 6.

and the private sector had substantially overfulfilled the planners' expectations.[1] Corporate investment reflected the new-found optimism, increasing nearly three times between 1953–4 and 1955–6.[2] The capital market experienced a new buoyancy: the Government found it possible to borrow;[3] capital issues sanctioned in the private sector quadrupled between 1952 and 1956; actual issues nearly trebled between 1953 and 1954; the sensitive initial issues market resumed after two years of inactivity; and stock markets were almost deliriously bullish.[4] So confident had business become that the Birlas went to great trouble throughout 1954 to enter the steel industry, and in fact were well on the way to doing so when an adverse and fortuitous mixture of too much proposed private control, too little proposed private funds, and a reassertion of state economic initiative finally put paid to the project in November 1954.[5]

The boom affected the labour market in a variety of ways. While the number of openly unemployed in the towns more than doubled to some two and a half million during the First Plan period,[6] employment also rose—by anything between five and seven million jobs.[7] Towards the end of the Plan, shortages of semi-skilled and technical personnel were being felt in an increasing number of industries. Wages were still shockingly low,[8] but were creeping up from their

---

[1] PC, *Review First Plan*, Table 3, pp. 202–3.

[2] See below, Appendix 3(e), p. 328.

[3] During the first three years of the Plan, the Central Government repaid, net, Rs 72 crores; in 1954–5 it borrowed, net, Rs 113 crores; and in 1955–6, together with the State Governments, Rs 89·4 crores (PC, *Review First Plan*, pp. 28–29).

[4] See Appendix 3, pp. 326 ff., below.

[5] See below, p. 93. The attempt was the more remarkable in that the Birlas had been consistently in favour of a state-run steel industry. As their journal, the *Eastern Economist*, put it in the early days of Independence: 'In fact, whether Government likes it or not, whether the Industrial Policy statement has reserved for Government the responsibility for new steel production or not, it is clear that the chances of the country putting up a new steel plant or plants lie virtually exclusively in Government entering this field and exploring special ways of raising finance, largely from external sources.' (6 May 1949, p. 730.)

[6] PC, *Second Plan*, p. 110; Malenbaum, 'Urban Unemployment in India', *PA*, June 1957, p. 138; Rangnekar, *Poverty and Capital Development*, p. 247 n.

[7] A. M. Khusro, *Economic Development with no Population Transfers*, Table 10, p. 36; refs. as on p. 314, below.

[8] The tripartite Committee on Fair Wages found the ruling wage for cotton textile workers in Bombay in 1954 to be Rs 105 per month, compared with their own estimate of Rs 176 per month for a 'living wage'. (Report cited in *EW*, 3 July 1954, p. 742.)

7

post-war slump of 1946, and had probably attained pre-war levels by 1951–2.[1]

Trade union activity naturally declined from the high point reached in 1948–9 and changed its character to some extent: while the number of registered unions nearly trebled between then and the last year of the Plan, membership increased by less than one-sixth to slightly more than two and a quarter million.[2] In other words, while the political leadership was busy pursuing and consolidating the fragmentation of the trade unions which followed Independence, they were being met by growing indifference on the part of their potential membership.

Indifference was deepened by the changed political complexion of the leadership. The Indian National Trade Union Congress, the fastest-growing federation and recognized as the largest already in 1948,[3] was officially committed to 'strengthen[ing] the hands of the Government of free India with the help of contented labour'.[4] The Hind Mazdoor Sabha leadership, while free to oppose Government policy, was engaged throughout this period in a battle for recognition, culminating in the general strike of textile workers in Bombay, August-September 1950, and in nation-wide campaigns against impending labour legislation. Whatever the merits of these latter, they were not the sort of activities that could generate much enthusiasm amongst ordinary workers. As for the Communist leadership of the All-India Trade Union Congress, they had forfeited a large measure of the goodwill that attached to that federation during their ultra-left period, 1948–51. The results were to be seen in the steady *decline*

---

[1] Myers, *Labour Problems*, Table 4, p. 10.

[2] Karnik, *Indian Trade Unions*, Appendix I, p. 259.

[3] Ministry of Labour, *Report . . . [on] Organized Workers in India*, 1948, p. 8. Recognition might well have overtaken the event by a few years.

[4] R. G. Soman, *Peaceful Industrial Relations*, p. 313, quoted in Karnik, *Indian Trade Unions*, p. 127. Kandubhai Desai, its first General Secretary, had laid down a collaborationist policy from the beginning: 'In the present context of Indian conditions, doctrinaire harping on the right of the working class to strike cannot be more than an indulgence in academic and theoretical discussion. The slogan of "strike" at such a critical juncture is not only unpatriotic but highly reactionary in its effect. . . . Society which gets its sustenance from continuous production cannot be expected to remain unconcerned when dislocation of production results from its theoretical vindication of the slogan of [the] right to strike which, as every union worker knows, has done the greatest harm to the working class in the country.' 'The INTUC: Its Role in the Trade Union Movement', in T. L. A. Acharya (ed.), *Planning For Labour*, New Delhi: Indian Labour Forum, 1947, p. 171, quoted in Venkatasubbiah, *Indian Economy*, pp. 330–1.

in strike activity, from 16·6 million man-days in 1947 to 3·4 million in 1954, and in a parallel loss in mass involvement, from two million to half a million workers.[1]

By the mid-fifties, social stability seemed to have been attained, and Indian capital regained its wartime self-confidence. 'What was new', commented the *Eastern Economist* of FICCI's 27th Annual Meeting in the spring of 1954, 'was the conviction which business men were able to convey that their philosophy could stand comparison in moral terms with that of any of their critics.'[2] Business was now in a position to review much of the thinking it had brought with it into Independence.

(b) The diminishing state:

The present investors' strike, as far as Government borrowing is concerned, can only be due to the deliberate desire to cause embarrassment and thus force the Government to change its policy.

Thus the *Economic Weekly* after the Government had made far-reaching concessions on income tax and import duties, after they had agreed to compound tax offences, and welcomed minimum profits at twice the rate payable on their own long-term borrowings.[3] The journal was right. Shaken by the social upheavals accompanying Independence, afraid of the Government's populist leanings and of its tendency to formulate policy from general principles, Indian capital's major preoccupation in the first years was to *set the limits* of state economic activity. For its part, the Government was only too conscious of the need to ward off social chaos with increased production and employment. Since more than nine-tenths of total output and employment and more than seven-tenths of output in modern industry, were within the private sector, it was clear that private capital held most of the cards.

The tone of the debate was set before the transfer of power. Moving a resolution at FICCI's Annual Meeting, March 1947, on the 'Need for Increased Production',[4] G. D. Birla gave a glimpse of the utter exasperation with the state felt by him and his colleagues:

[1] See Appendix 2, p. 325, below. 1950 was an exception, but 9·4 million of the 12·8 million man-days lost were on account of the general strike in the Bombay textile industry mentioned in the text.

[2] 12 March 1954, p. 425.

[3] The Crisis of Confidence', *EW*, 1 January 1949, p. 7.

[4] The resolution ended: '. . . The Federation, therefore, urges the Government of India to take immediate measures to maximise production within as short a time as possible by encouraging private enterprise to expand production through

All that I ask at this stage is that they ought to declare their policy. If it is their desire that for the next few years they will rely on private enterprise they should say so; if on the other hand it is their desire to start industries of their own and manage them through their own agencies, they should declare it. All I can say is that the spirit of suspense is hindering production; and when I say this I am not expressing any vague fears but only telling you what is today in every businessman's mind.[1]

Tone and content were repeated endlessly, and not only by purely Indian business. As the Fiscal Commission summed up in 1950:

Written and oral evidence placed before us referred to widespread misgivings about the policy of nationalisation laid down by the Government of India. It was contended that, owing to uncertainty in regard to future policy, capital could not be attracted to industries.[2]

The new Government hastened to reassure business. An Industrial Truce was arranged in December 1947;[3] parties to the Truce were told by Nehru that 'far too much attention is often paid to acquiring existing industries than to the building of new industries by the state or under state control'.[4] Sardar Patel, Deputy Prime Minister, told a working lunch in Calcutta a few weeks afterwards, 'our Finance Minister belongs to your own class. . . . We deliberately appointed him to create confidence in the industrial future. . . . Our Commerce Minister is also an experienced industrialist.[5] The Government opposed a resolution which called for the adoption of a 'socialist pattern' for the country.[6] Finally, on 6 April 1948, the Government published their Industrial Policy Resolution.

---

the utilisation of the existing capacity of the industry to the full, expansion of the existing industries and the establishment of new ones; Government should also extend the necessary assistance to the industry in the form of better transport facilities, adequate supplies of coal and raw materials and by stabilising wages, ensuring industrial peace through greater stress on higher standards of productivity of labour, and functioning of trade unions on right lines and recognition by them of their responsibility and obligations to the larger interests of the country.' (*Proceedings*, 1947, Vol. III, p. 42.)

[1] ibid., p. 47.　　　　[2] Fiscal Commission (1949–50), *Report*, Vol. I, p. 201.

[3] See above, p. 76.

[4] 'Production the First Essential', *Speeches*, Vol. I, p. 154.

[5] Quoted in Natarajan, *American Shadow over India*, 1st ed., pp. 247–8.

[6] The resolution, proposed (and withdrawn) by Kazi Syed Karrimuddin, read: 'This Assembly is of the opinion that the economic pattern of this country shall be socialist economy based on the principle of nationalisation of key industries and cooperative and collective farming and socialisation of the material resources of the country and that the Government of India shall adopt the said principle immediately.' (*CA* (*Legislative*) *Debates*, 17 February 1948, p. 825.) Replying to the debate Nehru told the Constituent Assembly: '. . . production comes first

The Resolution marked a considerable *retreat* from previously held positions. Where the Congress Economic Program Committee had envisaged a transfer of existing undertakings to the state within five years, 'the first five years [being] treated as a period for preparation, during which arrangements should be made to take over and run these undertakings efficiently',[1] the new Resolution announced that 'Government have decided to let existing undertakings . . . develop for a period of ten years, during which they will be allowed all facilities for efficient working and reasonable expansion'.[2]

Where the Interim Government's Advisory Planning Board had recommended the nationalization of coal, petroleum, iron and steel, motor, air, and river transport, amongst others,[3] the Resolution merely stated that the establishment of new undertakings in some of these fields would be the exclusive responsibility of the state, 'except where, in the national interest, the state itself finds it necessary to secure the co-operation of private enterprise. . . .' The Resolution's detail was less memorable than the shift it marked in the Government's approach: henceforth, nationalization was to be used as an expedient for increasing production, not a means for attaining a measure of social justice, or a different order of society:

A mere redistribution of existing wealth would . . . merely mean the distribution of poverty; . . . the state could contribute more quickly to the increase of national wealth by expanding its present activities . . . and by concentrating on new units of production . . . rather than on acquiring and running existing units.

And since 'the mechanism and the resources of the state may not permit it to function forthwith in Industry as widely as may be desirable . . . private enterprise, properly directed and regulated, has a valuable role to play.'

K. T. Shah, former Secretary of the Congress National Planning Committee, expressed 'utter disappointment with everything . . .

. . . everything that we do should be judged from the point of view of production first . . . when you come down to giving effect to [nationalisation] you have to think as to which to choose first and how to do it without upsetting the present structure and without actually interfering with production. . . . it is far better for the state to concentrate on certain specific vital new industries rather than go about nationalising many of the old ones . . . [and] interfering with the existing apparatus except where it is absolutely necessary.' (ibid., pp. 829–31.)

[1] See above, p. 78 and ref.

[2] Para. 4. The Resolution is reprinted in full as Appendix I of BOT, *India 1949*, pp. 220–4.

[3] See above, p. 19.

contained in this Resolution';[1] but business greeted it with approval: share prices which, early in the week, were 'down to rock bottom', staged a remarkable recovery;[2] *Commerce and Industry* welcomed the Resolution as a 'partial and somewhat fundamental reversal of some of the points contained in the Congress Economic Policy Report';[3] *Capital,* organ of the older British interests, explained that

those branches of industrial activity which the state reserves exclusively are, for the most part, spheres from which new private enterprise has long since withdrawn. Those industries in which the state reserves new enterprise to itself . . . call for the employment of capital on a scale which, in the present depressed condition of the market, it would be very difficult to mobilize through unaided private effort;[4]

Commerce thought the Resolution 'a necessary compromise';[5] and the Chairman of the Engineering Association of India welcomed it in his quarterly address as 'a ray of hope'.[6]

Capital remained hesitant, however, and the Government continued to woo business, repeating the Resolution's major themes at every opportunity. Dr. John Matthai, Minister of Finance, told the Associated Chambers of Commerce and Industry in December 1948: 'for so long a period as we can foresee, there will be not only a large but an increasing field for private enterprise in India'. Almost a year later he declared that the Government's aim was 'not to recast society but . . . to help move the wheels of production and to achieve economic stability'.[7] Prime Minister Nehru told the Advisory Council of Industries in January 1949:

. . . our policy is to direct our energies in increasing productivity and not in seizing hold of existing institutions and things which are functioning. . . .[8]

The following month Deputy Prime Minister Sardar Patel echoed with characteristic brevity:

Take it from me that this Government has not got the capacity and means to undertake nationalisation of any industry at present.[9]

---

[1] *CA (Legislative) Debates,* 7 April 1948, p. 3402.
[2] *Commerce,* 10 April 1948, cited in Gopal, 'Indian Industrial Policy', p. 327.
[3] 14 April 1948, quoted in Gopal, op. cit., p. 327.
[4] 15 April 1948, Gopal, p. 653.   [5] 17 April 1948, cited in Gopal, loc. cit.
[6] Gopal, p. 327.   [7] Quoted, ibid., p. 328.
[8] Quoted in BOT, *India 1952,* p. 103.
[9] Quoted in Spencer, *India, Mixed Enterprise and Western Business* p. 49.

Nehru followed with an assurance to the Federation of Indian Chambers of Commerce and Industry that March:

... we said, even in regard to certain basic and key industries, that we would not touch them for at least ten years, maybe more. It did not mean that we would necessarily touch them immediately after the ten-year period.[1]

And once more Patel:

Take it from me—if anyone talks of nationalisation, it is only for the sake of leadership.[2]

So it went on. There seemed to be no *concession* to which the Government might not be pressed. *Capital* reported at the time:

It was good to hear Congressmen [on the Standing Committee for the Ministry of Industry and Supply] pleading for a share of private enterprise in an already nationalised project [the Government drugs factory]. Two years ago they were threatening to nationalise all the industries in India.[3]

Even the limited initiatory function envisaged for the state in the 1948 Industrial Policy Resolution was circumscribed: following a demand from the All-India Manufacturers' Organization that 'the threat of nationalisation . . . be unconditionally withdrawn or its retention . . . explained to the public',[4] the Minister for Commerce and Industry, Harekrushna Mahatab declared:

. . . taking everything into consideration, the Government could not be expected to invest money in industrial undertakings. The impression had got round that the Government were starting industries. It was the people who must start industries and the Government would provide finance and technical personnel and give all kinds of assistance short of running them themselves.[5]

Successive Plan documents reflected the same trend. Where a paper prepared by the Planning Commission in 1950 read:

The objectives of planning are wider than those which private enterprise has normally in view. . . . The private sector has to become an agency for the furtherance of public ends,[6]

the actual First Plan document stated:

[1] Quoted in Natarajan, *American Shadow over India*, 2nd ed., pp. 60–61.
[2] *Capital* Annual Number, 22 December 1949, p. 11.
[3] 10 August 1950, p. 221.
[4] Sir M. Visvesvaraya, President, to the Third Quarterly Meeting of the Central Committee, A-IMO, Bombay, 7 January 1951, reported in *Hindu*, 9 January 1951.
[5] *Hindu*, 11 January 1951.
[6] *Planning in the Public and Private Sector—Scope and Method*, New Delhi, 9 September 1950, quoted in Cohen, *Economic Development in India*, III 7–8.

Private enterprise operating in terms of legitimate profit expectations and the efficient use of available resources has an important part to play in developing the economy. . . . The large volume of resources needed for all-round development of the economy can . . . be secured only if the public and the private sectors co-operate closely.[1]

Paradoxically, the final, perhaps most convincing, demonstration of legitimacy for the private sector came in 1954, at the Avadi Session of Congress. In his Report as outgoing President, Nehru said:

In our present state to limit resources to the public sector means restriction of our opportunities of production and growth. The main purpose of a socialised pattern of society is to remove the fetters to production and distribution . . . . It becomes necessary therefore to have a private sector also and to give it full play within its field.[2]

Confirmed in this way as an integral part of the 'socialistic pattern' to which Congress then subscribed, the private sector had won its doctrinal battle. Thereafter nationalization featured as a practical issue from time to time, or as a propagandist device, but never again as a fundamental difference in principle between the Government and private industry.

The Government did more than make encouraging noises in this period. The pro-labour bias of early Independence was reversed. Much of the legislation passed then, fell to the ground; compulsory recognition of unions was not enforced; implementation of the Plantations Labour Act, 1951, waited on the convenience of business until 1 April 1954; when the Employees' State Insurance Act, 1948, was eventually enforced in February 1952, it applied to a few States only—by September 1956 it covered thirty-one centres and slightly more than one million workers.[3] Where implemented, many legal requirements went by default for want of 'an extensive, well-trained inspectorate which India does not have and cannot yet afford'.[4] The Fair Wages Bill never got beyond the stage of 'eliciting public opinion' even though the Committee out of whose recommendations it came would not recommend payment of a 'fair wage' (less than a 'living wage') in all circumstances but, out of regard for industry's

[1] PC, *First Plan*, pp. 422–3.
[2] Quoted in *Capital*, 20 January 1955, p. 69.
[3] *The Indian Worker*, 3 September 1956, p. 1, cited by Myers, 'India', in W. Galenson, *Labour and Economic Development*, p. 73 n. 69.
[4] Myers, in Galenson, op. cit., p. 61. See also *EW*, 26 January 1955: 'Inadequate enforcement . . . has made labour lose faith in this kind of legislation.' (p. 149.)

'capacity to pay' opted for the even lower 'minimum wage'. And many of the welfare initiatives promised by the Government—notably the housing drive[1]—withered on the branch.

Amendments to earlier legislation reflected the new mood,[2] as did the growing body of 'case law' built up within the arbitration system.[3]

The trend in policy could be traced in the evolution of individual views. Once a trade union leader, V. V. Giri came to the conclusion in the middle of his term as Minister of Labour, 1952–4, 'much to my disappointment, that compulsory adjudication must continue to remain an important feature of labour-management relations for some time more. . . . We should avoid radical experiments for the present.' By early 1954, his transformation appears to have been complete. He wrote:

Trade unions should not merely pamper to the workers' demands, but must insist on their discipline inside and outside the walls of the industry and impart to them a sense of responsibility to do a satisfactory work for a satisfactory wage. . . . The unions must make every worker understand fully his duties and responsibilities before rights and privileges.[4]

Towards the end of the period, the Government felt able to probe one of labour's most cherished gains—job security. Instructions were issued to the Kanpur textile industry in 1955 to rationalize their use of labour. There followed a campaign by the national INTUC leadership that had long since accepted the need for such measures,[5] which resulted in their disaffiliating the local Kanpur

[1] See above, p. 77.

[2] The most important was probably the Industrial Disputes (Amendments and Miscellaneous Provisions) Act, passed in 1956 but formulated in 1954. Amongst other things, it deprived workers in dispute of their immunity from disciplinary action, as provided for in Section 33 of the original Act of 1947 (see Myers, in Galenson, op. cit., p. 63; Mrinal Kanti Bose, 'Industrial Disputes (Amendment) Bill', *EW*, 17 December 1955, pp. 1486–7).

[3] In a key decision in 1950, the Labour Appellate Tribunal ruled that bonus payments, while still a worker's by right until such time as he earned a 'living wage', were to be a residual charge on profits, secondary to depreciation charges and to a 'fair return' on capital (assessed at 6 per cent of paid-up capital and 2 per cent of reserves), the amount of bonus to depend on a firm's relative prosperity and on its need to attract or keep labour. In another key decision in 1951, labour's claim for above average wages in relatively prosperous firms (the case centred on the Buckingham and Carnatic Mills, Madras) was dismissed. (See Myers, *Labour Problems*, pp. 157–8; Myers, in Galenson, op. cit., p. 66.)

[4] Quoted by Morris, in R. L. Park and I. Tinker, *Leadership and Political Institutions in India*, p. 277.

[5] See, for example, the resolution on the subject adopted at their third annual Conference, October 1950: 'The INTUC is not opposed to proper rationalisation

branch. A similar attempt was made in Nagpur early the following year. Neither succeeded; both precipitated protracted strikes. But the fact that the Government was prepared to make them, despite the explosive nature of the issue, was eloquent of a new firmness in its approach to labour, one which the private sector found heartening.

A parallel could be found in the Government's growing leniency towards business. While making it clear that it saw in 'the regulated economy . . . the best alternative to both free economy . . . and also to nationalisation',[1] the Government took greater pains to define its powers in the legislation of the period and to limit its area of discretion.[2] Many of the regulations were of a precautionary nature, unlikely to be used under normal circumstances.[3] If found to stand in the way of production, they were willingly sacrificed, as became abundantly clear on the conclusion of the Refinery Agreements with the three foreign oil companies towards the end of 1951 and in March 1953.[4]

---

which does not merely mean reduction in the number of workers but includes adoption of improved and scientific methods of purchase, production and sale, reducing charges of management and stoppage of all leakages, wastes and corruption.' (Quoted in Urmila Devi, 'Rationalisation of Industry', *EW*, 15 June 1951, p. 597.)

[1] H. K. Mahatab, Minister for Commerce and Industry, to the Constituent Assembly, reported in *JIT*, January 1952, p. 6.

[2] Compare, for example, the Mines and Minerals Act, 1948, which is little more than an enabling measure for the Central and State Governments to make rules without the slightest hint as to the criteria to be followed in leasing and development, and the Industries (Development and Regulation) Act, 1951, a meticulously-framed document which sets out the Government's admittedly extensive powers exactly.

[3] See BOT, *India 1952*, pp. 105–6; *Hindu*, 13 May 1953.

[4] The Agreements, final negotiations for which began on 10 October 1951, were concluded on 30 November with the Standard Vacuum Oil Co., on 15 December with Burmah Shell, and on 28 March 1953 with Caltex. They quarantined the companies from nearly all the regulatory legislation and rules promulgated since Independence. Where the Industrial Policy Resolution of 1948 announced forthcoming legislation to ensure 'that, as a rule, the major interest in ownership, and effective control, should always be in Indian hands' (para. 10), the Agreements reserved a *maximum* of 25 per cent for Indian participation, and that in preferred, non-voting shares only. The companies were guaranteed against nationalization for 25 years from the commencement of operations and 'reasonable compensation' thereafter. Their imports of crude were exempted from customs duty and their machinery imports assigned a special, low, 5½ per cent *ad valorem* duty. They were specifically excluded from many provisions of the Industries Act which had just come on to the statute book as the Government's major regulatory device for the private sector, among them that the state might assume control under certain, stated circumstances. Finally, as the Damle Committee revealed at a later date, the Agreements were of indefinite duration. (See

The Government took to sounding out business opinion before acting. On the legislative front, to take an important example, the extensive rules-making provisions incorporated in the original Industries Bill of 1949—relating to production, the use of raw materials, standards, scope of production, development of an industry, and so on, and greeted with headlines like 'The Road To Serfdom'[1] or 'With Fangs Retained'[2]—were dropped from the final Act of 1951. On the economic front, formal conferences, continuing committees such as those listed in Chapter 5,[3] and informal consultations became the order of the day.

Consultation often had far-reaching effects. Developments in the machine-tool industry are a notable example. At the trade's annual gathering in 1952, K. C. Reddy, Minister of Production, reminded delegates:

You must recall that the division of spheres between the Government factory on the one hand and private industry on the other was settled after long discussions with the representatives of your Association. We had made it clear to them that the state factory will not undertake production of lathes less than $8\frac{1}{2}$ inches centre, and we have no intention of going back on this agreement. On the contrary, after reviewing the position, particularly in the light of your general fears about lack of demand, the Government have decided to produce only 400 of these lathes instead of the 1,200 originally envisaged.[4]

Explaining the year's delay in opening the Government-owned Hindustan Machine Tools Ltd. by reference to 'the adjustments and changes [made] in the layout of the factory' caused by its 'wholly commendable' policy of not producing 'tools that will be competitive with those produced by the private units in the industry', a report continued:

The factory is producing $8\frac{1}{2}$-inch lathes at present . . . but should the private sector develop extra capacity to produce these $8\frac{1}{2}$-inch lathes, the Government is reported to have given an assurance that it will reconsider

Ministry of Production, *Establishment of Oil Refineries. Texts of Agreements with the Oil Companies*, New Delhi, 15 September 1953; *EW*, 25 November 1961, p. 1762; below, p. 167.)

[1] *EE*, 8 April 1949, on the Bill's first presentation for debate.

[2] *EE*, 17 February 1950, p. 243, on its emergence from the Select Committee.

[3] See below, pp. 233–6.

[4] Speech to Indian Machine Tool Manufacturers' Association, Sixth Annual Conference, Bangalore, 1 October 1952, reported in *Hindu*, 2 October, *Capital*, 9 October 1952, p. 467.

its production program to avoid overlapping, and switch production to other specialised types.[1]

Machine tools were no exception. K. C. Reddy, Minister of Production, assured the Central Committee of the All-India Manufacturers' Organization that the Government's decision to build a plant for heavy electrical equipment would not affect the private sector in the industry, 'as the new venture would produce only non-standard items to supplement the output of the established industry'.[2] State Trading was held at bay until 1956, after an early Committee was dissolved because its continued work threatened to have 'an adverse effect on the "morale of the business community" ',[3] after a second had laid down too stringent criteria for the state to undertake trading at all;[4] and after a third had decided that even the limited scope allowed the state by its predecessor was too large and had recommended that the Government refrain altogether from trading directly.[5]

The most dramatic adjustment of Government policy in deference to the private sector's views occurred in the formulation of the First Five-Year Plan. It was puny—and recognized as such by professional bodies and business spokesmen equally: 'rather modest' wrote United Nations experts;[6] 'there may be a penalty to be paid for high promises and hope deferred', commented *The Economist*, London.[7] 'I do not call this document a Plan', echoed G. D. Birla. But he added significantly: 'This modesty does not weaken the Plan in any way; on the contrary in it lies the Plan's greatest strength.'[8] It bent over backwards not to encroach on the sensitive industrial sector by allocating to it a mere twelfth of total planned expenditure compared with over a half in the first of the three plans proposed by the Bombay Planners six years previously.[9] It went far enough in this direction to arouse criticism from business for neglecting in-

---

[1] *Capital*, 22 September 1955, p. 387.　　[2] *Capital*, 24 February 1955, p. 272.
[3] *EW*, 28 May 1949, p. 5.
[4] '. . . the most striking feature of the Committee's whole approach', commented *Capital*, 'is its profound disbelief in the competence of the state as a business organisation. . . . They . . . lay down criteria which must be satisfied before the state starts trading in a commodity—criteria which, in a market even remotely approaching normal, would successfully prevent the state ever trading at all.' (27 October 1950, p. 625.)
[5] See speech of Bimal Ghose, *LS Debates*, 19 December 1957, cols. 6579–80.
[6] ECAFE, *Survey 1953*, p. 59.　　　　　　[7] 20 December 1952, p. 802.
[8] Chairman's address to the 10th Ordinary Meeting of the United Commercial Bank, reprinted in *EE*, 27 March 1953, pp. 548, 549.
[9] *Bombay Plan*, Section 94, p. 59.

dustry.[1] Most significant of all, it was recast throughout its formative stages to meet the view of business.[2]

So far indeed did the Government go in meeting private sector demands that at one point it seriously considered opening the steel industry to private capital. The full story has yet to be told, but the outlines seem clear enough. After endless procrastination[3] a steel mission was sent to Britain to invite participation in a public sector project. 'Hovering between nationalisation and denationalisation', and without Government backing, the British industry refused, letting the contract go to Krupp-Demag of West Germany.[4] The point was taken and at the next round—when B. M. Birla arrived in the Autumn of 1954 to canvass support for a plant in the private sector— he found a willing audience. The Birlas were not working in the dark. The trend in Government policy in general, and the active lobbying on their behalf by T. T. Krishnamachari, then Minister of Commerce and Industry, seemed to outweigh anything said in the 1948 Industrial Policy Resolution about reserving steel for the public sector.[5] Indeed the Minister was himself so sure of getting the project cleared that its final rejection by the Cabinet in November 1954 prompted an immediate threat of resignation.[6]

By all accounts, had the Birlas offered more in cash and demanded less control over the venture, or had they presented it earlier, before the 'swing left' gathered momentum,[7] they might well have gained entry into the industry.

[1] See, for example, FICCI, *Memorandum on Draft Outline of the First Five Year Plan*, New Delhi, 25 September 1951.

[2] See, for example, above, pp. 87–88.

[3] Three consulting firms, appointed to advise on the establishment of works capable of an output of one million tons, were appointed in the second half of 1948 (*Report of the Ministry of Industry and Supply*, 1948–9); a decision in principle to set up two plants, in Madhya Pradesh and Orissa, 'as soon as finances permit' was taken the following year (*Report*, 1949–50); 'the difficult financial position' prevented a decision in 1950–1 (*Report*, 1950–51) and, from the official silence, during the next year as well. In February 1952, the Government decided to open negotiations with foreign firms and in February the following year it was decided to set up a technical mission to prepare a (revised) project report (*Report of the Ministry of Production*, 1952–3).

[4] The phrase is F. G. Connor's, Managing Director, Metallurgical Equipment and Export Co. Ltd. in a letter to *The Times*, 22 December 1953.

[5] See below, p. 143 n. 6.

[6] *MG*, 29 November 1954. Krishnamachari actually tendered his resignation the following January, after disagreement over steel policy had been augmented by disagreement over the adoption of a 'socialistic pattern' by Congress (see above, p. 88) and departmental wranglings (*Capital*, 3 February 1955, p. 157).

[7] See below, pp. 128 ff.

As important as any were the concessions made in fiscal and monetary matters. The 1948-9 Budget provided depreciation allowances and income tax exemption for a wide range of new industrial undertakings; in 1949-50 the Capital Gains Tax was abolished and in 1950-1 the Business Profits Tax; personal income and super-tax, together with company taxation were reduced at the same time. Promises were made to deal lightly with undisclosed income provided there was some response[1] and Government capital expenditure was cut.

It was in this period that the Government set up the first of the special financial institutions for extending long-term credit to private industry; the Industrial Finance Corporation in July 1948 and the State Finance Corporations from 1951 onwards. As one observer wrote: 'Nothing demonstrated more concretely the acceptance by the Government of India that private enterprise has a definite part to play in industrial development. . . .'[2] They were the beginning of a line of development that led ultimately to the Industrial Credit and Investment Corporation of India Ltd., the acme of business aspirations, early in 1955.[3]

Relations between state and private capital did not clear at once. Until it experienced the expansive effects of 1953-4, it was natural for the private sector to crib and carp at Government regulation, no matter that it was substituted for the more dangerous policy of nationalization. It was as natural for the Government to show impatience at the slowness with which business responded to encouragement and the narrowness with which it viewed larger, less immediate problems.

Naturally too, the dialogue continued in the old terms, if with less acrimony. Business spokesmen expatiated on the 'inconveniences and delays to which small and big industrialists are put due to greater

---

[1] A private offer of Rs 100 crores on condition the Government put an end to its inquiries into tax-evasion was refused by the Cabinet as being impolitic. (*EW*, 8 October 1949, p. 14.)

[2] Venkatasubbiah, *Indian Economy Since Independence*, p. 175.

[3] The ICICI received a very warm welcome: '[the] new institution epitomises in every lineament of its structure all the best features not only of the present Government's policy but of any rational policy designed to promote economic progress in India . . . [namely] the fostering of private productive initiative, the spread of technical and managerial skills, the close co-operation of private businessmen and Government officials, and the full support of the two leading countries of the democratic world, the United States and Britain.' (*Capital*, 3 February 1955, p. 141.)

centralisation of power in New Delhi', and spokesmen for the Government asked them to 'not chafe too much under New Delhi's control as the Government was, on the whole, a middle of the road, moderate administration'; they added that, 'if Parliament were given its head, there is little doubt that it would unerringly veer to the left. . . . Government had so far succeeded with pre-eminent success in diverting these tendencies.'[1]

Nehru continued to tilt verbally at the private sector:

I do not consider free enterprise has anything to do with the concept of democracy. . . . If private enterprise clashes with the interests of the country as a whole, it will have to be put down or perhaps have to go, root, trunk and branch.[2]

None the less, the private sector was not altogether unmindful of the Government's intentions. Quite early on, *Capital* noted that

business and political leaders are being given a more friendly hearing in New Delhi than heretofore, and are being made to feel that Government is not only anxious to have their advice, but to follow it in so far as it is considered to be politically possible. Remarkable also is the degree of agreement that has been reached.[3]

Early in 1949, FICCI

noted with satisfaction the growing realisation on the part of the Government of India of the gravity of the prevailing economic situation . . . and their refreshing realistic approach. . . . The Federation . . . particularly welcomes and appreciates the anxiety evinced by the Government to hold consultations with and seek advice of all the important sections of the community before finally enunciating their policy. . . .[4]

Speaking to the motion, and trying hard to convince a generally suspicious audience, G. D. Birla gave some of the reasons for their satisfaction:

We submitted a report in August last to Government; what did we find? Ninety per cent of the suggestions that we made to Government have been accepted. What more could you expect from the Government? They

[1] Exchange between the Vice-President of the All-India Manufacturers' Organization and the Secretary of the Ministry of Commerce and Industry, at a meeting of A-IMO, reported in the *All-India Manufacturers' Organization Journal*, May 1953, pp. 2, 4.

[2] Address to the Silver Jubilee session of FICCI reported in *NYT*, 30 March 1952.

[3] 25 November 1948, p. 807.

[4] Resolution on the 'General Economic Situation', 22nd Annual Meeting, *Proceedings 1949*, Vol. III, p. 115.

have given such enormous facilities for the establishment of new industries . . . after three or four years you will regret that you did not take advantage of the favourable situation.[1]

British interests echoed the sentiment:

A point on which Sir Paul [Benthall, President, Associated Chambers of Commerce and Industry] was able to pay Government a well-merited compliment was the latter's practice of consulting commercial interests on legislation and other matters affecting the trade and industry of the country.[2]

Approval was not confined to the Government's growing habit of consultation. Birla asserted at the time: 'The intentions of Government are of the very best. Their industrial policy on the whole is not unsound. . . . It is the execution of this policy that the Administration has muddled.'[3] And the Fiscal Commission found that 'towards the end of our tours it was conceded by prominent industrialists that the fears referred to had largely receded'.[4] Apart from a short lapse during the post-Korean War slump, marks of appreciation followed hard on one another. By 1953, business seemed confident on matters of economic policy: 'Fear of Nationalisation Baseless', *Commerce* assured its readers, and went on:

There are . . . sufficient grounds to feel that the Government of India is not likely to make any fresh move in regard to nationalisation of any sector of private enterprise . . . the Government is keen on securing the co-operation of private enterprise for the implementation of the Five-Year Plan. Our own enquiries in high Government circles reveal that the Ministers are quite aware that the Government machinery is not efficient enough to undertake additional responsibility in the sphere of trade and industry.[5]

Even in a matter as controversial as its labour policy, which had drawn criticism from the Finance Minister, C. D. Deshmukh,[6] from the President, Bombay Chamber of Commerce, in an annual address,[7]

---

[1] 'State and Private Enterprise', speech reprinted in *Path to Prosperity*, pp· 529–30.

[2] *Capital* reporting the annual session of ACCI, 14 December 1950, p. 917.

[3] 'Economic Conditions in India', 3 August 1949, *Path to Prosperity*, p. 561.

[4] *Report* (1949–50), Vol. I, p. 202. Some of the fears in question are quoted above, p. 84.

[5] 21 March 1953, p. 479.

[6] Budget Debate, 1954, reported in *Capital*, 1 April 1954, p. 459.

[7] The target for attack was the Industrial Disputes (Amendments) Act, 1953, which had made dismissals prohibitively expensive (*Capital*, 25 March 1954, p. 403).

from FICCI at its annual meeting that year,[1] the Government met with qualified approval. Analysing the results of a poll of leading businessmen, the Indian Institute of Public Opinion concluded: 'The present system of compulsory adjudication is generally believed to be working reasonably well.'[2]

(c) *Official policy towards foreign capital:* The Congress Government entered Independence confident that its existence was alone sufficient to release the springs of economic growth. Pre-Independence thinking in both business and political circles was agreed on this;[3] and the exceptional circumstances of the first months of Independence were not conducive to reappraisal. As a result, *little encouragement* was given foreign capital. On the contrary: India's first Ambassador in Washington, Asaf Ali, assured his hosts that there was 'no more than a limited field for private enterprise in an Independent India'.[4] And in the series of conferences preparatory to the founding of the International Trade Organization in 1947, it was the Indian delegation, all officials, who led the attack on 'national treatment' for foreign capital, and who insisted on freedom in backward countries to discriminate in favour of domestic capital and to place quantitative restrictions on imports.[5] Not long afterwards negotiations for a commercial treaty between India and the United States broke down on precisely this issue of non-discrimination in trade. The Industrial Policy Resolution of 6 April 1948 was drawn up in the same spirit. Although in many ways more liberal than previous statements,[6] the one short paragraph devoted to foreign capital promised legislation to regulate it 'in the national interest'. Such legislation 'will provide that, as a rule, the major interest in ownership and effective control, should always be in Indian hands. . . . [Further] in all cases . . . the training of suitable Indian personnel for the purpose of eventually replacing foreign experts will be insisted upon.'[7]

Events quickly conspired to *change* official attitudes. The loss of food-marketing areas to Pakistan coincided with poor harvests in

---

[1] The occasion was a resolution on compulsory arbitration which called for an upgrading of arbitration personnel and their selection by the Minister of Law rather than, as was the case, by the Minister of Labour (*Capital*, 11 March 1954, p. 331).

[2] IIPO, *Quarterly Report*, January 1955, p. 9.

[3] See above, pp. 71–72; also the Reports of the Industrial Panels which followed the publication of the Bombay Plan.

[4] *NYT*, 17 April 1947.

[5] W. A. Brown, *The United States and the Restoration of World Trade*, p. 98.

[6] See above, p. 85; below, p. 104.   [7] Para. 10.

8

the first years of Independence and imports of grain on a large scale
became necessary, rising from under one million tons valued at Rs 26
crores for undivided India in 1945–6 to a peak of 5¼ million tons
valued at Rs 254 crores in 1951–2.[1] Other consumer imports soared
as demand was released after the War. Dollar payments rose sharply
and, since some dollar earnings now went to Pakistan, India's deficit
on that account was some $200 million by 1948–9. A loan from the
International Monetary Fund, a draft on convertible sterling, and
other measures helped, but the following year, aggravated by devaluation, the deficit was still running at about $150 million.[2]

The need for foreign funds seemed obvious. At the same time,
something had to be done to start Indian industry moving lest social
and political chaos engulf the country; and since domestic capital
remained shy, Government began to look abroad.[3]

Other advantages soon suggested themselves: foreign capital
would provide many of the skills that the Government was beginning
to realize were necessary—and lacking; more important, as foreign
interests never tired of pointing out, a demonstration of foreign
confidence would probably do more to revive domestic capital's
spirits than any amount of official exhortation.[4]

Whatever the reasons—and these need to be augmented by more
purely political ones such as the Asian Communist Parties' new insurrectionary course[5]—interested observers were able to report as
early as October 1948, 'signs are not wanting that public opinion
has already veered somewhat from its previous attitude of rigid
opposition to all forms of foreign investment in India'.[6]

[1] Ministry of Food and Agriculture, *Food Situation in India 1939–53*, Tables
4.2, 4.3, pp. 28–33.

[2] Gurtoo, *India's Balance of Payments*, p. 144; *EW*, 25 June 1949.

[3] The link between the paralysis of domestic capital and official probings
abroad was explicit. *Capital* reported at the time: '. . . the Government of India
say that it will not be in the interests of the country to wait indefinitely until
Indian capital is forthcoming, and as it is their view that domestic capital is not
sufficient for India's multifarious industrial purposes "attempts should, therefore, be made to secure the maximum possible influx of foreign capital in the
shortest possible time".' (22 September 1949, p. 466.)

[4] *Capital* explained at the time of the World Bank's first mission to India early
in 1949: 'It is important to realise that assurances capable of satisfying the
foreign investor would certainly help to reassure the Indian investor, so that the
successful flotation of an International Bank loan might well be the prelude to
an overdue revival of the now inanimate internal capital market . . . foreign
capital is not likely to be forthcoming in any quantity from private sources until
indigenous capital shows itself willing to take risks.' (24 February 1949, p. 285.)

[5] See above, p. 75.   [6] *Capital*, 7 October 1948, p. 553.

By the time the first Plans were formulated—a six-year Plan was presented at a meeting of the Commonwealth Consultative Committee in London, September 1950—private foreign capital was given as much prominence as public loans and intergovernmental aid.[1]

In one important sense, the turn to foreign capital was *freely chosen* by the Government. Throughout the period and until the latter half of the fifties, India held reserves of foreign currency adequate to her known requirements. Reserves which stood at Rs 1,014 crores at the end of March 1949 were still some Rs 902 crores at the end of the First Plan, March 1956;[2] scarcely more than two-thirds of the foreign aid received for the Plan was actually used.[3] There were, it is true, contrary pressures. The British Government proved reluctant to release India's sterling balances and did so on onerous terms.[4] But they were not such as to impair India's financial independence. If the terms were stiff, as they proved on occasion to be, India could afford to reject them, as indeed, on occasion she did.[5]

During the period, the conditions attached to receiving public aid were such that self-sufficiency as a policy never moved far from official thinking. Still smarting from American pressure to have India modify her neutral stand in Korea during the Wheat Loan negotiations in 1950, the Planning Commission were convinced that only exceptional advantages could justify the risks inherent in receiving aid:

External assistance is acceptable [they wrote] only if it carries with it no conditions explicit or implicit, which might affect even remotely the country's ability to take an independent line in international affairs.

[1] *Capital*, 30 November 1950, p. 845.
[2] See Appendix 3(i) below, p. 330.
[3] PC, *Second Plan*, Table, p. 103.
[4] Press reports, quoting sources in the Ministry of Finance, implied that the Indian Government was persuaded to place imports under Open General Licence for a period of ten weeks, in exchange for the release of £80 million in the year ending 30 June 1949. This cost the country £42 million. (See, for example, 'Sterling Link is Costly', *EW*, 14 May 1949.)
[5] Indo-American relations are illustrative in this context. While the shift in active Cold War probings to Asia in 1948 brought American funds for development to the area for the first time (President Truman's 'Point Four' speech was made in January 1949), India's refusal, after a pro-Western wobble (symbolized by the decision to remain within the Commonwealth, May 1949; Nehru's visit to the United States, Autumn 1949; India's hesitancy in recognizing the People's Republic of China; and the initial support given the West during the Korean War, summer 1950), to commit herself utterly and militarily to the United States, denied her any gains of substance until well into the fifties.

There are also obvious risks in excessive reliance on foreign aid which depends on the domestic political situation in lending countries and which might be interrupted by any untoward international developments.[1]

Later, when the United States had concluded a military alliance with Pakistan, and Indo-American relations reached their lowest ebb yet, Nehru told the annual gathering of FICCI:

> It is becoming increasingly clear in the new atmosphere that real progress for us will depend on the progress we make ourselves. It is better if we progress a little more slowly rather than allow ourselves in any way to depend on others, for I fear real progress does not come if we go about on crutches all the time.[2]

C. D. Deshmukh, the Finance Minister, laid bare the bones of the matter: 'It is not likely that foreign assistance on an extensive scale would be available for the Second Five-Year Plan.'[3]

But private foreign capital was another matter. Besides its inherent advantages, it seemed easier to attract than public aid; the net could be drawn wider than the United States; and the political concessions required were of a general nature as would appeal to the large foreign sector already in the country and, in many respects, to domestic capital as well.

The Government set about *attracting* it very soon after Independence. While still restrictive, the 1948 Industrial Policy Resolution conceded that 'participation of foreign capital and enterprise . . . will be of value to the rapid industrialisation of the country'. In itself, this marked a substantial retreat from previous attitudes towards foreign business.[4] Liberalization was taken a step further in the Prime Minister's Statement to Parliament on 6 April 1949.[5] The earlier threat of legislation to cover foreign investment was dismissed: it 'arose from past association of foreign capital and control with foreign domination of the economy of the country. But circumstances today are quite different'. Where, before, foreign investment was thought to be merely useful, it was now considered necessary, not only to supplement Indian capital 'but also because in many cases scientific, technical and industrial knowledge and capital equipment can best be secured along with foreign capital'.

[1] PC, *First Plan*, p. 26.
[2] *NYT*, 7 March 1954. The dispatch was headlined, significantly, 'Nehru Suggests Ending US Help'.
[3] *Hindu*, 7 June 1954.   [4] See above, p. 97.
[5] Reprinted as Appendix II in BOT, *India 1949*, p. 225.

The statement announced the principles which would govern official policy in the future:

1. Existing foreign interests would be accorded 'national treatment': 'Government do not intend to place any restrictions or impose any conditions which are not applicable to similar Indian enterprise.'

2. New foreign capital would be encouraged: 'Government would so frame their policy as to enable further foreign capital to be invested in India on terms and conditions that are mutually advantageous.'

3. Profits and remittances abroad would be allowed, as would capital remittances of concerns 'compulsorily acquired'.

4. Fair compensation would be paid 'if and when foreign enterprises are compulsorily acquired'.

5. Although majority ownership by Indians was preferred, 'Government will not object to foreign capital having control of a concern for a limited period, if it is found to be in the national interest, and each individual case will be dealt with on its merits.'

6. 'Vital importance' was still attached to rapid Indianization of personnel, but 'Government would not object to the employment of non-Indians in posts requiring technical skill and experience, when Indians of requisite qualifications are not available. . . .'

The outcry from domestic interests was shrill, and official spokesmen made a number of verbal concessions to them. But the new policy remained. In July, an opportunity was found to elaborate on 'national treatment':

when protection is granted to a particular industry [went a Press Note] all the units of that industry, whether Indian-owned or not, will be automatically entitled to claim the benefits of such protection. . . .[1]

'(India) Ltds.' were held not to constitute a danger any more:

. . . the Government of India has no reason to believe that the growth of a foreign-controlled concern, even with the assistance of some protection that may be given to any particular industry in general, would be detrimental to the interests of the nation;[2]

---

[1] *Hindu*, 17 July 1949; *Capital*, 21 July 1949, p. 103.
[2] Quoted in US Government, Department of Commerce, *Investment in India*, 1st ed., 1953, p. 27.

and the relaxation on ownership was confirmed. As reported at the time:

The Government of India no longer think that a majority non-Indian interest in ownership, and in some cases effective control can be regarded as *ipso facto* detrimental to the interests of the country. It is, therefore, proposed not to insist too strongly on majority control residing in Indian hands in the formative stage of industries.[1]

The Indian Ambassador in Washington appealed for an Indo-American investment company, owned jointly by private interests in both countries, and promised a bright future for American capital in India.[2]

Practical steps were not lacking. The Government was prepared to put up much of the finance if only foreign firms would come in. A number of state plants—amongst them Hindustan Machine Tools, Hindustan Cables, Hindustan Shipyard, Indian Telephone Industries, and the first steel plant—date from this period. In most, the foreign collaborator was asked, initially, to put up some finance of their own, but only a little. More important in the long run, restrictions on repatriating investments were progressively relaxed;[3] foreign firms were encouraged to go into 'reserved industries' such as machine tools and fertilizers;[4] the oil companies were granted a substantial measure of extraterritoriality as an inducement to set up refineries;[5] and so on. By 1953 it was generally recognized that 'the terms on which capital can be invested in India now match almost exactly the conditions laid down in the "Code" ' published by the International Chamber of Commerce in the United States.[6]

The *response was poor*. Between mid-1948 and the end of 1953, exclusive of investments in oil refineries, 75 new foreign firms brought in a total of under Rs 11 lakhs, or an average of Rs 14,000-odd each.[7] While foreign assets rose by Rs 130 crores, half came from reinvested profits and most of the rest—Rs 45 crores—from a

---

[1] Press Note cited in *Capital*, 22 September 1949, p. 466.

[2] See below, p. 281 n. 1. Cf. an earlier Ambassadorial statement above, p. 97.

[3] Press Notes of 2 June 1950, 3 March 1953.

[4] US Department of Commerce, *Investment in India*, 1st ed., 1953, pp. 6, 28, *passim*.

[5] See above, p. 90 n. 4.

[6] 'Asia Thinks Again About the Capitalist', *New Commonwealth*, London, 23 November 1953, p. 545.

[7] From RBI, *Survey 1953*, pp. 80, 81. Cf. the retirement of nearly Rs 16 crores during roughly the same period (p. 54, above).

heavy, one-shot investment in new oil refineries.[1] Apart from oil, all that the Government had to show in five and a half years was Rs 15–25 crores of new capital and the continued presence of a large body of investment that might otherwise have been tempted to leave. None the less, and one or two lapses notwithstanding, the policy remained intact until the mid-fifties.

(d) *Neo-Swadeshism:* The attitude of Indian Business towards foreign capital throughout this period was an ambivalent one. While concessions to foreign private capital were seen as concessions to *private* capital, therefore welcome, they were at the same time concessions to *foreign* capital, and therefore threatening. Foreign investment in spheres in which Indian capital was not interested met with little antagonism; potential competition was opposed. Government-to-Government loans were welcomed for their neutral impact within the private sector; opposed for enlarging the resources of the state sector. Business saw reason to attract foreign capital; but still wished to be protected against it.

Normally the different strands co-existed uneasily, held by different sections of the business community at the same time. Sometimes one or another attitude took precedence and gave a temporary cohesion to that community. But at no time during the period did it exhibit the unanimity and clarity of aims it achieved during the Second World War or again during the latter half of the fifties. None the less, a mood of hostility towards foreign capital and of distrust towards the Government for entertaining it was apparent throughout. Throughout, too, Indian capital did its best to demarcate clearly between its sphere and that of the foreigners.

Hostility was muted at first. The Government was suspicious of foreign capital; Indian capital more than suspicious of the Government, and therefore inclined to be *tolerant*. Soon after the 1948 Industrial Policy Resolution, Birla's *Eastern Economist* reminded readers that even the Planning Advisory Board which had so strongly opposed the 'intrusion' of foreign firms, accepted foreign managerial control in the case of 'specialised industries'. It then went on to declare 'specialised industries' too limited a category; and that foreign capital should be encouraged to invest in 'light industries' and even 'service industries'.[2] Later, it is true, the journal realized how unrealistic its open invitation was; 'with our minds set upon a

[1] ibid., Table V–4, pp. 78–79, 80.   [2] *EE*, 23 April 1948, p. 762.

plan, we cannot now invite private foreign capital into the country except on terms which it is almost certain to dislike'; and called for negotiations on a Government-to-Government loan from the United States.[1]

But the decision was to be left to foreign capital. There were to be no discriminatory measures. On the contrary, as early as October 1948, it called on the Government to clarify policy towards foreign capital and to retract from the hostile posture adopted in the Resolution of the previous May. The policy needed 'can only be that no adverse legislation of any kind is contemplated; that there will be . . . assurance of . . . equal protection by the law and non-discrimination.'[2] As late as March 1949, with an official statement on foreign investments expected at any moment, the journal was still of the opinion that an Indian stake of 25 per cent in any investment

may be all that is necessary to secure the gradual and friendly 'infiltration' of the national element into the active ownership and management of joint enterprises. As regards the 'protection' to be given to domestic producers against unfair competition, we would urge that the only way to deal with the problem is through legislation controlling monopolies and unfair practices in business generally. . . .

Apparently, all that domestic business wanted at the time was an assurance that 'there would be no interference with terms privately negotiated'.[3] 'It is not impossible', echoed Lalji Mehrota in his Presidential address to FICCI early the following year, 'to devise means of economic collaboration with other countries, both on the Governmental and private levels' on mutually satisfactory terms.[4]

The *situation changed* radically on 6 April 1949 when the Prime Minister presented his long-awaited statement on foreign capital. The tolerance advocated hitherto in the knowledge that it would be rejected by the Government, was now official policy. It was now possible for Indian capital to conceive of a state-foreign line-up and with very few exceptions, domestic capital ran for protectionist cover. FICCI protested at the Government's 'open door' policy, demanded that 'majority interest in ownership and effective control' be assured to Indian interests, as provided for in the Industrial Policy Resolution of the previous year, and, indeed, that the Government return to the Advisory Planning Board's recommendation to

---

[1] *EE*, 25 June 1948, pp. 1122–4.   [2] *EE*, 15 October 1948, p. 656.
[3] *EE*, 25 March 1949, pp. 493–4.   [4] *EE*, 11 March 1949, p. 422.

limit foreign capital to specialized industries.[1] The All-India Manufacturers' Organization protested that blanket encouragement to foreign capital would destroy local industry's confidence and that the new statement went 'beyond the safety limit in some cases'.[2] Reassurance that it 'did not imply any discouragement to Indian capital'[3] was beside the point. Indian capital was more afraid of equal treatment than of the altogether remote prospect of anti-Indian activity on the part of their Government. As for the main official argument—'if the country needs foreign capital and if it is to be encouraged to come in it must be given an assurance of non-discrimination'[4]—it was as alarming in substance as it was impeccable in logic.

The Government strained to calm the fears. Opening an industrial exhibition in New Delhi, January 1950, Sardar Patel appealed for support for Swadeshi;[5] H. K. Mahatab, Minister for Industry and Supply, assured the National Chamber of Industries that Swadeshi 'would be the guiding policy of the Government of India today; and accordingly the entire policy will be formulated'.[6] More concretely, he assured Indian industrialists that they would be consulted before any foreigner was invited to invest in India and that their agreement would be necessary before any foreign firm could claim 'national treatment'.[7] The Government was even prepared, on occasion, to go back on their new policy, as when they retreated from a proposed joint Indo-British Shipping venture with P & O in 1949,[8] or when the Tariff Board permitted indigenous producers a price mark-up as an 'allowance for prejudice'.[9]

Nothing helped. Even as the first shock of debate spent itself under the influence of the Korean War boom, the Fiscal Commission was made acutely aware of widespread opposition to foreign investment and of the desire to limit it to clearly-defined spheres:

---

[1] *Capital*, 22 September 1949, p. 466; Madhukar Narayan, 'Fresh Overtures to Foreign Capital', *EW*, 17 June 1950.

[2] *EE*, 13 May 1949, p. 778.

[3] Finance Minister to the All-India Manufacturers' Organization, Bombay, 27 April 1949, reported in *EE*, 13 May 1949.

[4] Answer to FICCI, cited in *Capital*, 20 September 1949, p. 466.

[5] *Hindu*, 31 January 1950.   [6] *Statesman*, 28 June 1950.

[7] *Foreign Commerce Weekly*, Washington, 12 September 1949, quoted in L. K. Rosinger, *India and the United States*, pp. 79–80.

[8] M. A. Master to a joint meeting of Chambers of Commerce, Madras, 17 April 1948, reprinted in *Indian Ship*, pp. 38 ff.; *Capital*, 18 August 1949, p. 265.

[9] See below, p. 230.

The consensus of opinion is that, as a general rule, foreign capital should be confined to—

(a) projects in the public sector . . . which depend on the import of capital goods, plant, machinery, equipment, stores, etc. from abroad . . . or on foreign technical assistance in the establishment or management of new lines of manufacture;

(b) undertakings in the private sector which involve new lines of production, and where indigenous capital and management are not likely to be forthcoming.[1]

There were exceptions. G. D. Birla is on record as having welcomed the opportunity to 'supplement internal sources of capital with foreign capital . . . in our mutual interests'.[2] But his was a minority opinion at the time and despite the Birla group's size and special position in both the business and official worlds, it did not embark upon its first major joint venture—the Hindustan Aluminium Corporation Ltd. together with Kaiser—until 1958.[3] In practice, it behaved not very differently from other, lesser houses.

Once the initial shock had passed, foreign capital ceased to be an important issue for a time. The Korean War stimulated the domestic economy; other problems, particularly the labour situation, demanded attention; and foreign investors proved less eager to come to India than had been feared. The major investment of the period—the oil refineries—fell into the second category of investments mentioned by the Fiscal Commission and were widely welcomed,[4] particularly as 'Government were . . . alive to the desirability of

[1] *Report* (1949–50), Vol. I, p. 213.

[2] Chairman's Report to the Annual General Meeting, United Commercial Bank, reprinted in *Capital*, 5 May 1949, p. 721. He wrote in a paper for the India-America Conference later that year, 'I visualise collaboration only in big tasks . . . where large-scale investment amounting to a few scores of crores is needed and also where necessary technical skill is wanted in India. . . . The collaboration which I visualise is between agencies of private enterprise on both sides.' (*Industrial Cooperation between India and US*, (duplicated), p. 2, quoted in Natarajan, *American Shadow over India*, 2nd ed., p. 61.)

[3] See below, p. 198 n. 3.

[4] Shri Ram, industrialist and Chairman of the Industrial Finance Corporation proposed that the Government 'should restrict foreign private investment to such special and difficult lines as oil refining and not permit it in lines wherein Indian enterprise has already made a beginning'. (Address to the 5th Annual General Meeting of the IFC, *Hindu*, 1 September 1952.) The *Eastern Economist* went as far as to state: there is 'nothing that can be regarded as extravagant in the terms now offered to the oil companies considering the volume of the capital and the highly complicated nature of the refinery operations which require long-range planning and security.' (7 December 1951, p. 889. See above, p. 90 n. 4, for the Refinery Agreements.)

diverting a fair share of the business accruing from the proposed oil refineries to indigenous banking, insurance and shipping interests and [were making] efforts . . . for the advancement of these interests.[1]

The lull did not last. The post-Korean War slump coincided with the quickening of foreign interest in India as a field for investment, especially after the 1952 general election had given evidence of long-term political stability. Indian capital's fears were renewed, and with them its quarrel with the state. At their annual session early in 1952, the All-India Manufacturers' Organization called upon the Government 'to specify clearly the fields of Indian industry where foreign capital might participate directly'; demanded that 'the policy of non-discrimination between foreign and Indian undertakings . . . be modified'; that 'foreign capital . . . be controlled where it acted in a monopolistic manner detrimental to the interests of indigenous enterprise'; and urged the Government 'to prevent such foreign enterprise from taking advantage either of the assistance granted to indigenous industries or of facilities provided for consolidated import requirements in respect of components and raw materials'.[2]

Two months later a strong deputation of industrialists, including S. P. Jain, G. D. Birla, Lala Shri Ram, Tulsidas Kilachand, G. D. Somani (Chairman, Bombay Millowners' Association), Chandulal Parekh (President, Ahmedabad Millowners' Association), and G. L. Bansal (Secretary, FICCI), attended T. T. Krishnamachari, Minister of Commerce and Industry, to get a first-hand account of the Government's intentions towards industry, 'particularly those facing competition from foreign industries'.[3] Having drawn a blank, it was not long before the All-India Manufacturers' Organization appealed again to the Government 'to prevent foreign interests, particularly those with world-wide ramifications, establishing or expanding factories in India in the field of consumer goods and such other industries as had already been undertaken by national enterprises'.[4]

The Indian Merchants' Chamber snatched the baton in the autumn. Addressing its second quarterly meeting, the President, Pranlal Devkaran Nanjee, gave as clear and measured a statement of Indian capital's fears and demands as had ever been presented. It is worth quoting at some length:

[1] Indian Merchants' Chamber, *Report 1952*, p. 99.
[2] As reported in *Capital*, 3 March 1952, p. 477.
[3] *Hindu*, 17 May 1952.   [4] *Capital*, 25 September 1952, p. 420.

A number of foreign-owned undertakings manufacturing consumers' goods requiring no special skills and in spheres in which Indian units had developed and made striking progress, had expanded their production capacity in recent months substantially and to such an extent as to jeopardise not only the future plans of expansion of the corresponding Indian units, but even the continuance of their present level of output. . . . The fears about their future, because of this increasing competition from non-Indian establishments in certain lines of manufacture, had led to owners of corresponding Indian units selling their rights and the Indian-owned undertaking to their foreign compeers.

This brings to the forefront the question of a self-contained legislation covering, firstly, the terms and conditions governing the entry and participation of foreign capital; secondly, defining the sectors of industrial activity in which such foreign assistance should be enlisted; thirdly, formulating the safeguards necessary for preserving a fair field for expansion to Indian-owned industries in sectors in which they have made progress; fourthly, laying down minimum requirements in regard to the percentage of Indian holding in the capital structure and the proportion of Indian representation in the management which foreign-owned undertakings should be enjoined to observe; and fifthly, setting up the necessary machinery for securing the effective enforcement and implementation of the lines and basis of participation in terms of the overall policy.[1]

The following year—1953—brought the campaign to a *climax*. The Swadeshi League, formed to do battle in the soap industry with Lever Bros., focused attention on the general problem of protected foreign capital, and mobilized support far beyond the confines of the industry.[2] FICCI adopted its famous 'Swadeshi Resolution' deploring 'the present indifference to the importance of Swadeshi in the social and economic regeneration of the country', and urging 'that the purchase of [the] Government's own requirements . . . should be confined to goods of Indian origin, wherever available and possible, and more liberal price preference in favour of Indian goods and a substantial preference to Indian banking, Indian insurance and Indian shipping should be accepted as part of the official stores purchase policy.'[3] Two months later FICCI sent a memorandum to the Government drawing attention to the fact that new foreign firms were 'creating difficulties for indigenous industries', and demanding that foreign capital be excluded from spheres in which it 'would adversely affect parallel Indian interests' and be confined to industries where domestic capital 'is definitely shy over a period of years'.[4]

---

[1] *Hindu*, 22 October 1952.   [2] See below, p. 214.
[3] 26th Annual Meeting, *Proceedings 1953*, Vol. III, pp. 38–39.
[4] *Capital*, 28 May 1953, p. 715.

The matter was pressed at the meeting of the Central Advisory Council of Industries,[1] as it was wherever business met the Government throughout the year.

By 1954, the industrial economy had begun moving again and set the more alarmist fears at rest. Some of the weaker industries were still complaining, with the Indian ink-makers, that the 'Government have . . . allowed some foreign firms to participate in the field of ink-making . . . against the decared policy';[2] but larger capital was beginning to modify its stand. At least part of the problem was seen to lie with Indian industry itself. A FICCI Report on *Imports and Industrial Development*, while calling in general for a 'revival of the spirit of Swadeshi', omitted proposals for regulating foreign firms; instead it recommended measures to restrict imports, reorientate the Government stores purchasing policy, and, significantly, build up 'healthy relations between different wings of industry to ensure offtake of the indigenous product'.[3] H. N. Tata's message later that year to the annual conference of the Indian Soap and Toiletries Makers' Association, hitherto the launching site for the most extreme Swadeshist statements, was a model of *conciliation*. After making obeisance to the distinction 'between what is merely "made in India" and what is truly Swadeshi, which means "made in India with Indian capital and management" ', he went on:

We have no objection to foreign capital and foreign enterprise, nor are we worried about foreign competition, so long as . . . [the] foreign section of the industry does not dominate and dictate the price and policy of the indigenous section of the industry by sheer strength of international resources.[4]

By the following year Indian capital had swung round completely. In January 1955, a FICCI sub-committee, including B. M. Birla, J. R. D. Tata, A. Ramaswami Mudaliar, Tulsidas Kilachand, Shantilal Mangaldar, from amongst the top echelons of Indian business, met in Bombay to consider foreign capital. The Committee, stated one report,

[1] *Capital*, 4 June 1953, p. 751.

[2] N. Maitra, 'Indigenous Inks Achieve Quality', *Hindu Survey of Indian Industry*, 2 December 1954.

[3] *Hindu*, 15 May 1954. These views were also put to the Stores Purchasing Committee two months earlier (*Hindu*, 11 March 1954).

[4] *Hindu*, 21 September 1954.

generally welcomed the flow of foreign capital into India, particularly in those industries which are not pursued by Indian nationals even after due notice by the Government, like oil refineries, where there are difficulties of obtaining technical knowhow etc. It also welcomed foreign capital in the consumers' industries, like textiles, cement, paper etc., where India has already established herself.[1]

And a resolution at the Annual Conference of the All-India Manufacturers' Organization merely 'emphasised that an effective system of screening [foreign investments] should be laid down so that it may be purposefully canalised'.[2]

The new policy was not accepted wholeheartedly as yet. A FICCI press statement in March, while welcoming foreign capital 'particularly . . . in specialised industries requiring a high degree of technical skill and which have not been developed in the country and [in] any industry in which domestic capital shows definite shyness', recommended none the less that 'foreign interests should be persuaded to offer a part of equity capital to Indian investors'; although it thought that 'foreign capital may operate in consumer goods industries . . . where Indian units are fairly established', it added cautiously: 'In such cases Indian enterprises should be duly informed in advance of Government's program and if after due notice of, say, one year and notwithstanding such assistance as the Government might extend, Indian capital is not forthcoming, then foreign capital might be permitted to come.' In all cases, it demanded, 'the foreign investors should be prevailed upon to utilise Indian services such as banking, shipping and insurance.'[3] Cautious as was this press statement, *Capital* featured it as a 'New and More Favourable Attitude'.

(e) *Uneasy triangle:* Before business conditions eased, the Government had been hard put to defend its 1949 policy. It repeated the basic assumptions again and again: 'The wheels of industry, no matter who owns them, must be kept moving', T. T. Krishnamachari, Minister of Commerce and Industry, told the Lok Sabha. And on the same occasion: 'Our own capital resources are very limited and although our preference is in favour of Indian capital, we must be prepared to use foreign capital in developing industrial production.'[4]

---

[1] *Hindu*, 28 January 1955.   [2] *Hindu*, 28 March 1955.
[3] *Capital*, 10 March 1955, p. 348; 'Industrial and Foreign Investment Policy', *India News*, 22 April 1961, p. 5.
[4] *Capital*, 16 April 1953, p. 511.

Then again, in a debate on the foreign-dominated tea industry; 'while I would ask the House to . . . recognise the foreign element, I also beg of them not to stress that point because mere elimination of the foreign element does not produce something which is better.'[1] 'If Indian capital is available', he concluded, 'we give it first preference'.[2] Earlier he had pointed in some exasperation to the contradictions in which Indian capital had involved itself. Speaking to an All-India Manufacturers' Organization meeting, he said: 'You want the country to be rapidly industrialised. Indian capital is shy and you want me to prohibit foreign capital from seeking investment in India. What do you expect from Government in this situation?'[3] And on another occasion, in an address to the Central Advisory Council of Industries, he rounded on Indian companies that 'wanted free enterprise for themselves'.[4]

Indian capital was reminded that there were interests common to all capital, no matter what its nationality. As the Minister of Finance told the Lok Sabha, 'if we were to stop the remittance of dividends [abroad], then we might as well be driven to sequestrate the payments of dividends to Indian shareholders also'.[5] T. T. Krishnamachari took the argument to its logical conclusion when speaking to the Punjab and Delhi Chamber of Commerce: 'It is no use asking for interference with a British unit. . . . Once Government starts interfering in one unit there is no end of it. In your own interests it is not worth while permitting Government to do so.'[6] The Government did its best to reassure domestic capital: 'Once we find that foreign capital is likely to jeopardise national interests, we will not allow it to enter the country',[7] and told foreign capital to act circumspectly: it was advised to keep out of trading;[8] throughout 1953 it was told—ad nauseam—to get on with the Indianization of higher staff; and although it was assured continued 'national treatment' it was warned that discrimination could be applied for more reasons than one: 'there are foreigners and foreigners. . . . If at any time vested interests fight the Government, it is the vested interests that will suffer. . . .'[9]

[1] Hindu, 3 May 1953. [2] NYT, 5 May 1953.
[3] Hindu, 1 September 1952. [4] NYT, 30 May 1953.
[5] Capital, 10 July 1952, p. 43. [6] Hindu, 19 March 1954.
[7] T. T. Krishnamachari to the All-India Manufacturers' Organization, Bombay, reported in Hindu, 1 September 1952.
[8] T. T. Krishnamachari to the Annual General Meeting, ACCI, 1952, reported in The Times, 16 December 1952.
[9] T. T. Krishnamachari in the debate on tea, reported in Hindu, 3 May 1953.

All in all, Government, foreign, and domestic capital formed an uneasy triangle in the period. If the Government was satisfied that its 'industrial policy in respect of the participation of foreign capital provided enough safeguards for the prevention of unfair competition and the participation of foreign capital was not likely to cause any great hardship if the indigenous industry was organised on a sound basis and run efficiently',[1] Indian capital was not. As one delegate to FICCI's 1953 meeting put it: 'It is true that the Government is giving a sort of preference to Swadeshi-made articles, but the question is, is it enough?'[2]

Nor could foreign capital feel at ease where 'national treatment' was granted only in the letter, and then not consistently. As the US Ambassador, George V. Allen, said when opening Lederle Laboratories (India) Private Ltd.'s new plant—an occasion ostentatiously boycotted by the Government in protest at the company's refusal to associate Indian capital with the venture — 'American interests must be convinced that there is a reasonable chance of long-term hospitality. The Indian Government and people must be convinced that they are not being exploited. Neither side is entirely convinced at present.'[3]

[1] D. P. Karmarkar, Minister of Commerce, to the 45th Annual General Meeting of the Indian Merchants' Chamber (*Hindu*, 27 February 1953).

[2] Pranlal Devkaran Nanjee, representing the Indian Merchants' Chamber at FICCI, 26th Annual Meeting, *Proceedings 1953*, Vol. III, p. 44.

[3] *CSM*, 15 July 1953.

CHAPTER FOUR

COLLABORATION

I INTERNATIONAL BACKGROUND

(*a*) *Russian policy:* East-West relations entered a new phase with the agreement on Indo-China in July 1954. Both sides—each now armed with thermo-nuclear warheads—were becoming aware of the advantage in maintaining the rough balance of power that had been achieved in Asia. Disengagement did not occur at once. In Russia's case, the first signs were discernible as early as July 1950 with the exchange of letters between Nehru and Stalin on a possible settlement in Korea. It edged forward in Stalin's lifetime. With his death, a new policy of co-existence, the accent heavily on commercial competition, quickly established itself at the centre of Russia's relations with the outside world. Eastern Bloc trade with backward countries rose from $860 million in 1954 to $2,700 million in 1960;[1] agreements to supply long-term credit (and grants) rose from $6 million in 1953 to a peak of $1,542 million in 1960.[2] Russia had come of age economically. She could now buy her way into the world as it is: there seemed little reason to upset it.

India benefited early and substantially from the new turn. A trade pact, signed on 2 December 1953, was quickly followed by a first small shipment of oil products in January.[3] The old trade channels were soon deemed inadequate. By May 1954, Russia had invited a trade mission to Moscow, had offered technical assistance, and sent some tractors for testing. The great push came in August when the Russian trade commissioner intimated—through a Bombay businessman—that his Government was prepared to supply equipment and technical assistance for a steel plant. In September a steel team was

---

[1] USIS, *The Threat of Soviet Economic Policy*, p. 14.

[2] J. Berliner, *Soviet Economic Aid*, Table 3, p. 39; H. J. P. Arnold, *Aid for Developing Countries*, Table, p. 103.

[3] Press reports. An offer of capital equipment for rupees was made by the Russian Ambassador, M. Novikov, at an international industrial fair in Bombay as early as January 1952 (*Capital*, 24 January 1952, p. 102), but seems to have had no follow-up from either side. (References are not cited for material reported widely in the Press. Single reports and other sources are mentioned.)

appointed; it arrived late in November; had its reports accepted in principle before the year was out; and on 2 February 1955, barely one month before a crucial mid-term election in Andhra Pradesh,[1] an agreement for a million-ton plant was signed.

During the steel negotiations the Indian trade delegation had visited Moscow (September 1954) and reported, through Kasturbhai Lalbhai, a prominent industrialist member, that prospects for trade between the two countries were bleak. It was about this time, too, that Russia underlined, symbolically, its acceptance of the social *status quo* in India by selling equipment on deferred payment terms to a privately-owned firm, the Birlas, Hindustan Gas Co. Ltd.[2]

Further economic ties had to await the first political harvest. The Bandung Conference of Afro-Asian countries (end of April 1955) was followed by Nehru's spectacular reception in Russia (June). The first ('Big Four') Summit Conference, high point of the new policy, took place in July; and in November, Bulganin and Khrushchev repaid Nehru's visit to equally spectacular acclaim. It was then that the economic discussions resumed: November saw the Indian Government examining an offer of two oil tankers;[3] December—the signing of an agreement for the supply of twenty Russian coal-drilling rigs.[4] In March 1956 Russia offered technical assistance to the overwhelmingly privately-owned coal-mining industry; in May she reported on the feasibility of setting up an integrated drug industry,[5] and agreed to supply three oil-drilling rigs and facilities for training Indian crews; in June—an agreement to exchange mining equipment and geological training for industrial diamonds; in November—another agreement to undertake oil prospecting on a large scale, and to supply nearly two hundred oil technicians and training facilities for Indians. Also in November 1956, a preliminary agreement was reached covering the manufacture of heavy machinery, coal-mining equipment, fertilizer plants, and an oil refinery.[6]

Aid during the following year (1957) was largely a matter of working out the details of this large package deal: the report on the heavy machinery plant, submitted in January, was accepted in June, as was the report on the coal-mining machinery plant. Rs 10 crores were offered as a loan, repayable in rupees, for an amended drugs project.

[1] See below, pp. 116, 129.
[2] Berliner, *Soviet Economic Aid*, p. 200; information supplied privately.
[3] *Capital*, 10 November 1955, p. 613.   [4] Berliner, loc. cit.
[5] See below, p. 163.   [6] Berliner, loc. cit.

By now, the Eastern European countries had followed Russia's lead. An early agreement with Poland to supply railway wagons on credit (June 1955) was followed by a three-year trade pact (April 1956). In the course of 1956 Czechoslovakia supplied loans for three sugar refineries and steam power plants in the private sector, and a cement plant in Assam;[1] and—in 1957—made a major contribution to the large foundry-forge project at Ranchi. East Germany and Rumania also entered the field in 1956, the former with a raw film manufacturing plant, the latter with an oil-drilling rig and training scheme.[2] Hungary weighed in with aid for an aluminium cable plant in November 1959. By the beginning of 1963, Eastern Bloc countries (excluding Yugoslavia) had authorized a total of Rs 437 crores, predominantly in the form of loans repayable in rupees.[3] Trade followed the same course, rising more than twenty times between 1954 and 1963–4:

TABLE 2

Trade Between India and the European Eastern Bloc Countries 1954–1963/4

(Rs crores)

	1954	1955	1956	1957	1958	1959	1960	1961–2	1962–3	1963–4
Indian exports	5·12	4·36	17·59	25·44	31·11	45·05	49·36	63·70	93·24	108·75
Indian imports	5·70	8·38	26·65	38·27	34·89	36·03	36·60	80·79	106·19	123·74
Total trade	10·82	12·74	44·24	63·71	66·00	81·08	85·96	144·49	199·43	232·49

Sources: S. K. Verghese, 'Rupee Payments Arrangements', *EW* Special Number, July 1963, p. 1295, based on Ministry of Commerce and Industry, *Foreign Trade Statistics*, relevant years; Overseas Development Institute, Discussion Paper; Department of Commercial Intelligence and Statistics, *Monthly Statistics*.
Note: Yugoslavia included.

In keeping with their policy elsewhere, Eastern Bloc countries went out of their way to emphasize the unconditional nature of their aid— it was given without reference to the internal social or political régime of the recipient. Most of it naturally found its way to the public sector, as indeed did most Western aid; but some went to

[1] Berliner, *Soviet Economic Aid*, p. 204; K. Billerbeck, *Soviet Bloc Foreign Aid*, pp. 129–30.
[2] Berliner, op. cit., pp. 205, 206. The raw film project was later rejected in favour of a French alternative (see below, p. 165).
[3] *Economic Survey 1962–63*, Table 7.2.

strengthening individual, privately-owned firms. To repeat, the first Russian credit was granted in the private sector, to the Hindustan Gas Co.; Hindustan Files, Calcutta, a subsidiary, received Russian technical aid;[1] a private textile machinery plant was reported to be getting Russian help;[2] and, abortive though they proved, negotiations were begun for Russian aid in producing lorries in the private sector.[3] Other East European countries had entered into 70 collaboration agreements with privately-owned firms by the end of 1964: East Germany—38, Czechoslovakia and Poland—14 each, Hungary—9, and Yugoslavia—5.[4] In addition, Hungary has been reported willing to set up an aluminium plant in the private sector, first in Kerala,[5] then at Koyna, Maharashtra.[6]

Support for the *status quo* was made abundantly clear, clearer than the Indian Government could have hoped for in their wildest dreams. Mention has been made of the steel agreement, signed while a critical election campaign in Andhra was reaching its climax.[7] One week previously, *Pravda* greeted India's Republic Day, 26 January, by referring to 'the outstanding statesman, Mr. Jawaharlal Nehru' and to India as 'a peace-loving state upholding its national independence', and praising its achievements in liquidating colonialism and advancing the masses' standard of living.[8] Translated by Congress into Telugu and distributed in hundreds of thousands of copies, the *Pravda* editorial constituted the ruling party's major propaganda weapon against the local Communist challenge.[9] Add to it Molotov's speech to the Supreme Soviet on 8 February, three days before the commencement of voting—'there is no longer a colonial India but a Republic of India', in flat contradiction to the local Communist Party's own current thesis[10]—and Russia's commitment to supporting explicitly the Nehru régime appeared incontrovertible.

---

[1] Tariff Commission, *Report on the . . . Steel Files Industry*, 1960, p. 3.

[2] *Capital*, 29 November 1962, pp. 801–2.   [3] *Capital*, 1 June 1961, p. 864.

[4] Indian Investment Centre data, reproduced in All-India Seminar on Foreign Collaboration, *Factual Background Papers*, pp. 20–25.

[5] E. M. S. Namboodiripad, then Communist Chief Minister of Kerala, reported in *Hindu*, 17 April 1958.

[6] *ET*, 13 October 1962.   [7] See above, p. 114, below, p. 129.

[8] S. S. Harrison, *India, the Most Dangerous Decades*, pp. 189 n, 242; T. K. Chaudhuri, MP, 'What Would the Communists do Now? Political Implications of New Soviet Appraisals of India' (*The Call*, March 1955). *New Times* of the same date published an article, similar in all essentials, under the title 'India's Five Years of Progress'.

[9] T. K. Chaudhuri, loc. cit.   [10] See ibid.

Nor has she wavered since. An opportunity to do so presented itself towards the end of the Communist Party administration in Kerala, 1957–9. The campaign to overthrow the State Government, well-organized, well-financed, and ultimately successful, was already under way when the Chief Minister, E. M. S. Namboodiripad, left to attend the 21st Congress of the Communist Party of the Soviet Union in Moscow, January 1959. Were Russia to offer substantial aid—a contingency Namboodiripad undoubtedly had in mind at his eve-of-departure press conference—some of the sharpest conflicts might have been avoided. As he said at the time, 'I would certainly try to find out whether Soviet assistance that is now increasingly given to India can be used for the economic development of our State also'.[1] Questioned on his return, the best he could muster was: 'They did not show any discrimination in favour or against me'.[2]

Even more convincing was Russia's backing for India over the Himalayan War in the winter of 1962. Within days of the start of large-scale fighting, Russia dropped her initial support for China.[3] Within weeks a new air agreement had been signed.[4] And within months an Indian industrial exhibition in Moscow was arranged (early January 1963), talks were being conducted on doubling the volume of Indo-Russian trade (February),[5] and a massive increase in Eastern credits and technical aid agreed.[6] At the same time Russia set about piecing together the fragments of 'non-alignment' with military aid.

Arms supplies have been important in India's foreign relations since Independence. Quite early in this new phase of foreign policy—official denials notwithstanding[7]—Russia tried to reduce India's dependence on Western sources. A large offer of army equipment made at the time of the Russian leaders' visit in November 1955,

[1] *Hindu*, 16 January 1959.   [2] *Hindu*, 17 February 1959.
[3] An editorial in *Pravda*, 25 October 1962, called on India to accept China's 'constructive' proposals for a cease-fire and to negotiate on the border; a subsequent editorial (5 November), while calling for a cease-fire and talks 'without any condition attached', no longer implied, as had the first, that the MacMahon Line was invalid.
[4] *The Times*, 14 November 1962.
[5] A new Trade Agreement was signed on 10 June 1963.
[6] Manubhai Shah, Minister for International Trade, at a Press Conference on his return from Eastern Bloc Capitals (*ET*, 14 June 1963).
[7] See, for example, Nehru, in the 1957 Budget Debate: 'At no time in the past has there been any offer from the Soviet Union or any request from us for the purchase of aircraft.' (Reported in *Hindu*, 31 May 1957.)

was frustrated in its main outlines by a counter-offer brought by Admiral Mountbatten, the following March, on British initiative. A specially-equipped Ilyushin-14 had been presented to Nehru at the time, another in March 1956 in conjunction with a visit by the Russian Defence Minister, Georgi K. Zhukov, and an offer made of Ilyushin-28s at £60,000 apiece. After strenuous Western lobbying, it was decided early in 1957 to buy Canberras at £250,000 each and agreed that orders for military aircraft would be placed in the West only; and the first round went against Russia. Besides the Canberras ordered in 1957, French Mystères were bought, British Hawker Hunter jets ordered in quantity as the major air weapon in the autumn of 1957, and British Sea Hawk jets for the navy a year later. At the same time arrangements were concluded to manufacture under licence the Folland 'Gnat' jet trainer, and a German design team hired to develop an Indian supersonic fighter.

A second round took place in 1961. The design team at Hindustan Aircraft had been working on an air-frame in the knowledge that a British engine was being developed for NATO and would be made available to India in due course. In the event the engine was abandoned and the Indian fighter left to fly at subsonic speeds in its first trials (March). The matter could not be left there. The United States had upset the arms balance in the area by supplying supersonic fighters equipped with air-to-air guided missiles to Pakistan (end of 1961). And India, unwilling to spend the £2 million or so required to develop the new engine, looked elsewhere. By March, a number of high-altitude transport planes were bought from Russia, followed in September by six power units of the type fitted to the MiG supersonic fighter. The way was now open for negotiations on the supply of MiGs and their production in India.

Negotiations dragged on throughout the summer of 1962, the final decision being delayed with every move in the strenuous Anglo-American diplomatic offensive to block the deal. After much ado, and after Nehru had been led to protest in the Lok Sabha at Western blackmail—'We are not going to be influenced by pressure from outside. We want aid badly, but not at the cost of our independence'[1]— the decision was finally taken in July: India would buy Russian jet engines for her own fighter, would buy MiGs, and would go ahead with a plant to manufacture both.

The breakthrough had come and neither India's war with China

[1] Quoted in *The Observer*, 24 June 1962.

nor her near-military alliance with the West was allowed to inter-fere. Early in December, barely six weeks after the outbreak of large-scale fighting, Nehru told the Lok Sabha that there had been 'no question at any time of the Soviet Union backing out'[1] and in February 1963 the first, small shipment arrived. In December too, as a Western Air Aid Mission prepared to leave for New Delhi, Russia appears to have offered ground-to-air missiles. The offer was renewed in June the following year, and supplemented with one for light tanks and infantry equipment just before the details of the Western 'air umbrella' were settled, or, more pertinently perhaps, on the eve of the abortive Sino-Soviet peace talks in Moscow. By August, the line of supply was sufficiently secure for India to appeal for arms *aid* as distinct from *sales*.

Political circumstances had changed radically since the mid-fifties: arms from Russia were now to augment, not supplant, those from the West. But central to Russian foreign policy, then as now, stands political and material support for the Indian régime as at present constituted.

(*b*) *Western policy:* Russia's bid to win, rather than overthrow, the new governments in backward countries, shifted the locus of conflict from the periphery of Asia to its heart. India became central to Western strategy.

This did not happen overnight. At first it looked indeed as if India's growing friendship with Russia and the associated 'swing left' in internal policy[2] would work the other way. The United States concluded a military alliance with Pakistan in 1954; Executive requests for aid for India entered into a decline from which they did not recover for four years; and Indo-American relations deteriorated steadily.[3] Even after the corner had been turned, say in the summer of 1956, military aid to the region—primarily to South Korea, Formosa, and South Vietnam, but also to Pakistan—declined only gradually as a proportion of the total; and as late as 1962–3, India's receipt of some $1,000 million (loans mainly) from all Western sources including the World Bank scarcely topped the $8–900 million (grants mainly) received by the first three from the United States alone.[4]

[1] *LS Debates*, 4 December 1962, col. 4225.
[2] See below, pp. 128 ff.   [3] See above, p. 100.
[4] US Department of Defense, *Military Assistance Facts*, 1 March 1962, p. 15; Agency for International Development, *US Foreign Assistance*, 21 March 1962, pp. 31–54. Military support for South Vietnam rose greatly in 1964.

None the less, Western commitments increased dramatically from 1958 onwards. The occasion was provided by India's exchange crisis[1] and its real or imputed impact on internal stability;[2] the justification by the now apparent readiness of the Government to defer to Western wishes—a Russian arms offer had already been turned down—and the associated 'swing Right' in domestic policy;[3] and much of the impetus by the many Western industrial and trade missions that toured India throughout 1957[4] and by the return visit of the Indian Industrial (Birla) Mission in the late summer.[5] By the end of the year, a convertibility agreement providing for payment of profits in dollars had been concluded with the United States, a permanent World Bank mission established in New Delhi, and the first large injection of credit received—from the United States, West Germany, Britain, Japan, the World Bank, and the International Monetary Fund. Western aid took on a quasi-institutional form the following year with the inauguration of an 'Aid India Club'—a creditors' consortium—in August. It grew rapidly until 1961. Since then, despite increased membership[6] and the onset of the worst crisis yet in India's foreign exchange position, aid has fallen off. In 1961 the United

[1] See below, pp. 124–6.

[2] Official spokesmen found it useful to exaggerate the degree of social instability in India as part of the 'bloc blackmailing techniques' they were perfecting at the time. An early illustration was provided by T. T. Krishnamachari on the eve of his first tour of Western capitals as Finance Minister. Interviewed by a *New York Times* correspondent he said: 'We have to be strong enough to defend New Delhi. And it is not just Pakistan. . . . Take Dange [a leading member of the Communist Party]. Maybe some day he will say, "we are ready for a revolution". And maybe then the Soviet Union or China would like to help him. We could then turn to friends for help. But we have to be able to hold on, say for a month, until help comes.' (Quoted in *Hindu*, 7 November 1957.)

[3] See below, pp. 138 ff.

[4] Among the more important of these were the (British) Coates Heavy Engineering Mission (winter 1956–7), the US Trade Mission (March 1957), a West German team on machinery manufacture (May), and another American team on machine tools (June).

[5] See below, pp. 178 f.

[6] The original members—World Bank, United States, West Germany, Britain, Japan, Canada—held their second meeting in Washington, March 1959; their third in Paris, 12 September 1960. They were joined at their fourth (Washington, 31 May–2 June 1961) by the International Development Association and France; at the sixth (Washington, 30 July 1962—the fifth, attended by no new members, was held in Washington on 29–30 January) by Austria, Belgium, Italy, the Netherlands. No new members joined at the seventh (preliminary) meeting (Washington, 30 April–1 May 1963) or the eighth (Paris, 4–5 June), ninth (Washington, 7 August 1963), tenth (preliminary) meeting (Paris, 17–18 March 1964), and eleventh (Washington, 26 May 1964).

States put a ceiling on future contributions, to be reached only if there were matching credits from other countries; a year later she ostentatiously stopped soliciting on India's behalf in Europe.[1] The Club's fourth meeting, convened in June 1961 to raise funds for the first two years of the Third Plan, fell short of its target by a tenth; a fifth meeting scheduled for the autumn had to be postponed until January 1962, and still produced no further contributions; a sixth, again postponed from May to the end of July, added something but still not enough to reach the original target.[2]

The reasons for the decline are complex: the continuing see-saw weakness of the dollar and the pound, and a temporary decline in Western Germany's surpluses on foreign account had something to do with it as did—from 1962 onwards—the growing insularity of Franco-German Europe. Fed by the obvious failure of their (largely military) aid programmes in Asia, the US Congress's natural antipathy to foreign aid as such hardened irremediably throughout the sixties. While other countries, notably Pakistan, had been inspired by India's example to press for, and gain, Aid Consortia of their own, the purely book-keeping resources that sustained some of the initial contributions were quickly spent. India contributed to the growing discontent by rejecting, after protracted diplomatic parleys, Western counsels not to absorb Goa at the end of 1961, not to buy Russian military aircraft the following summer, and not to aggravate Pakistan—then beginning to chafe at the constraints of exclusive commitment to the West—over Kashmir. Overall, there was the unsteady, interrupted, but none the less substantial thawing of the Cold War between the Russian East and the West, and the rapid transition of the Sino-Indian development race into open hostilities.

Not even the Himalayan war has reversed the trend. After an initial Indo-Western honeymoon marked by an immediate, favourable response to India's request for arms aid and a number of concessions in return, Western policies came up against India's resistance to settling the Kashmir issue;[3] and, soon after the fighting ceased,

[1] 'The Indians have been politely told to do some of their own aid seeking.' (*NYT*, 29 June 1962.)

[2] IBRD Press Releases, Washington, 2 June 1961, 30 January, 30 July 1962.

[3] The importance of doing so was emphasized in the joint communiqué issued by President Kennedy and Prime Minister Macmillan after their talks in Nassau, December 1962; in Kennedy's State of the Union message to Congress the following January; and in the elaborate pains taken by representatives of the British and United States Governments to organize and perpetuate an abortive series of meetings between India and Pakistan during the first months of 1963.

many of the long-term trends reasserted themselves. The United States and Britain proved reluctant to meet many of India's requests for military equipment, refused to supply the supersonic fighters which topped her shopping list and left her to find, independently, the $1,400–1,700 million of *extra* foreign exchange she considered necessary for military purchases during the remaining years of the Third Plan. Consortium aid followed its downward course: the $1,250 million requested for 1963–4 was met by an offer of $850 million in April 1963, raised to $915 million in June and $1,052 million in August—still below the $1,070 raised the year before and the $1,295 the year before that; France and Germany cut aid drastically; the United States lowered their ceiling from $500 to $450 million while still making it conditional on 'matching contributions' from others; and the saga of negotiations on a United-States-aided steel mill at Bokaro[1] finally petered out in August, with an adverse decision in the American Congress. The following year, Consortium aid fell slightly further to $1,028 million, albeit on easier terms.

(*c*) *The flow of aid:* Since it is always 'subject as appropriate to legislative action or other necessary authorization,'[2] aid committed is not aid received. It is even farther from aid utilized—no more than three-fifths of total grants and loans allocated in any one year are actually taken up.[3]

Sometimes the lags, due to cumbersome regulations on the part of creditors[4] or inefficient programming or indecisiveness at the Indian end,[5] can stretch over years.[6] The form it takes—tied to individual

[1] See below, p. 237.
[2] Of the $930 million pledged at the first Aid India Club meeting, August 1958, for the completion of the Second Plan, no more than $800 million actually materialized (*The Economist*, 10 September 1960, p. 1004).
[3] See *EW*, 16 March 1963, p. 469; 29 June 1963, p. 1020.
[4] See, for example, A. K. Ghosh, 'External Assistance for Plan Programmes, Problems of Utilisation', *EW*, 27 October 1962, pp. 1699–1702.
[5] See, for example, 'HEC on the Mat' and 'Unplanned Lags', *EW*, 11 April 1964, pp. 671–2.
[6] For example: by mid-1962, a World Bank loan granted in 1958 for improvements to Calcutta Port was still not fully utilized; only Rs 6 crores out of the Rs 9·5 crores authorized in 1959–60 for the Koyna hydroelectric project had been drawn; only Rs 3 crores out of the Rs 33·4 crores authorized by the US Government for power projects; Rs 1·4 crores out of the Rs 14·3 crores for a fertilizer project in Bombay; one-fifth of a Rs 60 crores Russian credit announced in 1959; nothing out of the Yen credit of Rs 8·6 crores, also in 1959; and less than Rs 1 crore out of another Rs 38 crores Yen credit in 1961 (*Hindu*, 23 June 1962). A World Bank loan to the coal industry, authorized in July 1961, was

projects, individual suppliers, and specific commodities to the extent of 96·8 per cent of all loans authorized up to the end of March 1962[1] —makes it expensive: estimates vary, but suggest that India might normally be paying anything between 6 and 15 per cent, sometimes as much as 20–30 per cent, above ruling prices for aid-supported imports.[2] Nor is it all available for new or continuing projects, since servicing of past loans is absorbing an increasing amount of the credits received: Rs 23 crores in foreign currency in 1958–9,[3] Rs 90 crores in 1961–2, and an estimated Rs 130 crores in 1965–6.[4]

All this said, the transfer of capital on Government account over the past decade has been substantial. It permitted India to finance three-fifths of her import surplus during the Second Plan;[5] all of it and more in recent years.[6] It supplied one-eighth of public investment during the First Plan, 28 per cent during the Second,[7] and was expected to contribute slightly over half during the Third.[8] Beyond the bare figures, it has given the Indian Government independent resources and a measure of initiative which otherwise might have had to be won, by force, from within the country.

II DOMESTIC BACKGROUND

The boom which set in towards the end of the First Plan[9] did not run short of stimuli. A quickening tempo of development expenditure; the use of budgetary deficits to finance it; rising inflationary pressures in the United States and Western Europe; growing trade with Eastern Bloc countries; and many of the detailed measures adopted by the Government over and above the reassurance it was offering verbally, helped sustain expansion. Industrial production continued growing steadily;[10] the indices for important investment

---

'wholly unutilised' at the end of September 1962 (*EW*, 13 April 1963, p. 616) and 'almost totally undrawn' in March 1963 (*EW*, 16 March 1963, p. 469). For a general survey of the lag in aid utilization, see 'Strategic Shortfalls in Industry', *EW* Special Number, July 1963.

[1] RBI, *Balance of Payments*, Table VIII, p. 55.
[2] See *The Economist*, 28 January 1961, p. 344; *The Times*, 21 April 1961.
[3] NCAER, *Taxation and Foreign Investment*, p. xiv.
[4] *Statistical Outline of India*, 1963, Table 50, p. 51. The forecast for 1965–6 is an official one made in September 1962. See Table 19, p. 308, below.
[5] PC, *Third Plan*, p. 108.
[6] PC, *Mid-Term Appraisal*, Table 2, pp. 42–43.
[7] From PC, *Third Plan*, Tables 1 and 3, pp. 32 and 33.
[8] ibid., pp. 90, 109.   [9] See above, p. 80.
[10] For these and other economic indicators, see Appendix 3 below, pp. 326–31.

goods made predominantly in the private sector—cement, tyres, coal, iron, diesel engines, sulphuric acid—swept upwards. Corporate investment in the private sector rose uninterruptedly until 1958–9; capital issues consents, actual issues, initial issues, share prices, indicative of business confidence in different ways, all went up until 1957.

What with the narrowness of India's industrial economy, bottlenecks appeared early in the boom. Basic metals were the most important, steel prices rising by three-fifths in the six years from 1951–7 despite increasingly heavy imports.[1] But they were not the only problem. Coal, electricity, a variety of capital goods, were all in short supply by the end of the First Plan and hindering production.

Since foreign exchange was relatively plentiful at the time, demand was allowed to spill over into imports. With export receipts very nearly static, the trade deficit almost trebled between 1955–6 and 1956–7, and doubled again by 1957–8. Reserves of foreign currency took the strain, declining by nearly half between 1955–6 and 1957–8 despite lavish use of the borrowing facilities provided by the International Monetary Fund.[2]

A number of factors behind India's continued balance of payments weakness became apparent during this first major crisis. One was her vulnerability to the world economic climate: import prices which were rising noticeably during 1955 and 1956, jerked up by about a tenth during and after the Suez War,[3] while export prices and receipts fell during the period of slackness in world trade that followed it. Stagnation abroad shortened delivery dates for India's imports forcing her to make earlier, bunched payments; while the deterioration of India's external balance, coupled with the attraction of Britain's high post-Suez bank rate (for which India's run on sterling was partly responsible), induced some Rs 5 crores' worth of British capital to flow to London in 1957.[4]

Another factor was India's narrow food margin. Bad harvests in 1955–6 and the following year nearly trebled food imports, from Rs 67 crores in 1955–6 to Rs 195 crores in 1957.[5]

A third was the steadily worsening relations with her neighbours and would-be neighbours: on a background made up of the United

---

[1] ECAFE, *Survey 1957*, Table 36, p. 77.
[2] See Appendix 3 (f), (i), pp. 329, 330, below.
[3] PC, *Appraisal and Prospects*, p. 4; *EW*, January 1958, p. 98.
[4] 'Unofficial trade estimate' quoted in *The Times*, 22 December 1959.
[5] T. Mohan Chandar Menon, *ET*, 17 June 1962.

States–Pakistan Mutual Defense Agreement of May 1954, the outbreak of hostilities in Nagaland the following spring, the flare-ups on the Goa border throughout that year, and China's commitment to a full-scale colonial war in Tibet in 1957, pressures to increase the arms budget could not be contained. After remaining fairly steady for six or seven years, it jumped up by more than a quarter in 1957 to Rs 257 crores;[1] and since its import content is high,[2] some Rs 60 crores were added to that year's foreign exchange bill to make a total of some Rs 120 crores on arms account.

Finally, there was the administrative laxity and policy conflict within the Government which permitted lavish official expenditure abroad and a speculative boom in private imports. 'We were not fully seized of what was happening', admitted Nehru on the first count. 'Different Ministries went on ordering things without anybody knowing the entire picture for some time.'[3] The Planning Commission added a note on the 'lack of circumspection in the allotment of foreign exchange for marginal items in the shape of too many delegations going abroad and too many large government buildings being constructed involving foreign exchange for steel and non-essential electrical equipment'.[4]

On the second, and by far the more important factor, C. D. Deshmukh, Finance Minister during the early phases of the crisis, reported afterwards:

at least Rs 100 crores worth of exchange was wasted on things we do not want. . . . The use of the foreign exchange resources by the private sector was a sort of hoarding on their part when they realised towards the end of 1955 that the second Five Year Plan was going to be short by some Rs 800 crores of foreign exchange.[5]

This could not have happened without direct encouragement from the Ministry of Commerce and Industry, always responsive to private sector interests: 'Our businessmen [were allowed to] . . . stock their larder . . . by a sympathetic Ministry and even before the Plan was fully approved.'[6]

[1] See Appendix 4, p. 332, below.
[2] It has been estimated at 38 per cent for recent years compared with 15 per cent for Britain. (B. N. Ganguli, 'Defense Production and Defense Expenditure', *EW* Annual Number, February 1963, p. 152.)
[3] Speech in the Lok Sabha, quoted in *Capital*, 27 March 1958, p. 453.
[4] Quoted in *CSM*, 29 March 1958.
[5] 'Our Foreign Indebtedness', Symposium in *Kalki* (September 1958), quoted in D. Latifi, *India and U.S. Aid*, p. 61.
[6] ibid.

Deshmukh was not informed of the extent of import licensing. He began to suspect what had happened in May 1956 as the permits granted the year before took effect. Only after he had resigned did he grasp its full dimensions. The Government as a whole became aware of the impending crisis in the autumn of 1956 when the fruits of the two most prodigal licensing periods—those beginning in December 1955 and June 1956—began to be harvested. Even then no serious remedial measures were contemplated until after the elections in 1957 and after a number of important measures affecting the private sector had been adopted.[1] Then, in February, capital goods imports were cut and businessmen asked to seek deferred payment terms abroad. In July all import licences were suspended for three months; in September essential imports only were renewed. In August currency reserves had fallen below the legal minimum; in October the legal provisions relating to reserves were liberalized. That autumn, a major systematic effort commenced to seek aid from the West.[2] The drain continued into 1958 and in May the Second Plan was cut back by a fifth to a core of three steel plants, their ancillaries, and railway, coal, power, and port developments.[3]

After the initial shock in 1957 and 1958, during which the growth of industrial production slowed down, investment fell off, the capital market halved its activity, and share prices slumped,[4] the boom resumed. Restrictions at home and aid from abroad sustained it as did increasing Government expenditure and the operations of the Life Insurance Corporation and the statutory financial institutions.[5]

The boom was relatively short-lived. By the beginning of the current decade, many of the factors in the first exchange crisis had reasserted themselves. Military expenditure went up sharply from Rs 250 crores in 1960–1 to Rs 290, Rs 450, and a budgeted Rs 710 crores in the three following years.[6] Food imports were at their highest ever in 1960 and continued at a high rate into the decade as domestic production stagnated for three years.[7] Over-licensing added

[1] See Deshmukh-Nehru correspondence, *Hindu*, 22 March 1958. The measures are dealt with below, pp. 137–8.

[2] See above, p. 120, below, pp. 157 ff.

[3] PC, *Appraisal and Prospects*, Table 5, p. 17; Table, pp. 85–86; Annexure, pp. 88–89. Although the cut envisaged was only Rs 300 crores out of a total 'financial investment' of Rs 4,800 crores, real investment suffered very much more, prices having risen 14 per cent between April 1956 and August 1957 (ibid., p. 3).

[4] See economic indicators, Appendix 3, pp. 326–31, below.

[5] See above, p. 94.   [6] See Appendix 4, p. 332, below.

[7] See Appendix 3, p. 329, below.

substantially to the load: within nine months of the Third Plan, the foreign exchange component of Industrial licences granted by the Ministry of Commerce and Industry amounted to Rs 400 crores, and clearances by the Capital Goods Committee to Rs 190 crores, compared with a total foreign exchange allocation of Rs 450 crores for the entire Plan period.[1] There were now no foreign exchange reserves to cushion their effect as there had been at the beginning of the Second Plan, and India entered the worst balance-of-payments crisis yet. Reserves bumped along the legal minimum from 1961 to date, sustained by mounting drafts on the International Monetary Fund. The first of a run of increasingly drastic import restrictions was imposed in October 1960: by December 1962 an official survey reported that 75 industries were working at 65 per cent of capacity on average[2] —and an unofficial estimate put machine utilization in engineering at half of capacity due to the lack of maintenance imports.[3]

As early as August 1960, before the Third Plan started, it was feared that foreign exchange resources might be inadequate to see it through;[4] with the Himalayan War it became inevitable.[5]

The key years in this entire period were 1957-8. The drain of foreign exchange thrust India into a totally new dependence on foreign support. Coupled with the methods chosen to overcome the crisis, this dependence tilted the balance of economic and social power within the country heavily in favour of the private sector, particularly its modern corporate wing, and crystallized changes of a fundamental nature in the latter's attitude to foreign capital. When the Sino-Indian conflict finally broke in 1962, it added impetus to social and economic developments that were already well under way.

[1] *Capital*, 8 March 1962, p. 417. Within eight months of the Plan's formal inauguration, the Planning Commission found it necessary to warn the Ministry of Commerce and Industry that their 'desire to encourage new entrepreneurs to enter the field of industrial activity, and to avoid undue concentration . . . should not lead to new pressures for setting up of new capacities in industries where already adequate capacity has been licensed.' (*Hindu*, 27 December 1961.) See also pp. 300 f., below.

[2] *ET*, 1 December 1962.

[3] Survey made by the Engineering Association of India, reported in *Hindu*, 5 January 1963.

[4] Morarji Desai, Minister of Finance, Lok Sabha debate reported in *The Times*, 26 August 1960.

[5] See, for example, 'Rephasing the Third Plan', *EW* Special Number, July 1963, pp. 1099–1101; PC, *Mid-Term Appraisal*, pp. 39–40, 50, 178, *passim*; two years before the end of the Third Plan, official instructions were sent out to hold in abeyance such Plan projects as had not yet been started (Prem Bhatia in *The Guardian*, 14 August 1964).

III SWING LEFT[1]

(a) *Background:* Open urban 'unemployment began to show a marked upward trend when the first Plan was half way through'.[2] By the beginning of the Second Plan it had more than doubled the 1951 figure to some two and a half million;[3] one-fifth of the urban labour force was thought to be either totally unemployed or underemployed 'in the sense of having work for "a quarter or less" of the time' it would be willing to work; and in the larger, politically more advanced cities as many as one-quarter or a third were thought to be in that position.[4] Literate unemployment formed a substantial part of the total,[5] and was the more significant for sharpening the linguistic and regional agitations that first came to a head at about this time[6] and for manning the opposition parties. The danger to Congress became overt when the Praja Socialist Party, having already doubled their parliamentary fraction through the adherence of practically all Independents, won a crucial by-election in Agra, July 1953. Thereafter, and until the Second Plan, the provision of jobs dominated politics.

The fact that the political challenge came from the Praja Socialists and Communists, not from the Right, determined to some degree both Congress's choice of solution—industrialization—and of method—state production. Congress had to compete, on their terms.

---

[1] 'Left' in India normally denotes support for economic growth through state capitalism: 'Right'—support for orthodox, private-ownership capitalism with a large but subsidiary role for the state. Although there is, or was, a large measure of agreement between the two wings on the necessity for Indian economic independence, the 'Left' has generally shown a more uncompromising economic nationalism and a surer opportunistic flair for exploiting 'non-alignment' for Indian ends. The 'Right', linked to private capital in the West, has been softer on both counts. The issues between them are often obscured and overlaid by terminologies and ideologies imported from the developed world; talk of 'socialism' and 'capitalism', 'working class' and 'bourgeoisie' abounds. But the issues rarely correspond to a conflict of interest sustained by an organized conflict between classes. While these exist and lend colour to the phraseologies, they are as alien to the aims of the 'Left' (including Communists, both 'Russian-wing' and 'Chinese-wing') as of the 'Right'.

[2] PC, *Second Plan*, p. 110.

[3] Malenbaum, 'Urban Unemployment in India', *PA*, June 1957, pp. 138–50. PC, *Second Plan*, p. 110.

[4] Malenbaum, 'Unemployment in Urban Areas', *EW*, 8 September 1956, p. 1073.

[5] ibid.; B. T. Ranadive, *The Call*, December 1959, p. 13.

[6] See Harrison, *India*, pp. 74, 91, *passim*. The States Reorganization Commission reported in October 1955.

Already in May 1953, the Congress Working Committee warned: 'The major test of the success of any plan is the measure in which one deals with the problem of unemployment.' As yet, however, they still believed that it 'should . . . be tackled on all fronts and more particularly by the organised growth of cottage and village industries'.[1] In July, at Agra, at the time of the by-election, the All-India Congress Committee expressed 'its concern at the increase in unemployment . . . notwithstanding the fact that generally there has been an upward trend of production'. By now, however, they had come round to the view that 'the state must accept an increasingly active and positive role in regard to the development of industries'.[2] After the defeat, pressure in the Congress ranks brought the 'industrialisers' under T. T. Krishnamachari to join battle with the 'Gandhians' at the Congress Working Committee meeting in September;[3] the National Development Council gave employment priority over food the following month;[4] and the Plan was expanded in December. Resolutions continued to pour out: at Ajmer, July 1954, the All-India Congress Committee viewed 'with concern the unemployment that exists more especially in the urban areas';[5] at Avadi, January 1955, one month before the critical electoral battle with the Communist Party in Andhra,[6] the famous resolution on the 'Socialistic Pattern of Society' called for 'full employment within a period of ten years'.[7] And so on through to 1956.[8]

Pressures for rapid industrialization came from other quarters as well. The boom of the mid-fifties did not get very far before running into production bottlenecks.[9] Indian businessmen were reminded of the frustrations they had experienced during the Second World War and returned to some of the solutions they had proffered then. J. R. D. Tata told a shareholders' meeting: 'Bold planning and determined execution of large schemes of development are essential if we are to raise living standards, relieve unemployment, give opportunities to all and ensure a reasonable degree of social justice.'[10] They realized again, as they had before Independence, that such

[1] INC, *Resolutions 1924–54*, pp. 79–80.   [2] ibid., pp. 82, 83.
[3] *Capital*, 17 September 1953, p. 393; *Hindu*, 18 January 1955.
[4] *Capital*, 14 October 1953, p. 535.   [5] INC, *Resolutions 1924–54*, p. 89.
[6] See above, pp. 114, 116.   [7] INC, *Resolutions 1955–56*, p. 2.
[8] See Shriman Narayan, *A-ICC Economic Review*, 11 February 1956, p. 7; INC, *Resolutions 1955–56*, p. 9.
[9] See above, p. 124.
[10] Chairman's Address, Eighth General Meeting, TISCO (Tata Iron and Steel Co. Ltd.), 25 August 1955, quoted in N. Das, *Industrial Enterprise in India*, p. 171.
10

large schemes—'the industrial reconstruction of India'—were beyond the capacity of the private sector and required state action.[1] In part this was a matter of resources; in part it was because Indian capital was not organized for the job; it was too monopolistic, operated with too few and too narrowly-held funds, was biased towards trade rather than production.[2] Perversely enough, the very success of the private sector in the closing months of the First Plan, its optimism, fed the pressures for more state initiative. The anti-capitalism which the Congress rank-and-file had inherited from pre-Independence times but which had lain dormant, now had something on which to latch. As one commentator wrote: 'The complaint is that private capital wants to do too much and has to be restrained from trespassing into the public sector.'[3]

The complaint was the shriller for the private sector's patent inability to spread its fortune to the unemployed. At the same time the success undermined official resistance to the idea of rapid growth. The three per cent per year increase in incomes originally set as the Second Plan target, and mentioned as late as December 1954 by the Finance Minister,[4] lost much of its appeal when it became clear that it might actually be attained in the course of the First. By the time the *Draft Plan-Frame* was completed in March 1955, the target was set at five per cent.[5]

Little might have come of all these if India were dependent on her own resources. But, just as the pressures were mounting, Russian policy underwent the reappraisal and change which provided India with some of the wherewithal for state investments,[6] and a lot of room for manœuvre in her relations with the West. Russian aid naturally added prestige and influence to the planners and public-sector industrializers who led the drive for heavy industry.

(*b*) '*Pattern*' *and Practice:* For a time it looked as if India had embarked on a course of fundamental social and political change. Arguments for and against rapid industrialization, for and against state economic initiative, tended to be couched in traditional doc-

---

[1] See, for example, PTI interview with G. D. Birla, *Hindu*, 24 December 1954.

[2] See Planning Commission, Panel of Economists, *Papers*, Section VII, 'Policy and Institutional Implications', *passim*.

[3] *Capital*, 21 January 1955, p. 69.

[4] C. D. Deshmukh, Statement to Lok Sabha, 20 December 1954, cited in Malenbaum, *Prospects for Indian Development*, p. 72.

[5] Malenbaum, *Prospects*, p. 73.   [6] See above, pp. 113 ff.

trinal terms—'socialism' versus 'private enterprise' or 'individual freedom'; 'left' versus 'right'—and not only for reasons of political expediency. In July 1954 the All-India Congress Committee resolved: in order to attain Congress's objectives of a 'co-operative common-wealth and a Welfare State . . . the present social structure, which still continues to be partly based on an acquisitive economy, has to be progressively changed into a socialised economy'.[1] In November Nehru pressed the National Development Council to adopt the 'socialistic pattern' as the country's goal.[2] In December, pressure from Congress back-benchers led the Government to amend its own motion to read, *inter alia*, that 'the objective of our economic policy should be a socialistic pattern of society'.[3] In January 1955, at its Avadi session, Congress resolved that 'planning should take place with a view to the establishment of a socialistic pattern of society, where the principal means of production are under social ownership or control'.[4] The new Industrial Policy Resolution of 30 April 1956 was formulated partly in response to the new trend as was the Second Five Year Plan, published shortly afterwards but in preparation from April 1954.[5]

The 'ideological' formulations encouraged what was even then considered to be extremist thinking, as when the Taxation Enquiry Commission under John Matthai recommended an income ceiling of one lakh of rupees a year;[6] or when the Parliamentary Consulta-tive Committee on Planning called, in January 1956, for wholesale nationalization of named industries (including such as were left to the private sector in the Second Plan), for an upward revision of heavy industry targets, for prohibiting Indo-foreign joint-ventures in the private sector, and for profit sharing and workers' participation in management;[7] or when the Uttar Pradesh State Assembly called for the 'abolition of capitalism in all its forms'.[8] It added zest to the

---

[1] INC, *Resolutions 1924–54*, p. 87.   [2] *Hindu*, 10 November 1954.
[3] *LS Debates*, 20–21 December 1954, col. 3692. According to C. D. Deshmukh, the decision to accept the obscure back-benchers' resolutions as an amendment to the Government's own motion was taken by Nehru and him in the Chamber without prior discussion or Cabinet decision (from discussion at an interview). For Nehru's opposition to a similar resolution on an earlier occasion, see above, p. 84. n 6.
[4] INC, *Resolutions 1955–56*, p. 1.
[5] See Resolution, para. 2; PC, *Second Plan*, pp. 21–24.
[6] Reported in *CSM*, 23 May 1955.   [7] *Hindu*, 16 January 1956.
[8] *Capital*, 2 February 1956, p. 163. Similar demands were canvassed within the Congress Party on the eve of its Amritsar session (*MG*, 7 February 1956).

labour offensive mounted during 1956–8, contributing something to its gains; and was reflected in the prestige accorded at the time to the Planning Commission's Panel of Economists, manned almost entirely by 'leftists' prepared to accept far-reaching social change in the interests of rapid development.[1]

Yet these *political* lunges to the left formed no part of the Government's intention. As was made clear on every possible occasion, their aim was to increase production, not change society. The pattern for the period was set at the Congress Committee meeting at Ajmer, July 1954, when the resolution calling for a 'socialised economy' hastened to add: 'the private sector is both important and necessary in the industrial development of India . . . [and] should be given adequate freedom to develop, within the limits of the National Plan.'[2] It was endorsed later that year when Nehru extolled the virtues of pragmatism to a restive Congress Parliamentary Party, telling them in effect, not to take the Government's resolution on the 'socialistic pattern' too seriously: 'In a country like India . . . socialism and a real socialist basis of society can only come gradually',[3] and in the Lok Sabha debate; 'I see a lot of good in the private sector functioning'.[4] The famous Avadi Resolution was not without its grain of comfort: 'The private sector or the non-State and voluntary enterprises will . . . continue to have importance.'[5] Moving it, Maulana Azad stressed that the 'main consideration was to increase production';[6] and referring to it in his report as outgoing president, Nehru elaborated:

in our present state to limit resources to the public sector means restriction of our opportunities for production and growth. . . . it becomes necessary, therefore, to have a private sector also and to give it full play within its field. We have to remember always that within the larger framework that we lay down, the test always is fuller production and fuller employment.[7]

Full legitimacy for the private sector came finally in the Government's Industrial Policy Resolution of 30 April 1956: '*as an agency*

---

[1] See Planning Commission, Panel of Economists, *Papers, passim*, particularly the memoranda prepared by Professors K. N. Raj, B. N. Ganguli, and D. R. Gadgil.

[2] INC, *Resolutions 1924–54*, p. 90.

[3] Report of a speech delivered on 22 December 1954 (*Hindu*, 3 January 1955).

[4] *Hindu*, 22 December 1954.   [5] INC, *Resolutions 1955–56*, p. 3.

[6] *A-ICC Economic Review*, 21 January 1955, quoted in Wiggins, *Private Foreign Investment*, p. 86.

[7] ibid.

for planned national development . . . the private sector will have the opportunity to develop and expand.'[1]

Reassurances were carried into every business gathering throughout the first crucial months of the 'socialistic pattern'. The Associated Chambers of Commerce and Industry, the Indian Merchants' Chamber, its Central Committee, the Indian Chamber of Commerce, the Federation of Indian Chambers of Commerce and Industry, all had one at least of the economic Ministers address them within three months of the key resolutions—all in roughly the same vein. To quote one at random, the Government did 'not visualise any change during the next twenty-five years in the private sector or private enterprise, so long as the latter acted within limits and did not harm the building up of an egalitarian society.'[2]

An important element in official and quasi-official pronouncements, one derived from the 'production-first' approach, was the clear distinction drawn between state enterprise and nationalization. More of the first did not necessarily entail more of the second. To go back to the Congress Committee at Ajmer, July 1954, 'the resources of the country should be utilised in building new state industries and not in nationalising existing private industries, except where this is considered necessary in the national interest.'[3] The most definitive expression came with the Industrial Policy Resolution, 1956, which finally drew the limits of the two sectors.[4] Beforehand, proposals for nationalizing particular industries or firms had been quashed time and again: TELCO in October 1954, commercial banking in December 1954, foreign trade, cement, jute, and plantations early in 1956.

The way in which the major acts of nationalization of the time were implemented—air transport in 1953, the Imperial Bank in May 1955, life insurance in January 1956, and the Kolar Gold Fields in November of that year—carried even greater conviction. While the temptation to make political capital out of them was not always resisted,[5] in each case nationalization was undertaken for specific and strictly defined objectives, not as part of an over-all anti-private-

[1] Para. 5. Emphasis added.

[2] T. T. Krishnamachari, Minister of Commerce and Industry, to the Silver Jubilee meeting of the Indian Merchants' Chamber, Coimbatore, quoted in *Hindu*, 31 December 1955.

[3] INC, *Resolutions 1924–54*, p. 90.   [4] Paras. 7, 8. See below, pp. 143–4.

[5] See, for example, C. D. Deshmukh's broadcast over All-India Radio, the day the Ordinance relating to life insurance was published: 'The nationalisation of life insurance will be another milestone in the road this country has chosen in order to reach its goal of a Socialist Pattern of Society. . . .' (*Hindu*, 21 January 1956).

sector strategy. Air transport was weakly organized, unable without Government support to extend services to many cities within India, let alone abroad. When the companies themselves requested such aid —long-term loans at nominal interest—the Government took them over, appointing as Chairman of the new Air Corporation J. R. D. Tata, largest air-line operator at the time. The Imperial Bank was nationalized after three or more decades of agitation in order to create a small-town credit structure other than that provided by money-lenders.[1] On the admission of A. D. Shroff, implacable critic of state intervention, nationalization was provoked by the 'unresponsive attitude of bankers to the nation's requirements' for a network of small-town branches.[2] On no account was it to be thought a prelude to nationalization of commercial banking, which, to quote T. T. Krishnamachari at the time, 'should be the last thing in nationalisation'.[3]

Life insurance was taken over partly in order to clean up an unusually corrupt and inefficient industry[4] for which 'legislative controls have become finally ineffective [and for which] we could devise no legislative hedge which could not be jumped over'.[5] Mainly however, it was done in order to concentrate savings for the large industrial investment that was about to begin. As Deshmukh said in the radio message already quoted:

With a second Plan in the offing involving an accelerated rate of investment and development, the widening and deepening of all possible channels of public savings have become more than ever necessary. Of this process the nationalisation of insurance is a vital part.

Private industry would not suffer and would continue to receive 'at least as much money as today made available to it'.[6]

---

[1] See, for example, C. D. Deshmukh, Minister of Finance, LS Debates, 30 April 1955, col. 7091, passim.
[2] Speech at the Rotary Club, Ahmedabad (Capital, 6 January 1955, p. 16).
[3] Press conference, Madras (Hindu, 1 January 1955).
[4] During 1954–5 over one-quarter of the operating companies either went into liquidation or failed to submit accounts as required by law (M. N. V. Nair, 'Nationalisation of Life Insurance', The Call, March 1956; Joint . . . India, p. 40); since the war Government administrators had to be appointed to eleven companies because of fraudulent transactions, defalcations, fictitious loans, and reckless expenditure (Joint . . . India, loc. cit.). See also C. D. Deshmukh, Minister of Finance, LS Debates, 19 March 1956, cols. 2917, 2918.
[5] T. T. Krishnamachari, quoted in Nair, The Call, March 1956, p. 8.
[6] C. D. Deshmukh, quoted in EW, January 1956, p. 52. The Life Insurance Corporation is today the largest single investor in the private sector.

The declining Kolar Gold Mines are a somewhat different case. Here nationalization was undertaken at the instance of the Mysore State Government in furtherance of its pre-Independence pledge to clear up a notorious area of exploitation. It was done against the advice of the Centre; and John Taylor and Sons, the managing agents, were retained as technical advisers at Rs 4 lakhs a year.[1] Even in this case, the nearest India ever came to punitive nationalization, it was clear that 'there [was] no ill will behind the Indian moves'.[2]

At no time was there any hint of confiscation. On the contrary, compensation was generous. The valuation of assets under the Air Corporation Act was such as to create a minor boom in air shares when the terms became known early in 1953.[3] Imperial Bank shares were taken over at the average market price of the previous twelve months—too generous an assessment in the opinion of many Congress members of the Lok Sabha.[4] Life insurance assets were assessed under a complicated formula which 'many in the business community felt [to be] . . . all things considered, a reasonable and fair basis of compensation'.[5] And the Government of Mysore's original offer of £650,000 was raised at the instance of the Centre to £900,000 and finally to £1,230,000—a 'fair and reasonable' sum in the opinion of the Kolar group's managing Director.[6]

(c) *Economic strategy:* Two things needed doing quickly to break production bottlenecks and absorb unemployment: one was for the Government to tackle the less profitable tasks itself; the other was to adapt the country's economic and legal institutions to rapid industrialization and to gear the private sector to it. Both upset entrenched interests; both aroused opposition; and both encouraged, as a result, doctrinal formulations in what was, essentially, a quarrel over the organization of the social *status quo*. That the formulations themselves became material political factors at the time is not denied;

[1] *Link,* 28 July 1963, p. 17.

[2] K. S. Shelvankar, *Hindu Survey of Indian Industries,* 24 December 1956.

[3] *Joint . . . India,* pp. 38–39.

[4] *Joint . . . India,* p. 39; Wiggins, *Private Foreign Investment,* p. 89.

[5] *Commerce,* 24 March 1956, p. 542, cited in *Joint . . . India,* p. 42.

[6] *FT,* 10 October 1956. The Lok Sabha's Ad Hoc Committee on Compensation thought that 'some consideration is also due to shareholders, particularly when they are non-Indians, for the disturbance caused to their investment and the expenditure they will be put to in reinvesting what they receive by way of compensation'. (*Hindu,* 22 December 1957.)

they were less important, however, than the concrete measures adopted by the state to increase production.

The Government's own intentions were charted in the *Second Five Year Plan*. Prepared during the height of the swing left from April 1954 and presented in mid-1956, it bore all the hallmarks of the new strategy (although not to the same degree as Professor Mahalonobis's *Draft Plan-Frame* of March 1955).[1] It was a 'big' plan, on which the Government expected to spend nearly two and a half times as much as on its predecessor.[2] It was a plan for industrialization, with seven times as much projected for industry as was spent in the First,[3] and with a strong bias in favour of large projects.[4] Above all, it was a plan for the public sector, which was to increase its share of total investment from an actual 44 per cent in the first to a projected 61 per cent in the second.[5]

The second arm of the Government's strategy is less amenable to statistical description. It required the concentration of larger resources in the hands of the state, and increasing state control over the economy. To this end the Imperial Bank and life insurance were nationalized; to this end, too, a thorough inquiry into taxation revenue and tax administration was instituted, first at the hands of the Taxation Enquiry Commission which reported in March 1955, then at the more radical hands of Nicholas Kaldor who reported in May the following year. While not all of their recommendations were implemented, least of all the far-reaching, closely-interrelated reforms proposed by Kaldor, revenue took a sharp turn upwards with the 1955–6 Budget;[6] a number of the more obvious and traffic-laden loopholes were closed;[7] and some radical innovations—a wealth tax, an expenditure tax, and, once again after ten years, a capital gains tax—were adopted in 1956 and 1957.

A further requirement of the new strategy was for the state to free

---

[1] The major differences lay in the increased allocation for transport of Rs 400 odd crores and a Rs 200 crore cut in heavy machine-making capacity.

[2] Rs 4,800 crores as against Rs 2,000 crores (PC, *Review First Plan*, p. 18; PC, *Second Plan*, pp. 51–52).

[3] From PC, *Review First Plan*, p. 21; PC, *Second Plan*, p. 53.

[4] During the First Plan, no one industrial project absorbed more than Rs 8·30 crores (PC, *Review First Plan*, p. 204). In the Second, the three steel plants alone were expected to absorb Rs 350 crores (PC, *Second Plan*, p. 417) and ended by claiming very much more.

[5] See below, pp. 142–3.   [6] See Appendix 4 below, p. 332.

[7] Primarily those relating to tax-free 'perquisites' and tax-avoidance through non-distribution of profits.

itself from a number of legal restraints on its economic initiative. The most eventful step in this direction was taken with the enactment of the Fourth Amendment to the Constitution in April 1955.[1]

A third requirement was to rid Indian capital of its hobbling organization, primarily the managing agency which was increasingly held responsible for the 'financial orientation' of private capital, its lack of resources, its timidity in production, and so on. The major instrument here was the Companies Act of 1956.[2] But it was not the only one. Individual industries came in for close inspection: the Plantation Enquiry Commission, set up in April 1954, recommended (August 1956) the abolition of managing agencies on Indian-owned plantations, control over dividend payments, turnover, and salaries; the Pharmaceutical Enquiry Commission, appointed in March 1953, recommended (September 1954) that the Government look into the Patent Laws 'whose working hinders development of the synthetic drug industry [and] consider if the international patent regulation can be abrogated to enable the manufacturers to make essential pharmaceuticals . . . without having to pay heavy royalties to foreign firms'.[3] Coal mining was under close scrutiny throughout the

---

[1] The Amendment was introduced after a Supreme Court decision had cast doubt on the legality of much of the regulatory legislation passed since Independence (including the Industries [Development and Regulation] Act of 1951). It removed from the jurisdiction of the courts questions of compensation for property compulsorily acquired by the state. As Nehru argued before the Lok Sabha at the time: 'the ultimate authority to lay down what political, social and economic law we should have is Parliament and Parliament alone. It is not the function of the judiciary to do that.' (*TOI*, 15 March 1955.)

[2] See above, pp. 51 f. The evolution of the Act is instructive in showing the Government's growing resolve to control the private sector. The Company Law Committee, appointed in 1950, 'necessarily based [its inquiry] on a tacit acceptance of the fundamental postulates and assumptions of private enterprise' (*Report*, p. 11), which, in India, meant the postulates and assumptions of the managing agencies. Although it recommended a number of reforms, the *Report* and later, the Bill as introduced in the Lok Sabha in mid-1954, in no way questioned these postulates. It was during its passage through a Joint Select Committee that the implications of the Government's new strategy were felt: Chapter X of the Bill, relating to Managing Agencies was substantially altered and made more stringent; more important in the present context, the administration of the Act was brought firmly under Government control: the Company Law Committee had recommended that control lie with a central statutory authority on the lines of the American Securities and Exchange Commission; the Bill left the matter open; the Select Committee introduced a lay Advisory Commission with real powers in the hands of the state, while the Act finally provided for a new Department of Company Law Administration within the Ministry of Finance, with a fully-fledged Secretary responsible to the Minister.

[3] Quoted in *Hindu*, 26 September 1954.

first half of 1955, from January when nationalization was under discussion until the summer when the Government reiterated its intention of developing new fields, and placed limits on the concession areas and leases of private collieries although it undertook not to nationalize existing firms.[1] The Banking Companies (Amendment) Act, 1956, empowered the Reserve Bank to regulate the appointment and remuneration of banking executives, to appoint observers at Scheduled Bank Board meetings, and to obtain information over a wider range than hitherto.[2] The list could be extended.

At the same time, the Government set about buttressing the private sector with finance and technology. Besides many of the measures mentioned in Chapter 2,[3] most of which struck root during this period, the National Industrial Development Corporation was set up. Incorporated in October 1954, it was to have been a specialist entrepreneurial body in the purest sense, setting up new industries and processes and operating them until private capital came forward to take over, acting as a repository of skills and consultancy for private industry, and so on. In the event, the original conception was lost in the ebb-tide of state initiative which followed soon after.[4] The Government also overcame in 1956 its long-standing hesitations and set up a State Trading Corporation.[5] In one sense this was a pragmatic response to a growing need since India's trade abroad was branching out into new areas, particularly the Eastern Bloc countries; in another, it was indicative of the Government's new willingness to supplement and augment private capital where it found difficulty in adapting it to the task in hand.

IV SWING RIGHT

(a) *Domestic opposition:* The impetus behind the swing left soon ran out. The Andhra elections of February–March 1955 alerted Congress

[1] See *Capital*, 27 January 1955, p. 105; 9 June, p. 849; 7 July, p. 13; 18 August, p. 223.
[2] See Sukumar Chakrabarty, 'Banking Undergoes Structural Changes', *EW*, January 1957, p. 201.
[3] See above, pp. 48–50.
[4] It became 'in effect . . . an agency of the Ministry of Commerce and Industry to make loans for the modernisation of the cotton and jute textile industries' (Rosen, *Aspects of Industrial Finance*, p. 83), and by 1961 was considered redundant. (Report of the Estimates Committee, Lok Sabha, *Hindu*, 3 April 1961.)
[5] See above, p. 92.

to the fact that its own tactics and acceptance by Moscow had pulled the teeth of the Communist opposition; deep cracks appeared in the Praja Socialist Party later that year. By then many of the reforms and economic programmes the Government had launched were either completed or well under way. At the same time, private sector opposition grew with every manifestation of the new policy.

Indian capital took the *announcement* of a 'socialistic pattern' calmly, in marked contrast to its foreign counterpart.[1] 'As far as the Avadi Resolution goes', said G. L. Bansal, Secretary General of the Federation of Indian Chambers of Commerce and Industry, 'there is no question of an antithesis between the private sector and a movement towards a socialistic pattern. . . . it would be safe to say that even in a socialistic pattern of society, the private sector will have an important and growing role to play.'[2] 'Dalal Street wants more of this socialism', reported the *Economic Weekly*'s stock exchange correspondent from Bombay;[3] and J. R. D. Tata, despite the caution engendered by years under a hostile Government, was willing to give it a try:

If it means a society in which all have equal rights and opportunities, the underprivileged are protected and helped to a better life, economic activities are harnessed to constructive nation-building purposes and controlled by the state for the common good, and selfish abuses and antisocial acts are checked, then we should all support it.[4]

They were willing to back their judgement with finance. Although faltering now and again—the last quarter of 1954 was a particularly bad period—the bull market continued advancing on a broad front.[5]

This is not to say that they were happy with every manifestation of the Government's strategy. On the contrary, while the general statements were accepted calmly, detailed proposals—nationalization, the Plan, increased taxation and recasting the tax structure, the Fourth Amendment, state trading, the Companies Bill and Act—met with increasingly bitter and co-ordinated resistance. By August 1956 the first business organization with an openly political orientation, the Forum of Free Enterprise, had been formed. Significantly—for

---

[1] See below, p. 152.
[2] Quoted in N. Sreekantan Nair, 'The Myth of Congress Socialism', *The Call*, November 1955, p. 9.
[3] *EW*, 5 March 1955, p. 325, commenting on the post-Avadi budget.
[4] Chairman's address, Annual General Meeting, Tata Iron and Steel Co. Ltd., 25 August 1955, quoted in Prasad, *Economic Problems*, pp. 120–1 note 5.
[5] See Appendix 3, pp. 326–31, below.

mounting business opposition within received powerful reinforcement from abroad[1]—its literature featured as a motto the article of faith of the President of the World Bank, Eugene Black: 'People must come to accept private enterprise not as a necessary evil but as an affirmative good.'[2]

(b) *Climacteric 1957–8:* The Government gave some ground to its critics even in the high days of the swing left. The original plans for the Industrial Credit and Investment Corporation of India envisaged a state body to help finance the private sector. By the time it was registered in January 1955 it had become, at the instance of the World Bank, a private-sector body financed by private subscription in the United States, Britain, and India, as well as by the United States and Indian Governments, and enthusiastically welcomed in business circles.[3] When copper mining was reserved for the state in June 1956, the Indian Copper Corporation, the only active firm in the industry, was expressly exempted.[4]

The turn towards state enterprise in steel, marked by the Krupp-Demag contract of August 1953, the rejection of the Birla proposals for a steel mill in November 1954, and the negotiations for a Russian plant throughout the last quarter of that year, did not prevent the Tata Iron and Steel Co. Ltd. getting a Rs 20 crore loan from the Government in September 1954 and having its plans for expansion approved the following January. Electricity generation and distribution, strictly controlled under the terms of the Electricity (Supply) Act, 1948, regained considerable freedom with the Electricity (Supply) Amendment Act, 1956.

Partly in recognition of organizational realities, partly as an exercise in accommodating the critics, many of the early plans to refashion whole industries were not proceeded with. Coal, most sensitive gauge of state-private relations, was spared nationalization; and the private collieries were allowed successive increases in targets, from eight million tons in October 1955 (as against an increase of fifteen million in the public sector)[5] to ten million in May 1956 (twelve million in the public sector).[6] Plantation industries were left

---

[1] See below, pp. 152 ff.
[2] Quoted in Shonfield, *Attack on World Poverty*, p. 135.
[3] See above, p. 94 n. 3.   [4] *Capital*, 21 June 1956, p. 865.
[5] *Capital*, 3 November 1955, p. 579; 8 March 1956, p. 322.
[6] *Capital*, 3 May 1956, p. 637.

pretty much alone despite the far-reaching proposals of the Enquiry Commission.[1]

Coming when it did, the Industrial Policy Resolution of 30 April 1956 also marked a concession to the Government's critics. It made no bones about 'the state [having] . . . to assume direct responsibility for the future development of industries over a wider area'. But the fact that it recognized 'limiting factors' in this; that it accepted as desirable the development of private undertakings 'with as much freedom as possible, consistent with the targets and objectives of the national plan'; and offered aid to the private sector through developing services, fiscal measures, and finance, was balm to private capital. It 'has given perhaps the largest single fillip to Indian private industry in recent times', wrote the Minister of Finance;[2] 'Stock Market Welcomes The Industrial Policy Statement', was *Capital's* headline in Calcutta;[3] and in Bombay, the positive response of share prices was explained by the 'absence of any rigidity in implementing this policy within a given time limit and [the] scope given to the private sector to contribute its quota to the development of the country'.[4] The Federation of Indian Chambers of Commerce and Industry offered very moderate criticism,[5] as did the Chairman of the All-India Manufacturers' Organization.[6]

None the less, these were concessions. The fabric of the Government's economic policy remained. As late as the autumn of 1956, when the outlines of the foreign exchange crisis were beginning to be perceived, T. T. Krishnamachari, then Minister of Finance, was still able to take on the World Bank and reject its ultimatum.[7]

Within a year, however, the scene had changed. The acute shortage of foreign exchange strengthened the Government's critics at the same time as it enhanced their awareness of common interest. Concessions became so substantial as to affect, in practice, the Government's entire economic strategy.

(c) *Abridgement of the public sector:* In May 1958, the Second Plan was cut by a fifth. By 1961 the cut in real terms was more like two-

---

[1] See above, p. 137.

[2] In a letter to Eugene Black, Chairman, IBRD, 16 September 1956. See below, p. 156.

[3] 3 May 1956, p. 633.

[4] *EW*, 12 May 1956, p. 562. The market report was headlined: 'Operators Reconciled to New Policy'.

[5] As reported in the *Hindustan Times*, 7 May 1956.

[6] *Capital*, 10 May 1956, p. 678.   [7] See below, pp. 154 ff.

fifths. The Third Plan, 1961–6, suffered a similar fate; by the time it was finally presented, accounting changes and price rises had reduced it to three-quarters of its original size.[1] Prices have not stood still since with consequent reductions in the Plan's real volume, while foreign exchange stringencies and the impact of the Himalayan War have been such that the target itself has been generally written off as unattainable.[2]

The abridgement has not affected all branches of the economy equally. Since planning began, private capital has consistently overfulfilled its targets. In the First Plan, private investments reached Rs 1,800 crores[3] excluding transfers from the state, or Rs 200 crores more than anticipated.[4] In the Second, according to a rough official estimate, private investment overshot the mark of Rs 2,400 crores by no less than Rs 900 crores or nearly 40 per cent.[5]

Exception made for the heavier end of production,[6] its record in large-scale modern industry was as good. At Rs 850 crores, actual fixed investment during the Second Plan was one-quarter more than anticipated.[7] In a number of lighter industries—power-driven pumps, diesel engines, electric motors, ACSR cables, for example—production exceeded plans substantially.[8]

The projected shift towards state dominance in investment did not materialize. Originally it was thought that the state might undertake 53 per cent of all monetized investment during the First Plan[9] and 61 per cent during the Second.[10] In the event, state investment formed 43·7 per cent of total monetized investment in the First,[11] and even during the Second it reached no more than 51·1–54·1 per cent.[12]

---

[1] An early report projected a target outlay of Rs 9,900 crores at 1952–3 prices, in order to double national income by 1967– 8 and *per capita* income by 1973–4. In the event, the Third Plan target is Rs 9,950 crores at current prices, or some Rs 7,500 crores of 1952–3 value. Some Rs 1,350 crores (18 per cent) of this discrepancy is due to price increases, the rest to accounting changes. See A. K. Dasgupta, 'The Concept and the Size of the Third Plan', *EW*, June 1960, p. 851; also Little, in NIESR, *Review* No. 9, pp. 20–21.

[2] See above, p. 127.

[3] These are 'monetized' investments. For a discussion of the significance of the figure, see Malenbaum, *Prospects for Indian Development*, pp. 78–79, *passim*.

[4] PC, *Third Plan*, Table 1, p. 32.

[5] ibid., Table 5, p. 105. Including Rs 200 crores transferred from the State.

[6] See ibid., Table 1, p. 454.   [7] ibid., Table 2, p. 456.   [8] ibid., p. 454.

[9] Malenbaum, *Prospects*, Table 4, p. 81, and p. 215.

[10] From PC, *Second Plan*, pp. 56, 57.   [11] Malenbaum, *Prospects*, p. 215.

[12] The higher figure combines transfers to the private sector with state investment, the lower brackets them with private investment (see PC, *Third Plan*, pp. 32, 105).

As a proportion of total gross capital formation, monetized and non-monetized, planned and unplanned, the state's share was naturally smaller: 24·3 and 34·1 per cent during the First and Second Plans respectively.[1]

Nor did the anticipated shift of private savings to the state occur. It was to have amounted to between Rs 2,450 and Rs 2,850 crores during the Second Plan.[2] In the event, no more than Rs 2,360 crores were transferred, and that in an increasingly devalued currency.[3] At the same time, private resources in the crucial modern industries sector were augmented by Rs 230 crores or 37 per cent above planned targets, the largest single increase—Rs 100 crores—being from foreign sources.[4]

(d) *Encroachment by the private sector:* The relative diminution in its own resources and investment, coupled with the pressing need to increase production quickly, by whatever method, as well as the weight brought to bear by interested parties at home and abroad,[5] led the Government to condone a growing encroachment of private capital into spheres reserved—as late as April 1956—for the public sector. Of the seventeen industries listed in Schedule A of the Industrial Policy Resolution,[6] 'industries, the future development of which will be the exclusive responsibility of the state [and in which] all new units will be set up only by the state', seven at least have been opened to private interests since 1958 or thereabouts. These include *arms,*[7] *heavy plant and machinery,* an important part of whose output comes from ACC-Vickers-Babcox Ltd., Larsen and Toubro Ltd.,

[1] CSO, *National Income Statistics,* Table 8.2, p. 57.
[2] PC, *Second Plan,* p. 82.
[3] From PC, *Third Plan,* Table 2, p. 95, using the method outlined in PC, *Second Plan,* p. 82. Prices rose 30 per cent during the Second Plan (PC, *Third Plan,* p. 122).
[4] PC, *Third Plan,* Table 2, p. 456.   [5] See below, pp. 152 ff.
[6] 'Arms and ammunition and allied items of defense equipment; atomic energy; iron and steel; heavy castings and forgings of iron and steel; heavy plant and machinery required for iron and steel production, for mining, for machine tool manufacture and such other basic industries . . .; heavy electrical plant including large hydraulic and steam turbines; coal and lignite; mineral oils; mining of iron ore, manganese ore, chrome ore, gypsum, sulphur, gold and diamonds; mining and processing of copper, lead, zinc, tin, molybdenum, and wolfram; minerals specified in the Schedule to the Atomic Energy (Control of Production and Use) Order, 1953; aircraft; air transport; railway transport; ship building; telephones and telephone cables, telegraph and wireless apparatus (excluding radio receiving sets); generation and distribution of electricity.'
[7] See below, p. 151.

and Walchandnagar Industries Ltd.—all licensed early in 1959;[1] *heavy electrical plant*, whose already substantial private sector was further strengthened by the addition of a new English Electric plant near Madras early in 1959 and by a later decision to allow that company and others to undertake production of 'reserved items'.[2] They include the *processing of lead and zinc* in which new facilities were licensed in the private sector in 1958–9; the production of *telephone cables and telegraphic equipment*;[3] the *generation and distribution of electricity* and *coal* in which the target for private production has risen from 43·8 million tons a year at the end of the Second Plan, to some 61 million at the end of the Third.[4]

The greatest shift towards the private sector took place in 'Schedule B' industries which, by the terms of the 1956 Industrial Policy Resolution, were to be 'progressively state-owned and in which the state will therefore generally take the initiative in establishing new undertakings'. Twelve industries are listed.[5] In at least nine, the private sector has made most of the running since 1957–8; and in some of them all the running.

While expansion in *aluminium* production was allocated to the public sector in the Second Plan document,[6] a private sector project was announced in March 1958[7] and a collaboration agreement reached early in October between Kaiser and Birla interests to set up a 20,000-ton plant.[8] The industry has since then been handed over almost entirely to the private sector.[9] Early in 1956, the

---

[1] See below, p. 207.

[2] See below, p. 202 and refs. Licences to produce *large transformers* have been granted the Kirloskar Electric Co. Ltd. Bangalore; Hackbridge-Hewittic and Easum Private Ltd. Madras; Hindustan Electric Co. Ltd. Bombay; Transformers and Switchgear Ltd. Madras; Electric Construction and Equipment Co. Ltd. Calcutta; Gandhi Electric Co. Ltd. Bombay; Hitachi Transformers and Electricals (Kerala) Ltd. Trivandrum. Licences for *high tension switchgear* were granted English Electric Co. Madras; Jyoti Ltd. Baroda; Mysore Electrical Industries Ltd. Bangalore; Electric Construction and Equipment Co. Ltd. Calcutta; Hindustan Electrical Co. Ltd. Bombay. (*Capital*, 30 August 1962, p. 310.)

[3] See below, pp. 202–4.   [4] PC, *Third Plan*, pp. 511, 519, 520.

[5] 'All other minerals except "minor minerals" as defined in Section 3 of the Minerals Concession Rules, 1949; aluminium and other non-ferrous metals not included in Schedule "A"; machine tools; ferro-alloys and tool steels; basic and intermediate products required by chemical industries . . .; antibiotics and other essential drugs; fertilizers; synthetic rubber; carbonization of coal; chemical pulp; road transport; sea transport.'

[6] p. 404.   [7] It was not followed through. See above, p. 116.

[8] Announced by Edgar F. Kaiser in Bombay, 9 October 1958 (*FT*, 10 October).

[9] See below, pp. 197–9 ff.

Thacker Committee on *machine tools* allocated new products between the six principal manufacturers, responsible for some four-fifths of total output by value.[1] Three of these were private sector firms. Industrial Policy Resolution notwithstanding, the allocation of Second and Third Plan targets shows the Government to be committed to parity in development between the two sectors in this rapidly growing industry.[2] Plans for *ferro-alloys and tool steels* have been drawn and redrawn since 1958. The *Draft Third Plan*, published in June 1960, allocated just over a third of target capacity to the private sector,[3] as did a Ministry of Iron and Steel Press Release dated 26 September. By the time the *Third Five Year Plan* was published in 1961, the target ratio was altered to 50 : 50.[4] By then, however, licences had been issued for 261,000 tons capacity, some 160,000 tons of which were in the private sector.[5]

Plans for *basic chemicals and intermediates* followed a similar course. In 1956 the Government looked as if it would take advantage of a Russian offer to help set up an integrated drug industry, an important component of which would have been a new chemical intermediates plant of 94,000 tons a year capacity.[6] Opposition to the scheme was fierce and well organized. By the time a second Russian team was invited to report in February 1958, their terms of reference had been narrowed and the plant abandoned. A revised project—a 25,000 ton per year unit planned at Panvel, near Bombay, with West German aid—was abandoned in its turn in 1963 leaving considerable scope for private production. Plans for *antibiotics and other essential drugs* are closely related to those for chemical intermediates. Here again, state projects were drastically curtailed in 1957–8, and the private sector given its head.[7]

Evidence of rethinking the allocation of *fertilizer production* appeared with the appointment in 1959 of Dr. G. P. Kane to investigate future requirements and production. His report proved to be a turning point for the industry. Satish Chandra, Deputy Minister

[1] M. K. Mathulla, Managing Director, Hindustan Machine Tools (Private) Ltd., 'The Vital Importance of Machine Tools', Supplement to *Capital*, 27 June 1957, pp. 43–45; *EE*, 8 March 1957, p. 347; Supplement to *Capital*, 23 June 1960, p. 53.
[2] *EE*, 8 February 1957, p. 197; PC, *Third Plan*, p. 474.
[3] PC, *Third Five Year Plan. A Draft Outline*, p. 225.   [4] p. 469.
[5] Ministry of Iron and Steel cited in Supplement to *Capital*, 28 June 1962, p. 17.
[6] S. S. Sokhey, *The Indian Drug Industry and its Future*, p. 10.
[7] See below, pp. 163 ff., 211 ff.

for Commerce and Industry, called on United States interests to fill the 'gap of 600,000 tons between the expected installed capacity in 1962 and the target fixed for the third Plan';[1] the Government accepted a Ford Foundation offer 'to create interest among US investors in collaborating with Indian industrialists in the establishment of fertilizer plants in the private sector';[2] and over one-quarter of target capacity was allocated to private industry in the Third Plan.[3] Production of *synthetic rubber* is wholly within the private sector.[4]

Official policy on *road transport* has changed as radically. Accepted in principle in 1950–1,[5] nationalization was kept in abeyance for the period of the Second Plan and private operators assisted to form viable units.[6] It was finally rejected in the first half of 1958 and the States' share for the Third Plan pegged at 30 per cent—the proportion ruling in 1961.[7] Policy towards *sea transport* has been and still is complicated by the predominance of foreign shipping in India's international trade, and by its strength even in home and adjacent waters.[8] However, despite somewhat stormy relations with the Government, the Indian private sector has been helped to grow through the Shipping Development Fund, has been able to influence policy through the National Shipping Board and, in 1961, was enabled to increase its size by half at one *coup* when the Jayanti Shipping Corporation was licensed and loaned Rs 20 crores for the purchase of a fleet.

These examples complete the tally of industries listed in Schedules A and B of the 1956 Industrial Policy Resolution. They do not reveal the extent to which such encroachments are self-perpetuating. By over-licensing the private sector;[9] by allowing investments in specified industries to take place freely; by condoning delays of three or four years in every major state unit while simultaneously permitting the private sector to overreach its targets, the Government constantly adds to the backlog in public utility output.[10] The result is that pressure builds up for the 'Government [to] concentrate its full attention on augmenting rail transport capacity, power and services such as telephones and telegraphs instead of dissipating its limited

---

[1] *Hindu*, 13 May 1960.   [2] *FT*, 7 September 1960.   [3] PC, *Third Plan*, p. 479.
[4] See below, p. 216.   [5] See PC, *First Plan*, p. 483.   [6] PC, *Second Plan*, p. 479.
[7] *EW*, July 1958, p. 95; PC, *Third Plan*, p. 554.
[8] See below, pp. 218 ff.   [9] See, for example, p. 125.
[10] Some of the shortfall is noted in PC, *Third Plan*, pp. 453–4.

resources of personnel on a wider front.'[1] If successful—and the Government is open to pressure from a number of directions at once[2]—the private sector has even greater incentive to encroach on 'reserved' industries, greater need for services from the public sector, with the result that the backlog grows.

The Rihand power project to Uttar Pradesh might illustrate the process. Conceived largely as a means of providing power to the 4,000 tube-wells in the State and a large number of river pumping stations which, together, were to irrigate some two million acres by the end of the Second Plan, the project's output was pre-empted for other purposes well before it went on stream: 55,000 kW were allocated to the Kaiser-Birla Hindustan Aluminium Corporation, 40,000 kW to the railways for a factory at Moghulserai, 10,000 kW for Madhya Pradesh to compensate for submerged land in that State. Nothing was left for the original purpose and a very large additional thermal power station had to be planned at Moghulserai.[3]

(e) *Ideological retreat*: The recital of physical encroachments on public sector spheres does little justice to the change in the Government's *attitude* towards private capital. Although there was nothing new in their continued rejection of nationalization,[4] a new tone of apology crept into their argument for state enterprise. Opening Tata's ferro-manganese plant in the Joda valley early in 1958, H. K. Mahatab, Chief Minister of Orissa, 'pointed out that even the three steel plants under the public sector would have gone to the

[1] From a Resolution at FICCI's 1962 Session, quoted in *Capital*, 29 March 1962, p. 557. The passage begins: 'there is considerable scope for industrial expansions and development and . . . businessmen are willing and capable of shouldering additional responsibilities. . . .'

[2] Following closely on the Centre's refusal to allow expansion in private electricity undertakings (September 1962), M. N. Lakshminarasiah, Andhra Industries Minister, assured business: 'The Andhra Government will allow any private industrialist to produce power in the State whatever the Central Government may say.' (*Hindu*, 18 October 1962.)

[3] *Capital*, 9 April 1959, p. 481; 6 August 1959, p. 177.

[4] See above, pp. 133 ff. To resume the dossier of official denials, the tea industry was reassured about the Government's intentions in May 1957, road transport early in 1958, the banks by the Finance Minister in April 1959, road transport by the Minister of Transport and Communications again in July, industry in general by the Prime Minister that month, general insurance by the Finance Minister in August, banking again by the Minister of Revenue and Civil Expenditure that month, coal by the Minister of Steel, Mines, and Fuel in November, and general insurance again in March 1960. The dossier is by no means complete.

private sector if [a] sufficient number of private people had come forward'.[1] If there was any reason for the Government to undertake production at all, it was, as Lal Bahadur Shastri, then Minister for Commerce and Industry, told a business gathering, because the investment was too large or complex for the private sector or 'because the Government were able to get more reasonable terms than the private sector could manage'.[2] Nehru crystallized the new tone at the 1962 Session of the Federation of Indian Chambers of Commerce and Industry: 'Private enterprise is a good thing in India. The suppression of private enterprise was bad.'[3]

The Government began toying with the idea of associating private capital more closely with state enterprise. In April 1958, they embarked on a process of 'non-officialisation' of public sector projects and went some way[4] before being halted at the instance of a Congress Committee chaired by Krishna Menon. Later the Planning Commission recommended that 20–25 per cent of shares in profitable public sector projects be sold on the market.[5] Although finally rejected by the Cabinet as unworkable,[6] the fact that it was made and considered shows how far official thinking had swung round from the state capitalist trend of two or three years earlier.[7]

(f) *Labour policy hardens: The Second Five Year Plan* promised to evolve a 'wage policy which aims at a structure with rising real wages', and laid down 'principles to bring wages into conformity with the expectations of the working class in the future pattern of

[1] *Hindu*, 21 April 1958.

[2] Meeting of the Federation of Andhra Pradesh Chambers of Commerce and Industry (*Hindu*, 1 January 1961).

[3] Quoted in *ET*, 25 March 1962.

[4] Chandulal Parekh was installed as Chairman of the State Trading Corporation, and D. P. Goenka and P. S. Lokanathan came on to its Board; A. R. Bhatt, President of the Maharashtra Chamber of Commerce, became chairman of Hindustan Antibiotics; Mehar Chand Mahajan, a retired Judge, was proposed for the Chair of Nangal Fertilisers and Chemicals; and K. K. Birla for the Chair of Hindustan Cables Ltd. (*Capital*, 10 April 1958, p. 540.)

[5] The Planning Commission's study group—D. L. Mazumdar, S. Bhoothalingam, S. Ranganathan, Tarlok Singh—was appointed in August 1960; its proposals accepted by the Commission as a whole in January 1961.

[6] B. R. Bhagat, Deputy Minister of Finance, to the Rajya Sabha, reported in *Hindu*, 5 November 1962. The paper commented: this 'cannot be regarded as the last word on the subject'.

[7] The trend towards state-run industry had always been weaker at the State level, and the retreat more precipitous. See, for example, 'Public Sector on Sale', *EW*, 14 December 1963, p. 2029.

society'.[1] It ruled that 'rationalisation should . . . be attempted [only] when it does not lead to unemployment, is introduced in consultation with workers, and is effected after improving working conditions and guaranteeing a substantial share of gains to workers'.[2] It even suggested a system of workers' 'association with management'.[3] These were notable advances on the First Plan's virtual wage freeze[4] and its recognition of the 'imperative need to reduce costs by rationalising industrial processes'.[5] They completely reversed the dominant trend in labour legislation throughout the first half of the decade.[6]

Growing industrial unrest from 1956, and in particular the wave of strikes by Government workers, railway and port workers, and in the coal and steel belt, in 1957–8, carried these promises a long way towards consolidation at the 15th and 16th Indian Labour Conferences in December 1957 and May 1958. At the same time, together with the formation of a Communist Ministry in Kerala on 1 April 1957, they led to a fundamental review of the new labour policy. The Central Pay Commission, August 1957–December 1959, was crucial to this review.[7] Its recommendations were quickly adopted and widely regarded as a definitive statement of a new and hard official attitude to labour in general, as indeed they were.[8] The 17th Labour Conference, July 1959, anticipating the *Report* by six months, was remarkable chiefly for the Government's obstructive attitude towards the unions;[9] and the Central Government Workers' strike called in July 1960 in protest at its recommendations was met head on with the Essential Services Ordinance, a refusal to parley,

---

[1] PC, *Second Plan*, pp. 578, 579.   [2] ibid., p. 581.   [3] ibid., p. 577.
[4] PC, *First Plan*, p. 583.   [5] ibid., p. 590.   [6] See above, pp. 88–89.
[7] The Commission was appointed under threat of a strike by Government workers. Its deliberations were closely watched and its conclusions guided. One example will do. Early in its work, towards the end of April 1958, it learned through a Secretary to the *Ministry of Finance* that 'the recommendations of the Labour Conference should not be regarded as decisions of Government', that they had 'not been formally ratified by the Central Government', and that 'Government have, at no time, committed themselves to taking executive action to enforce their recommendations'. Eight months later the Minister of *Labour* was still of the opinion that 'the decisions of the Conference . . . are to be taken as binding on the parties'. (See Report of the Secretariat, United Trade Union Congress, Fourth All-India Conference, Hasimara, West Bengal, excerpts published in *The Call*, May 1960, p. 12; *Five Glorious Days*, p. 11; Karnik, *Indian Trade Unions*, p. 183).
[8] See, for example, Karnik, op. cit., pp. 245–7.
[9] See official and trade union documents reprinted in *Seventeenth Tripartite*, All-India Trade Union Congress, New Delhi, 1959; UTUC Report, loc. cit.

full mobilization of the Home Guard and Territorial Army, mass arrests, suspensions and dismissals—all in marked contrast to the treatment meted out the same body of workers three years previously.[1]

By the time *The Third Five Year Plan* was published, labour policy had turned full circle. Real wage increases were again linked to increases in productivity and workers were exhorted 'to insist on and not resist the progress of rationalisation in their own interest and in the larger interest of the country'.[2]

(g) *Indian capital responds:* The private sector boom regained its former vigour under the new treatment.[3] Its spokesmen took it upon themselves to reassure foreign investors.[4]

Its leading figures did their best to lay the ghost of runaway state capitalism at home. G. D. Birla told a Federation luncheon: 'industry should welcome [the 'socialistic pattern of society'] in its own interest. Socialism must depend on production of more wealth.'[5] He assured his shareholders 'that the public sector is, even now, helping to give a tremendous push to the private sector', and drew attention to the large number of 'ancillary industries [that] have already been set up in the private sector to cater for the requirements during the period of erection of the industries set up in the public sector'.[6]

The most eloquent testimony to Indian capital's new mood came at the Federation's 31st annual meeting in March 1958. Considered an 'outstanding' session, it was conspicuous for the fact that, to quote a report, 'businessmen have recovered their confidence and are speaking their minds freely and unafraid'.[7]

Indian capital has continued expressing satisfaction with the Government:

the business community is in complete agreement with the socialistic objectives of the Government and there are no two opinions on that score;[8] there is no fundamental or ideological difference between the business community and the Government;[9] over the years, much of the seeming cleavage in the approach of the

---

[1] See *Five Glorious Days*, Chapter 3.   [2] p. 262.
[3] See above, p. 126.   [4] See below, p. 158.   [5] *Hindu*, 11 March 1958.
[6] Address to the Annual Meeting of the United Commercial Bank, *Capital*, 9 April 1949, p. 493.
[7] *EE*, 14 March 1958, p. 561.
[8] Tulsidas Kilachand, moving the Resolution on Economic Policy at the Federation's 1962 session (quoted in *Hindu*, 25 March 1962).
[9] G. D. Somani, quoted in ibid.

Government and the private sector to the problems of economic development has narrowed down to matters of detail.[1]

At the same time it has shown increasing dissatisfaction with the balance of the mixed economy. Already at the crucial 1958 session of the Federation, Babubhai Chinai, the President, felt confident enough to demand denationalization of life insurance.[2] Claims for private entry into iron and steel and petroleum were advanced the following year.[3] They reached a crescendo after the 1962 elections while the economy was seizing up through lack of foreign exchange. 'We must produce more', demanded G. D. Birla, 'never mind who produces it. Cut the controls and turn a Nelson eye to the policy resolutions that lay down that certain developments . . . belong only to the public domain.'[4] The Federation followed with a demand for private participation on the manufacture of power-generating equipment.[5] It was suggested that panels of businessmen be formed to advise the State Trading Corporation,[6] and much more on the same lines.

In step with this change of mood, a new party, Swatantra, the first political organization devoted almost exclusively to the furtherance of private enterprise, was formed in the summer of 1959. Significantly, it was the first split Congress had suffered from the Right.

(*h*) *Himalayan War:* The trends outlined in this section gained powerful impetus from the war. For the first time, private capital was associated with military production: munitions components, radar and electronic equipment, army vehicle parts.[7] The Government discontinued investments in its own Shipping Corporation and diverted funds to the private sector.[8] Detailed administration of price controls was handed over to the controlled industries.[9] A number of

[1] *ET*, 25 March 1962, commenting on Nehru's speech to the Federation's annual session (see excerpt, p. 148, above).

[2] *EE*, 14 March 1958, p. 561.

[3] Federation of Indian Chambers of Commerce and Industry, *The Third Five Year Plan—A Tentative Outline*, published on the eve of the All-India Congress Committee session at Chandigarh, September 1959.

[4] *Guardian*, 8 March 1962.   [5] *ET*, 17 April 1962.

[6] S. S. Sharma, President, at the second annual meeting of the Bharat Chemical Importers' and Distributors' Association, Calcutta (*ET*, 28 April 1962).

[7] *ET*, 16 May, 21 May, 9 June, 1963; Romesh Thapar, *EW*, 20 April 1963, p. 661.

[8] *ET*, 4 March 1963.

[9] Vanaspati, rubber, textiles in May 1963 (*ET*, 22, 27 May).

state projects were dropped—a phytochemical plant in Kerala, a big chemical intermediates plant at Panvel, Maharashtra—and some of their programme handed to the private sector.[1] While taxation rose phenomenally with the 1963–4 Budget, the Super Profits Tax was progressively modified to limits acceptable to business.[2]

The shift to the right, marked by the third general election in 1962, was confirmed in a number of key by-elections in the summer of 1963. It was even more pronounced within Congress, where the 'Left' or state capitalist wing sustained heavy losses: first Krishna Menon, Minister of Defence, then K. D. Malaviya, Minister for Mines and Fuel, were forced out of the Cabinet, while Bijoyananda Patnaik, Chief Minister of Orissa, was effectively prevented from entering it.[3] Finally, Indian labour has been trapped between rising prices, deteriorating conditions, and the legal inhibitions of protest embodied in the Defence of India Regulations, the constitutional amendments, and many of the other rules and ordinances promulgated in the name of the Emergency and still—summer 1964—in force.

V GOVERNMENT AND FOREIGN CAPITAL

(a) *Swing Left:* Congress's policy swings did more than reflect changes in the international scene. They also effected minor changes in it.

The swing left was greeted with alarm in the West. Cause and effect were pointedly, and unscrupulously, reversed to derive the new policy from Nehru's visit to China in November 1954 rather than the other way about.[4] The financial press featured ominous headlines: 'More State Control in India, Government Industrial

[1] See below, p. 164.
[2] See I. S. Gulati, 'Modified SPT', *EW*, 4 May, 11 May, 22 June, 1963.
[3] Menon went at the end of October 1962, Malaviya in mid-June 1963. Nehru was compelled to deny any intention of including Patnaik in the Cabinet in March 1963. In each case charges of nepotism or corruption were made to justify their exclusion; but these were clearly items in a brief rather than the fundamental motive. For the ubiquity of such corruption in Government circles see *The Times*'s Delhi correspondent, 'India Fights Against Corruption' (*The Times*, 5 August 1964).
[4] See, for example, *MG*, 29 November 1954: 'There is a growing feeling among industrialists that the Government's policy in the last two weeks, especially since Mr. Nehru's return from China, has hardened against private enterprise and vigorously shifted in favour of national control'; *FT*, 23 May 1955: 'The move to the Left in India began last Autumn when Mr. Nehru returned from China'.

Monopolies Doubled'.[1] Indian experts warned that the country was 'moving away from its earlier middle-of-the-road course'.[2] The United States Government made it known that 'help to India would be based on licensing or investment arrangements "for mutual profit" between US and Indian private enterprise instead of through loans and grants'.[3]

More important at the time, since it was first in the field with development finance and was to play a key role in coordinating Government aid, was the response of the World Bank. The Bank had never hidden its active espousal of private enterprise, particularly foreign private enterprise. From its inception its role 'was to be marginal—marginal to private international investment, and marginal to domestic investment in the member countries themselves'.[4] And since India now became the first borrower of importance to appear to threaten the Bank's assumptions, it was in India that the direct, public confrontation of ideologies took place.

The first intimations of battle came early in the swing left. In the course of the negotiations between Krupp-Demag and the Indian Government over the Rourkela steel plant,[5] the Bank appeared willing to lend one-third of the required capital if Krupp and the Government each took a like share. One study ran:

It was the Bank's expectation that eventually the loan would be converted into stock and sold on the Indian market to private investors when the steel mill becomes a proven enterprise. At the same time, Krupp would have a sufficiently large stockholding in the enterprise to permit it to be in control of the technical and managerial aspects.

The Government of India, however, would not accept virtual IBRD-

---

[1] *FT*, 1 May 1956, featuring a story on the Industrial Policy Resolution, 1956.
[2] Geoffrey Tyson, Secretary, India, Pakistan, Burma Association, 'Role of Foreign Investments', *FT* Survey of India, 13 August 1956.
[3] *EE*, 8 March 1957, p. 347, reporting a meeting between machine-tool manufacturers and the US Department of Commerce.
[4] 'A Note on the World Bank', prepared by the staff of the IBRD, Appendix to Eugene R. Black, *The Diplomacy of Economic Development*, p. 62. Eugene Black's views were uncompromising: 'if the real benefits of industrialisation are to be obtained . . . Governments should undertake [industrial] ventures, if at all, only as a last alternative and only after a full examination of other alternatives that exist. And even in cases where a government may go as far as to start an industrial enterprise, I think every effort should be made to put the venture into the hands of private capital and private management as quickly as possible.' (Address to Annual Meeting of IBRD, *IFNS*, 23 September 1955, p. 103.) See also A. H. Hanson, *Public Enterprise and Economic Development*, pp. 19–20, for a summary of IBRD attitudes as expressed in its country surveys.
[5] See above, p. 93.

Krupp control of a steel mill in India. Krupp, in turn, was willing to reduce its equity to ten per cent of the paid-up capital. This, however, was unacceptable to the IBRD as it was contrary to its policy of not financing government-controlled industrial enterprise.[1]

Relations worsened steadily thereafter, but it was not until the autumn of 1956, with the swing left in full flood, and after it had received its Mission's report on India, that the Bank issued a public ultimatum. A letter from Eugene Black, Chairman, to T. T. Krishnamachari, Minister of Finance, set out the Bank's over-all policy, none the less forcefully for being couched in personal terms:

In making my own comments [wrote Black], I should like first to emphasise once again that India's interest lies in giving private enterprise, both Indian and foreign, every encouragement to make its maximum contribution to the development of the economy particularly in the industrial field. While I recognise that the Government of India itself must play an important role in India's economic development, I have the distinct impression that the potentialities of private enterprise are commonly underestimated in India and that its operations are subjected to unnecessary restrictions there.

Turning to the report of the Bank's Mission to India, it continued:

The Bank . . . shares the Mission's conviction that in so far as the public sector is concerned, the program is too large to be completed in five years. Quite apart from possible financial limitations, it seems inevitable in the light of past experience in India and elsewhere that the execution of projects will be delayed by administrative difficulties and by a lack of trained managerial and technical personnel with experience of large-scale construction and industrial operations. This makes it all the more important that every effort should be made to secure the technical co-operation and financial support of foreign private enterprise in carrying out the development program. The Bank welcomes the arrangements that have been made to associate foreign firms with the construction and operation of a large number of major undertakings, both in the public and the private sectors, but hopes that more positive measures will be taken to facilitate foreign investment, and that consideration will be given to the suggestions made by the Mission in its Memorandum.

The Bank did not confine itself to *hoping* for a change of heart:

We feel that we would have to consider the pace and scale of our further loan operation in India from time to time in the light of economic conditions and prospects and taking into consideration the economic policies pursued by your Government. On the one hand, we should have to take into account the extent and the character of the impact on India's balance

[1] Friedmann and Kalmanoff, *Joint International Business Ventures*, p. 420.

of payments of the service of external debt contracted from sources other than the Bank. On the other hand, our disposition to lend would be favourably influenced by the amount of external financial assistance which India obtains without incurring fixed foreign exchange obligations.[1]

For a time, the Government appeared unshaken by criticism from abroad. The severity of the foreign exchange crisis had yet to be appreciated,[2] and Government spokesmen continued in an independent vein. Thus T. T. Krishnamachari, Minister for Commerce and Industry: 'as far as private [foreign] investment is concerned, India is not a country which was likely to attract "venture capital". That would want far more than what the country could afford to give.'[3] Thus too, in sharp rejoinder to a foreign journal's complaint of 'continuous sniping and carping at private enterprise', an authoritative spokesman of the Ministry said, 'it is too late to ask India to believe that she "needs capital and capitalism desperately".'[4] And again Krishnamachari: 'I do not subscribe to the view that the need for foreign capital is as great as India's poverty.'[5] Ministers felt free to reprimand foreign interests: C. D. Deshmukh, Minister of Finance, 'advised' that it would be in their interests to allow a 'certain amount of Indian participation';[6] and Krishnamachari, while reassuring his audience about the consequences of the Constitutional Amendment, went on to berate the Associated Chambers' annual gathering for trying to hold on to India as an export outlet and for their 'hesitancy to entrust the Indian concerns with . . . knowhow'. Turning to particular industries, he said: 'Vested interests in shipping are not merely slow in recognising the need of Indian shipping, but would like to see that Indian shipping does not develop.'[7]

Not all Government statements were couched in these harsh tones; nor was there ever any suggestion of keeping foreign capital out. On the contrary, it was invited to invest in a number of industries such as heavy chemicals, pharmaceuticals, synthetic oil, heavy machinery, iron and steel, and aircraft manufacturing.[8] The

---

[1] Letter dated 5 September 1956.   [2] See above, p. 126.
[3] As reported in *Hindu*, 1 January 1955.
[4] In reply to the *Investors' Chronicle*, London, *Hindu*, 19 January 1955.
[5] To the Annual Meeting of the Associated Chambers of Commerce and Industry, as reported in *Hindu*, 13 December 1955.
[6] *FT*, 17 November 1955.   [7] As reported in *Hindu*, 13 December 1955.
[8] See, for example, Gulzarilal Nanda, Minister of Planning, speech to the Colombo Plan Consultative Committee, Singapore, October 1955 (*CSM*, 27 October 1955).

dominant theme was, however, one of independence and reluctance to admit the necessity of compromising with foreign interests. For example, the Government shied away from concluding an Investment Guarantee Agreement for which the United States were pressing throughout this period. Agreement seemed within reach in the autumn of 1955 when opposition to its compensation clause, voiced by the Minister of Commerce and Industry, managed to shelve it for two years, by which time conditions and attitudes had changed fundamentally.

(b) *Swing Right:* By the summer of 1956 the Government was sufficiently perturbed at the foreign exchange position to survey prospects abroad. In June and July, B. K. Nehru toured Western Europe in search of private loans; in August, following discussions with the Minister of Commerce and Industry, a Federation delegation set out on the same tour 'to find out what was the attitude of . . . big industry in these countries towards India and her plans for industrialisation'.[1] In December, the Prime Minister visited the United States.

At the same time a new emphasis was discernible in official statements. While rejecting the World Bank's ultimatum, Krishnamachari did not engage with Black ideologically. In his reply he merely emphasized 'that in Indian conditions the maintenance of social stability—which is even more important than financial stability—depends wholly on the pace at which development proceeds', and drew attention to the fact that the Government's most recent Industrial Policy Statement had been welcomed enthusiastically by Indian Business.[2] In relation to foreign capital he found it expedient to stress an earlier theme: as he told an Indian business audience in May, 'it is not the Government but Indian capital who opposes the participation of foreign capital in Indian enterprises';[3] and to a largely foreign audience he repeated in December, 'so far as the Government are concerned, it would welcome foreign capital, but foreign capital would have to make its terms with indigenous capital and enterprise'. It was at this meeting that he revealed that the

---

[1] *Hindu*, 26 September 1956.
[2] Letter dated 16 September 1956. See excerpt quoted above, p. 141.
[3] Speech at the opening of the Indian Exchange Building, Calcutta, reported in *Hindu*, 11 May 1958. The theme itself harks back to the period of domestic capital shyness soon after Independence; see above, pp. 78 f.

Government was not wedded to Indian majority holdings in foreign-initiated firms.[1]

These early feelers did not go unnoticed. One observer wrote early in 1957:

For foreign capital, the future appears more favourable than it has done for some years. Recent foreign exchange difficulties have reaffirmed the need for it. The difficulties under which it has to operate are better appreciated than they were. Even the impossible burden of taxation under which the foreign executive has to work is receiving attention.[2]

Nor were they unreciprocated. It was at about this time, impelled by the sharpening of competition internationally as well as by the expansion of the Indian market, that Western business started showing real interest, and a number of major contracts were signed.[3]

The first massive effort to attract Western finance had to await the summer of 1957. The occasion was a loan-raising tour of Western capitals by T. T. Krishnamachari, Minister of Finance, concerted with another by key business figures, the Indian Industrial Mission. Both parties set out to dispel any misgivings about the 'socialist pattern' and to project India as a safe and desirable haven for foreign capital.

The message was put over unadorned. 'Let me say quite categorically', begged Krishnamachari in New York, 'that Socialism in India indicates nothing more sinister than a society in which there is equality of opportunity. . . . The basic desiderata of an egalitarian society as we understand it are precisely those of the American society as it now exists'.[4] H. V. R. Iengar, Governor of the Reserve Bank, echoed:

The 'Socialism' contemplated in India does not, by any stretch of the imagination mean communism; it does not mean state capitalism. . . . It is a system under which private competitive enterprise has and will

[1] Speech at the Annual Meeting, Associated Chambers of Commerce and Industry, Calcutta, reported in *Hindu*, 11 December 1956. Krishnamachari returned to the subject at a meeting held under the auspices of the Indian Council of Public Affairs in Madras (*Hindu*, 16 February 1957).

[2] *FT*, 9 January 1957.

[3] See above, p. 120 n. 4. British observers were particularly anxious about losing out to commercial rivals; see, for example, Stephen Garvin's report of a tour undertaken for the Federation of British Industries in January–March 1956, *India: A Survey for British Industrial Firms*; see also Daniel Duxbury in *FT*, 21 March 1956.

[4] Address to a meeting of the Far East Congress, quoted in *The Call*, December 1957, p. 5.

continue to have a vital role to play; it is a system which respects private property and provides for the payment of compensation if such property is acquired by the state. I submit there is nothing in the system which should be repugnant to the social conscience of the USA.[1]

The private delegation followed suit: the Government's attitude to foreign capital, G. D. Birla told the Far East America Council for Commerce and Industry, 'is favourable and indeed much more receptive than in 1948'.[2] General propagandist statements were of course not enough. 'It is no secret that the attempts by capital goods exporters to raise lines of credit for Indian business in the City have met with little success in the past two months', *The Times* warned the visitors to London;[3] 'If India wants new private investment from abroad, she must be ready to treat existing private capital less unfavourably', confirmed the *Financial Times*.[4]

The point was taken. As an earnest of the Government's announced intention not to require majority Indian ownership of joint ventures under the so-called '51 per cent rule',[5] Ceat Tyres of India Ltd. were licensed in February 1958 on a 60 : 40 Italian : Indian basis;[6] the Indo-US Convertibility Agreement was signed on 19 September 1957;[7] and the first of a series of tax concessions to foreign firms were made—affecting salaries (May 1957), wealth tax (July), and supertax (September). It was at this time too that foreign firms were invited to take up the more profitable parts of state-reserved industries, notably

---

[1] Speech at an international conference of industrialists, California, delivered at the same time, quoted by Tridib Kumar Chaudhuri, MP, Lok Sabha, 20 April 1959, and reprinted in *The Call*, May 1959, p. 14.

[2] *Hindu*, 13 September 1957. Cf. Krishnamachari to the Lok Sabha before leaving the country: Government 'wanted to encourage the flow of [foreign] capital not retard it. The Government's attitude towards foreign funds was totally different today from what it was in 1948.' (*The Times*, 5 September 1957.)

[3] 26 August 1957.   [4] 27 August 1957.

[5] The announcement was first made in India in December 1956 (see above, p. 157). It was repeated abroad throughout the tour during the summer of the following year, and by business leaders in capital exporting countries thereafter. See, for example, Sir Norman Kipping, Director General, Federation of British Industries, addressing the Indian Chamber of Commerce in Great Britain (*FT*, 1 March 1958). Kipping also revealed that British investors were invited to join with the Indian Government on a minority ownership basis and yet with full managerial control, the Government transferring its share to the Life Insurance Corporation after the project began to make profits, or in any event, within five years. (*Financial News*, cited in *EW*, 15 March 1958, p. 368.)

[6] Ceat Tyres' application was widely regarded as a test case at the time. See, for example, *EW*, 15 February 1958, p. 243; Sharokh Sabavala, *CSM*, 5 May 1958.

[7] See above, p. 120.

in drugs, aluminium, heavy electrical equipment, fertilizers, and synthetic rubber.

The response was gratifying. The World Bank organized a relief operation which brought India more than $600 million in loans within six months;[1] private capital began to flow in increasing quantities.[2] Foreign interests in India seemed satisfied; the Associated Chambers' President, W. H. S. Michelmore, was notably conciliatory at the annual meeting in December 1957.[3]

Outside comment ranged from the approving—'the climate for American private investment is basically good'[4]—to the ecstatic: 'In a surprising turnabout, India, while still preaching socialism, is giving an exciting demonstration of the unique power of free enterprise to build its economy.'[5]

In broad outline, Government policy has remained very much the same since. The flow of encouraging noises has continued. Corporate taxation on income and royalties was reduced in the 1959 and 1961 Finance Acts (until reversed after the Himalayan War); and exemption for foreign technicians—a loose and rather all-embracing term —was standardized at three years. Double taxation avoidance agreements have been concluded with a number of creditor countries including Sweden, Norway, Denmark, West Germany, and Japan; another, with the United States, has been ratified by India and is awaiting American approval (summer 1964). The processing of foreign investment projects has been streamlined: in April 1960 much of the red tape connected with sanctions for manufacturing investments was cut; in February 1961, the Indian Investment Centre, an autonomous, high-powered body with branches abroad, was inaugurated to ease and advise on collaboration ventures between foreign and Indian capital;[6] in May, a senior official of the Ministry

[1] See above, p. 120.   [2] See below, p. 301.

[3] *Capital*, 19 December 1957, pp. 837–8. Nehru's presence at the meeting for the first time in a number of years showed that conciliation was not all one way.

[4] Nathaniel Knowles, Deputy Director, Bureau of Foreign Commerce, US Department of Commerce, commenting on a nine-week tour (*NYT*, 7 January 1959).

[5] *Readers' Digest*, US edition, December 1957, p. 111. The article did not appear in the Indian edition of that date. It continued: 'Today, T. T. Krishnamachari, Minister of Finance, and Morarji Desai, Minister of Commerce and Industry, both conservative and practical men, are dominant figures in the government.' (p. 113.)

[6] See Indian Investment Centre, *Investing in India*, New Delhi, 1961, particularly Chapter 5, 'Objects and Functions'. A New York office was opened in October 1961; and a Common Market office planned for 1963 (*The Times*, 10 August 1963), although it appears not to have been established by the summer of 1964.

of Commerce and Industry was seconded to 'undertake co-ordinated consideration of all aspects [of official sanction] at the same time, in consultation with the authorities concerned,[1] and a special agency set up in the Ministry of Commerce and Industry for him to work with.[2] Foreign firms have been invited to fill 'industrial gaps', 'as a rule . . . not . . . in the industries listed in Schedule "A" of the Industrial Policy Resolution of 1956 . . . [except] where, after full consideration, this is found to be in the public interest'; and no particular ratio between foreign and domestic capital is specified—an 'Indian majority holding would be generally welcome' but the extent of foreign shareholding would 'be judged on merits'.[3] The response from abroad since 1957–8 has likewise been relatively constant. Although aid showed clear signs of flagging in 1962,[4] and might have fallen off considerably were it not for the Himalayan War, private investment has kept up. And the lines drawn during the crisis years of the fifties have guided Indo-Western relations ever since.

(c) *Non-alignment and its critics:* Not everything was conceded to official Western views during and after the exchange crisis. The Indian Government insisted on maintaining at least the 'core' of the Plan—the heavy industrial and technological base for further development. They insisted, too, on their right to break any foreign private monopoly in the country. In both, Eastern Bloc aid was invaluable (over and above its importance in helping to plug the foreign exchange gap), and so was a key argument for maintaining the policy of non-alignment, or political neutrality between East and West, despite mounting pressure from within the country and abroad to abandon it.

Russian aid started flowing in quantity in 1955, too late to be listed with the public sector industrial projects of the Second Plan.[5] By the beginning of the Third Plan, Eastern Bloc aid covered between seven and eight of the sixteen Central Government projects carried over from the Second, and twelve of the twenty-two new projects for which external credits were already assured. It accounted for more than half the foreign exchange expected to be spent on these

---

[1] Government of India *Press Note*, 8 May 1961.

[2] Raj. K. Nigam, 'Flow of Foreign Investments', *Company News and Notes*, 1 August 1964, p. 23.

[3] ibid. Many of the industries listed were included in Schedule B of the Resolution. For the significance of the Schedules, see above, pp. 143 ff.

[4] See above, pp. 121–2.   [5] As in PC, *Second Plan*, pp. 417–19.

projects (some Rs 270 out of 435 crores) and nearly one-third of the total investment envisaged (Rs 794 crores). They were key items in India's programme of heavy industrialization.

TABLE 3

Government of India Third Plan Industrial Projects[a]

(Rs crores)

Project	Location	Total Investment	Foreign Exchange	Loans and Technical Aid from:
A. Projects under execution and carried over from the Second Plan				
1. Hindustan Steel (three plants)	a. Rourkela b. Bhilai c. Durgapur	50	20	West Germany Russia Britain
2. Rourkela Fertilizer factory	Rourkela			uncertain
3. Heavy Machinery plant	Ranchi	80	55	Russia
4. Foundry Forge shop	Ranchi			Czechoslovakia
5. Mining Machinery plant	Durgapur			Russia
6. Heavy Electricals plant	Bhopal	16	7	Britain
7. Drug Projects: a. synthetic drugs plant b. antibiotics plant c. phytochemicals plant d. surgical instruments plant	Sanatnagar, AP Rishikesh, UP Munnar, Kerala Guindy, Madras	30	15	Russia
8. Organic Intermediates plant	Panvel, Maharashtra	11	6	West German Consortium
9. Expansion of Hindustan Antibiotics	Pimpri, Maharashtra	neg.		US
10. Trombay Fertilizer factory	Trombay, Maharashtra	25	13	US
11. Nahorkatiya Fertilizer factory	Nahorkatiya, Assam	12	7	Britain
12. Neiveli Fertilizer factory	Neiveli, Madras	16	12	Italo-W. German Consortium
13. Briquetting and carbonization plant		14	9	US
14. Thermal Power plant		10	6	Russia
15. Nunmati Oil Refinery	Nunmati, Assam	9	5	Rumania
16. Barauni Oil Refinery	Barauni, Bihar	23	8	Russia
B. New projects in the Third Plan				
1. Expansion of Heavy Machinery plant	Ranchi	14	11	Russia
2. Expansion of Foundry forge project	Ranchi	10	6	Czechoslovakia

12

Project	Location	Total Foreign Invest-ment	Ex-change	Loans and Technical Aid from:
3. Expansion of Mining Machinery plant	Durgapur	15	10	Russia
4. Second and third Heavy Electricals projects	a. Hyderabad, AP b. Hardwar, UP }	} 69	45 {	{ Czechoslovakia Russia
5. Heavy Machine Tools project	Ranchi	11	9	Czechoslovakia
6. Precision Instruments project	Kotah, Rajasthan Palghat, Kerala	8	6	Russia
7. Ophthalmic Glass project	Durgapur	3	2	Russia
8. Raw Film project	Ootacamund	8	5	France
9. Watch factory	Bangalore	3	2	Japan
10. Expansion of Steel plant	Bhilai	138	56	Russia
11. Expansion of Steel plant	Durgapur	56	27	Britain
12. Expansion of Steel plant	Rourkela	90	50	West Germany
13. Expansion of Hindustan Machine Tools	Bangalore	3	2	France[b]
14. Basic Refractories project	Bhilai	3	2	Russia
15. New Machine Tools works	Pinjore, Punjab	5	3	East Germany
16. Gujerat Oil Refinery	Koyali, Gujerat	30	15	Russia
17. Expansion of Praga Tools	Secunderabad, AP	1	1	Poland
18. Heavy Structurals works 19. Heavy Plate and Vessels works }	} Undecided	12	17 {	{ uncertain
20. Fertilizer factory	Gorakhpur	18	8	Japan
21. Security Paper Mill	Hoshangabad, MP	6	4	Britain
22. Expansion of Hindustan Cables	Rupnaraianpur, WB	4	1	Britain

Notes: a. The list has been amended in the course of the Third Plan, a number of items having been dropped, others added, and others changed in their physical and financial details. The changes are noted in the text where appropriate.

b. A number of smaller agreements on individual tools have been concluded with British firms.

Sources: PC, *Third Plan*, pp. 493–5; *India*, 1963, Table 140, pp. 258–60; the financial press.

The Eastern Bloc's disproportionate contribution to public sector industrial projects is no reflection of Indian Government wishes. But such has been the reluctance of Western aid- and credit-giving agencies to back state-run industries, which in the circumstances often means industries *tout court*, that the Government has been forced to accept whatever was available from the East.[1] Where an alternative existed or was created, the Government has been quick to choose a Western-sponsored project, even at the price of quality.

India's costly rejection, between 1955 and 1961, of Russian arms offers is one example.[2] Another is provided by the drug industry.[3] After early attempts to set up a number of state-run drug plants with Western, primarily American, help had foundered on issues such as secrecy of processes, scale of royalties, and so on, the Indian Government was persuaded to take advantage of a Russian offer of technical aid. Early in 1956 a party of Russian experts was invited to survey requirements and make recommendations. By May the Government had received a report proposing an integrated, state-owned industry of sufficient scope to cover three-quarters of likely requirements. It was to have consisted of a greatly enlarged and diversified Hindustan Antibiotics at Pimpri, a second and larger antibiotics plant, subsequently sited at Rishikesh, UP, a large synthetics drugs plant to manufacture sulpha drugs, sedatives, vitamins, and such like at Sanatnagar, Hyderabad, AP, a large plant for the production of chemical intermediates for both the drugs and the dyestuffs industries, and one for the manufacture of endocrines.

Indian and Western pharmaceutical firms were naturally unenthusiastic. They found a champion in the Ministry of Commerce and Industry. The Ministry opposed the original invitation to the Russians and, after they had arrived and reported, postponed consideration of the Report until it had sent its own team to Moscow (September). The Indian team recommended that the industry remain in private hands and that aid be sought in Italy, West Germany, and the United States. The Russians, kept fully informed of the state of

---

[1] Western reluctance to support industrial projects embraces aid already 'obligated': while 14 per cent of the total aid authorized under the Indo-US Technical Assistance Program remained unutilized at the end of September 1959, 34 per cent of the allocation to 'industry and mining' remained untouched: (from Ministry of Finance, *External Assistance*, 1959, pp. 4–5).

[2] See above, pp. 117 f.

[3] The following paragraphs rely heavily on conversations with Major-General Dr. S. S. Sokhey, MA, MD, FNI, early in 1962, and on the many articles and pamphlets he has written on the subject, notably, *The Indian Drug Industry and Its Future*, May 1959. Dr. Sokhey was Director of the Haffkine Institute, Bombay, until he joined the staff of the World Health Organization, Geneva, as Assistant Director General in 1948. He played a leading role in the negotiations leading to the Russian offer of aid for the Indian pharmaceuticals industry, and has remained a persistent critic of the Government for not following it through.

battle, responded in February 1957 with an offer of an eighty million rouble (Rs 10 crores) loan on exceptionally easy terms to cover the cost of imported equipment: repayment to be in *rupees*, in easy instalments at the usual low rate of interest ($2\frac{1}{2}$ per cent); and no charge for knowhow. No Indian response was forthcoming for a full year. Then in February 1958, a second Russian team was invited to make proposals within very much narrower terms of reference: no mention was made of Hindustan Antibiotics, the second antibiotics plant was assigned low priority, the chemical intermediates plant was dropped altogether, and the synthetic drugs plant reduced to one-quarter of what was originally envisaged.

By the time this second team arrived—August 1958—an agreement to extend Hindustan Antibiotics had been concluded with Merck & Co. Inc. of the United States, parent of the largest drug firm in India. It provided for fairly high royalty payments in foreign currency ($2\frac{1}{2}$ per cent after tax on sales in India; 5 per cent on sales abroad), screening of scientists and classifying of information supplied, to Merck's satisfaction; it also envisaged production costs very nearly double those of the Russian proposal—Rs 267 a kilogram of streptomycin compared with Rs 157. Subsequently the chemical intermediates plant at Panvel, Maharashtra, was allotted to a West German consortium[1] and foreign private firms encouraged to undertake production of antibiotics and synthetics at considerable cost in royalties, foreign exchange, and secrecy. The cost structure and supply position in the industry were modified to such an extent by these changes that the consortium felt it necessary to urge the Government to abandon the plant at Panvel in mid-1963 (at the same time as one of its members was reported to be negotiating for the manufacture of intermediates in the private sector).[2]

A bare recital of events does little justice to the bitter bargaining that accompanied demarcation in the industry between public and private interests, East and West. Something of its flavour can be gained from the following extract out of an American trade journal:

Drug officials started looking at India about two years ago, just as the Russians began a big push to have India freed from the dependence on Western chemicals and pharmaceuticals. Soviet engineers, loans, and all else needed would be provided if the Indians would take USSR help and build the state-owned industry.

[1] Members of the consortium were Farbwerke Hoechst *AG*, Badishe Anilin und Soda Fabriken *AG* (BASF), and Farbenfabriken Bayer.
[2] *EW*, 6 July 1963, p. 1056; Special Number, July 1963, p. 1284.

Fortunately for the Free World, Merck and other US and Western drug and chemical firms have not been idle since.

Merck's efforts have helped in part to stall this Soviet offensive; however, Knoppers fully admits that eventually some products in this area will be produced using Russian knowledge and aid. But the original Soviet offer, which was all-embracing (and somewhat obsolete technologically, some say), is shelved, and the Indian Pharmaceutical Industry will not be a government monopoly.[1]

Another less well-documented illustration is provided by the raw film project at Ootacamund. Early attempts to interest the major producers in the United States, Britain, Belgium, West Germany, and Japan in production in India met with, to quote the Minister of Commerce and Industry, unacceptable 'lame duck' offers.[2] For a time it looked as if the Government would 'be driven to accept the aid offered by the East Germans'.[3] Then, after four years of waiting and searching, after negotiations with East Germany on technical aid had been opened[4] and an offer of finance received (and favourably reviewed by the Planning Commission),[5] an agreement was concluded with Messrs. Bauchet et Cie of France early in 1960. That the French company was known to be one of the smaller ones, that the agreement provided for the production of only 50–60 per cent of requirements and not, it appears, for the better-quality ranges, were less important than that the Indian Government were not obliged to take up the East German offer.[6]

Other examples could be adduced from almost every sphere of industry in which the state showed interest.[7] Enough has been said

[1] *Chemical and Engineering News*, 14 November 1958, p. 73, quoted in Sokhey, *Indian Drug Industry*, p. 3.

[2] See below, p. 289.

[3] *Capital*, 3 January 1957, p. 15. The passage which concludes with the phrase quoted in the text is interesting, the more so as it occurs in a journal wedded to foreign (British) interests. It reads:
'India is often blamed for accepting Communist aid in industrialisation. The fact, however, is that she is sometimes driven to accept such aid. The raw film industry illustrates the point. India is the second largest consumer of raw films. She has been wanting to develop a raw film industry of her own. The only offer of help so far has come from Eastern Germany. Even now, India is open to offers. As things stand, she may be driven to accept the aid offered by the East Germans.'

[4] *Capital*, 22 August 1957, p. 255.   [5] *Capital*, 6 February 1958, p. 189.

[6] *EW*, 16 April 1960, p. 609.

[7] For example, the Ophthalmic Glass Project, Durgapur: 'Enquiries show that the [West] Germans have not taken much interest in the project, while the British quotations were regarded as on the high side' (*Capital*, 3 January 1957, p. 16); the Mining Machinery Project, Durgapur, on which both a British and a Russian Mission submitted Reports (ibid.); the ill-fated US-aided steel mill at Bokaro (see above, p. 122, below, p. 237); oil prospecting (see below, pp. 168 f.).

however, to show that Eastern Bloc preponderance in building up the heavy state-run industrial sector has been despite, rather than in consequence of, the Government's own inclinations. Had Western aid agencies and Governments been less inflexible doctrinally or Western firms able to offer better terms, the public sector map in India might well have taken on a different colour.

Paradoxically, Eastern preponderance in heavy industrial aid has made the West overcome its antipathies in some cases, and so added a booster to its own direct contribution. It is naturally difficult to adduce direct evidence. But it is more than coincidental that the markedly unenthusiastic response in London to India's first request for aid in building a steel plant in 1953 should give way to one of readiness and a formal offer (3 January 1955) once it became clear that a similar Russian offer was about to be accepted.[1] As Khrushchev is reported to have told Nehru: 'Rourkela and Durgapur should also be put in our account.'[2] Nor can it be coincidental that dark hints about Russia's willingness to step in with aid have accompanied almost every request for project support in the West.

The second major effect of Eastern Bloc aid has been in enabling the Indian Government to weaken, or remove entirely, foreign control over key industries. None illustrates the case better than oil. To this day the industry is very much controlled from abroad.[3] But since 1956 the state has come increasingly to challenge the foreign monopoly in all its aspects, from prospecting to marketing. It is scarcely conceivable that the challenge could have been made without Eastern Bloc aid.

Very early on the Government showed signs of concern at the foreign companies' large claims on Indian resources. Product prices were high and justified by complex arithmetic.[4] About the time of Independence, the Government was reported to be

---

[1] See above, p. 93.   [2] *EW*, 28 April 1962, p. 692.

[3] The three major foreign groups are Burmah Oil, including the Assam Oil Co. Ltd., Burmah Oil Co. (India Trading) Ltd., Burmah Shell Oil Storage and Distributing Co. of India Ltd., and Burmah Shell Refineries Ltd.; Esso-Standard, replacing the Stanvac group (Standard Vacuum Oil Co. Ltd. and Standard Vacuum Refining Co. of India Ltd.) and Caltex, including Caltex (India) Ltd. and Caltex Oil Refining (India) Ltd.

[4] At the time of Independence, notwithstanding the fact that three-quarters of India's supplies came from the Anglo-Iranian Oil Company's refinery at Abadan, prices in India were based on the landed cost of crude, compounded of the Mexican Gulf price of crude plus the cost of freight to India minus imputed freight charges from India to the Persian Gulf. One price list showed the landed

considering . . . an intensive oil prospecting program with the aid of up-to-date machinery and experts imported from America and Russia, . . . contacting [the] Russian authorities . . . to find out if and how imports of Russian oil could be revived, securing a share in the management and control of oil companies and in the distribution and fixation of prices for petrol, and obtaining facilities for Indians to receive training in the business as well as the operational side of the oil industry.[1]

By the end of the year, it narrowed its aims to inviting the companies active in India to build refineries. Negotiations dragged on for three years, breaking down ultimately when the Government baulked at allowing the companies to raise product prices by the tenth they considered necessary to break even.[2]

Conditions changed radically when the Abadan refinery was nationalized—temporarily—by Iran. Prices rose anyway, the Government wanted an assured supply of products, and the companies became interested in alternative refining capacity. A second approach was made in November 1951 and by the end of the month the first Refinery Agreement—with Stanvac—was signed.[3]

The Agreements marked the apex of the companies' fortunes. The third, with Caltex, had scarcely been concluded (March 1953) when the Government began to question their terms; a Cabinet sub-committee was appointed to inquire into product prices, particularly in Assam, the only State with a working refinery and yet the one in which product prices were the highest;[4] Government spokesmen took the lead in hammering the companies on the floor of the Lok Sabha, imputing to Assam Oil a profit of 'from 100 to 300 per cent', rejecting the Company's own figures as useless 'in determining the cost structure on the retail price of petrol . . . [because] whatever the cost of production of indigenous oil, the price is based on the [Mexican] Gulf price.'[5]

Within two months of the debate prices were lowered by 4 annas a gallon in Shillong and by 2 annas elsewhere in Assam,[6] a reduction

---

cost of crude in India to be 160s. a barrel compared with 32s. a barrel in Abadan and 18s. a barrel 'of Russian oil'. (*EE*, 9 May 1947, p. 838: see also *Capital*, 10 July 1947, p. 67.)

[1] ibid.

[2] The invitation was extended in November 1947; a technical survey committee toured the country in 1948, and submitted its report early in 1949. The report, which envisaged an annual loss of Rs 2 crores at prevailing product prices, was under active consideration late that year.

[3] See above, p. 90.   [4] *Hindu*, 27 June 1953.   [5] *Hindu*, 29 August 1953.
[5] *EE*, 9 October 1953, p. 615.

made possible, according to the company's press statement, 'by the greater availability of these products from nearer sources and the fall in freight rates'.[1]

Little more was heard for a time. The companies invested heavily in their refineries, the first of which came on stream in January 1955, followed in March by Burmah-Shell's, the largest; and the Government smarted under the memory of the Agreements. It could not do much to alter them; neither persuade the companies to reduce prices nor, in the absence of alternative supplies, force them to. It had tried to interest other Western companies in prospecting in India but with no success.[2]

The deadlock was broken in 1955. In September, K. D. Malaviya, Minister for Natural Resources, led a delegation to Moscow to seek help in exploration.[3] He returned with the outlines of an agreement. By January 1956 Russian technicians had reported favourably on oil prospects in the Cambay region, Gujerat; by March they had come to similarly favourable conclusions on the general reserve position, and an agreement for the supply of technicians and of a drilling rig had been signed with Rumania. By May three Russian rigs had been bought, a special directorate—the Oil and Natural Gas Commission —set up, and plans formulated to extend the Government prospecting effort to the Jaisalmer region in Rajasthan; Saurashtra; the Cauvery Basin, Madras; the Jwalamukhi area of north-east Punjab; and the Borsad region, Gujerat. Russian and Rumanian crews featured largely in these plans although, by this time, it had been found possible to hire a Canadian (official) crew.

With the Russian deal in the offing the Government was in a position to press the companies for concessions. State partnership be-

---

[1] *Hindu*, 2 December 1953.

[2] *NYHT* (European Edition), 21 July 1955. Only three relatively small tracts out of a sedimentary area of over 400,000 square miles had been prospected at all, and that not too successfully. Assam Oil, with its old Digboi field facing exhaustion, was active elsewhere in the State. Early in 1953 they struck what was to become an important field in Nahorkatiya, 20 miles to the west. Burmah Oil, the parent company, had made some test drillings at Lakhra, Rajasthan, but abandoned them in 1950. Stanvac, now Esso-Standard, surveyed the Bengal Basin from 1951 and went on to test drilling in 1953. They also had a shot at the Rajasthan border region around Jaisalmer. Both came to nothing, the Bengal concession being abandoned in 1960 after ten dry holes and an expenditure of Rs 7 crores.

[3] Unless otherwise stated the following paragraphs are based on press reports and trade journals (of which the most important is the *Petroleum Press Service* [*PPS*]).

came a condition for obtaining a new prospecting licence: Stanvac agreed (March 1955) to associate with the Government in exploitation once commercial quantities were struck in West Bengal; Assam Oil agreed (June) to become a rupee company with a one-third Government stake in exchange for a twenty-year prospecting licence covering an 800 square mile area near their new Nahorkatiya field.[1]

Initially, the Government assumed a threatening posture. Fortified by the Russian estimate of India's reserves, Maulana Azad, then Minister of Education (including scientific research and natural resources), demanded (March 1956) 'not one farthing less than 51 per cent' Indian ownership. Soon afterwards, the Industrial Policy Resolution (April) reserved oil as a state enterprise under Schedule A.[2] Later, it drew back a bit: new, simplified licensing rules were published in November 1959 together with a formal general invitation to foreign private companies 'to join the quest for oil in India, subject to mutually acceptable terms'. Even then, however, its insistence on 'state partnership, half or more than half the profits, and [the Government] itself having undivided control of any oil found', to quote an industry interpretation,[3] proved too onerous for private operators. Reports of renewed interest abroad proved groundless, and it was found necessary to prolong the deadline for offers by two months to the end of March. A year later, negotiations were still proceeding with six companies for prospecting rights either in partnership with the Commission in reserved areas or alone elsewhere. In practice, with the exception of a new licence for Oil India in exchange for a rise in the Government's stake from one-third to one-half,[4] private companies have been virtually excluded from prospecting for, and producing, Indian crude.

From 1956 the Government also tried a less oblique approach to company profits and prices—with some success: in August 1956, Swaran Singh, Minister for Works, Housing, and Supply told the Lok Sabha that refinery profits would be scrutinized to ensure that no

---

[1] It was not until February 1959, after complex and strenuous bargaining and as part of the general easing in Government relations with foreign capital, that the joint company—Oil India (Private) Ltd.—was incorporated.

[2] See above, p. 143 n. 6.   [3] *PPS*, June 1961, p. 217.

[4] The new area covers 1,886 square miles to the east of the earlier concession area. In this case, the Government possessed powerful leverage as Assam Oil's refinery was faced with exhaustion of crude from its Digboi field (cf. *FT*: 'Burmah Oil appears to have purchased a valuable lease on life by accepting the 50:50 formula', 29 June 1961), but also had good reason to deal gently with the company at this stage. (See below, pp. 172 f.)

avoidable drain occurred. Six weeks later, Burmah-Shell and Stanvac surrendered their right to duty protection on motor spirit of
2 annas (12·5 *naye paise*) per gallon, at a total cost to them of some
Rs 10 crores. In August 1957, after pointing out in the Lok Sabha
that prices rose after the Suez War even though supplies were drawn
east of the Canal, Malaviya pressed the companies to replace the
existing price formula, based on assumed costs (unaudited by the
Government), by one based on 'actual . . . cost plus reasonable
profit'.[1] In October, they were asked to justify their product prices
which were higher than in neighbouring countries that did not have
the benefit of refineries. Six months later, having told the Lok Sabha
that talks on price reductions had been in progress for more than a
year, Malaviya confessed 'to a deep sense of frustration and disappointment at the fact that we are not able to get a conclusive
decision, although we requested the parties to let us know their
proposals by today'.[2] In May 1958, the Companies were informed
'that the Government considered it necessary to examine the quantum and propriety of all charges . . . included by them in their selling prices of each product'.[3]

No real dent could be made in the companies' pricing formula until
alternative supplies were found, however. In practice, this meant
augmenting indigenous crude with imports, building state refineries
with Eastern Bloc aid initially, and breaching the companies' monopoly of marketing—all of which the Government proceeded to do.

The first moves came towards the end of 1958. In October, Malaviya returned from a four-week tour of Eastern Europe with a firm
agreement for a refinery at Nunmati, near Gauhati, Assam, to be
built and financed by Rumania, and with the hint of another to be
built by Russia. Within six months the second materialized as the
Barauni, Bihar project.[4] Simultaneously, the problem of distribution
was taken up. Direct assault on the companies' monopoly was clearly
ruled out: they shared 95 per cent of the market, while as yet the
Government had no regular supplies, lacked storage, transport, and
marketing facilities and stopped short of expropriation. Accordingly,
from the start, the Government disclaimed any intention of super-
seding them: while planning to have the distribution of petroleum

---

[1] *Damle Report*, p. 14.   [2] Reported in *Hindu*, 2 April 1958.
[3] *Damle Report*, p. 14.
[4] A third refinery, at Koyali, Gujerat—again with Russian help—was agreed
to in 1961. It was only with the fourth public sector refinery, at Cochin, that an
alternative to Eastern Bloc aid was found (see below, p. 174).

products in the public sector, this was to be 'in due course and in agreement with the oil companies'.[1] For the moment, the new Indian Oil Co. Ltd., floated in June 1959, would limit itself to supplying Government requirements, or about one-tenth of the total.

The only immediate threat to the companies lay in the Government's stated intention to operate through Indian Oil before the public sector refineries came on stream.[2] The source of supplies now became crucial, and the companies pressed for permission to increase production. In June 1959, Burmah-Shell offered to forego another *tranche* of 'duty protection' in exchange for an additional 300,000 tons a year throughout. This was accepted. A similar bargain was struck with Stanvac, as from 1 October.[3] As yet neither side had made any decisive gain. Pressure on the companies mounted substantially the following summer. Internationally, the industry was suffering from surplus capacity. Russia made an offer of crude at 15–25 per cent below ruling prices in May[4] just as the seemingly rich Ankleshwar field in Gujerat was struck. In June, an agreement was concluded for the supply of $1\frac{1}{2}$ million tons of products at a discount with payment in rupees, the quantity being raised to $2\frac{1}{2}$ million tons in December. It was now that the Government raised official objection to the pricing, training, and by-products clauses of the Refinery Agreements. The companies were approached to refine Russian crude—and refused. After Burmah-Shell and Stanvac had countered with an unsatisfactory offer of $7\frac{1}{2}$ per cent discount on Persian Gulf posted prices of crude—a saving of Rs 3 crores on a total annual fuel bill of Rs 100 crores—the Government set up the Oil Price Enquiry (Damle) Committee to examine the principles which should guide pricing policy. Before the appointment was officially announced, the companies declared a further discount in posted prices, making $12\frac{1}{2}$ per cent in all.[5] This was still not enough. In August, Malaviya

[1] Nehru at a press conference (*FT*, 7 March 1959). See also Malaviya to the Rajya Sabha: 'It will be our effort to control and have a fair share in the work of oil distribution and at the same time to examine it and consult the foreign companies to see that a reasonable scheme is produced so that this work of distribution might be taken up by Government in a satisfactory manner.' (*Hindu*, 14 March 1959.)

[2] Malaviya to the press (*Hindu*, 3 June 1959).

[3] An agreement with Caltex in the same vein followed in November 1960.

[4] Press accounts of the Russian discount vary from 15–20 to 20–25 per cent, without any detail being given.

[5] The $12\frac{1}{2}$ per cent discount was later reduced once again to $7\frac{1}{2}$ per cent when Middle Eastern posted prices came down by 4–14 cents a barrel in mid-August,

regretted in the Lok Sabha that a 'more attractive' Russian offer had had to be turned down because of the companies' refusal to handle crude from that source. He thought their prospects 'not bright'; and rejected a Burmah-Shell offer to exchange the Refinery Agreement for permission to raise throughput from 2¾ million to 4 million tons a year. The first regular Russian shipments were now being received. Indian Oil, the state marketing company, found itself engaged in a silent rate war for the municipalized Bombay Electrical Supply and Transport Co.'s custom—the first of many. Defeated by the heavy discounts offered by the companies, the Government had to suspend shipments for a time.

The battle continued well into the spring of 1961. In March, Malaviya accused the companies of stalling in negotiations over refining Indian crude. The managers of Burmah-Shell and Stanvac protested that they were not. Malaviya counter-protested that they had every right not to refine Indian crude or Russian for that matter, but that state refineries would continue to claim priority over their own expansion. A month later, permission to increase throughput was again stated publicly to have been refused.

By now, however, pressure was being put on the Government to modify its oil policy. A World Bank Mission had suggested in the summer of 1960 that 'a change in this policy could free significant amounts of foreign exchange for other uses during the third Plan by attracting additional foreign capital into the oil industry.'[1] Thereafter, 'oil company diplomats' went to work and 'the "Aid India Club" . . . politely suggested . . . that it is hardly its job to make good foreign exchange deficits that could be avoided by a different oil policy'. In April, six weeks before the Club's crucial fourth meeting, B. K. Nehru flew back to Delhi from Washington in an attempt

---

still less than the 30 cents a barrel discount that had become common enough. (See *The Economist*, 18 November 1961, p. 679.)

[1] Quoted in *Capital*, 8 September 1960, p. 353. The full passage reads: 'There is a good prospect that the inflow of business capital will be larger in the third Plan than in the second, but apart from oil, private foreign investment cannot be expected to make a major contribution to the financing of the Plan—the amounts involved are still much too small. The policy pursued by the Indian Government over the past few years of excluding private capital from further investment in oil and refining has added very considerably to the immediate pressure on India's foreign-exchange resources. A change in this policy could free significant amounts of foreign exchange for other uses during the third Plan by attracting additional foreign capital into the oil industry.'

to secure modifications in that policy.[1] That he succeeded became clear during the ensuing months. An agreement with Burmah-Shell, signed on 31 May, the day the Club met in Washington, made far-reaching concessions to the company;[2] a few days later, Malaviya opened a chink for bargaining by stating that the Government would consider offers for new refineries on condition that the foreign share would be a minority one. At the same time, an upward revision of the estimates for future needs made by the Oil Advisory Committee added to the pressure to allow the companies increased throughput, since the state sector could not, by any stretch of the imagination, be expanded quickly enough to take up the extra demand. Burmah-Shell was still willing, it appeared, to throw in the Refinery Agreement as its contribution to a bargain.

The tenor of the struggle was now changing. While accepting the Damle Committee recommendations (September 1961), including the proposal to cut prices by Rs 15 crores, or 8–10 per cent, the Goverment did so only after discussions at Cabinet level lasting some ten weeks, and with circumspection. The companies, while rejecting the recommendations, made it known that they had little choice.[3] After they had done so they were still granted foreign exchange to buy their crude requirements abroad, 'the situation [was] not regarded as altogether critical in London',[4] and the agenda for the meeting to discuss the recommendations included an item on refinery throughput, previously considered 'a separate issue' by Malaviya. For good measure, a proposal to nationalize the refineries, made in the Rajya Sabha (December), was turned down.

Since the summer of 1962, a measure of stability has been reached in the relations between the Government and the companies. First the critical foreign exchange shortage, then the inexorable rise in

---

[1] Rawle Knox in the *Observer*, 16 April 1961. The story was substantially confirmed by Malaviya in the Rajya Sabha, 28 April.

[2] The Government withdrew its demand for a special Director with the power of veto on the Board of the new joint Oil India Ltd.; a return of 9–13 per cent was guaranteed to Oil India's shareholders; and the company was to supply crude at prices related to Persian Gulf posted prices—an early report mentioned 25 per cent below landed cost at Calcutta—rather than at cost plus a 'reasonable profit' as the Government had originally intended.

[3] One report put it in this way: 'The companies . . . have picked or accepted a quarrel, and if they cannot expect to win here, perhaps they reason that their willingness to fight will help them in areas where their stakes are bigger.' (*The Times*, 17 October 1961.)

[4] *FT*, 21 November 1961.

domestic demand (and with it in demand projections), and finally the Himalayan War have made the Government more amenable to persuasion. While still rejecting, throughout the summer and autumn of 1962, the companies' offer to abandon the Agreements and turn their marketing organizations into rupee companies in exchange for greater permitted throughput,[1] it renewed without difficulty the temporary increases already sanctioned, totalling nearly 50 per cent since they first went on stream.[2] In May, the Cabinet asked the Planning Commission to review the private sector's role in the industry. Revising their demand projections upward, they recommended that the refineries be allowed to expand further—by three million tons.[3]

At the same time, the policy of establishing new refineries wholly in the public sector came in for liberal reinterpretation. An agreement to build and operate a new 2·5–3·5 million ton/year plant at Cochin was concluded with Phillips Petroleum of the United States in April 1963: the Government was to hold 51 per cent of the shares, 25 per cent was to go to Phillips, 2 per cent to Duncan Bros., and the rest to the Indian public; for ten years after the formation of the new company or until such time as all foreign exchange debts were retired, whichever is the later, Phillips would appoint the managing director; they would act as purchasing agents of crude for fifteen years, as chartering agents (using Indian flag tankers 'if and when available at competitive freight rates'), and as construction agents; would receive a high processing margin of $1·35 per barrel, declining

[1] For example, Malaviya to the press: 'Only if Western oil companies are willing to import cheaper crude than at present and accept payment in non-convertible rupees will I consider any proposal for expansion in their refineries.' (*FT*, 24 September 1962.)

[2] Throughput capacity is at best a loose concept. The Refinery Agreements allowed Burmah-Shell 2 million tons a year for an investment of £25 million; by the time their plant was on stream (March 1955), throughput was 2·8 million tons with only £18 million invested; from July 1962, throughput rose to 3·5 million tons without any additional investment having taken place. Esso's planned throughput of 1·2 million tons a year had risen to 1·9 million by the time their refinery went on stream (August 1954), and to 2·4 million tons in 1962. For the Caltex refinery at Vizakhapatnam, the quantities were 0·657 million tons, 0·9, and 1·1 million respectively.

[3] Esso had asked to increase throughput by 2·5 million tons a year to 4·9 million, Burmah-Shell by 2·5 to 5·5 million, and Caltex by 1·5 million tons to 2·5 million. Malaviya opposed the increase. He told the Lok Sabha that it would be 'suicidal' for the public sector refineries if the private companies were allowed to grow (April); he fought it in the Cabinet (May) and in the press (June). But in mid-June he ceased to be Minister of Mines and Fuel (see above, p. 152).

to $1·30 after ten years, irrespective of the price paid for crude; and would receive royalties and fees for research and for the services of twelve technicians seconded by them.[1] This agreement set the pattern of negotiations between the Government and some eight foreign companies towards the end of 1963 for two further refineries—at Madras and Haldia, near Calcutta.

There is plenty of life yet in the foreign companies, and Government action has proved less compelling than appeared likely a few years ago. None the less, the companies have been made to share, if only in a limited way, the local market for crude and products; to distribute some of their profits within India; and—although they appeared to be having second thoughts on the matter in the autumn of 1963—they have been made to come very near indeed to relinquishing the extraterritoriality written into the Refinery Agreements. That they are in the forefront of the drive to diversification into petro-chemicals in India is as surely a sign of their waning confidence in traditional activities as of profounder trends within the oil industry.

While oil is the paradigm for the use of non-alignment in underpinning economic independence, it is not the only case. In one way or another, Eastern Bloc aid has sustained the state in many of its efforts to release industries from utter dependence on tightly organized foreign private interests—in heavy electrical equipment, drugs, and dyestuffs, mining machinery, and much else.[2] So important is this aspect of the policy, that despite the clear shift Rightwards within the Government and elsewhere since the Himalayan War, every effort has been made to recover the formal stance lost during the first panic reaction. Agreement for a Western 'air umbrella' was accompanied by 'discussions with the USSR regarding the assistance for strengthening our air defense that can be provided by that country';[3] a request for Western arms aid was matched by another addressed to Moscow;[4] and a hasty decision to serve as a base for Voice of America broadcasts was annulled (finally in November 1963).

The stance is a frail shadow of its former self, the result of East–

[1] Malaviya to the Lok Sabha as reported in *Hindu*, 8 May 1963; *PPS*, June 1963, p. 229.

[2] See below, Chapter 5.

[3] Statement issued by the Ministry of External Affairs quoted in *The Times*, 27 July 1963.

[4] See above, p. 119.

West accord rather than the symptom of discord it once was. It has been overlaid by the Rightward drift that has settled within the country. None the less, so long as it is sustained internationally—India is reported to have asked informally for a joint U.S.-Russian declaration on the Sino-Indian conflict[1]—it can continue to serve its original functions: to supply resources for state industry and provide a means for weakening foreign private control over Indian industry.

(d) *Foreign critics:* Western critics of India's swing left were not fully satisfied by her arrested swing back. The tones have softened, and the blanket attack on economic policy generally ceased. But the questioning of state activity in any of the spheres in which foreign private capital is particularly interested continues unabated, as does the championing of private sector causes in a general way.

The World Bank's more recent statements are representative of official opinion. Their 'Bankers' Mission' which toured India and Pakistan in February and March 1960, recorded that 'the issue of public versus private enterprise has lost some of its sharpness . . . because it has become more widely recognised that both sectors of the economy have their contribution to make'.[2] At the same time they suggested that if aid-seeking Governments 'are to use the potential sources of aid to the full they will need to create conditions which will attract private capital from abroad.'[3]

Another Bank report spelled out these conditions: a change in the Government's oil policy to enable private interests to participate in the industry's expansion; a change in coal policy—'The private collieries should . . . be encouraged to raise all the coal they can, restrictions on the issue of new mining leases should be lifted, and prices should be adjusted to provide the industry with larger resources for re-investment';[4] and a change in steel policy with regard to the proposed fourth public steel plant at Bokaro, since 'the case for having the plant in the public sector [cannot] be established until alternative possibilities of obtaining a further expansion of production in the private sector have been thoroughly explored, [which]does not appear to have been done'.[5] And an even later one came very

---

[1] *The Times*, 11 September 1963.

[2] *Report of the Bankers' Mission to India and Pakistan*, Washington DC, IBRD, 1960, pp. 17–18. The Bankers were Hermann J. Abs, Chairman, Deutsche Bank, Frankfurt; Sir Oliver Franks, Chairman, Lloyds Bank, London; Allan Sproul, formerly Chairman, New York Federal Reserve Bank.

[3] ibid., p. 25.   [4] Quoted in *Capital*, 8 September 1960, p. 353.

[5] Quoted in ibid., p. 354.

close to suggesting World Bank participation in Indian planning.[1]

Private opinion has followed similar lines. 'What is to be feared at the moment', wrote a spokesman for British capital in India on the eve of the current Plan, 'is not the threat of further general nationalisation, but the doctrinaire use of existing powers by the state'. He cites 'four leading cases': motor-car manufacture; road transport; 'the future relations between the oil industry and the Government'; and 'whether the private sector of the coal industry is to be allowed to exploit, not only areas physically contiguous to existing coal-bearing properties, but other coal-bearing areas also'.[2] The argument has become one about details.

VI THE PRIVATE SECTOR

Indian capital's first stirrings towards liberalism during 1954-5 were strengthened by the Government's swing left. It heard its arguments echoed and amplified abroad; if it feared the state's aggrandizement, so did foreign capital. Both sides campaigned for reduced taxation, against state trading, against the Companies Act, and the Fourth Amendment.

The old enmities did not die at once. The wave of take-overs affecting old-type British capital had not entirely subsided;[3] pockets of traditional opposition like the Swadeshi League held out amongst mainly smaller firms and continued to attract attention;[4] Eugene Black's crude ultimatum to Krishnamachari was widely rejected as a piece of gun-boat diplomacy that could interest foreign capital only.[5] Yet as one leading daily admitted in tones that might have done for a growing number of businessmen, 'the amount of agreement that seems to exist between the criticisms and doubts expressed by the

[1] See, for example, *EW*, 4 April 1964, p. 631.

[2] T. Gregory, *India on the Eve of the Third Five Year Plan*, p. 161. The book is particularly significant for having been commissioned and published by the Associated Chambers of Commerce of India.

[3] See above, p. 43 ff.

[4] 'Nothing should be done', begged the League's President of Nehru, 'which would have the result of foreign capital supplanting the existing Indian units or activity in any particular line of manufacture or coming in the way of future expansion of such existing units.' (Babubhai M. Chinai at the Annual General Meeting, 1956, *Hindu*, 1 June 1956.)

[5] One mouthpiece of Indian business commented: 'The Banks' plea for further concessions to the private sector can be more sympathetically considered in respect of the Indian than in that of the foreign private sector.' (*Indian Express*, 9 October 1956.) For the *affaire* itself, see above, pp. 153-5.

13

World Bank mission on the Second Five-Year Plan and the views expressed in these columns from the time the "Plan-Frame" was published, is so great that it is somewhat embarrassing'.[1] The exchange crisis of 1957-8 brought this liberalism to rapid maturity. Domestic firms were made acutely aware of their own poverty in knowhow and finance just as the Indian market looked as if it was finally about to open out; imports became contingent on finding foreign partners, or foreign intermediaries with foreign credit agencies; medium-size 'outsiders' could exploit the situation to pole-vault into the tight circle of Indian big business with the help of foreign collaborators; all sizes and sorts of companies found association with foreign firms an advantage in internal competition; and so on. And, on a different plane, the political advantages of a united private-sector front became obvious.[2]

As a result, for the first time, the overwhelming body of Indian capital called openly for a reappraisal of its traditional hostility. As G. D. Birla put it to his shareholders:

the time has now . . . come to revise our attitude towards private foreign investment which, if freely encouraged, could go a long way to solve our problem of the exchange gap . . . we can build up India quickly only through the help of foreign capital and, since we are an independent nation, I do not see why we should be afraid of it. I feel, therefore, that not only should we allow foreign investment without any restriction but we should welcome it, improve the climate for it and make the investor feel that the opportunities for profitable utilisation of capital here compare favourably with those available anywhere else in the world. Some time ago the Finance Minister stated that he was not against foreign capital but that it had to make peace with Indian capitalists. I hope Indian industrialists will not take a narrow view of the situation but, in the higher interests of the country, make it absolutely clear that they welcome foreign capital.[3]

By the summer, Indian business had assembled the most impressive delegation ever to have travelled abroad—the Indian Industrial (or Birla) Mission—to back their Finance Minister's first tour abroad for aid.[4] It went abroad 'to create a climate' in the words of its

[1] *Hindu*, 31 July 1956.   [2] See below, p. 273.
[3] Chairman's address to the Annual Meeting, United Commercial Bank, *Capital*, 25 April 1957, p. 583.
[4] Members of the delegation were: G. D. Birla (Leader), Babubhai M. Chinai, Madanmohan R. Ruia, Ramnath A. Poddar, Shriyans Prasad Jain, S. L. Kirloskar, B. D. Garware, D. P. Goenka, S. S. Kanoria, R. Venkataswami Naidu, C. H. Bhabha, Kasturbhai Lalbhai, Madanmohan Mangaldas, and G. L. Bansal (Secretary-General, FICCI), *Hindu*, 29 July, 12 September 1957. A later list excludes Kasturbhai Lalbhai and includes Gordhandas J. Ruparel (ibid., 9 December 1957).

leader and, more specifically, to encourage foreign, particularly American, firms to invest in industry jointly with Indian capital. In both it was moderately successful: some of the major private projects of later years, notably in aluminium, drugs, cement, fertilizers, and machine tools, had their origins then.

More important, it returned convinced that Indian and foreign capital had common and complementary interests. Their specific fears were the same: the 'spate of recent fiscal and taxation measures', 'fear of nationalisation', 'doubts about the role of the private sector', 'the scheme of compulsory deposits and heavy taxation in the last Budget', 'too much interference by Government', 'restrictions on the quantum of royalty and the licence to manufacture'—all were cited as specifically foreign fears on their return.[1] The complementarity carried even greater conviction: 'There is no limit . . . to the amount of commercial credits that may be available from abroad, provided the climate is made favourable here for the raising of matching rupee capital.'[2] In their report to the Government, they spelled out the policy corollaries:

For the raising of this rupee capital, it is essential that both personal and corporate savings should be promoted. In order to promote them the Government of India should suitably modify the present tax structure, reorganise the country's existing credit institutions and banking system so as to create a capital market, and leave royalties on joint enterprises to be settled between the concerned foreign and Indian manufacturers.

They drew attention to the importance of encouraging 'productive projects as against projects which contain a very large welfare element'.[3]

The Mission marked a transition in the attitude of Indian to foreign capital such as had not yet been experienced. If the protagonists of collaboration had before constituted a minority, sometimes viewed with hostility by their colleagues, at best enjoying their tolerance,[4] they now became the authentic voice of Indian business. 'Nowadays', wrote *Capital*, 'criticisms [of foreign capital] come mainly from indigenous units which are inefficient and, therefore, cannot compete.'[5] The old policies were progressively jettisoned.

[1] *Indian Industrial Mission Press Statement*, Bombay, 18 November 1957 (*Hindu*, 19 November 1957).
[2] Quoted in *Capital*, 12 December 1957, p. 797.
[3] An extensive summary of the Report may be found in *Hindu*, 9 December 1957.
[4] See above, pp. 103 ff.   [5] 30 April 1959, p. 592.

First to go was the bias towards Government-to-Government loans:

I am averse to the idea of continued borrowing from abroad [said G. D. Birla to his shareholders] because, ultimately, the problem of repayment would become acute. . . . It would be better to create a favourable atmosphere in which foreign capital would feel encouraged to invest in our enterprises. . . . the question of repatriation of capital would normally not arise so long as private enterprise is allowed to function with a reasonable degree of freedom.[1]

The Federation took up the matter. A resolution on the 'Problem of Economic Development' adopted at its 1959 session read in part:

[The Federation] is of the opinion, and feels that Government concurs in its view, that as far as possible [the transfer of] foreign exchange should be less in the form of loans and more in the form of investments. The Federation, therefore, feels that in consultation with those foreigners who are willing to invest in India . . . any reasonable difficulties felt by them should be removed to facilitate their investments. The Federation notes with satisfaction the efforts made by individual industrialists . . . to get foreign collaboration and foreign exchange aid as far as possible through their own efforts, to start or expand various industries, and trusts that Government will make it easy for them to make such arrangements, without, of course, undue loss to the country.[2]

Given the basic premise that foreign private capital was in fact willing to flow, everything else followed: 'The authorities must recognise that a condition precedent for attracting and augmenting foreign capital in India is the building up of similar internal savings or capital', went a plea for lower taxation;[3] 'in order to attract [foreign private capital] the private sector must be able to maintain its prestige abroad. A private sector that has to be perpetually apologising for its existence cannot command prestige in the eyes of foreigners', went a more general request.[4]

The tables were completely turned. Where before the Government had reassured Indian business with the continued presence of foreign

---

[1] Chairman's address, Annual General Meeting, United Commercial Bank, *Capital*, 17 April 1958, p. 566. Cf. above, p. 72.

[2] *Proceedings 1959*, Vol. III, p. 43. Birla returned to the subject at the United Commercial Bank's annual meeting the following month: 'We must . . . plan for less of foreign loans and more of foreign investments. For attracting foreign investment we must create a proper climate.' (*Capital*, 9 April 1959, p. 492.)

[3] Resolution on 'Savings, Investment and Taxation Policy', FICCI, 1958 Annual Session, quoted in *Hindu*, 12 March 1958.

[4] Report of a FICCI Mission abroad, quoted in *Hindu*, 14 June 1959. See also FICCI, *The Third Five-Year Plan—A Tentative Outline*.

capital,[1] now Indian business used foreign capital's nervousness as a perpetual bogeyman to keep the Government on good behaviour, and the Government's behaviour as an argument to allay foreign capital's nervousness.[2] Yet it did not embrace foreign capital blindly. In the uneasy triangle formed by the Government and the two wings of the private sector, foreign capital could count on being isolated whenever it attempted to retain or create a monopoly position for itself to the total exclusion of Indian interests. Oil is one example;[3] others will be adduced in the next chapter. In the microcosm of the private sector they represent a residue of non-alignment.

[1] Cf., for example, T. T. Krishnamachari's address to the Central Advisory Council of Industries after passage of the Fourth Amendment: 'There are many reasons why compensation would always be reasonable and in no case illusory. For instance . . . to fulfil our plans we shall continue to need foreign investment in several fields. It is only common sense that the foreign investor should feel that in the case of acquisition, reasonable compensation would be available.' (*Hindu*, 23 July 1955.)

[2] At its first annual session after the Himalayan War, the Federation called for 'consistent efforts to attract foreign capital for the country's economic development', and demanded also that 'the preoccupation with taxation as the key to development must give place to a purposive program of financial and fiscal encouragement to private industry' (Resolution on the 'National Emergency and Planning'); at the same time Morarji Vaidya, 'one of the moving spirits in opposition to India's Congress Party', was telling the American Management Association that the Government 'are trying to build a pragmatic, free enterprise system with a well-planned basis for the economy'. (*Hindu*, 11 May 1963.)

[3] 'Burmah-Shell Refineries might find the Government more responsive if they could couple their plans for expansion with an offer to provide for Indian participation in the equity capital of the company.' (*Hindu* leader, 27 June 1961.) 'They jolly well deserve the squeeze'—the phrase is A. D. Shroff's, arch-critic of the Government—seems representative of the views held throughout the Indian business community.

PART III

THE FOREIGN SECTOR TODAY

CHAPTER FIVE
SCOPE AND IMPORTANCE OF FOREIGN INVESTMENT

SINCE Independence the output of official statistics has grown tremendously, yet it remains difficult to map the contours of foreign investments. Questionnaires are often loosely framed and data badly presented. Official series often contradict each other. Mostly, however, the difficulty arises from government policy which normally permits foreign investment 'national treatment' in statistics as well as in law. With few exceptions they are indistinguishable from purely Indian investments; within these exceptions, the most important of which are the Reserve Bank's periodic *Censuses* and *Surveys of India's Foreign Liabilities and Assets*,[1] the identity of individual investors and firms is effectively concealed. As a result, the meagre official diet needs to be supplemented privately, hence inadequately.

I SCOPE

(*a*) *Volume:* Officially there were Rs 580 crores of foreign private business investments in India at the end of 1961.[2] These are long-term investments. They do not include banking capital;[3] capital engaged in construction;[4] or the growing investment in patents and similar claims to royalty payments.[5] They do include funds owned but not controlled from abroad, and private loans.

The computation itself is not free from ambiguities,[6] nor is it adequate to assessing the full weight of foreign investments in the

[1] There have been four to date, relating to 30 June 1948, 31 December 1953, 31 December 1955 and 31 December 1961. A fifth, relating to 31 December 1962, was reported to be in progress in February 1965. The Reserve Bank also published an annual article on foreign investments in their *Bulletin* between 1958 and 1962 inclusive.

[2] Excluding official funds invested in the private sector. RBI, *Survey 1961*, Statement 13, pp. 80–82.

[3] i.e., foreign liabilities of the banking system—Rs 58 crores on 31 December 1961 (ibid., Statement 29, p. 100).

[4] Work done, contracts obtained, and work outstanding by British companies in India, Pakistan, and Burma (mainly India) in the twelve months ending 31 March 1959 totalled £11·4 million, £6·3 million, and £9·8 million respectively (Treasury *Bulletin for Industry* No. 125, December 1959).

[5] See below, pp. 268 ff, 308.

[6] See Mazumdar, *Business Saving in India*, pp. 64–66.

economy. To do this one would need to measure the value of total assets employed by foreign-controlled companies. One such estimate for 1953 showed total *foreign-controlled assets* as something more than twice the Reserve Bank's figure for *foreign investments*.[1] Since then, official data have become less detailed and preclude a fully-independent estimate; but if some of the crucial economic relationships can be assumed to have remained relatively stable in the intervening seven years,[2] total written-down foreign-controlled assets in 1961 might be something over Rs 1,400 crores.[3]

Crude though it be, this figure indicates that foreign-controlled assets formed slightly more than two-fifths perhaps of the total in the organized or large-scale private sector at the end of 1961,[4] or one-quarter of the modern sector as a whole.[5]

(*b*) *Distribution:* Foreign investments are concentrated in a small number of industries. Together tea, petroleum, and manufacturing account for more than three-quarters of the total. Within manu-

[1] Includes banking investments (Mazumdar, op. cit., pp. 64–71). A later estimate for the same year gives foreign-controlled assets at just about double foreign-owned investment (Bettelheim, *L'Inde indépendante*, pp. 91, 118).

[2] The most important are those between net worth and total assets; and between total assets as defined by the Reserve Bank and as defined more generally (see Mazumdar, op. cit., pp. 64–66).

[3] Mazumdar (loc. cit.) found the Reserve Bank's figure for investment in foreign branches undervalued by a factor of 36/232. Assuming no change here and substituting the Bank's 1961 figures for investment in branches and foreign-controlled equity (*Survey 1961*, Statement 13, p. 80), the corrected figure for the foreign investment stake at the end of the year would be 272 + (36 × 272)/232+257 or Rs 571 crores.

From a Reserve Bank sample of 207 foreign branches and 117 controlled rupee companies accounting for some two-thirds of foreign investment, it appears that net worth as a proportion of total assets (net of depreciation) was 343/654 or 52·5 per cent at the end of 1959 (from 'Finances of Branches of Foreign Companies and Foreign Controlled Rupee Companies in 1957 to 1959', RBI *Bulletin*, March 1962, Table 1, p. 346; the ratio remained constant in 1960 and 1961—from articles of that name in RBI *Bulletin*, January 1963, pp. 31–46, and March 1964, pp. 268–80). This factor needs correcting since the foreign proportion of 'paid up capital plus reserves' in the Bank's 117 controlled rupee companies might be anything between 40 (or below under certain circumstances) and 100 per cent. Assuming the 1955 average of 57 per cent (RBI *Survey 1955*, p. 15), the factor would be 263/654 or 40·2 per cent.

Net foreign-controlled assets at the end of 1960 would be then of the order of Rs 1,420 crores.

[4] I have followed Mazumdar, pp. 72–73, as further elucidated in correspondence, using later data.

[5] From 'Estimates of Tangible Wealth in India', RBI *Bulletin*, January 1963, Table 2, p. 10. The proportions given in the text indicate rough orders of magnitude only, and cannot pretend to accuracy.

facturing, chemicals and drugs, cigarettes and tobacco, textiles (mainly jute), and electrical goods account for over half the investment. The distribution is very different from that of private capital as a whole and accounts to some extent for foreign capital's commanding position in a number of industries:

TABLE 4

India: Distribution of Foreign Business Investment from Private Sources by Industry, 31 December 1961, roughly compared with the Distribution of Paid-up Capital of Joint-Stock Companies at Work in the Private Sector, 1958–9

	Foreign Capital Investment % (Rs crores)		Private Sector %	
Plantations (mostly tea)	103·8	17·9		
Mining	12·4	2·1	2·9	Agricultural and allied activities
Petroleum (processing and trading)	148·6	25·6	4·1	Mining and quarrying
Manufacturing	219·4	37·8	1·5	Manufacture of petroleum products
			65·3	Processing and manufacture
Food, beverages, etc.	36·1	16·0	2·0	Tobacco
Textile products	20·7	9·4	20·8	Textiles
Transport equipment	13·0	5·9		
Machinery and Machine Tools	11·4	5·2		
Metals and Metal Products	32·1	14·6		
Electrical Goods and Machinery	14·7	6·7		
Chemicals and allied products	50·5	23·0		
			9·0	Chemicals and allied products
Others	40·9	18·6	68·2	Others
Trading	29·3	5·1	7·4	
Construction, Utilities, Transport	41·3	7·1	6·8	+Communications and Storage
Financial (excluding Banks)	6·3	1·1	10·4	Finance, property, Insurance, Banking, etc.
Miscellaneous	9·3	3·3	1·6	Miscellaneous
Total	580·4	100·0	100·0	

Sources: RBI *Survey 1961*, Statement 13, pp. 80–82. Central Statistical Organization, *Statistical Abstract 1961*, Table 54, pp. 154–9.

Notes: Percentages do not add up to 100 due to rounding. The private sector totals include a substantial amount of foreign-controlled investments. The table shows a distribution of foreign *investments* and of *paid-up capital* of Indian joint-stock companies in the private sector which are not easily comparable.

A more detailed breakdown of foreign investments as on 31 December 1961 adds the following:

	Rs crores	per cent
Within manufacturing:		
Cigarettes and tobacco	24·3	13·2
Medicines and pharmaceuticals	17·0	9·2
Building and building materials	6·8	3·7
Rubber goods	12·2	6·6
Total (including others)	184·3	100·0
Other than manufacturing:		
Managing Agencies	23·3	4·1
Total business investment (including others)	566·3	100·0

Source: 'Foreign Investments . . . 1960', RBI *Bulletin*, October 1962, Statement II, p. 1540.

(*c*) *Foreign-dominated industries:*[1] In *agriculture*, foreign interests are concentrated almost entirely in *plantation products*, of which *tea* is the most important. In the mid-fifties, 80 per cent of the acreage under tea was foreign (British)-controlled, the bulk of this in North India.[2] In the seven years 1955–61, slightly under one-tenth of the foreign-controlled area in North India changed hands, presumably into Indian ownership,[3] leaving some seven-tenths of the total acreage under foreign control in the early sixties. Foreign firms dominated

[1] There are three major difficulties in drawing the contours of foreign control over Indian industries. One lies in the nature of official published data and, in particular, the complete absence of central statistics relating to individual firms: the degree to which ownership is held abroad; output; capital or labour employed; the relevance of capacity ratings to performance; and so on. The second is the rapidity with which the industrial scene is changing. The third lies in the nature of control and influence: to take a 40 per cent share in the equity of a firm as the threshold of control, as is done here in conformity with Reserve Bank practice (see below, p. 274), is arbitrary enough. It becomes intolerably rigid when a firm has large 'non-controlling' interests in complementary units in an industry—as is the case with Parsons and Whittemore, the paper group, for example; or when a controlling interest in one part of an industry is coupled with consultancy interests elsewhere—as is the case with AEI or Phillips; or when the holder of a minority interest is an industrial giant, very much larger than its majority partners—as happens again and again in India.

Nevertheless, while admitting to the crudity inherent in such an attempt, it is still possible to discern the large features of the landscape.

The sequence of industries adopted here is, with minor exceptions, that of the International Industrial Classification recommended by the United Nations.

Except in a few instances, shifts in control are not traced beyond 1962.

[2] From *Report of the Plantation Enquiry Commission*, Part I, Tables VII, VIII, pp. 17–18, 22.

[3] From information supplied by J. L. Llewellyn, Deputy Chairman, Indian Tea Association.

the industry to an even greater extent than might appear from these figures: in the mid-fifties, thirteen leading British managing agencies controlled three-quarters of North Indian tea production, seven of them more than half, and five of them no less than 36 per cent.[1] All processing factories were foreign-controlled as late as 1960.[2] Two British firms—Lipton (a Unilever concern) and Brooke Bond (Finlay)—handled 85 per cent of retail distribution within India;[3] and the export trade remains very much a British monopoly.[4]

The foreign stake in other plantation industries is less overwhelming but still considerable. In 1953 one-third of the acreage under *coffee* and three-fifths of the area under *rubber* were foreign-controlled.[5]

Amongst the ancillary industries, *tea machinery* manufacture is foreign-controlled. The major producer, licensed to cover almost the entire range of equipment, is Davidson of India (Private) Ltd., subsidiary of the Belfast firm. Of the four others producing items of specialized machinery only one is Indian.[6]

General *agricultural machinery* is as much a foreign preserve. Of four firms licensed to achieve the Third Plan target of 10,000 *tractors*, the only one to have actually started production by mid-1962 is Tractors and Farm Equipment Ltd., Madras, controlled by the Massey-Fergusson organization. Originally licensed for 3,500 per year, it planned to produce double that number with two-shift working.[7] The tractor manufacturers are joined by Marshall and Sons (India) Ltd., apparently foreign-controlled, in the manufacture

[1] *Report*, p. 23. [2] *Capital*, 8 September 1960, p. 355.
[3] *Report of the Plantation Enquiry Commission*, p. 24. Names supplied privately.
[4] See above, p. 43; 'External Transactions of Foreign-Controlled Companies—1958', RBI *Bulletin*, January 1960, Table II, p. 14.
[5] From *Report*, op. cit., Part II, Table XII, p. 13; Part III, Table IX, p. 9.
[6] The four other licensees are Britannia Engineering Co. Ltd., Titaghur; British India Electrical Construction Co. Ltd., Calcutta; Port Engineering Co. Ltd., Calcutta; and Steelworthy Ltd., Assam (*Capital*, 19 February 1959, p. 238). Of these the first is now Indian-controlled.
[7] *Capital*, 6 April 1961, p. 539; 28 September 1961, p. 480. Tractors and Farm Equipment started out as Amalgamations (Private) Ltd. Of the other three, Goodearth Co. Ltd., New Delhi, is foreign-controlled, and licensed for 2,000; Tractors and Bulldozers (Private) Ltd., Bombay, Indian-controlled, licensed for 1,000; and Mahindra and Mahindra, Indian, licensed for 3,500 (ibid., 6 April 1961, p. 539). Mahindra might have lost control of a proposed joint venture to the International Harvester Co., Chicago (*Capital*, 3 May 1962, p. 752), the company having previously negotiated unsuccessfully with David Brown Corporation (*Capital*, 22 October 1959, p. 535) and a Czech firm (*Capital*, 29 June 1961, p. 1019).

of *tractor-drawn agricultural implements*; and one firm, the Danish-controlled East Asiatic Co. (India) Private Ltd., has been licensed to produce 24,000 tillers out of the planned total of 26,400–31,200.[1]

Although the importance of foreign capital in *mining* has declined, it is still considerable. In *coal*, the largest producers in the private sector are still controlled by British managing agencies: Andrew Yule, Macneill and Barry, Jardine Henderson, and Bird.[2] Amongst other mining activities, the Indian Copper Corporation Ltd., British-controlled, is at present the sole producer of virgin *copper*, and owns the only copper smelter.[3] On present plans, it will share production equally with the National Mineral Development Corporation by the second half of the sixties.[4] *Lead* production is the monopoly of the Metal Corporation of India Private Ltd., whose mines and ore-dressing plant at Zawar, Rajasthan, and smelter at Tundoo, Bihar, meet something over one-quarter of estimated demand.[5] Financial control over the company is divided equally between the substantial Rio Tinto International Metal Co. Ltd., and Indian Steel and Wire Products Ltd., a domestic concern;[6] but technical control rests with the foreign partner and its associates, Krebs and Pennoria of France.[7] The Metal Corporation is also the sole producer of *zinc* at present, although the Consolidated Mining and Smelting Co., of Canada have announced plans to set up a 20,000-ton capacity smelter and sulphuric acid by-products plant in Kerala by 1965–6. The proposed company, Conminco Binani Zinc, will be Canadian controlled.[8] Of the two aluminium producers active in 1961, the foreign-controlled Indian Aluminium Co., Ltd., is a major producer of *bauxite* ore, the industry's basic raw material.[9] Amongst *quarrying* industries, *silliminite*, an important refractory, is produced solely by Assam Silliminite Ltd., formerly a subsidiary of the British firm, Pilkington Bros. Ltd.,[10] but now probably Indian-controlled.[11]

Mining machinery became a primarily state-run industry with the inauguration of a plant for coal machinery at Durgapur in the

---

[1] *Capital*, 29 June 1961, p. 1019.
[2] Venkatasubbiah, *Indian Economy Since Independence*, p. 154.
[3] PC, *Third Plan*, p. 470.   [4] Sreelekha Basu in *EW*, 19 January 1963, p. 89.
[5] *Capital*, 12 February 1959, p. 196.
[6] *Hindu*, 5 May 1959; *Capital*, 14 May 1959, p. 659.
[7] *Hindu*, 17 October 1960.
[8] *Capital*, 27 September 1962, p. 480; *EW*, 25 May 1963, p. 837.
[9] S. Kannapan and E. W. Burgess, *Aluminium Limited in India*, p. 32.
[10] *Capital*, 28 August 1952, p. 279.   [11] Information supplied privately.

autumn of 1963. What remains for the private sector appears to be pre-empted for foreign-controlled firms: A-V-B Ltd., the giant engineering firm controlled by Vickers and Babcock & Wilcox has been licensed to 'produce a fair amount';[1] McNally-Bird Engineering Co., Private Ltd., an American subsidiary, is to set up a plant for making complete coal washeries at Kumardhubi, Bihar;[2] and Cobmin Ltd., a British firm, is to set up in conjunction with Meameco Ltd., at Dhanbad, Bihar.[3]

Except for Burmah Oil through its half share in Oil India Ltd., private foreign companies are no longer active in *prospecting* and in the *production* of crude oil, the Government having taken up most of the new areas.[4] They are in a stronger position in supplementing local production with imports. Current *imports of crude* are entirely on their account and the import of products is overwhelmingly theirs.[5] Whether their dominant position in this sphere will remain, is an open question. On the one hand, plans for refineries in the public sector, particularly in the case of the Cochin Refinery, rest to some extent on importing crude independently of the established companies;[6] and the Government has already made arrangements for buying 2·5 million tons of products from Russia, to be handled at the rate of one million tons a year by 1964.[7] On the other hand,

---

[1] *Capital*, 19 February 1959, p. 238.   [2] *Capital*, 13 July 1961, p. 43.
[3] *Capital*, 13 July 1961, pp. 55–56.

[4] *Prospecting:* Oil India, a joint venture with the Government of India since 1961, has a concession in the Nahorkatiya-Hugrijan-Moran area of Assam and an as yet unexplored concession area of 1,886 square miles in north-eastern Upper Assam. Other than that, all exploration work is being undertaken by the Government's Oil and Natural Gas Commission, normally with foreign technicians and equipment: in Assam, with Russian help, where promising strikes have been made at Rudrasagar, near Silsagar; in Gujerat, with Russian and Rumanian help, where three fields have been struck, at Cambay (September 1958), Ankleshwar (May 1960), and Kalol (June 1961), and where exploration is continuing; in the Jawalamukhi area, north-east Punjab, with Russian help, where a promising gas find was reported in June 1958; in the Jaisalmer area, Rajasthan, with French Government help; in the Cauvery Basin, Madras, with Russian help; and in the Gangetic basin with Italian (ENI) help. Negotiations for Yugoslav help in prospecting the promising area along the Himalayan foothills between Jammu and Uttar Pradesh have also been reported.

Production: The Government is the sole producer of Indian crude, either in conjunction with Burmah Oil in Oil India (three-quarters of a million tons in 1962) or through the Oil and Natural Gas Commission (half a million). Current plans (June 1963) provide for 3–3·5 million tons from Oil India by 1966, another 0·75 million tons from the Commission's operations in Assam, and 3 million tons from Gujerat.

[5] See Table 5, p. 194, below.   [6] See above, p. 174.
[7] *PPS*, August 1960, p. 297; December 1960, pp. 460–1; above, p. 171.

pressure from the companies to allow increases in refining through-put and, by implication, their import of crude, mounts with every upward revision of future demand estimates,[1] every worsening in the foreign exchange position, and every concession made to the private sector. In all probability, the foreign-controlled share of imports will decline as a proportion of the total while increasing absolutely over the coming decade.

The same might be said of *oil refining*. Until January 1962 when the first state-owned refinery came on stream at Gauhati, Assam, the industry was shared by four foreign plants: Assam Oil's fifty-year-old refinery at Digboi, Assam, Burmah-Shell's and Esso-Standard's in Bombay, and Caltex's at Vizakhapatnam. Officially, more than half a greatly-expanded refining capacity is to be in the public sector by 1966;[2] unofficially, this is recognized as improbable: so bad has been the public sector's record of performance to date,[3] and so good the companies' tally of lobbying successes, that many of the plans are likely to follow K. D. Malaviya, their official author. As it is, the Planning Commission has recommended a substantial increase in private refining capacity (May 1962).[4] Whether or not the permission matches the companies' wishes—a near-doubling of current, ex-panded capacity to 14·9 million tons—it is likely to confirm their control of over half indigenous output for many years to come. At the same time, their full monopoly will have been breached by the growing public sector.

It is in *oil distribution* that the foreign companies are most strongly entrenched. Until June 1959 when the state-owned Indian Oil Co., was registered, the field was exclusively theirs.[5] They have been forced to give ground since, although very little by any standard. By the end

---

[1] As estimated in the *Draft Third Plan*, demand for petroleum products in 1965–6 would be under 10 million tons (PC, *Third Plan*, p. 483). By mid-1963, the Planning Commission was estimating demand at 17·69 million tons in 1966, rising to 30·35 million by 1971 (*FT*, 22 May 1963). See above, p. 173.

[2] *Public sector*: Gauhati, Assam—1·25 million tons; Barauni, Bihar—3 million; Koyali, Gujerat—3 million; Cochin, Kerala—2·5 million. Total public sector: 9·75 million tons. *Private sector* (see above, p. 174): Burmah-Shell—3·75 million; Esso-Standard—2·75; Caltex—1·25 million; Assam Oil—0·5 million. Total private sector: 7·75 million tons (sources as in Table 5 below, p. 194).

[3] See above, pp. 146–7.   [4] See above, p. 174.

[5] Burmah-Shell alone reported seven main ocean installations, 553 upcountry storage depots, over 3,000 retail petrol outlets, nearly 6,000 agencies and dealer-ships, besides another 1,300 agencies and about 40,000 dealerships exclusively for kerosene. (*Background to Burmah-Shell* [1955], pp. 21–22; *Burmah-Shell, Sur-vey of Activities 1956*, 1957, p. 5).

of 1962, Indian Oil had accomplished little beyond supplying relatively small quantities to some Government agencies and the armed forces. Port storage facilities—at Bombay, Cochin, and Vizakhapatnam—were so inadequate as to interrupt shipments;[1] inland depots were even more exiguous; and only one public sector service station had been opened. Some public authorities have been reluctant to change over to state supplies,[2] and while plans exist to utilize rural co-operatives as outlets on the lines of the Egyptian Oil Co-operative Society, and the Planning Commission has been asked to treble the allocation for oil distribution to this end, the state of the co-operative movement and the organizational effort required[3] give rise to serious doubts as to their feasibility.

Developments in the oil industry as a whole are summarized in the table on page 194:

It shows an industry still largely controlled by foreign capital, but in which the state is applying increasing pressure. Whether this pressure will result in Indian control within the time-span assumed in public is open to doubt, particularly in view of the recent developments outlined elsewhere.[4] None the less, further progress in that direction is likely as current, irreversible plans mature.

The first public intimation of plans for a *petrochemicals* industry came at one of Malaviya's press conferences in July 1961. While a number of negotiations were reported immediately afterwards—with the Italian ENI, with Esso-Standard, and Phillips Petroleum—they remained in abeyance until the Kane and Henny Committees reported early in 1963. If experience abroad is anything to go on, it is likely to be a fast growing industry; and if a third Report (summer 1964), of the Planning Commission's working group on the industry, is to set the pattern of development, it is likely to be overwhelmingly a private-sector industry, controlled from abroad, particularly at the

---

[1] See above, p. 172. Indian Oil's two main installations at Bombay and Cochin had capacities for 12,000 and 6,000 long tons respectively at the end of 1960 (*Damle Report*, p. 12). The lease for the third, naval installation at Vizakhapatnam, was made over from Burmah-Shell to Indian Oil in March 1961. (Malaviya in the Lok Sabha, *Hindu*, 24 March 1961.)

[2] See above, p. 172.

[3] Referring to the 3 million tons of products which Indian Oil was expected to handle in 1964, the Damle Committee reported: 'This will entail building up of an organization comparable to that built by Burmah-Shell during the last several years.' (p. 53.)

[4] The industry's estimates for 1966 appear the more realistic. See above, pp. 173 f.

14

TABLE 5

Indianization of the Oil Industry: approximate achievements and plans, 1951–1966
(metric tons to the nearest 0·1 million)

	1951	1956	1961	1966 Est.	1966 Plan
Consumption of products (excl. bunkers)	**4·0**	**4·8**	**7·9**	**17·5**	**17·7**[a]
Indigenous production of crude	0·3	0·4	0·4	5·0	7·3[b]
Foreign private	0·3	0·4	0·2	1·5	1·8
State	—	—	0·2	3·5	5·5
Imports of crude	—	3·8	5·9	12·0	9·8
Foreign private	—	3·8	5·9	6·3	7·4
State	—	—	—	5·7	2·4
Imports of products	4·0	1·4	2·4	1·9	0·3
Foreign private	4·0	1·4	2·3	1·9	—
State	—	—	0·1	—	0·3
Refining capacity (end of year)	0·3	4·9	6·7	17·5	17·5[c]
Foreign private	0·3	4·9	6·7	7·9	7·8[c]
State	—	—	—	9·6	9·7[c]
Distribution (excl. bunkers)	4·0	4·8	7·9	17·5	17·7
Foreign private	4·0	4·8	7·8	12·2	7·8
State	—	—	0·1	5·3	9·9

Note: Figures for 1951 to 1961 inclusive and the *estimate* for 1966 were made
available (December 1963) through the courtesy of Shell International
Petroleum Co. Ltd.; the *planned* configuration of the industry in 1966
relates to plans existing in the summer of 1963 as they appeared from the
following:
  a. Planning Commission estimate reported *FT*, 22 May 1963.
  b. *Hindu*, 4 June 1963.
  c. Oil Ministry target reported *EW*, 15 December 1962, p. 1903; *FT*,
  4 January, 24 May 1963.

processing end, where Esso-Standard Eastern and Union Carbide
are well set to be the major producers.[1]

By and large, foreign capital is not strongly represented in *food
industries* except where the manufactured content of a product is
relatively high or complex. This is the case in *vanaspati* production
(hydrogenated vegetable oil similar to margarine). It is dominated by
Hindustan Lever Ltd., whose sales in 1959 and 1960 of some 80,000
metric tons formed more than one-quarter of the total.[2] Cadbury Fry

---

[1] Press reports, particularly *PPS*, November 1962, p. 429; *Capital*, 20 December 1962, p. 919; *EE* Annual Number 1964, 27 December 1963, pp. 1344–5; and
EW, 27 June 1964, p. 1043.
[2] *Capital*, 30 March 1961, p. 475.

(India) Private Ltd., and Parry and Co., Ltd., are important in *sweets*, as are Huntley and Palmer Ltd., and the Britannia Biscuit Co., Ltd., in *biscuits*, but no figures are available. *Yeast* production is a monopoly of the Indian Yeast Co., Ltd., a new foreign firm set up in 1962 by Shaw Wallace and Co., Ltd., with the collaboration of the Distillers Co., Ltd.[1] The newer *prepared-foods* industry is, as might be expected, foreign-dominated: the three *milk powder* manufacturers are Hindustan Lever Ltd., Glaxo Laboratories (India) Private Ltd., and Horlicks Ltd.;[2] Horlicks is further licensed to manufacture *butter* and *ghee*, *baby foods*, and *malted foods*; and Nestlés Menton Co., of Switzerland appears to be the sole manufacturer of *sweetened full cream* and *condensed milk*.[3] Amongst *beverages* other than tea and coffee,[4] Coca Cola, Schweppes and some other foreign brands of *soft drinks* seem ubiquitous enough although figures to show their relative importance are not available.

Some 65 per cent of the Indian *cigarette* consumption (1961–2) is supplied by a group controlled, ultimately, by the British American Tobacco Co., Ltd. It includes the Imperial Tobacco Co., of India Ltd., largest Indian producer, and the Vazir Sultan Tobacco Co., Ltd., another major firm. Its interests extend to ancillary fields: in Molins of India Private Ltd., it controls the only *cigarette-making machinery* firm, and, with Wiggins Teape and Co., Ltd., the only *cigarette-paper* firm (Tribeni Tissues Private Ltd.). The group is also well represented, although to a decreasing extent, in the export of leaf tobacco.[5]

Foreign capital is not very important in *cotton textiles*, although it controls a few of the larger units such as the Buckingham and Carnatic, the Finlay, and the Madura Mills. The same holds true generally of *cotton textile machinery manufacture* except that the prevailing pattern is for the major Indian firms to seek foreign technical collaboration and, perhaps, some minority financial participation.[6] Foreign capital is more apparent in *woollen textiles*, the *wool combing* branch of which is dominated by foreign firms: Isaac Holdens (India) Private Ltd., set up in 1959 by Isaac Holdens and Sons Ltd.,

[1] *ET*, 9 February 1962; *Capital*, 15 February 1962, p. 269.
[2] *Capital*, 21 August 1958, p. 257; 9 March 1961, p. 352.
[3] *Capital*, 21 August 1958, p. 257.   [4] See above, p. 189.
[5] Information supplied privately. Bidi (a form of cheap indigenous cigarette) production is wholly Indian.
[6] See, for example, R. L. Rajgarhia, 'Textile Machinery Industry', *Capital Survey of Industry*, Supplement to issue of 24 June 1954, p. 73.

Bradford, the Anglo-Indian Jute Mills Ltd., and Duncan Bros., and now a public company, is capable alone of supplying one-third the total estimated requirement for wooltops.[1] Of the four remaining units in the industry, one—Modella Woollens Ltd., Chandigarh—is very closely tied financially to Robert Jowitt and Sons Ltd., Bradford;[2] another—Dhruva Woollen Mills Ltd., Bombay—is linked to a British firm through a technical collaboration agreement.[3] In the late forties *jute textiles* were still British-controlled;[4] today control has passed to Indian hands, although British interests are still powerful.

Jute mill machinery manufacture, a recent industry, is, however, British-controlled. Of the three firms which together are reputed to supply the entire world demand,[5] James Mackie and Sons is in production through its subsidiary, Lagan Jute Machinery Co., Private Ltd.;[6] Low and Bonar Ltd., is also in production;[7] and the third, Fairbairn Lawson Combe Barbour, is supplying the Textile Machinery Corporation Ltd., the big Birla textile complex, with technical knowhow.[8] Together they constitute the overwhelming bulk of the Indian industry.[9]

While *artificial fibres* are predominantly Indian-controlled, some sections constitute a foreign monopoly—notably the manufacture of 'Terylene' by the Alkali and Chemical Corporation of India Ltd., an ICI subsidiary.

The Bata Shoe Co. Private Ltd., is the largest *footwear* producer in the country, disposing of nearly three-fifths of capacity in the modern sector in 1956.[10] Bata is also so much the largest producer of *boot polish* that smaller firms have found it difficult to survive.[11]

Of the *basic metal* industries, *iron and steel* is very nearly a purely

---

[1] *Capital*, 16 July 1959, p. 75; Supplement to issue of 28 June 1962, p. 65.

[2] *Capital*, 4 January 1962, pp. 4, 16–17.

[3] *Capital*, 8 February 1962, p. 229.   [4] See above, p. 4.

[5] 'The Manufacture of Jute Machinery in India', Supplement to *Capital*, 30 June 1955, p. 35.

[6] *Capital*, 19 February 1959, p. 237.   [7] *Capital*, 2 February 1956, p. 159.

[8] Chairman's Report as printed in *Capital*, 27 September 1956, p. 431.

[9] One Indian firm, Britannia Engineering Co., Ltd., is reported to be manufacturing deffing sliver spinning frames with French and Italian technical collaboration (*Capital*, 19 February 1959, p. 237).

[10] S. R. Mohnot, *Concentration of Economic Power in India*, p. 68. The organized modern sector provided no more than six of the thirteen million pairs of western-type shoes manufactured in that year, and practically none of the 70 million pairs of indigenous-type shoes (ibid.).

[11] *Capital*, 18 June 1959, p. 845.

Indian industry, largely within the public sector, but with foreign technical guidance. *Ferro-manganese*, while predominantly Indian, will have as its largest unit, the only foreign firm, Electro-Mettallurgical Works Ltd., on the maturation of current plans.[1] Until Hindustan Steel's plant at Rourkela started producing *tinplate* in the public sector in 1962, its manufacture was a monopoly of The Tinplate Co. of India (Private) Ltd., a subsidiary of India Trading (Holdings) Private Ltd., itself a subsidiary of Burmah-Oil. The Tinplate Co. is still the only major producer in the private sector, with more than nine-tenths of total capacity.[2] *Tungsten carbide metal* and *cutting edges* are essential to the tool industry. Of the three licensees, with an aggregate capacity of 64 tons a year, two—Sandvik Asia Ltd., Poona, and Saka Industries Ltd., New Delhi—are foreign subsidiaries (of the Swedish Sandviken Steel Co., and the German Krupps group respectively) with a combined projected output of 44 tons a year; and the third, India Hard Metals Private Ltd., New Delhi, a Shri Ram enterprise, is in collaboration with the British Wickman Ltd.[3]

Other *non-ferrous metals* present a consistent picture. Domestic *copper refining*, *lead dressing*, and *zinc smelting* are, as has been shown, foreign monopolies. Although not fully foreign, the vastly more important *aluminium* industry is dominated by one very large foreign subsidiary. With an annual capacity of 15,600 ingot tons in 1961, the Indian Aluminium Co., Ltd., a subsidiary of the US-controlled Aluminium Co., of Canada Ltd.,[4] held some 88 per cent of the total. Indian Aluminium is a fully-integrated firm: it is a major producer of bauxite, the only firm engaged in the highly capital-intensive process of extracting *alumina powder*, the largest *ingot* producer and producer of *aluminium sheets and circles* (85 per cent of total capacity), and the only manufacturer of *extrusions and paste*. Although not engaged in manufacturing *aluminium products* directly, its wholly-owned subsidiary, Jeewanlal (1929) Ltd., is its main manufacturing customer.[5] The industry is in the process of rapid

[1] *Capital*, 17 May 1962, p. 841.

[2] Tariff Commission, *Report on* . . . *Tinplate*, 1958, p. 4. Tata Steel has a one-third interest in the company.

[3] *Capital*, 12 October 1961, p. 560; Shri Ram prospectus 1961.

[4] Three-quarters of Alcan's equity is held in the US (Kannapan and Burgess, *Aluminium Limited in India*, p. xi).

[5] Kannapan and Burgess, op. cit., p. 32; Tariff Board, *Report* . . . *Aluminium*, 1951, pp. 15–17.

expansion. The Third Plan called for a fivefold increase in capacity to 87,000 tons—later almost doubled to 160,000 tons a year[1]—by 1966, when Indian Aluminium, with 31,000 tons will still be the largest producer.[2] The rest of the scheduled capacity was expected to arise from the expansion of the existing Aluminium Corporation of India and from three new Indian-controlled units to be built with the technical and, to some extent, financial participation of foreign firms.[3] At the time, the Government could not foresee the euphoria in the industry which resulted in four firm new proposals being put within the first six months of the Plan,[4] nor the subsequent depression

---

[1] *EW*, 4 May 1963, p. 735.   [2] PC, *Third Plan*, pp. 469–70.

[3] The Aluminium Corporation also has a consultancy agreement with a foreign firm—Aluminium-Industrie *AG*, Zurich (*NZZ*, 13 January 1960).

The three new units referred to but not named in the Plan document are:

    (1) The Hindustan Aluminium Corporation Ltd., Rihand, UP, a 20,000 ton capacity plant owned by Birla (Gwalior) Private Ltd., and with a minority interest (assigned in payment for technical services) held by the Kaiser Aluminium and Chemical Corporation, US, which also handled a loan from the US Export-Import Bank. Building started in March 1960 and the plant began operating in October 1962.

    (2) The Madras Aluminium Co., Ltd., near Salem, Madras, a 10,000 ton capacity plant licensed in May 1960, in which the foreign consultant and minority shareholder (assigned shares for technical services) is Montecatini, Italy, and for which the foreign currency component was raised by a Rs 4 crore, ten-year bond issue in Italy. The Equity breakdown is: Montecatini—Rs 1·2 crores; the Madras State Industrial Investment Corporation—Rs 1·5 crores; the statutory Industrial Finance Corporation—Rs 1·2 crores; and Directors and the public—Rs 2·1 crores.

    (3) A 20,000 ton capacity plant at Koyna, Maharashtra, for which Tendulkar Industries (Private) Ltd., were reported to have been negotiating with the Aluminium Co., US (Tariff Commission, *Report . . . Aluminium*, 1960, p. 5), and then with the West German, state-owned VAW (*Capital*, 30 November 1961, p. 803). Later reports mentioned negotiations with Reynolds, US, which broke down, leaving the entire venture in jeopardy (*ET*, 13 October 1962).

[4] (1) A 25,000 ton smelter in the public sector based on the Korba thermal power station and built with Hungarian credit and collaboration—approved in principle (*Capital*, 12 April 1962, p. 649); and backed by a Rs 8 crore loan in May 1963 (*ET*, 1 June 1963).

    (2) A 33,000 ton smelter (rising to 90,000 tons in ten years) based on Sharavathi power, the Bharat Reynolds Aluminium Corporation Ltd., in which Reynolds International Inc., US, will hold 40 per cent of the equity and the Mysore State and Indian private interests the rest. (*Capital*, 3 August 1961, p. 173; 2 November 1961, p. 643.)

    (3) A 20,000 ingot ton plant at Annapur, MP, built for J. K. Industries by Aluminium-Industrie *AG*, Zurich, as a parallel venture to that group's existing Aluminium Corporation (*Capital*, 3 August 1961, p. 173.)

    (4) An extension to Hindustan Aluminium at Rihand which will bring capacity up to 50,000 tons (*Capital*, 3 August 1961, p. 173).

during which foreign collaborators drew back, and then sat on the negotiations they had begun, and on their industrial licences.[1] On present form, it looks as if the industry will still be foreign-controlled until well into the Fourth Plan.

Licences issued up to the summer of 1962 promise to break Venesta Foils Ltd.'s exclusive hold on the *aluminium foil* industry, but not its dominance: it will have 6,000 odd tons capacity, the foreign giant Indian Aluminium another 2,500 tons, and the two Indian licensees, The General India Society and the Aluminium Corporation of India Ltd., 1,200 and 500 tons respectively.[2]

Foreign capital predominates in the manufacture of some major *metal products*. Acrow India Private Ltd., is the largest firm in the manufacture of *steel framework, scaffolding,* and *construction equipment.*[3] Although large-diameter *steel tubes* are made in the public sector, small tubes are foreign-produced by the Indian Tube Co. (1953) Ltd., (jointly-owned by Stewarts and Lloyds Ltd. and Tata at Jamshedpur), and by Tube Products of India Ltd., a Tube Investments subsidiary at Avadi, Madras. The former has a capacity of 140,000 tons and is the only plant in the country making precision tubes (13,000 tons) and seamless tubes (40,000) tons; the latter has capacity for 5,000 tons.[4] Together they account for over half existing capacity.[5]

Steel ropes, made in small quantities by the Indian firm, National Rolling and Steel Ropes Ltd., might well turn into a foreign-controlled industry when two new units go into production: the Japanese-controlled Hindustan Kokoku Wire Ltd., (6,000 tons capacity) and Usha Martin Black (Wire Ropes) Ltd., an Indian firm with a one-fifth foreign holding (3,600 tons).[6]

Of the 120,000 tons of *cans* produced annually, half are *four-gallon cans* made by the foreign oil companies for their own products and half are *consumer cans*; half of these again are four-gallon bulk-produce cans made indigenously for the 'bazaar trade', and half by

---

[1] See, for example, Lakshmipat Singhania, Chairman, Aluminium Corporation of India Ltd., addressing the company's annual general meeting (*Capital,* 27 September 1962, p. 471).

[2] *Capital,* 24 May 1962, p. 880.   [3] *Capital,* 14 January 1960, p. 43.

[4] *Hindu,* 28 January 1960; *Capital,* 15 March 1956, p. 358; 25 May 1961, p. 808.

[5] 248,700 metric tons (A. W. F. Hamilton, Supplement to *Capital,* 2 July 1963, p. 41).

[6] *Capital* Supplement, 24 June 1954, p. 74; 12 January 1961, p. 47; 1 December 1960, p. 776; 5 January 1961, p. 3. Usha Martin Black is expected to double capacity at some future date.

the Metal Box Co., of India Ltd., a foreign subsidiary which has dominated the industry since 1923.[1] Although there were twenty-three registered producers of *wood screws* and eleven of *machine screws* in 1960, Guest, Keen, Williams Ltd., the British subsidiary, was in command of the industry with over two-fifths of output (on a base of one-fifth capacity) in wood screws and a large, unspecified proportion in machine screws.[2]

The heavier and more expensive items of *transport equipment—ships and boats, railway equipment, aircraft*—are made predominantly in the public sector, normally in conjunction with foreign technical consultants. The private sector, with foreign firms well to the fore, rules at the lighter end. Tube Investments of India Ltd., a British subsidiary, dominates the important *bicycle* industry. Its controlled associates, T.I. Cycles of India Ltd., and Sen-Raleigh Industries of India Ltd., produced some half-million of the 1961 total of 1¼ million; together with Diamond Chain Inc. of Illinois, US, it controls T.I. Diamond Chain Private Ltd., the only *bicycle chain* manufacturer in the country; it produces its own *steel tubes* at its neighbouring factory, Tube Products of India Ltd., its own *saddles*, and a large number of other parts. In T.I. and M. Sales Ltd., it has a far-flung distribution network. Such major *bicycle accessories* as are not manufactured within the T.I. group or under its close control, normally come from other foreign-controlled companies: Dunlop Rubber Co., (India) Ltd., is the major here with a complete monopoly of *cycle rims* and *cycle tyres and tubes*.[3]

Although only Ashok-Leyland Ltd., of the five civilian *motor vehicle* manufacturers is formally under foreign financial control, the industry as a whole is very much dependent on its foreign collaborators: of the four *passenger models* manufactured in the country in 1958, only one had an indigenous content of over half; the others ranged from 30 to 37 per cent. *Commercial vehicles* were in a like state, ranging from 9 to 58 per cent indigenous content and averaging about 37 per cent.[4] By the end of 1961, the position had improved, but in no case was the import content less than one-fifth, and it still ranged up to one-half.[5] In this industry, even a small import content

[1] Information supplied privately, early in 1962.
[2] Tariff Commission, *Report . . . Wood Screws*, 1960, pp. 6–7.
[3] Information supplied privately; also see below, p. 216.
[4] *Capital*, 18 December 1958, p. 839.
[5] K. C. Reddy, Minister of Commerce and Industry, quoted in *ET*, 12 November 1961.

restricts the freedom of local manufacturers; those of the order normal in India reduce it to a shadow.[1] The *motor accessories* industry is more explicitly dominated by foreign firms. *Tyre production*, dealt with below, is an outstanding case.[2] *Motor vehicle batteries* is another, with Associated Battery Makers (Eastern) Ltd., a subsidiary of Chloride Electrical Storage Co., England, supplying the bulk of local output[3] and other foreign (British)-controlled firms, such as Oldham and Son (India) Ltd., also in the picture.[4] The first, and still the largest *fuel injection equipment* firm is the Motor Industries Co., Ltd., Bangalore, a subsidiary of Robert Bosch *G.m.b.H.*, Stuttgart.[5] The manufacture of *electric components* is very much concentrated in the hands of Joseph Lucas Ltd., Birmingham (through Lucas-TVS [Private] Ltd.), Simms Motor and Electronics Corporation, and Robert Bosch *G.m.b.H.*—although to what extent it is difficult to say. In 1959, production of *sparking plugs* was divided between Motor Industries Co., Ltd., Bangalore, and the Indian-controlled Auto Accessories (India) Private Ltd., Bombay.[6] In Wheels India Private Ltd., Dunlop controls the largest single *wheels* producing unit, capable, without further expansion, of supplying one-third of the projected demand at the end of the current Plan, and all truck wheels.[7] Guest, Keen, Williams Ltd., another major producer, holds, together with its British associate, Joseph Sankey and Sons Ltd., a controlling 45 per cent of shares in the third major unit, Sankey Wheels Ltd.[8] With some 38 per cent of the equity in Napco Bevel Gear of India Ltd., the largest single shareholding, Napco Industries Inc. of Minneapolis appear to control the major potential *gears* producer.[9]

---

[1] See below, pp. 292–3.   [2] See below, pp. 215–16 f.

[3] Associated Battery Makers took over Associated Battery Makers (Eastern) Private Ltd., and Chloride and Exide Batteries (Eastern) Private Ltd., (*Capital*, 7 January 1960, p. 3), the latter alone having marketed two-fifths of the quarter million units sold in 1951 with only 16 per cent of capacity. (Tariff Commission, *Report . . . Motor Vehicle Battery Industry*, 1952, Table, p. 17.)

[4] *Capital*, 7 February 1952, p. 183.

[5] Tariff Commission, *Report . . . Sparking Plug Industry*, 1960, p. 5.

[6] *Capital*, 26 May 1960, p. 783.

[7] *Capital*, 22 October 1959, p. 535; 1 December 1960, p. 776; *ET*, 12 November 1961.

[8] *Capital*, 22 October 1959, p. 535; 1 December 1960, p. 776; *EW*, 24 August 1963, pp. 1439–40. A merger of the two firms was being considered at the end of 1961 (K. C. Reddy, Minister of Commerce and Industry, *ET*, 12 November 1961).

[9] *Capital*, 27 September 1962, p. 464.

In *motor cycle* manufacture, Enfield India Ltd., Madras, a British subsidiary, was the sole producer as late as 1960. A licence granted Ideal Jawa India Private Ltd., an Indo-Czech venture in the public sector, promises to break that monopoly, but the British firm will remain in a strong position.[1] Indian firms with Italian and Japanese technical collaboration were first off the mark in *motor scooter* production,[2] but were soon followed by Enfield and T.I. of India Ltd.[3] Foreign command of the mechanized two-wheeler field as a whole is greatly enhanced by the concentration of *motor-cycle-engine* and *scooter-engine* production in a joint venture of Enfield and Villiers Engineering Co., Ltd., Wolverhampton.[4]

Heavy *electrical equipment* is dominated by the public sector plants built and a-building. Lighter equipment, made in the private sector, is dominated by a handful of foreign firms. Of the sixteen private units making *transformers* in 1960, nine with three-fifths the industry's capacity and labour force, and with four-fifths of the allotted licences for expansion, had some degree of foreign participation.[5] At least seven of these were foreign-controlled, some by the giants of the industry in Britain.[6] One—English Electric—is also expected to meet one-fifth of the country's needs for *generating*, *transmission*, and *distributing equipment* from its new plant at Pallavaram, Madras.[7] The *electric cables* industry presents a similar picture: the Government featured largely as a producer before the Second World War, and the private sector, then comprising two firms, was dominated by the foreign one, Indian Cable Co., Ltd., a subsidiary of the British Insulated Callendar Cable Co., Ltd.[8] The

---

[1] *Capital*, 8 December 1960, p. 812.   [2] *Capital*, 8 September 1960, p. 354.
[3] *Capital*, 14 July 1960, p. 42.   [4] *Capital*, 13 July 1961, p. 55.
[5] Tariff Commission, *Report . . . Power and Distribution Transformer Industry*, 1960, pp. 8, 9, 38–41.
[6] The seven are: Associated Electrical Industries (India) Private Ltd.; British India Electric Construction Co., Ltd.; Crompton Parkinson (Works) Private Ltd.; English Electric Co. of India Private Ltd.; General Electric Co. of India Private Ltd.; Greaves Cotton and Crompton Parkinson Private Ltd.; J. Stone and Co., (India) Private Ltd.
Since the Commission reported, and following a recommendation by the Economic Secretaries' Committee that the private sector be permitted to manufacture transformers and switchgear in ranges hitherto reserved for the state, Hackbridge-Hewittic and Easum Private Ltd. has been added to the list of major manufacturers. (*Capital*, 3 August 1961, p. 173; 30 August 1962, p. 310.)
[7] *The Times*, 16, 17 February 1959.
[8] *Capital* Supplement, 27 June 1957, pp. 75–76; Tariff Commission, *Report . . . Base Copper Conductors*, 1957, pp. 7, 8; Appendix III, pp. 62–64.

number of producers has grown since and is continuing to grow, but the basic relationship between the Government, foreign private and domestic private capital remains very much what it was. The largest of the four units producing *power cable* and the sole producer of *co-axial cable* in 1962 was the state-owned Hindustan Cables Ltd., at Rupnarainpur, West Bengal (with technical collaboration of the US-controlled British Standard Telephones and Cables Co., Ltd.); the three others, in the private sector, were the Indian Cable Co., Ltd., a British subsidiary, the Cable Corporation of India, in which West German interests are heavily involved,[1] and the Asian Cable Corporation, an Indian-controlled firm with a technical collaboration agreement with the British Enfield Corporation.[2] A number of other firms engaged in specialized lines have been added to the list in recent years or are preparing to be, all with foreign knowhow and some with foreign equity or loan capital: Henly Cables (India) Ltd., formed in 1959, is a subsidiary of Associated Electrical Industries Ltd., through its product division, W. T. Henly's Telegraph Works Co., Ltd.;[3] Universal Cables Ltd., a Birla concern for *paper-insulated lead-covered cables* has a technical collaboration agreement with British Insulated Callendar Cables;[4] Madras Cables (Private) Ltd., controlled by P. S. N. S. Ambalavana Chettiar and Co., is linked to Krupps through a technical collaboration agreement and a long-term loan;[5] Indian Aluminium Cables Ltd. was set up in the private sector in 1959 with the help of Technoimpex, Hungary;[6] Traco Cable Co., Ltd., Japanese-controlled, is to make *VIR cables* in Kerala;[7] and Omega Insulated Cable Co. of India has an agreement with Antony Gibbs and Sons.[8] Many of the foreign technical collaborators are also heavily involved in the public sector, notably AEI and BICC.

While the Government is the sole producer of *telephone equipment*, its company, Indian Telephone Industries Ltd., Bangalore, is partly owned by the Automatic Telephone and Electric Co., Ltd., of Britain

---

[1] Rs 31·2 lakhs of the Rs 1 crore issued capital is shared between Siemens Schukertwerke *AG* and Felton Guilleaume Charlswerke *AG*; and the rest between D. M. Khatau and Krishnaraj M. D. Thakersey and their associates (*Capital*, 20 February 1958, p. 249).

[2] *Capital*, 12 November 1959, p. 648; 15 February 1962, p. 283.

[3] Source as in p. 239 n. 5, below; *Hindu*, 25 May 1959; *Capital*, 17 September 1959, p. 404.

[4] *Capital*, 2 February 1961, p. 164.   [5] *Capital*, 23 March 1961, p. 434.

[6] *Capital*, 3 December 1959, p. 764.

[7] *Capital*, 2 June 1960, p. 825; 2 February 1961, p. 164.

[8] *Capital*, 2 June 1960, p. 825.

with which it also has a technical collaboration agreement. The manufacture of *teleprinting equipment* will be a foreign monopoly when the Olivetti Co.'s plant starts production.[1]

Although eleven producers are listed in the *electric lamp* industry,[2] it is completely controlled by the international consortium, organized in India since 1938 as the Electric Lamp Manufacturers (India) Private Ltd.[3] This company acts as main supplier to the big firms: Philips India Ltd., subsidiary of one of the consortium members, and Hind Lamps Private Ltd., and Osler Electric Lamp Manufacturing Co., Ltd., controlled collectively by the consortium.[4] In 1952 these firms were reported to be supplying three-quarters of the offtake;[5] five years later the President of the Indian Lamp Factories Association, the domestic manufacturers' body, devoted much of his annual address to the 'very undesirable' contrast between the expanding foreign part of the industry and its stagnating indigenous one.[6] A new ancillary industry is the manufacture of *tungsten and molybdenum wire* for incandescent filament—expected to be a monopoly of N. V. Philips Gloeilampenfabrieken.[7]

State production is increasingly responsible for *electric motors* at the higher ratings, say 200 h.p. and above. The lower end is private with foreign firms well represented. Of the twelve manufacturers listed in 1954, five had foreign connexions; at least three of these, accounting for just under half total capacity, were foreign-controlled;[8] one—Crompton Parkinson—held more than one-quarter —27 per cent—of capacity.[9]

Electric tools production was until recently a monopoly of Ralliwolf Private Ltd., jointly owned by the British firm Wolf Electric Tools (Holdings) Ltd., and Rallis India Ltd., also British-controlled.[10]

---

[1] *Hindu*, 26 February 1960.   [2] *Monthly Statistics*, April 1962.

[3] Member firms include Associated Electrical Industries Ltd., Crompton Parkinson Ltd., General Electric Co., Ltd., and N. V. Philips Gloeilampenfabrieken.

[4] *Capital*, 7 August 1952, p. 175; *ET*, 27 November 1961.

[5] *EE*, 8 August 1952, p. 216.

[6] H. Sinha in *Capital*, 2 May 1957, p. 623; 6 June 1957, p. 792.

[7] P. C. Vink, Managing Director, Philips India Ltd., Supplement to *Capital*, 29 June 1961, p. 81; *ET*, 27 November 1961.

[8] They are: Crompton Parkinson (Works) Private Ltd., Associated Electrical Industries Manufacturing Co., Ltd., and General Electric Co. of India Private Ltd.

[9] Tariff Commission, *Report . . . Electric Motor Industry*, 1955, p. 10.

[10] *Capital*, 15 November 1956, p. 648; 19 March 1959, p. 386.

It was to have been joined, at the end of 1962, by another foreign firm, Portable Electric Tools (India) Ltd.[1]

Electric furnace production is entirely foreign-controlled, the major producer, Associated Electrical Industries Ltd., having recently been joined by Ofu Lynx Private Ltd., a West German-controlled firm,[2] and Wellman Incandescent (India) Ltd., a British subsidiary.[3] The only major manufacturer of *x-ray equipment* is the German-controlled Siemens Engineering and Manufacturing Co. of India Ltd., inaugurated in 1962,[4] although General Electric (through Elpro International Ltd.) and Westinghouse (in collaboration with Escorts Ltd.) are reported to be interested.[5] Many of the largest firms licensed for the production of *compressors and refrigerators* are foreign-controlled;[6] and the Indian ones are invariably buttressed with foreign technical aid and financial participation.[7] There is, however, no basis for distributing total output between foreign and domestic manufacturers.

Radio receiver production has been foreign-controlled since its inception. One company alone—Philips India Ltd.—accounted for 35 per cent of output in 1953.[8] No less than ten British firms are reported in the industry, many of them—Murphy Radio Co., Ltd., Marconiphone Co., Ltd. (an AEI subsidiary), Gramophone Co., Ltd. (an EMI subsidiary), General Electric Co., Ltd.—household names.[9] Philips have started producing a number of hitherto imported *radio components* while its parent firm is collaborating with Bharat Electronics Ltd., the state firm in Bangalore, in the manufacture of the most difficult items—*valves and transistors*.[10] *Dry*

---

[1] *Capital*, 14 December 1961, p. 780.

[2] Information supplied privately; and *Capital*, 24 March 1960, p. 423.

[3] *Capital*, 25 October 1962, p. 597.   [4] *ET*, 9 February 1962.

[5] *EW*, 29 June 1963, p. 1023; 11 May 1963, p. 792. By mid-1964, Escorts were reported, privately, to have started production.

[6] For example, American Refrigerator Co., Private Ltd.; Air Conditioning and Refrigeration Private Ltd.; General Electric Co. of India Ltd.; Lightfoot Refrigeration of India Ltd. (*Capital*, 7 November 1957, p. 617; 19 November 1959, p. 683.)

[7] For example, Kelvinators India Ltd. is connected with the Kelvinator International Corporation, US; Kalinga Industries Ltd., with Electrolux of Sweden; Blue Star Engineering Co., Ltd., with Worthington of the US; Goodhouse Co., Ltd., with Gesellschaft für Linde Eismaschinen *AG*, West Germany; Usha Refrigeration Industries with Westinghouse. (*EW*, 29 June 1963, pp. 1022-3.)

[8] *Capital*, 19 November 1953, p. 666.   [9] *Capital*, 7 November 1957, p. 617.

[10] P. C. Vink, Chairman and Managing Director, *Capital* Supplement, 23 June 1960, p. 51.

batteries are the near-monopoly of the United States subsidiary, Union Carbide India Ltd., to the extent of four-fifths of total output.[1] The company also meets the industry's requirements for *rolled zinc* and *flashlight cases*.[2]

Some branches of *specialized non-electrical industrial machinery* production have been touched on in connexion with the industries they serve. Others will be taken up later.[3] Of the rest, *dairy machinery* is, and promises to remain, foreign-controlled with not one Indian firm among the four expected to be in production by the end of the Third Plan.[4] Now that the only active *printing machinery* maker, Britannia Engineering Co., Ltd., has passed into Indian hands, foreign capital is not directly involved in the industry. Plans for another five firms include one foreign-controlled one—Oriental Electric and Engineering Co., Ltd., Calcutta—and foreign collaboration in the case of at least three others.[5]

Two consortia of three companies each were set up in 1959 to share the manufacture of twelve complete *sugar mills* a year: one, known as Sumaco, comprises the New India Development Corporation Ltd., a Krupps' subsidiary through Buckau R. Wolf *A G*, Binny and Co., (Madras) Ltd., a British-controlled firm collaborating in this venture with Mirrlees Watson and Co. of Glasgow, and KCP Ltd., an Indian firm with French technical collaboration. The other—Walistex—is a purely Indian consortium, each member of which has

---

[1] Tariff Commission, *Report . . . Dry Battery Industry*, 1950, p. 8; *EE*, 27 March 1953, p. 538. The company was known as the National Carbon Co. (India) Ltd., until December 1959. Its most famous brand—'Ever-Ready'.

[2] *Capital*, 8 January 1959, p. 6.

[3] See above for tea machinery (p. 189), mining machinery (p. 191), cigarette-making machinery (p. 195), cotton textile machinery (p. 195), and jute mill machinery (p. 195). See below for chemical plant (p. 213) and paper-making machinery (p. 216), gas-making machinery (p. 217).

[4] APV Engineering Co., Private Ltd., a British firm in Calcutta, already producing a limited range, but undergoing expansion; Vulcan Trading Co., Private Ltd., Pimpri, a subsidiary of the Swedish Match Co., Ltd., (see below, p. 215) in collaboration with Graham Enock Manufacturing Co., Ltd.; Larsen and Toubro Ltd., the largest, in collaboration with Silkeborg Maskinfabrik Ltd. and Wright Hargreaves Engineering Co., Ltd.; and Alfa Laval India (Private) Ltd., Pimpri, with AB Separators of Stockholm. (*Capital*, 19 February 1959, p. 239; 24 December 1959, p. 893.)

[5] Britannia Engineering, Titaghur, with Dowson, Payon and Elliot Ltd., Britain; Printer House (Private) Ltd., New Delhi, with Nederlandsche Shelpersen Fabriek; Sahu Jain Ltd., Bihar, with Hamada Printing Manufacturing Co., Ltd., Japan (*Capital*, 13 September 1962, p. 397).

some form of technical collaboration from abroad.[1] In 1960, another foreign firm, the Triveni Engineering Works Ltd., subsidiary of Booker Brothers, McConnell and Co., Ltd., was permitted to enter the field as well.[2] Finally, *cement-making machinery*: by the end of the Third Plan, capacity to produce six or seven complete 500–600 tons-per-day plants a year is expected to be ready. Of these, four will be produced by the British-controlled A-V-B Ltd., at Durgapur.[3]

In *general machinery*, foreign firms might dominate the production of *industrial boilers* once current plans mature; there being three new foreign units—A-V-B Ltd., Larsen and Toubro Ltd., and Nestler Boiler (Private) Ltd.—as against one old Indian concern—Texmaco, the Birla firm—and a new entrant—Walchandnagar Industries Ltd.[4] *Ball-bearings* production at the end of 1962 was shared by the Birlas' National Engineering Industries Ltd. and the Associated Bearing Co., Ltd., a subsidiary of the Swedish SKF group, sole manufacturer of *tapered bearings*. The foreign weight in the industry was expected to decline with the planned entry of nine new firms before 1966,[5] but would remain at some two-fifths of capacity.[6] Production of *materials handling equipment*, rudimentary at present, promises to develop rapidly with the formation of Tata-Robins-Fraser Ltd., in which Hewitt-Robins Inc. of the United States, and Fraser and Chalmers Engineering Works Ltd. of the British General Electric group, will share 49 per cent of the investment.[7] The largest firm—of five—manufacturing *abrasives* and *grinding wheels* is the foreign-controlled Carborundum Universal Ltd., which supplies (1964) two-fifths of the former and half the latter.[8] *Belt conveyors* production is a near-monopoly of foreign firms, notably Dunlop Rubber Co., (India) Ltd. and Firestone Tyre and Rubber Co. of

---

[1] *Capital*, 15 January 1959, p. 52; 19 February 1959, p. 237; Supplement to 25 June 1959, p. 43.

[2] *Capital* Supplement, 28 June 1962, p. 21.

[3] *Capital* Supplement, 28 June 1962, p. 23.

[4] *Capital*, 19 February 1959, p. 238; 16 July 1959, p. 87; 9 March 1961, p. 352.

[5] Tariff Commission, *Report . . . Ball Bearings Industry*, 1956, p. 5; *Capital*, 20 April 1961, p. 608; 18 January 1962, p. 96; 8 February 1962, p. 228; 23 August 1962, p. 255; 30 August 1963, p. 310; *ET*, 5 January 1962.

[6] From Tariff Commission, *Report . . . Ball Bearings Industry*, 1962, pp. 5, 6–7; International Finance Corporation, *Press Release*, Washington DC, 1 May 1963.

[7] Foreshadowed in Report of the Directors, Tata Iron and Steel Co. Ltd., for the year ending 31 March 1962 (*EW*, 1 December 1962, p. 1860).

[8] Tariff Commission, *Report . . . Abrasives*, 1955, pp. 4–5; information supplied privately.

India Ltd.[1] Although there are about eight firms producing *weighing machines* 'against orders', only Avery of India Co., Private Ltd., a British subsidiary, is of any size. A new Indian firm—Trident Industries Ltd.—with West German technical collaboration and loan capital, formed in mid-1961, might ultimately offer some competition, but not for a few years yet.[2] The dominant *lift* manufacturing firm is the US subsidiary Otis Elevators Co., (India) Private Ltd.[3]

Although initial Swiss proposals for setting up an Indian *watch-making* industry were rejected as too modest,[4] and the industry is being set up largely under Indian control with Japanese, French, and West German technical collaboration, the first unit in the private sector actually to produce watches and one which, on current showing, will ultimately supply one-quarter of total output, is the foreign-controlled Indo-French Time Industries Ltd., Bombay.[5] An important ancillary industry, the making of *synthetic gems*, is a foreign monopoly in the hands of the Indo-Swiss Synthetic Gem Factory near Ootacamund.[6]

In the *office equipment* range, *calculating machines* are the exclusive province of the big international firms—IBM and British Tabulating Machine Co., Ltd. (through its subsidiary Hollerith (India) Private Ltd.)—and *typewriters*, while made by both foreign and domestic firms, are dominated by the former. Surprisingly, foreign firms are important in the manufacture of *fountain pens* and *inks*: two foreign-controlled producers—Pilot Pen Co., (India) Ltd., and Parker Pen Co., (India) Ltd.—accounted for one-fifth of the ink-making capacity shared by the forty-four largest units in 1953, and certainly more than that proportion of output, as twenty-three units were working at under one-quarter of capacity;[7] amongst the other forty-four there were at least two other foreign firms: Stephens Inks (India) Private Ltd., and Waterman Pen Co., Ltd.; there were probably others. Pilot and Parker are, as their names denote, primarily pen-making firms, and as such are important in the Indian industry. No data are available, however.

---

[1] *Capital* Supplement, 25 June 1959, p. 23.
[2] *Capital*, 16 July 1959, p. 87; 27 July 1961, p. 120.
[3] *Capital*, 7 November 1957, p. 617.   [4] *Capital*, 30 April 1959, p. 603.
[5] *Capital*, 1 February 1962, p. 118.   [6] *Hindu*, 21 December 1957.
[7] Tariff Commission, *Report . . . Fountain Pen Ink Industry*, 1953, pp. 10–11. Formally Pilot does not qualify as a foreign-controlled company since only 30 per cent of its equity is held abroad (in Japan). However, since the rest is widely spread, and technical control rests with the foreign collaborator, it may be considered foreign-controlled in practice (see *Joint . . . India*, p. 126).

Except for heavy chemicals, the *chemical and allied industries* are an important and growing sphere for foreign capital. It is a difficult industry to analyse because it is an unusually fast-growing one, because the lines of demarcation between its branches are fluid, and because many of the firms involved—ICI, Du Pont, American Cynamid, the heirs of I. G. Farben—are very large, very diversified, and very secretive. *Fertilizer* production is not the most representative branch since about one-third of the capacity licensed for the end of the Third Plan is reserved for state plants, and most of current production takes place in the public sector. None the less, the one firm actually producing in the private sector in July 1964 was East India Distilleries-Parry Ltd., foreign-controlled; and of the capacity licensed in this sector by that date (including two joint public-private plants) half was on account of foreign-controlled firms, and the rest with foreign technical collaboration.[1] EID-Parry have the 'largest private *fertilizer manufacturing-cum-marketing* organization' in the country;[2] and Utkal Machinery Private Ltd., a West German subsidiary (in which Larsen and Toubro Ltd. has an interest), and Simon Carves Ltd. of Britain are the only large-scale manufacturers of *fertilizer plant*. One, perhaps both, of the schemes licensed for the production of *carbon black* appears to be foreign controlled.[3] *Blasting explosives* are a monopoly of Indian Explosives Ltd., Gomia, Bihar, in which ICI hold 80 per cent of the ordinary capital and the Government the rest. The company is also the main producer of *nitric acid*, *ammonium nitrate*, and *nitroglycerine*, and has been licensed to produce *safety fuses*.[4]

The *dyestuffs* industry has expanded tremendously in recent years, from ten manufacturing units, four of which of 'substantial size' early in the Second Plan,[5] to twenty at its end.[6] The industry was

[1] From J. P. de Sousa, *History of the Chemical Industry in India*, p. 262; PC, *Third Plan*, p. 478; *Capital*, 2 March 1961, p. 327; 11 January 1962, p. 70; 'Progress in Heavy Chemical Industry', Supplement to *Capital*, 2 July 1964, p. 91; Ajoy Gupta, 'Development of Fertiliser Industry', *EW*, 28 September 1963, p. 1645; H. Venkatasubbiah, *Hindu*, 27 August 1963.

[2] de Sousa, p. 261.

[3] Phillips Petroleum of New York is the minority, but apparently deciding partner in Phillips Carbon Black Ltd., a joint venture with Duncan Bros. at Durgapur (13,000 ton capacity); the second project, an 11,000 ton capacity plant in Assam is shared between Cabot Inc. and Kasturbhai Lalbhai, without the proportions being known (de Sousa, p. 247; *Capital*, 8 June 1961, p. 885; 4 October 1962, p. 521; *PPS*, July 1961, p. 262).

[4] *Capital*, 12 November 1953, p. 642; de Sousa, p. 127; ICI handout, p. 4.

[5] *FT*, 26 October 1956.   [6] de Sousa, p. 280.

15

expected to grow beyond the processing of imported primary products as soon as *organic intermediates* became available from the state-owned Basic Chemicals and Intermediates plant at Panvel, Maharashtra. Now that the project has been scrapped, organic intermediates will probably be produced by foreign-controlled firms.[1] In the dyestuffs industry proper, Atic Industries (Private) Ltd., half-owned but controlled by ICI, has been the dominant firm in the industry since its inception in 1956.[2] It claims to be able to supply 'nearly 60 per cent' of India's requirements,[3] or some eight million lb. (of mainly *vat dyes*), out of a total 1960–1 production of 11·5 million lb.[4] It is, however, only one aspect of ICI's activities in the industry. ICI's *dyestuffs sales network* is probably second only to Burmah-Shell's oil distribution system, while at Sewri in Bombay, they have a *packing and mixing* plant capable of handling 450,000 tons of colour a month, in which, in addition, 'auxiliary production amounts to about the same figure, including *weighing agents, cleaning and scouring agents, dyeing and printing agents* and *textile finishing products* for softening, stiffening and waterproofing.'[5]

No other firm can match ICI in scope or scale of operations, (although Montecatini of Italy, with interests already in Amar Dye-Chem Ltd. and Indian Dyestuffs Industries Ltd., and growing interests in explosives, plastics, aluminium, and other fields might be considered a likely outsider). But some are important none the less: the Swiss subsidiary, Sandoz Products Private Ltd., and Suhrid-Geigy Trading Ltd., also foreign-controlled, account for a large proportion of the *optical bleaching agents* produced;[6] Reckitt and Colman of India Ltd., a British subsidiary, produce all the *ultramarine blue* made in the country and will continue with over half licensed capacity when present plans mature.[7] Where foreign finance is unimportant, foreign technical collaboration usually is: Atul Products Ltd., ICI's partner in Atic Industries, and the biggest Indian firm in the field, has a technical agreement with the American Cynamid Co. for some dyestuffs;[8] Farbenfabrik Bayer *AG* has a technical agreement with, and through its 30 per cent share in the equity probably controls, Textile Pigments Ltd., Bombay; Amritlal

[1] See above, p. 164.   [2] *FT*, 26 October 1956.   [3] ICI handout.
[4] de Sousa, op. cit., p. 218; PC, *Third Plan*, Table, p. 506.
[5] ICI handout, p. 5.   [6] de Sousa, op. cit., p. 217.
[7] *Capital*, 10 November 1960, p. 656.   [8] de Sousa, pp. 216–17.

Co., Ltd., is associated with Hilton Davis Co. of the United States; Amar Dye-Chem with a number of Italian firms; and so on.

Drugs and pharmaceuticals present all the complexities of the chemical industry as a whole with the addition of a strong dose of hard political bargaining.[1] The industry is new and growing rapidly: its major branches—antibiotics, sulpha drugs, phytochemicals, anti-tuberculosis drugs—barely existed before the 1950's; output which, in 1948, was valued at some Rs 10–12 crores, had risen to Rs 70–75 crores by 1960–1 (as against a planned Rs 55 crores) and was expected to have reached Rs 175 crores by 1963.[2] It had not struck roots until quite recently: when the Pharmaceutical Enquiry Committee reported, June 1954, production still consisted largely of encapsulating and packing, and very nearly three-fifths of the industry's raw materials bill was spent abroad.[3]

The industry has been dominated by foreign firms from its inception: of the 1,600 registered units in 1954, there were only 93 large ones (including 11 government plants), 28 of which, producing two-fifths the value of finished drugs with one-tenth the labour force, were under foreign control.[4] Among these 28 are the largest firms in the country, starting with Merck, Sharp and Dohme India Private Ltd., of the United States, and including such household names as Johnson and Johnson Ltd., May and Baker Ltd., Boots Pure Drug Co., Ltd., the Glaxo Group, Burroughs Wellcome and Co., Ltd., British Drug Houses Ltd., and Beecham Group Laboratories (India) Ltd. Nor is control from abroad exercised through direct investment alone: patents and the provision of knowhow are more important here than in probably any other industry—and whereas foreigners held over nine-tenths of the patents granted in India up to 1958, almost all patents for essential drugs were theirs.[5] The industry is expanding too fast and plans have already proved too ephemeral for anything but the most general statements to be valid for more than a couple of years. Suffice it that what was conceived as an integrated state-run near-monopoly during the 'swing left' has made way for a mixture of state and private units, the latter almost invariably foreign-controlled. *Antibiotics*, which accounted for more than two-fifths expenditure on drugs during the mid-fifties and which, if the

---

[1] See above, pp. 163 ff.   [2] J. P. de Sousa, op. cit., p. 221.
[3] *Report*, Table 4, p. 21.   [4] ibid.
[5] Justice N. Rajagopala Ayyangar, *Report on the Revision of the Patents Law*, Appendix A, Tables 2 and 5, pp. 303 and 305.

experience of other countries is any guide, might form 70 per cent in the future, is a good illustration. Production in the state sector will be undertaken at Rishikesh, UP, when the Russian credit for it is finally taken up,[1] and at the expanded Hindustan Antibiotics plant at Pimpri.[2] Amongst the major private firms licensed in this sphere are Dumex (Private) Ltd., Chandigarh, controlled by the American Pfizer Corporation, for tetracyclin;[3] Lederle Laboratories (India) Private Ltd., an American Cynamid subsidiary, whose plant for aureomycin, achromycin, Ledermycin, and other antibiotics was opened early in 1962;[4] Parke, Davis and Co., (India) Private Ltd., another US subsidiary, for chloromycetin, and a plant controlled by E. R. Squibb and Sons for tetracyclins.[5] *Synthetic drugs* present a similar picture: the original plan for a state-owned plant of 2,300 tons capacity producing 52 items has been pruned to one of 831–868 tons producing 15–20 items;[6] and private firms have been encouraged to fill the gap. Among them are May and Baker Ltd., a British branch company ultimately controlled from France; Ciba Pharma Private Ltd., a Swiss subsidiary; the Glaxo Group, British; Roche Products Ltd., Swiss; and Sarabhai-Merck Ltd.[7] The same might be said of the other major drugs, as can be seen from Table 6.[8]

TABLE 6

India: Drugs manufacture: Distribution of Licensed Capacity Between State and Private Producers, as at the end of 1962
(metric tons per annum)

	Private		*State*	*Third Plan Target*
Antibiotics	74·6		373·5	322
Synthetics and Vitamins	1,719·8		1,551·0	2,500
Drugs of vegetable origin	49·6		71·4	126
Glandular products (insulin)	1,500	megaunits	—	1,000 megaunits

Source: 'Rapid Progress in Manufacture of Drugs and Pharmaceuticals', Supplement to *Capital*, 20 December 1962, Tables, pp. 155, 157.

[1] Offered originally in 1957, it was still almost unutilized in mid-1963 (*EW* Special Number, July 1963, p. 1282).

[2] See above, p. 163.   [3] *Capital*, 10 March 1960, p. 360.

[4] *ET*, 12 February 1962; Lederle changed its name to Cynamid India Ltd. in the autumn of 1962.

[5] S. S. Sokhey in *EW* Annual Number, February 1962, p. 235.

[6] Lower figures from de Sousa, *History of the Chemical Industry*, p. 227; higher from Sokhey, *Indian Drug Industry*, p. 19.

[7] *ET*, 10 January, 12 February, 8 November 1962. Roche Products started producing at its Rs 2 crore plant in Thana, October 1962 (*Capital*, 15 October 1962, p. 209).

[8] The fact that licensed capacity is consistently larger than planned capacity

Closely related is the manufacture of *insecticides, pesticides,* and *fungicides.* First in the field was ICI's subsidiary, Alkali and Chemical Corporation of India Ltd., at Rishra, West Bengal, with the *benzene hexachloride* range from April 1952.[1] A Government plant, run by Hindustan Insecticides Ltd. at Delhi, followed (March 1955) to make *DDT.* ICI was then (1957–8) joined by Tata Fison Private Ltd., in which the British partner, Fison Ltd., hold half the capital and a technical agreement for the production—in four plants—of BHC and a number of other products. While another state plant—for DDT production—has been set up at Alwaye, Kerala, most of the expansion in the industry is to be undertaken in the private sector: a Japanese-controlled company, Pesticides Ltd., is projected at Thana, near Bombay, for BHC, Malathion, mercury compounds, and other products;[2] and American Cynamid have combined with their associates Atul Products in a Rs 1 crore plant to be run by Cynamid India Ltd., at Bulsar, Gujerat, to produce a wide range, notably Malathion.[3]

Foreign firms dominate the capital-intensive branches of the *plastics* industry and are present as technical advisers and minority investors throughout: 85 per cent of *polyethylene* capacity is shared between ICI's Alkali and Chemical Corporation and a new (1961) Union Carbide plant at Trombay, near Bombay.[4] In other lines, *PF and UF moulding powders, polystyrene, PVC*—foreign capital is more important in a technical capacity: Japanese interests are reported to have no more than one-fifth of the capital (and technical control) in the largest PVC plant yet to be set up;[5] the American Dow Chemical Co. is heavily involved in the Kilachand Devchand plastics enterprises;[6] Montecatini is reported to be preparing massive involvement in the industry.[7] The only *injection moulding machine and mould* makers to have been licensed up to the end of 1962 is Engel India Machines and Tools Ltd., Austrian-controlled.[8] *Fibre glass plastics* will be entirely foreign-controlled when two plants

---

portends an even greater bias towards private production than would appear from the table.

[1] 'Development and Use of Insecticides in India', Supplement to *Capital,* 24 June 1954, p. 54.

[2] The Japanese interests are Kureha Chemical Industry Co., Ltd., and Itoh and Co., Ltd. (*Capital,* 6 October 1960, p. 457).

[3] *Capital,* 15 February 1962, p. 268; *ET,* 26 May 1962.

[4] *Capital,* 22 June 1961, p. 976; 31 May 1962, p. 909.

[5] *Capital,* 3 August 1961, p. 161.   [6] *FT,* 4 January 1961.

[7] *FT,* 25 October 1961.   [8] *Capital,* 27 September 1962, p. 464.

licensed so far start production. Their parent firms are BTR Industries Ltd. and Fibre Glass Ltd., the two major British manufacturers.[1] Industrial *laminates* output is also foreign, with Formica (India) Ltd., Poona, jointly controlled by Formica International Ltd., London, and the foreign-controlled Bombay-Burmah Trading Corporation Ltd., expected to be responsible for more than half total output.[2]

Paint is virtually a foreign province, peopled by giants such as ICI, which makes 'Dulux' and 'Duco' at the Alkali and Chemical Corporation plant at Rishra, and distributes through its 83 paint stockists; Shalimar Paint, Colour and Varnish Ltd., subsidiary of the largest paint manufacturing firm in the world, Pinchin, Johnson and Co., Ltd.; Jensen and Nicholson (India) Ltd., subsidiary of the British firm of that name; British Paints (India) Ltd., another British subsidiary; Goodlass Wall (India) Ltd., yet another; and many others. Production of *titanium dioxide,* essential ingredient for paints and pigments, is in the hands of two foreign firms, Travancore Titanium Products Ltd., and Botanium Ltd.[3]

One foreign company, Hindustan Lever Ltd., has occupied a commanding position in the *soap and detergents* industry for many years. As Lever Bros. (India) Ltd., it was producing nearly one-third total factory output in the period immediately preceding the Second World War.[4] With the end of soap rationing in September 1950 and on the crest of a wave of price-cutting, it engrossed some 70 per cent of the market in the early fifties,[5] with the results that the largest indigenous producers were operating at one-half to one-third of capacity compared with 94 per cent at Lever,[6] and the Swadeshi League was formed.[7] Improving demand since the mid-fifties and a more conciliatory policy on the part of the company have tended to hold back its relative growth, but it still dominates the modern sector, selling in 1960 over 83,000 tons[8] of the 152,000 produced (1960–1).[9]

[1] *Capital,* 8 February 1962, p. 230.

[2] *Capital,* 4 January 1962, p. 6; *EW,* 24 November 1962, p. 1829.

[3] J. P. de Sousa, *History of the Chemical Industry,* p. 243; TC, *Report on . . . Titanium Dioxide,* pp. 4–5.

[4] *EE,* 11 May 1945, pp. 630–1.

[5] S. Ghosh, Presidential address, Indian Soap and Toiletries Makers' Association, annual meeting, cited in *EW,* 6 June 1953, p. 639.

[6] T. T. Krishnamachari, Minister of Commerce and Industry, at Central Advisory Council of Industry (*Capital,* 4 June 1953, p. 751).

[7] See above, p. 108.   [8] *Capital,* 30 March 1961, p. 475.

[9] PC, *Third Plan,* Table, p. 506.

Developments in the *match* industry have been rather similar. Prompted by the imposition of a small protective tariff in 1924, the Swedish Match Co. Ltd. began manufacturing through its two subsidiaries, Western India Match Co. Ltd., and Assam Match Co. Ltd. It became almost co-extensive with the industry, supplying from its eleven factories some 80–85 per cent of offtake in 1945.[1] It provided the necessary chemicals to what remained of the cottage industry[2] and supplied many of them with Swedish wood.[3] Together with Hindustan Lever, it became the paradigm 'imperialist investor' during the fifties; but in this case, primarily because the small-scale cottage industry suffered most from the competition, the Government intervened and made Western India Match restrict its output.[4] As a result, the cottage industry expanded three and a half times between 1949 and 1961, and Swedish Match subsidiaries now contribute under three-fifths of total output.[5] The company is in an even stronger position as a supplier of *potassium chlorate*, the chief chemical ingredient for matches (as well as an important item in the manufacture of fireworks and some explosives), with more than nine-tenths of registered capacity.[6]

In *rubber manufacturing*, Dunlop Rubber alone disposed of more than half (53 per cent) of total capital employed in 1961–2, accounted for two-thirds the turnover and three-quarters of gross profit.[7] While motor vehicle *tyres and tubes* are no longer the foreign monopoly they were when investigated by the Tariff Commission in 1955,[8] foreign dominance remains. On present form, the four foreign-controlled companies now active[9] will be producing three-quarters of total output in 1966—2·6 million pieces out of 3·5 million. If all current licences are ultimately taken up, foreign companies will still be producing just under three-fifths of the total, about one-fifth each

[1] *EE*, 21 June 1946, p. 1050; 30 April 1948, pp. 829–30.
[2] *Capital*, 4 January 1951, p. 2.   [3] *EE*, 30 April 1948, p. 829.
[4] *Capital*, 2 September 1954, p. 319.
[5] *Capital* Supplement, 28 June 1962, p. 50.
[6] J. P. de Sousa, *History of the Chemical Industry*, p. 240.
[7] *ET*, 16 July 1962.

[8] TC, *Report . . . Rubber Tyres and Tubes*, 1955. The Commission was explicit about the monopolistic nature of the industry. 'All the [four] producers have denied the existence of any price ring among themselves, but . . . the industry is so organized that the producers have to act in unison in their own interest. The tyre industry provides a typical instance of an oligopoly which, so far as prices are concerned, functions virtually like a monopoly.' (p. 94.)

[9] Dunlop Rubber Co. (India) Ltd., Firestone Tyre and Rubber Co. of India Ltd., Goodyear Tyre and Rubber Co. (India) Ltd., and Ceat Tyres of India Ltd.

by Dunlop and Firestone.[1] Amongst other rubber industries, Dunlop is the sole producer of *bicycle tyres and tubes*, and together with Firestone dominates the entire field of belt conveyors.[2] Firestone is heavily involved in, and probably controls, the only *synthetic rubber* plant, run by Synthetics and Chemicals Ltd., at Bareilly, UP.[3]

Over one-third of the *paper* output—and most high-quality products—came from British-controlled firms in 1953.[4] Production has gone up more than three times since,[5] and the share of foreign-controlled companies has undoubtedly gone down. But foreign interest has not abated: the giant American paper firm, Parsons and Whittemore Inc., is involved as a minority shareholder in three major new paper and pulp ventures—The Mandya National Paper Mills Ltd., Nagpur (in which the foreign partner has 35 per cent of equity), Seshasayee Paper and Boards Ltd., Madras (19 per cent), and Bilaspur Paper Ltd., Calcutta (20 per cent).[6] Foreign capital is stronger in the specialist paper industry: *security paper* is a monopoly of Portals Ltd. of Britain;[7] *carbon paper* dominated by Caribonum Ltd.[8] It is especially strong in the new *pulp and paper machinery* industry. Present plans indicate that annual capacity for making four or five complete 50-ton-per-day plants will be shared among three foreign-controlled partnerships or consortia: a project started by Tata and Johnson of Sweden (2½ plants), Utkal Machinery Private Ltd., the West German consortium (1 plant), and Bertram, Scott Ltd., a British-controlled syndicate (1 plant).[9] Parsons and Whittemore are also reported to be putting up—through their associate, Black-Clawson Co.—a foundry and machine shop at Ennore, near Madras (and near the Seshasayee mill in which they have an interest).[10]

One-third of the total output of *scientific and laboratory glassware*

[1] K. M. Philip, Former President, India Rubber Industries Association, *ET*, 8 July 1963.
[2] See above, p. 207.
[3] Firestone has taken up one-quarter of the initial issues and has organized the foreign loan financing which accounts for Rs 7·5 crores out of a total Rs 13·5 crores. It also exercises technical control (*Capital*, 8 October 1959, p. 495; 26 May 1960, p. 781).
[4] Eddison, *Industrial Development . . . Pulp and Paper Industry*, Table XIII, p. 225.
[5] PC, *Third Plan*, Table, p. 507.   [6] Source as in n. 5, p. 239, below.
[7] Shelvankar in *Hindu Survey of Indian Industry*, 29 December 1956.
[8] *Capital*, 13 July 1961, p. 55.
[9] *Capital* Supplement, 28 June 1962, p. 25; *Capital*, 31 March 1960, p. 478.
[10] *Capital*, 28 September 1961, p. 481.

is expected to come from the US-controlled Borosil Glass Works Ltd.;[1] *plate glass* is to be a foreign monopoly held by Hindusthan Pilkington Glass Works Ltd.;[2] *glass fibre* is also expected to be undertaken by foreign firms.[3] The major branch of the industry, *sheet glass* manufacture, is also largely foreign: over two-thirds of registered capacity was in the hands of Hindusthan Pilkington and Indo-Asahi Glass Co., Ltd., a Japanese subsidiary, in 1958.[4] Their share of output was probably greater.[5]

Since its registration in 1925, so complete has been Indian Oxygen Ltd.'s monopoly over the manufacture of *industrial gases* that it was bound to run foul of the Government in much the way the oil companies, Hindustan Lever, Western India Match, ICI, and one or two others have done. From 1960 a number of small and medium-size firms have been licensed and at least one major consumer—the Tata Iron and Steel Co., Ltd.—pushed into producing bulk oxygen in an attempt to weaken British Oxygen's giant subsidiary. However, all but one of the newcomers are single-plant firms; none can hope to challenge the foreign one. As the *Economic Weekly* wrote of the industry: 'It is a picture of expansion certainly, and of considerable variety also, but does it not have a little bit of the texture of jet planes and bullock carts?'[6] The ancillary industries present a similar picture: Indian Oxygen is *the* producer of *arc-welding electrodes*;[7] it also looks like becoming the major *gas-making machinery* manu-facturer now that its articles of association have been amended to allow that development.[8]

In general, foreign investment plays a relatively small part in the broad *services* sector; there are a few special fields, however, in which its influence is overwhelming. *Construction*—a natural transition to this sector—is illustrative. Overwhelmingly Indian, it takes on a strong foreign complexion in some of the more specialized aspects of its civil engineering side: for example, the laying of the 720-mile oil pipeline between Nahorkatiya, Assam, and Barauni,

---

[1] *EW*, 18 May 1963, p. 826.
[2] *Capital*, 1 November 1962, p. 641; *EW*, 10 November 1962, p. 1744.
[3] See above, p. 213. [4] *Capital*, 11 September 1958, p. 370.
[5] Production was expected to double during the Third Plan, but not in the foreign-controlled sector: recent licences have been granted Indian-controlled firms collaborating, in three cases out of five, with East European plants. (*Capital*, 23 June 1960, p. 951; 4 August 1960, p. 148; 20 July 1961, p. 80; 30 November 1961, p. 804; TC, *Annual Report 1962–3*, p. 10.)
[6] 13 January 1962, p. 34. [7] Information gained privately.
[8] *Capital*, 30 August 1962, p. 291.

Bihar, is in the hands of Burmah Oil Co. (Pipelines) Ltd., main contractors for whom are Mannesmann of West Germany, and Saipam, of the Italian ENI group;[1] the complex civil engineering items for the Durgapur steel plant were contracted out to British firms; and so on. *Design, development*, and *consultancy* services are even more a foreign preserve. There is only one Indian firm of any size in the field—M. N. Dastur and Co., Ltd., Calcutta—in a country booming with new, non-traditional construction and engineering activities. Until quite recently the same could be said of less technical services such as *advertising*. Now, however, although many of the largest firms are still foreign, Indian firms have challenged them successfully.[2] *Managerial services, managing agencies* in particular, are controlled by foreign interests to a considerable extent, but foreign influence is declining.[3] There is one crucial complex of services over which foreign capital still exerts an overwhelming—albeit slowly declining—influence: *foreign trade, exchange banking*, and *shipping*. T. T. Krishnamachari, then Minister of Commerce, explained to a meeting of the Export and Import Advisory Councils:

Foreign trade has developed in a particular way. . . . export trade in the past has been more or less the monopoly of foreign companies. All these foreign companies have had some relationship with the shipping companies, their travel agents or some other people. They were agents for foreign insurance companies, marine insurance companies, etc.[4]

Not long beforehand, a Reserve Bank study had shown that about two-fifths of India's *international trade* was handled by foreign firms and nearly three-quarters of *foreign trade financing* by foreign banks.[5] At about the same time, *shipping* was to all intents and purposes a foreign industry, dominated by Peninsular and Orient's gigantic subsidiary, British-India Steam Navigation Co., Ltd., the world's largest passenger carrier. *Overseas trades* to other continents was carried in foreign bottoms to the extent of 95 per cent of the total; the *adjacent* and *coastal trades* to the extent of three-fifths and two-fifths respectively.[6]

---

[1] *PPS*, February 1961, pp. 68–69.   [2] Information gained privately.
[3] See above, pp. 5–11, for a detailed discussion of the foreign managing agencies.
[4] Quoted in *Capital*, 2 June 1955, p. 815.
[5] See above, p. 4.
[6] The figures for overseas and adjacent trades relate to 1955 (PC, *Second Plan*, p. 481); for coastal trade, to 1949 (K. C. Neogy, Minister of Commerce, to the Lok Sabha, cited in *Capital*, 16 February 1950, p. 271.)

Indian interests have made inroads since the early fifties; but not as deeply as might have been expected. A later study by the Reserve Bank shows that 29 per cent on average of private exports and imports were put through foreign companies in the three years from 1956–8.[1] In shipping, plans to further Indian interests have made even less headway. While the Government resolved as early as July 1947 to assist the indigenous industry to reach two million gross registered tons within five to seven years, giving it control of the entire coastal trade, three-quarters of the adjacent trades, half the long-distance overseas trades, and a third of the trades 'formerly carried in Axis vessels in the Orient',[2] total tonnage at the end of the Second Plan in 1961 was under 900,000, and was then expected to do no more than top the one million mark by the end of the Third Plan.[3] More important in the present context is the distribution of the different trades between foreign and domestic lines: coastal shipping—reserved by law for Indian shipping from 1950—was still two-fifths foreign as late as 1957–8,[4] despite the 'full enforcement' of coastal reservation from 15 August 1951 and despite repeated official assurances that this was so. In fact very nearly that proportion of traffic was automatically excluded from the coastal reservation by the Refinery Agreements which allowed the oil companies to carry products in tankers of their choice.[5] Although there were four Indian tankers by March 1963—two in the private and two in the public sector—the situation had not altered appreciably. Equally, Indian participation in the adjacent trades has fallen short of target: instead of the 75 per cent envisaged for 1954 at the latest, the Second Plan started in April 1956 with no more than 40 per cent carried in Indian

[1] 'External Transactions of Foreign-Controlled Companies in India—1958', RBI *Bulletin*, January 1960, Tables II and III, pp. 14 and 15. These figures are not fully comparable with those given on p. 43 above, since they relate to 'merchandise and service transactions of all kinds . . . involving transfers of foreign exchange to and from the country' and not trading transactions only as in the previous case.

[2] Resolution dated 12 July 1947 quoted by M. A. Master, 'Shipping Policy—Its Evolution and Progress', *Commerce* Annual 1960, p. 3 of the offprint.

[3] PC, *Third Plan*, pp. 556, 557; M. A. Master, 'Seven Wrongs Against Shipping', *Swarajya* Special Number 1962, p. 213; *Capital*, 6 July 1961, p. 19. But see below, pp. 220 f., for new developments.

[4] Jaya Chamaraja Wadiyar, Governor of Mysore, 'Indian Shipping Under the Five Year Plans', *EE*, 4 November 1960, pp. 828–9. The percentage is based on figures for traffic through Bombay and Calcutta which together handle more than three-quarters of total coastal cargo.

[5] See above, p. 90 n. 4. At the time, oil products accounted for more than 1·5 million tons out of a total of 4 million.

bottoms, and a scaled-down target of 50 per cent.[1] But it is in the overseas trades that Indian performance has lagged most: the 50 per cent target gave way early on to a modest 12–15 per cent to be achieved by 1961.[2] Actual attainment was no more than 9 per cent.[3] With this dismal record, it is not surprising that the Government ceased publishing targets for the Indianization of shipping, or that the Third Plan document deals with tonnages and not percentages,[4] or indeed that by the end of the Second Plan, Indian shipping experts were expressing doubts about the feasibility of retaining even 9 per cent of overseas trades for Indian shipping during the Third Plan.[5]

Recent developments have run counter to this view. First, as a result of the latter-day spirit of compromise within the ruling Conferences which, in turn, reflects the growth of state-supported fleets outside the Conference system, Indian shipping has found it easier to gain a larger share of some of the more important overseas trades: by virtue of an agreement reached late in 1962, the three Indian members of the India/United Kingdom/Continent Conference—Scindia Steam Navigation Co., Ltd., and India Steamship Co., Ltd., in the private sector, and the state Shipping Corporation of India—will be permitted to increase their share of the trade from 30·5 per cent to 48 per cent in 1971.[6] Second, after a long period during which shipping was pretty well ignored, the Government came round to helping the industry: besides the normal financial help in the form of loans and subsidies through the Shipping Development Fund, tax concessions and suchlike, it has, since 1958, concluded bilateral shipping agreements which reserve half the growing trade with Russia, Poland, East Germany, Rumania, Egypt, the Levant, and some other areas, to Indian ships. It has also developed, in the Shipping Corporation of India,[7] a powerful

---

[1] PC, *Second Plan*, p. 481.   [2] ibid.

[3] M. A. Master in *Swarajya* Special Number 1962, p. 213.

[4] 'The [National Shipping] Board, we understand, hold the view that no attempt should be made to lay down some specific target for eventual attainment.' (M. A. Master, in *Transport*, March 1960, offprint, p. 3.)

[5] See, for example, M. A. Master in *Swarajya*, loc. cit.; *Transport*, October 1959, offprint, p. 3.

[6] Sir Ramaswami Mudaliar, Chairman, Indian Steamship Co., Ltd., to the annual general meeting, *EW*, 29 September 1962, p. 1552; M. A. Master, 'Indian Shipping Crosses Million-ton Mark', *ET*, 31 December 1962.

[7] Formed 2 October 1961 out of a merger between the Eastern Shipping Corporation and the Western Shipping Corporation, founded in 1950 and 1956 respectively, the former as a mixed state-private enterprise.

merchant fleet that has grown from 42,000 gross registered tons in 1956 (under one-twelfth the total)[1] to 228,000 gross registered tons in April 1963 (or one-fourth), and a possible 273,000 gross registered tons by the end of 1963 or 1964 if outstanding contracts are honoured;[2] and one that led the assault on the Conferences.[3]

The growth of state tonnage stopped suddenly after the Himalayan War, making way for the third, major recent development—the Jayanti Shipping Co., Ltd. Registered in 1961, it has announced and begun to implement plans for a fleet of 350,000 gross registered tons (750,000 tons d.w.) by 1965, when it expects to be the largest Indian carrier.[4] It has received generous help from the Government: a Rs 20 crore loan and an adjustment of official policy to allow a 40 per cent foreign shareholding in an Indian shipping company. If its plans materialize, and if the company turns out not to be controlled in practice by foreign shipping interests (two propositions which have encountered an unusual degree of public scepticism),[5] Indian shipping will have taken a considerable step towards fulfilling its traditional aims. Even then, however, the revised target of 1·5 million gross registered tons will be able to cope with no more than 12 or 12½ per cent of foreign trade by the end of the Third Plan.

(*d*) *Conclusions:* As an exercise in mapping the contours of foreign control, this sort of listing has severe limitations. They reside, as has been said, in the inadequacy of data both as regards relevance and

[1] From *Indian Ship*, Appendix E, pp. 112–16.

[2] M. A. Master in *ET*, 31 December 1962; PC, *Mid-term Appraisal*, p. 144.

[3] The new aggressive tone on shipping in official quarters was met with glee by the 'development wing' of Indian business opinion. Cf., for example, the *Economic Weekly*: 'The advantages of being a Government Corporation are many, but so far they have never been used. The Managing Director of the Shipping Corporation is therefore to be congratulated that, like Thomas of Becket [sic], he has learnt to "beat the barons at their own game".' (6 October 1962, pp. 1562–3.)

[4] From notes prepared by the company's insurers, 29 April 1963.

[5] The National Shipping Board, representing both public and private shippers, opposed registration of the company's first tanker, *Adi Jayanti*, at its meeting in Madras, 2 December 1961, on the grounds that too little was known about its sponsors; the Maritime Union of India opposed on the grounds that it carried a Norwegian crew. (*EW*, 13 January 1962, p. 36. See also, M. A. Master, letter in *ET*, 23 February 1962; idem., 'Indian Shipping Crosses Million-ton Mark', *ET*, 31 December 1962.)

The first Capital Issue Consent—for Rs 1·5 crores in 1961–2—permitted 100 per cent foreign subscription (Capital Issues Control data). At the end of April 1963, Michael Kulukundis, the Greek shipowner, held about one-quarter of Jayanti's equity, but was reported willing to sell out (Insurers' notes).

reliability, in the 'drag-net' method of collecting it, in the arbitrary criterion of control necessarily used, and in the almost equally arbitrary demarcation between industries. Yet some of the landscape's major features do emerge. One relates to the type of industry in which foreign control is fairly likely: the newer, technologically complex, and patent-protected industries with large, uncontrolled profit margins, such as the electrical and chemical industries. Although some traditional industries are still foreign-controlled, foreign firms are increasingly likely to be found in the specialist machinery-making side rather than in actual production. This is true as much of jute and other textiles as of tea or mining. However, where massive investment is required, whether in technologically-intensive industries or not, foreign firms are unlikely to venture more than knowhow. Steel-making, heavy transport equipment, heavy electrical and mechanical equipment, for example, have all been left largely to local capital, in these cases through state financing, with foreign firms participating as technical advisers.

A second feature which emerges is the extent to which a small number of major foreign firms hold a key position in a number of industries. A full inquiry into the ramifications of such firms is beyond the resources, if not the scope, of this study, yet it appears fairly normal for a company like Burmah Oil to be the sole producer of tin-plate in the private sector and until recently in the country, a major producer of cans, a shipper, civil engineering designer and contractor, besides running the largest oil refinery and marketing organization. There are others in the same class: Hindustan Lever in food products and toilet articles; ICI in explosives, paints, chemicals, pharmaceuticals, insecticides, plastics, and so on; Dunlop; Firestone; the Swedish Match Co.; Montecatini. The list could be extended. They illustrate a thesis as commonplace in India as elsewhere: the big, successful firm is better able to utilize institutional and other factors which encourage further growth than the smaller one.

A third feature, possibly less pronounced but none the less important, is the frequency with which large foreign firms act as technical consultants and suppliers in Government projects. In many cases their position here lends them unique advantages in their private operations. One case is illuminating, although not exhaustive of the range of possibilities. Early in 1958, the English Electric Co. gained a Rs 2 crore contract to supply the electrical equipment for the fertilizer and heavy water plant at Nangal. When members of the Rajya Sabha questioned the award in view of a substantially lower tender by an Italian firm, it was justified by reference to the company's agreement to take immediate payment in rupees, to receive less of the contract price in sterling, and their willingness to use one-tenth of the advance paid in rupees to start an electric switchgear factory near Madras.[1] The plant later became the largest in the private sector and one of the largest in the country.[2] Other examples have been mentioned in passing: Merck and Co., Inc., parent of the largest pharmaceuticals firm in India acted, *inter alia*, as consultants in the expansion of Hindustan Antibiotics, Pimpri; ICI has been associated with, *inter alia*, Hindustan Fertilizers and Chemicals at Sindri; AEI with Heavy Electricals, Bhopal; Vickers with the military tank factory, Madras; Philips with Bharat Electronics, Bangalore; and so on. The list could be lengthened to cover almost every major foreign investor in Indian industry. Naturally rumours of favouritism in the granting of licences, allocations of raw materials, and suchlike abound. Doubtless they are greatly exaggerated. But there is no denying the benefits of technical collaboration with the Government for a firm operating on its own account, even if they go no further than early and accurate knowledge of the formulation of projects, the workings of state plants, and so on.

Finally, the constraints placed on foreign capital emerge quite clearly. Wherever it appears to exercise unchallenged control in an important industry, whether as a single firm (matches, *vanaspati*, soap, tin-plate, aluminium, transformers, some drugs, industrial gases, shipping), or as a group of firms acting in concert (oil, rubber tyres, electrical equipment), the Government has attempted to curtail that power. It has done so by entering the industry on its own account (oil, tin-plate, electrical equipment, drugs, shipping) or by encouraging Indian and other foreign firms to enter, or to increase their share in, an industry (matches, soap, *vanaspati*, industrial gases, rubber tyres). The method and the timing have varied, the fact of intervention not.[3] Writing after the Himalayan War, it looks as if this ultimate sanction against foreign control will be more sparingly used than hitherto. There is little doubt, however, that it exists as the major ingredient of Indian economic independence.

---

[1] *MG*, 10 May 1958.   [2] See above, p. 202.
[3] Some aspects of the part played by the state are discussed below, pp. 317 ff.

II IMPORTANCE

(*a*) *Scale of operations:* In shared industries foreign firms are larger on average than Indian firms. In traditional spheres this is still true of plantations or mining, but no more the case in jute or cotton textiles, or paper. It is invariably true of modern industry which, for technological and managerial reasons, very often requires large minimum starting sizes. Official figures offer no guidance in the matter and one is left with the evidence adduced in the previous section and some indirectly related bits of information, official and unofficial.

The Ministry of Commerce and Industry listed the hundred biggest companies by total net assets in 1956–7:[1] subtracting Government companies, the twenty-seven foreign firms formed just under one-third of the private sector total (eighty-three). A later (1962) unofficial ranking of the hundred largest companies by volume of sales and net profits includes thirty-three foreign companies (and only one Government company), two of which—Hindustan Lever and Imperial Tobacco—are among the first five.[2] Were subsidiaries of companies grouped together, the relative weight of the foreign aggregates would be even more marked.

(*b*) *Relative profits, foreign and Indian:*[3] There is ample evidence to support the common-sense conclusion that returns on foreign investments in India are higher than average for Indian industry as a whole. A Reserve Bank study of United States and British investments shows that gross profits were 12·1 and 9·9 per cent of total capital employed in 1953 and 1955 respectively, compared with 6·8 and 9·4 per cent for Indian joint-stock companies in the same years.[4] Later, more accurate studies show that foreign-controlled firms were earning some 20 per cent more than Indian firms in the five years 1957–61, or an average of 10·1 per cent compared with 8·4 per cent.[5]

[1] Nigam and Chaudhuri, *The Corporate Sector in India*, Appendix IX, pp. 130–2.

[2] IIPO, *Monthly*, January 1962, pp. 9–12.

[3] Foreign firms' profits at home and in India are compared below, pp. 246 ff. Here foreign and Indian profits *in India* are dealt with.

[4] 'Return on Foreign Investments in India, 1953–1955', RBI *Bulletin*, May 1958, p. 537.

[5] 'Finances of Branches of Foreign Companies and Foreign Controlled Rupee Companies—1957 to 1959', '. . . 1960', '. . . 1961', RBI *Bulletin*, March 1962, January 1963, March 1964. These studies correct a bias imparted to the previous

Their performance is not uniformly better. The later studies draw a rough distinction between foreign branches, heavily weighted towards 'old type' investments like tea (half the total) and trading firms (one-fourth), and foreign-controlled rupee companies, over half of which were in manufacturing. It shows that the former, at an average of 7·5 per cent, were doing a shade worse than purely Indian firms (8·2 per cent), while the latter, at 12·7 per cent, were earning between one-half and three-quarters as much again as both Indian companies and foreign branches. Even in modern manufacturing industries, examples of Indian firms making higher profits in shared industries are not unknown.[1] They are rare, however.

These official figures minimize the difference in returns to foreign and domestic capital in two ways. First, they do not register the impact of new-type, high-earning investments from abroad which *began* precisely during the period covered by the second inquiry and did not generally add to the flow of profits until later.[2] More important, they do not allow for the widespread understating of earnings for tax or other purposes.

It can be taken as axiomatic that the bulk of business in India evades taxation, 'a lot of [it] by fairly well-known methods, including the keeping of two sets of books,'[3] or by managers appropriating directly the 'considerable gap between the profit shown and the actual profit [in the] very large number of . . . concerns [in which it] appears nowhere in the accounts.'[4] Nicholas Kaldor estimated the sum lost to Revenue in 1953–4 to be between Rs 200 and 300 crores, of which perhaps Rs 70–100 crores was due from the modern business sector,[5] and even the Revenue authorities admitted to Rs 31 crores at the time.[6] In many branches of industry, the Ministry of Finance

---

one by excluding foreign-controlled companies from the sample of Indian companies. Their conclusions are supported indirectly by a yet earlier study devoted to part of the foreign-controlled sector—'India's Annual Liability on Investment Income Account', RBI *Bulletin*, February 1952.

[1] See, for example, the Tariff Commission's comparison between National Insulated Cable Co., Ltd., and the British-controlled Indian Cable Co., Ltd. (*Report . . . Base Copper Conductors*, 1957, p. 26).

[2] This factor might be offset to some extent by the bias of Reserve Bank samples towards older, less profitable industries and firms.

[3] *The Times*, 16 January 1957. See also Rosen, *Aspects of Industrial Finance in India*, pp. 39 n., 108 n.; *Industrial Change in India*, Indian ed., p. 126 n.

[4] A. D. Gorwala, article in *The Illustrated Weekly of India*, 27 January 1957, p. 38, quoted in Rosen, *Industrial Change*, Indian ed., p. 126 n.

[5] *Indian Tax Reform*, pp. 104 and 105.   [6] *DT*, 31 May 1956.

estimated, only one-third of profits are declared for taxation;[1] and an inquiry into a group of Indian companies revealed known evasion and avoidance of taxes between 1946 and 1956 by ten companies only to be very nearly Rs $1\frac{1}{2}$ crores.[2]

Foreign firms are generally thought to have a cleaner record than indigenous ones in this respect; and indeed their greater size and the fact that they are exposed to special, politically-inspired scrutiny make it unlikely that they would resort to the more blatant methods known. At the same time there is less incentive for them to do so, since many of them are in a uniquely favourable position to modify their accounts to their advantage.

There is a great deal of indirect evidence for this. The *Damle Report*[3] drew pointed attention to the oil companies' inability to quote the price paid for crude supplied by their foreign associates (or indeed the names of their original suppliers):

The oil companies do not have access to the invoices of the original producers/suppliers of crude oil and remittances of foreign exchange are settled by them on the basis of the invoices of their immediate consignors, who are not the original producers/suppliers of crude oil. . . . Remittance of foreign exchange on the basis of the invoices of the immediate consignors only would not be conducive to absolute control, without a reasonable basis of satisfaction that such invoices represent no more than the true prices paid for purchases of crude oil at the source of supply.[4]

The importance to the level of profits in the oil industry of the price paid for its basic raw material needs no explaining. Under the conditions of payment allowed the companies in India it is even more important: a large part of the investment in the industry has been through imports of crude on a consignment basis[5] so that any inflation in their value magnifies the apparent investment and reduces the apparent rate of profit in the industry.[6]

---

[1] *The Times*, 16 January 1957.

[2] *Vivian Bose Report*, pp. 39–40. Examples of profit understatement to fleece shareholders or deny the Government taxes, occur throughout.

See also *EW*, 15 June 1963, for the Finance Minister's appeal to film stars to own up to the 75 per cent of income never declared: 'If you allow me to get the income tax from this black money, then I am prepared to consider your request to reduce the excise levy on films.' (pp. 946–7.)

[3] *Report of the Oil Price Enquiry Committee*, July 1961.

[4] ibid., pp. 21–22.

[5] RBI, *Survey 1953*, p. 84; ECAFE, *Bulletin*, June 1962, p. 7.

[6] ECAFE, loc. cit.; 'On account of the close links between the subsidiaries and branches of the oil companies operating in India and their affiliates abroad, the

Tea is another industry in which a profit-depressant can be seen at work. Again, the key link is in the price paid abroad to an intermediary, although, in this case, for the product. In his Minute of Dissent to the *Report of the Plantation Enquiry Commission, 1956*, K. G. Sivaswamy dealt with it as one aspect of exchange control evasion. He found that

The best quality tea was sent by direct consignment. Valuation of tea directly consigned was in the hands of producing companies and the customs officer and the Reserve Bank had to check whether it tallied with the actual realization in the UK market. Loopholes were many for mal-practices and checking could not discover them.

He quotes the Company Law Committee to the effect that

Many . . . managing firms also earn large amounts as buying and selling agents either direct or through their associate companies. For instance, company X sells the produce of the gardens under their control to their opposite numbers in the UK. Company Y in their turn sell some of this tea to the USA on contract with the parties there. The profits earned on these transactions are credited to company Y, although their functioning as an intermediary may not be necessitated by marketing conditions. . . .[1]

In the rubber-tyre industry the evidence is more direct. Each of the four foreign producers were found by the Tariff Commission to have consistently undervalued profits in their balance sheets: Dunlop by 28 per cent on average between 1946 and 1953; India Tyres by 18 per cent; Firestone by 10 per cent; and Goodyear by something under that.[2] In this case, the Commission felt unable to recommend

fixing differential prices in such a way as to eliminate the excess profits made by some units, e.g. Firestone . . . [since] Firestone (USA) can make up the loss of profits resulting from such action by charging suitably higher prices for materials or equipment supplied to its subsidiary in India.[3]

Evidence is harder to come by in other sectors of foreign interest, largely, one presumes, because, being less uniform or important, they have not been subjected to such detailed scrutiny. None the less, as is shown in another context below,[4] it is common enough for

---

reported price of imported crude oil may not represent the actual price paid. To that extent, the profits accruing to these enterprises, and remitted abroad, may be larger than they are shown to be.' (pp. 7–8.)

[1] *Report*, Part I, pp. 337–9.

[2] From *Report . . . Rubber Tyres and Tubes*, 1955, Statements LIII a–d, pp. 107–10.

[3] ibid., p. 124.   [4] See p. 265 f.

foreign manufacturing firms in a wide range of industries to prefer a high revenue from sales to their Indian branches and subsidiaries to high profits made in India. Manufacturing firms are also exceptionally well placed to transmute profits into royalties (paid for the acquisition of knowhow, patent rights, etc.) and fees (for drawings, technical assistance, purchase of goods on an agency basis or supply of goods at less than ruling rates). As royalties have been taxed at a lower rate than profits since 1961, and fees are completely tax-free, the inducement to do so is considerable.

If anything might be inferred from the annual summer rush to Western capitals of Indian businessmen, living well above their foreign exchange allowance, they are no strangers to over- and under-invoicing, and their related arts. It is none the less true that foreign firms are better equipped for this type of operation at the point where the Government is least able to reach them.

While official figures minimize the difference in profitability between Indian and foreign investments, they give no indication of the causes for the difference that they do show. An important one lies in the distribution of foreign capital between industries. Two-thirds of it is in petroleum and manufacturing, each of which has shown a greater than average yield in the post-war period. Within manufacturing, although some relatively depressed industries—jute and cotton textiles—are still strongly represented, foreign investments are concentrated in high-yielding branches like cigarettes and tobacco, electrical goods, drugs and other chemicals.[1]

In some industries, foreign firms have been able to exploit a monopolistic position. Of The Metal Box Co., then sole beneficiary of a Rs 500 per ton subsidy for tin-plate, the Tariff Commission reported:

We see little justification for the Company, which increased during the last three years its sales and profits by more than 50 per cent and 100 per cent respectively and dividends by more than 50 per cent, to have raised . . . the price of open top cans by more than Rs 15 per 1,000 in spite of the recommendation on this subject in our last report (1954). In the case of the preserved fruits industry, the price of open top sanitary cans accounts, on an average, for 20 to 33 per cent of the ex-works cost of the finished product. . . . We are convinced that it should be possible for Metal Box Co., without undue sacrifice of its profits, to reduce the prices of cans used by the preserved fruits industry substantially. . . .[2]

[1] See above, Table 4, p. 187.
[2] *Report . . . Preserved Fruits Industry*, 1957, p. 16.

TABLE 7
India: Profits after Tax as a Percentage of Net Worth, Selected Industries, 1955–62
(financial year)

	1955	1956	1957	1958	1959	1960	1961	1962	average 1955–62
All joint-stock companies	**9·0**	**8·7**	**6·2**	**7·1**	**10·5**	**10·9**	**10·0**	**9·0**	**8·9**
Mineral oil	14·7	28·8	16·7	14·7	15·5	11·0	12·0	7·1	15·1
Electrical goods and machinery*	10·5	9·7	8·3	9·7	14·3	14·2	13·4	11·5	11·5
Medicines and pharmaceuticals**	6·1	6·2	5·5	6·3	9·4	17·8	16·4	12·0	13·9 (10.0)
Basic industrial chemicals**					10·0	14·2	13·1	11·4	12·2 (9·1)
Other chemicals**					15·0	11·2	10·1	9·8	12·1 (9·1
Matches	9·1	8·0	3·5	9·5	14·8	13·1	12·3	13·4	10·6
Machinery and machine tools*	10·5	9·7	8·3	9·7	12·2	14·5	12·6	10·7	11·0

Source: 'Finances of Indian Joint Stock Companies', RBI Bulletin, August 1959, Table 7, p. 968; September 1960, Table 8, p. 1260; June 1962, Table 4, p. 851; June 1963, Table 4, p. 762; July 1964, Table 4, p. 854.

Notes: * Together with non-ferrous metals and transport equipment, 1955–8 inclusive.

** Average 1959–62 inclusive; in brackets, average for the whole period including combined average for 1955–8 inclusive.

The Metal Box Co. is not alone. From rubber tyres to matches, oil to electric motors, as will be shown in the next chapter,[1] the prices charged by foreign firms have contained a sufficiently large element of monopolistic rent to draw official notice and intervention.

In shared industries, foreign firms enjoy a number of advantages. An important one is the xenophile prejudice which suffuses Indian society. An imported article is *ipso facto* preferable to one 'made in India'; a foreign brand manufactured locally by a foreign firm is better than one made by an Indian firm; and so down the line with decreasing value accompanying receding foreign-ness. This is not altogether surprising: 'the quality of indigenous [wholly Indian] bicycles varies from one consignment to another', noted the Tariff Commission,[2] and what goes for bicycles can be said of most industries. Justified or not, so strong is this feeling and so general, that

[1] See below, pp. 250 ff.
[2] *Report . . . Bicycle Industry*, 1954, p. 17.

producers have succeeded in arousing official assessment and action. Tariff Commission reports, the early ones in particular, are studded with recommendations to have 'prejudice' (conceived as a percentage of retail price), incorporated as an element in the 'fair price': to the extent of 20 per cent in the case of motor vehicle batteries[1] and sodium thiosulphate,[2] 11–14 per cent in that of bicycles,[3] 12½ per cent in that of ring frames,[4] 17 per cent in that of sewing machines,[5] to name a few. While later Reports tend to play it down as an item of assessment, this is presumably because it has become impolitic not irrelevant.

Foreign firms are generally—not always—more efficiently run. To understand in detail why and to what extent this is so would require information not normally volunteered by firms or revealed by the Government. But some direct evidence exists. To take one example, the ratio of assets to turnover for a Reserve Bank sample of 83 foreign-controlled companies was 15 and 12 per cent less than for its sample of 745 Indian companies in 1959 and 1960 respectively.[6] And indirect evidence is plentiful. At least until the latter half of the fifties, when foreign exchange stringency turned the country into a naturally protected market, industry frequently called on the Tariff Commission to initiate the costings preparatory to making recommendations for protection.[7] Invariably the request came from Indian firms. In one case aluminium, a counter-request for a *reduction* in protection was made by the foreign producer.[8] Before 1952, when the Commission was vested with powers to subpoena witnesses and documents, foreign firms made a practice of boycotting its hearings and refusing to co-operate in any other way. In a *Report on the Electric Motor Industry*, the Commission considered the problem:

It is possible that the costs of production of the two non-Indian concerns, *viz*. Associated Electrical Industries and Crompton Parkinsons, are substantially lower than those of other producers; and this is probably the

[1] *Report . . . on the Motor Vehicle Battery Industry*, 1948, p. 9.

[2] *Report . . . Sodium Thiosulphate*, 1949, p. 7.

[3] *Report . . . on the Bicycles Industry*, 1946, p. 9; mentioned again in the 1954 *Report*, p. 23 (8½ per cent) and the 1960 *Report*, p. 32.

[4] *Report . . . on the Cotton Textile Machinery Industry*, 1949, pp. 31–32.

[5] *Report on . . . the Sewing Machine Industry*, 1949, pp. 16, 17. The 1960 *Report* still recommended a sum of Rs 50 per machine.

[6] From S. Kumarasundaram, *Foreign Collaboration and* [the] *Indian Balance of Payments*, Table, p. 8.

[7] These costings are confidential documents not published together with the *Reports*.

[8] Tariff Commission, *Report . . . on the Aluminium Industry*, 1955, p. 27.

reason why these firms have made no representation for any increase in the quantum of protection already enjoyed by the Indian industry.[1]

Foreign firms are also privileged, by and large, in gaining access to cheap finance. They naturally benefit from the bias shown by almost all Indian lending institutions towards big, established borrowers.[2] In addition, they almost all have access to special loan funds set up or supported by their home governments to encourage exports.[3] It is this ease in gaining loans (coupled with a reluctance to commit too much of their own resources),[4] that explains the exceptionally high gearing ratios (between owned and owed capital) featured by foreign firms. They are high not merely in relation to their parent firm but even in the Indian context. Again, evidence is sparse and scattered: in 1955, the Tariff Commission found two foreign tyre manufacturers, Firestone and Goodyear, with an annual turnover of Rs 7 and Rs 4 crores respectively, operating with a paid-up capital of Rs 20,000 and Rs 15,000.[5] Not all companies would go to these lengths—and the two have since strengthened their capital structure—yet a sufficiently large number have gone sufficiently far to excite comment.[6]

[1] loc. cit., 1949, p. 17.

[2] See Rosen, *Aspects of Industrial Finance*, pp. 13–14, 31, 32–33, 39–40, 45, and on the Life Insurance Corporation (p. 77), the IFC (p. 89), the ICICI (p. 100), and the Refinance Corporation (p. 104).

[3] These include the Export Credits Guarantee Department and the Commonwealth Development Finance Co., in Britain; the Export-Import Bank and Development Loan Fund in the United States; the Kreditanstalt für Wiederaufbau, Hermes Versicherung *AG*, and Deutsche Revision und Treuhand *AG* in West Germany; the Compagnie Française d'Assurance pour le Commerce Exterieur in France; and similar institutions in almost every capital-exporting country. Although geared primarily to fostering home country exports, they are often involved in medium- to long-term investment financing abroad with the accent heavily on their own nationals' undertakings. An important special source of loans is formed by the 'counterpart funds' held by the United States Government as payment for surplus food aid. Following the 'Cooley Amendments' of 1957, a condition for receiving such aid has been that 25 per cent of these funds 'be earmarked for being handled through the Export-Import Bank of USA for loans . . . to US business firms and branches and subsidiaries or affiliates of such firms' (Indo-US Technical Co-operation Program, *Third Report*, 1959, pp. 7–8). One-third by value of the 'Cooley loans' disbursed during the Second Plan went to American-controlled firms, and almost all the remainder to firms associated with American companies.

[4] See below, pp. 264, 309 f.

[5] *Report . . . Rubber Tyres and Tubes*, 1955, pp. 12, 25, 32.

[6] See, for example, *EW*, 8 October 1955, p. 1191, for comment on US companies; 'India's Annual Liability on Investment Income Account', RBI *Bulletin*, February 1952, p. 105 n., for Canadian companies; p. 248 n. 2, below, for British companies.

In line with experience elsewhere (see, for example, E. T. Penrose, 'Foreign

Foreign firms are equally favoured in attracting local equity. Yields on foreign shares are among the lowest in the market. New foreign issues are almost always sold at a heavy premium: to take a few instances at random from the financial press, Hindustan Lever marketed its first public issue at 65 per cent above par in November 1956; Guest, Keen, Williams at 100 per cent above in June 1957; British Paints at 50 per cent above in November 1960; Goodyear India at 70 per cent above in April 1961. When Hindustan Twyfords went to the market early in 1961, its issue was over-subscribed some 75 times; the Indian Carbon issue towards the end of that year, 125–150 times. Again, shares in foreign-controlled companies are the market leaders in capital appreciation: taking the leading 30 of the 130 issues made between January 1959 and July 1962, no less than eleven, including the first three and four of the first ten, were foreign scrips. There were no foreign companies among the fifty odd quoted at a discount.[1] In fine, the dividend cost to foreign capital of local financing is less, on average, than it is for Indian capital.

(*c*) *Channels of influence:* Enough has been said in this chapter to sustain a view that foreign capital wields considerable influence with the Government. The direction in which it has been exercised was touched on in Chapter 4; some of the results will be taken up in Chapter 7. Here interest centres on the channels through which it is exerted.

Documentation is naturally difficult. It is impossible if anything approaching comprehensiveness is aimed at. Such interrelated developments as the growth of government, the absorption of many former ICS men—not all expatriates—into foreign firms, the centering of head offices or strong 'industrial embassies' in the capital, and the development of a Delhi 'cocktail-party round' embracing business, government, and foreign aid missions, are scarcely amenable to formal description. And yet the channels of influence embedded in

---

Investment and the Growth of the Firm', *EJ*, June 1956, p. 227 n.) views expressed in discussions early in 1962 supported similar conclusions: US firms were usually singled out as more prone than others to substitute loans for equity, but the foreign sector as a whole was thought to be doing so more than Indian firms as a whole.

Government control of gearing ratios, exercised in one form or another since 1954, seems to have had little effect. The explanation lies perhaps in the exclusion of 'temporary loans taken for genuine working capital' (private communication from the Ministry of Finance) from the computation of debt.

[1] *ET*, 10 July 1962.

them are almost certainly more important than many others which are more easily demonstrated.[1]

One such channel is the advisory bodies to the Government. In its *Report* for 1960–1, the Ministry of Commerce and Industry lists 113 commissions, committees, statutory and advisory bodies, and directorates of state undertakings, together with their members' names.[2] Many of these, perhaps fifty, are relatively unimportant, or are purely technical or have no non-official members. Of the rest, *at least* 34 have among their members representatives of foreign-controlled firms or associations.

TABLE 8

India: Representation of Foreign Business Interests by Foreign Residents on Official Bodies Advisory to the Ministry of Commerce and Industry, 1960–1

Body	Foreign Member	Business Affiliation
1 Tea Board	N. S. Coldwell	James Finlay & Co.
	E. W. Emmett	Williamson Magor & Co. Ltd.
	J. R. Henshaw	Bombay Burmah Trading Corp. Ltd.
	I. F. Morriss	Jardine Henderson
	R. G. Peirce	Forbes, Ewart & Figgis Pte Ltd.
	R. R. L. Pennell	Williamson Magor & Co. Ltd.
	J. G. Robinson	Brooke Bond (Finlay)

[1] Professor D. R. Gadgil, Director, Gokhale Institute of Politics and Economics, Poona, dealt with the wider aspects of relations between business and government in his Convocation Address at Nagpur University, 20 January 1962. Some of his observations have direct relevance here:

'. . . the range and field of activity of Indian businesses are now so large that they constitute to-day overwhelmingly the most important group of employers of personnel commanding high salaries. . . . the relative position of Government and Business in this regard . . . greatly changed within the short span of eight years between 1948 and 1956. The direction of effort of those who want to get into the top salariat has consequently changed. Their goal is no longer to get into the highest official ranks but into the highest ranks of managers and technicians employed by large Indian and foreign businesses in India. This applies, among others, to sons and relatives of the highest officials as well as of prominent politicians. The pattern of behaviour of officials on retirement has changed simultaneously. Formerly, these usually sought no employment and almost never employment with Indian business. To-day the most highly placed officials very readily find highly rewarding positions within business. . . . We have thus arrived at the curious position that most officials who exercise large discretionary powers in relation to regulation of business might yet look on businessmen as potential employers or patrons of their sons and relatives and even of themselves.' (pp. 8–9.)

[2] Appendix V, pp. 306–70.

Body	Foreign Member	Business Affiliation
2 Coffee Board	R. Radcliffe R. K. Renfer E. H. Stanes	Ossoor Estate (Pte.) Ltd. Volkart Bros. T. Stanes & Co.
3 Coir Board	K. Newton	Not Available
4 Import Advisory Council	B. D. Hall H. M. L. Williams	Not Available President, Associated Chambers of Commerce and Industry; Guest, Keen, Williams Ltd.
5 Export Promotion Advisory Council	D. C. B. Pilkington	Chairman, Indian Jute Mills Association; Bird & Co.
	H. M. L. Williams (*ex officio*)	As in 4.
6 Standing Committee of the Export Promotion Advisory Council	H. M. L. Williams	As in 4.
7 Committee of Administration for the Cotton Textiles Export Promotion Council	W. A. Foges	United Traders Ltd., (a Hindustan Lever subsidiary)
8 Committee of Administration for the Shellac Export Promotion Council	M. Russell	Not Available
9 Committee of Administration for the Tobacco Export Promotion Council	E. G. Willis	Director, Imperial Tobacco Co. of India
10 Cotton Textiles Fund Committee	E. J. M. Leigh	Binny & Co. (Madras) Ltd.
11 The Advisory Committee for the Office of the Director General of Commercial Intelligence and Statistics, Calcutta	Geo. Barrell, Representative	Editor, *Capital* ACCI
12 Central Advisory Council of Industries	G. N. Noel-Tod D. C. B. Pilkington H. M. L. Williams	Parry & Co., Ltd. As in 5 As in 4
13 Standing Committee of Central Advisory Council of Industries	G. N. Noel-Tod H. M. L. Williams	As in 12 As in 4
14 Reviewing Sub-Committee of the Central Advisory Council of Industries	H. M. L. Williams	As in 4

Body	Foreign Member	Business Affiliation
15 National Productivity Council	B. F. Goodchild	Saxby & Farmer (India) Private Ltd
16 Development Council for Heavy Electrical Industries	J. Nicholson B. J. Woodley	AEI (India) Private Ltd. BICC Ltd.; Indian Cable Co., Ltd.
17 Development Council for Light Electrical Industries	S. Dorresteyn H. R. Gregson J. E. Reid	Not Available Associated Battery Manu-facturers (Eastern) Ltd. GEC of India (Manu-facturing) Private Ltd.
18 Development Council for Internal Combustion Engines and Power Driven Pumps	J. H. Langdon J. W. Whitaker	Greaves Cotton & Crompton Parkinson Private Ltd. Not Available
19 Development Council for Machine Tools	J. Hodikinson	Associated British Machine Tool Makers (India) Ltd.
20 Development Council for Non-Ferrous Metals and Alloys	T. L. Holdsworth W. J. Woodhouse B. J. Woodley	Indian Aluminium Co., Ltd. Eyre Smelting (Private) Ltd. As in 16
21 Development Council for Bicycles, Sewing Machines, and Instruments	B. A. Forsythe	Works Director, T.I. Cycles of India Ltd.
22 Development Council for Automobiles, etc.	A. E. L. Collins	Managing Director, Ashok Leyland Ltd.
23 Development Council for Leather, Leather Goods, and Pickers	B. B. Dodd	Madras Chamber of Commerce
24 Development Council for Alkalis and Allied Industries	S. Gothberg	Western India Match Co. Ltd.
25 Development Council for Drugs and Pharmaceuticals	W. R. Thompson	Glaxo Laboratories (India) Private Ltd.
26 Development Council for Organic Chemical Industries	J. Dick Hewitt	Additional Director, Alkali and Chemical Corporation of India Ltd. Not Available
27 Development Council for Sugar	M. J. Edwards M. N. Pittie	W. H. Brady & Co. Ltd. Vice-President, Indian Sugar Mills Association
28 Development Council for Oils, Soaps, and Paints	T. Korner S. H. Turner S. L. G. Wright	East Asiatic Co. (India) Pte. Ltd. Hindustan Lever Ltd. Andrew Yule and Co., Ltd.; Blundell Eomite Paints Ltd.; Elephant Oil Mills Private Ltd.

Body	Foreign Member	Business Affiliation
29 Development Council for Paper, Pulp, and Allied Industries	A. I. Fleming L. Shuttleworth	Not Available Bird and Co. (Private) Ltd.; Titaghur Paper Mills Co., Ltd.
30 Development Council for Woollen Textiles	E. B. Whitley	International Wool Secretariat
31 Panel for the Clocks and Watches Industry	H. I. Cormack	P. Orr & Sons Pte. Ltd.
32 Standing Committee for Engineering Industries	A. J. Lund	Simpson & Co. Ltd.
33 Standing Committee for Ferrous and Non-Ferrous Metals and Metallurgical Industries	R. I. Chisholm S. D. Pirks	Venesta Foils Ltd. Not Available
34 Standing Committee for the Machine Tools, Transport, and Communications Industries	A. E. L. Collins E. W. H. Scaife	As in 22 Machine Tools (India) Private Ltd.

Note: The Ministry of Commerce and Industry does not give members' affiliations, nor differentiates between official and lay members. Since Indian business directories and *Who's Whos* are less than rudimentary, the table has had to be compiled from fragmentary personal knowledge and private communications.

By not picking out the *Indian* representatives of foreign firms, of whom there must be very many, the table grossly understates the degree of formal representation enjoyed in practice by foreign capital. At the same time, it gives no insight into foreign firms' unique role as representative of the general interests of the private sector, able to act as such because of their relative immunity from Government pressure and their freedom from the family, community, and caste distractions which cut across the Indian business community.

Another formal channel of influence, more effective certainly although more clouded in conjecture, runs through foreign aid- and credit-giving agencies. Examples have been given of successful lobbying to modify the Government's policy in oil, drugs, pharmaceuticals, and dyestuffs.[1] It appears too that American aid for a state fertilizer plant at Trombay, near Bombay, towards the end of 1961 was conditional on New Delhi's acceptance of American (and Indian) private capital in the industry, and on a review of fertilizer

[1] See above, pp. 160 ff.

prices to make this possible.[1] Among the many other cases that might be quoted, the most significant perhaps is that of the proposed American-aided fourth public sector steel plant at Bokaro, first mooted in 1959 and dropped finally in September 1963. Prompted by an active Indo-American private sector steel lobby,[2] the United States objected at various times to it being a state project, to having the feasibility studies and designs undertaken in India, to locating the overall authority for supplying equipment and supervising construction and operation in the country, to having the Indian authorities take over operational responsibility within ten years, and so on. More important than these individual instances, however, is the general tenor of the advice proffered to donor- and creditor-governments by their home business communities. When acted upon, it can exert a powerful influence on Indian policy by virtue of that country's dependence on foreign aid.

[1] *EW*, 7 January 1961. Announcing the loan, the Development Loan Fund 'took cognisance of the Indian Government's announced intention to enlist the co-operation of private enterprise to help produce further fertilizer supplies'. The announcement went on to say that 'five sites have already been identified as suitable for fertilizer plants and other sites are under consideration'.

[2] See, for example, *The Economist*, 22 June 1963, p. 1280.

CHAPTER SIX

BEHAVIOUR OF FOREIGN CAPITAL

I NEW FOREIGN CAPITAL

(a) *Size:* Foreign-controlled firms are large not only in Indian terms.[1] Of the 368 active British *branch companies* listed by the Ministry of Commerce and Industry in 1957–8,[2] 268 had companies quoted on the London Stock Exchange as principals. That is to say, more than seven out of ten companies with branches operating in India—and nine-tenths of the invested capital—were among the three thousand-odd large 'quoted' companies, compared with one out of one hundred and thirty for British companies as a whole. The same is true of British companies with *subsidiaries* in India:[3] 55 of the 84 active in the same year (or between six and seven out of ten) were controlled by 'quoted' British companies.[4]

Since branches and subsidiaries account for all but a minute portion of foreign 'direct investment', and 'direct investment' for nine-tenths of all foreign business investments from private sources, the typical British-controlled firm in India is clearly part of a substantial organization.[5] This is probably even more true of other foreign firms, most of whom have not had long association with the country, nor

---

[1] See above, p. 224.

[2] Ministry of Commerce and Industry, *Information Broadsheet No. 12/1958.* A defective copy, containing only 368 out of 390 active British branches, was available for consultation.

[3] Official classification perpetuates the legalistic and artificial distinction between foreign branches and subsidiaries. In practice there are 'no significant operational differences between a branch and a subsidiary', the choice between them being made 'on the basis of legal and taxation grounds' (Barlow, *Management of Foreign Manufacturing Subsidiaries*, pp. 77, 78). 'The main difference between the two is that while branches are legally part and parcel of the parent company abroad, the subsidiaries by virtue of their incorporation under the Indian Companies Act, have an independent legal status.' (RBI *Bulletin,* May 1958, p. 535.)

[4] From Ministry of Commerce and Industry, *Information Broadsheet No. 1/1960.* Only subsidiaries other than nominee companies or those engaged in gathering or disseminating information are considered.

[5] The bias towards bigness is grossly understated in the text since no attempt was made, in all but three cases, to trace the parentage of companies beyond that listed in the *Information Broadsheets.*

the benefits of a large resident expatriate population, unrestricted entry for personnel, and similar factors.[1]

Since investment in manufacturing is growing as a proportion of the whole, it is particularly interesting to show the bias towards bigness in this sector. Towards the end of 1959, the British Trade Commission, New Delhi, listed 213 ventures involving 184 home manufacturing companies.[2] More than half of these (ninety-four) were among the 1,900 British companies with net assets of £0·5 million and above in 1960.[3] Twenty-seven were among the top hundred British companies with net assets of £24 million and above; forty-one were companies with assets of £10 million and above; and no less than sixty-eight, more than one-third of the total, were amongst those with assets of £5 million and above. Even more interesting is the ranking of these home firms within their main industrial groupings: in the chemical and allied industries, nine out of the first ten British companies (including the first six) were active in India; in electrical engineering, six of the first ten (including the first five); in non-electrical engineering, six out of the first ten (including the first); in vehicles four (including the second); in textiles two (including the second); 'other manufacturing' two (the first two); tobacco two, including the first (overwhelmingly larger than any others); 'metal goods not elsewhere specified' two (the first two); metal manufacture two (the second and third).[4]

The bias towards bigness is growing stronger. Of the one hundred and seven British principals other than financial companies to have received capital issues consent for new companies between April 1956 and December 1964,[5] seventy-six were among the 1,900 companies

---

[1] Direct investment abroad was reported by less than one-half of one per cent of all United States corporations in 1949, but by 6 per cent of those with assets of $1 million and above (Mikesell, *Promoting United States Private Investments Abroad*, p. 23, citing Barlow and Wender, *Foreign Investment and Taxation*, Prentice-Hall, 1955, Chapter 2).

[2] *List of Manufacturing Concerns.* The list is not exhaustive.

[3] BOT, *Company Assets . . . 1960*. Since the Board of Trade excludes, amongst others, companies wholly or mainly operating overseas and most unquoted companies, including private ones, both of which are well represented amongst the 184, the bias towards bigness is understated in this comparison and in those that follow.

[4] ibid.

[5] Marginally adjusted for parent-subsidiary relations. Unless explicitly stated, all analysis relating to capital issues in this chapter is based on the replies to Unstarred Questions Nos. 3896, 4 May 1959, 2711, 27 April 1960, Lok Sabha; and on data supplied by the Office of the Controller of Capital Issues.

with net assets of £0·5 million or more; forty-seven among those with assets of £5 million or more; thirty-four among those with assets of £10 million or more; and twenty-four were among the top hundred British companies.[1] Some of these ratios are significantly higher than in the Trade Commission's list, indicating a growth towards bigness. The same holds for the ranking of these principals by industry. Taking the first ten firms in an industry again, new ventures in electrical engineering were undertaken by the first, second, third, and fifth; in non-electrical engineering by the first, second, and eighth; chemicals and allied industries by the first, sixth, and ninth; tobacco by the first; drink by the first; 'other manufactures' by the first; 'paper, printing, and publishing' by the fourth and eighth; vehicles by the fourth and tenth; textiles by the second and ninth; metal manufacture by the second and third; metal goods by the first; and bricks, pottery, glass, etc. by the fifth.[2]

(b) *International scope and origins:* An aspect of their great average size is the international scope of the typical new investing company's operations. Using a somewhat primitive index—the number of countries in which a firm is engaged in its main occupations—it has been possible to discover the international spread of 36 of the 60 British firms financially involved in new ventures during the first five years of the period. The drag-net method used[3] is as crude as the index; if anything it understates the spread of the companies. None the less the results are of some interest (Table 9, p. 241).

One aspect of this wide international spread is the gap between local and total turnover or investment in most of the firms. Although one of the top five companies active in India, Hindustan Lever accounted for scarcely more than 2 per cent of the total turnover of the parent concern (Unilever) in 1962, less than that percentage of net profit, net worth, or capital employed;[4] Alkali and Chemical Corporation of India, a giant amongst Indian companies, accounted for 0·8 per cent of the assets of its principal (ICI) in 1960; Boots Pure Drug Co. (India) Private Ltd., another local giant, and the largest of the parent group's overseas subsidiaries, contributed less than 1 per cent of total group turnover in 1962.[5] These are not exceptions.

[1] BOT, *Company Assets . . . 1960.*   [2] ibid.
[3] *Stock Exchange Yearbooks* and Company Chairmen's *Reports* were dragged for the data.
[4] *Company News and Notes,* 1 August 1963, p. 41.
[5] Chairmen's Annual Statements.

TABLE 9

Distribution of 36 British Principals (out of a possible 60) by Number of Countries in which they are engaged in Their Main Occupation(s), 1956/7–1960/1

No. of countries	No. of firms	No. of countries	No. of firms
At least 2	4	More than 10 and at least 11	1
More than 2 and at least 3	1	" " 11 " " " 12	1
" " 3 " " " 4	6	" " 12 " " " 13	1
" " 4 " " " 5	7	" " 13 " " " 14	0
" " 5 " " " 6	2	" " 14 " " " 15	1
" " 6 " " " 7	2	" " 15 " " " 16	0
" " 7 " " " 8	3	" " 16 " " " 17	1
" " 8 " " " 9	1	" " 17 " " " 18	1
" " 9 " " " 10	1	" " 25	3

Sources: Company *Reports*; *Stock Exchange Yearbook*; Financial Press.

Another aspect of the international spread is that British and foreign investments are no longer the near-synonyms they once were.[1] If at the end of 1961 British business investments still constituted 77 per cent of total investments from private sources,[2] the position is rapidly changing: between 1948 and 1953, 90 per cent of the net inflow came from Britain; it fell to 70 per cent in 1954 and 1955, and to 57 per cent in the period 1956–61.[3] The decline is even more precipitous if the flow of public funds to the private sector is taken into account: the share of British capital having fallen from 90 per cent in 1948–53 to 33 per cent in 1956–61.[4]

Something of the new diversity in national origins can be seen from the list of new issues with foreign participation sanctioned by the Capital Issues Committee in recent years. Of the 324 sanctions in the five-year period already dealt with, national origin was recorded unambiguously in 311 cases. They are analysed in the table on the following page.

---

[1] Nationality with regard to capital is often as impossible to pin down in practice as it is obscure in concept. Indian Aluminium, for example, is registered as a Canadian subsidiary, but three-quarters of the shares in its parent, the Aluminium Company of Canada Ltd., is held in the United States (Kannapan and Burgess, *Aluminium Limited in India*, p. xi). A firm, held to be Dutch at the Ministry of Commerce and Industry in the morning, turned out to be fully Anglo-American-owned at the US Embassy in the afternoon.

[2] From RBI *Survey 1961*, Statements 8, 13, pp. 70, 80-82.

[3] From 'Recent Trends in Foreign Investment in India', RBI *Bulletin*, September 1958, p. 1012; RBI *Survey 1961*, Table IX, p. 38.

[4] RBI *Survey 1961*, Table IX, p. 38.

17

TABLE 10

India: Breakdown of New Capital Issues Sanctioned April 1956–December 1964 by National Origin of Foreign Participant

(Rs crores)

	No.	Cases Per cent	Authorized Capital Amount	Per cent	Foreign Stake Amount	Per cent
Britain	107(105)	34·4 (34·0)	98·94 (67·44)	36·5 (28·1)	45·23(27·89)	47·1 (35·5)
United States	73	23·5 (23·6)	87·37	32·2 (36·4)	27·76	28·9 (35·3)
West Germany	44	14·1 (14·2)	21·27	7·8 (8·9)	7·30	7·6 (9·3)
France	16	5·1 (5·2)	16·96	6·3 (7·1)	2·31	2·4 (2·9)
Japan	15	4·8 (4·9)	9·28	3·4 (3·9)	1·71	1·8 (2·2)
Switzerland	13	4·2 (4·2)	10·06	3·7 (4·2)	4·12	4·3 (5·2)
Italy	12	3·9 (3·9)	12·36	4·6 (5·1)	3·21	3·3 (4·1)
Others	31	10·0 (10·0)	14·95	5·5 (6·2)	4·35	4·5 (5·5)
Total	311(309)	100·0(100·0)	271·19(240·19)	100·0(100·0)	95·99(78·65)	100·0(100·0)

Source: As on p. 239 n. 5.

Notes: National origin could not be attributed in thirteen cases in the period covered. Figures in brackets show the effect of excluding two exceptionally large authorizations in the oil and petrochemicals industries: of Rs 21 crores, of which the British stake was Rs 14 crores, for Oil India (Private) Ltd., in 1958–9; and of Rs 10 crores, of which the British stake was Rs 3·34 crores, for National Organic Chemical Industries Ltd., in 1964–5.

There is nothing surprising in the multiplicity of national origins revealed. It is partly due to the loss of the special privileges for British firms that occurred with Independence;[1] partly to the diffusion of economic power in the world; partly to official efforts at encouraging aid and investment from wheresoever. Partly too it derives from the identity of the new investors, and their growing national agnosticism as size and technical leadership bring international operation in their train.

(c) Manufacturing and technological bias: The distribution of foreign investments by industry has changed greatly since Independence, petroleum, manufacturing, and finance having gained as a proportion of the total compared with all other branches. If it is borne in mind that perhaps half of the increase in petroleum investments has been on manufacturing account (refining) rather than trading,[2] and

[1] See above, Chapters 1 and 2.
[2] The total originali nvestment in refineries is reported to have been between Rs 45 crores (above, p. 102 n. and Rs 55 crores (Wiggins, Private Foreign Investment, p. 38).

some of the rest on account of asset revaluation,[1] and that there has been a substantial shift towards industrial financing in both the managing agency and financial sectors,[2] manufacturing will be seen to have gained even more than appears from Table 11. Indeed, of the 324 consents granted for new capital issues with foreign participation between April 1956 and December 1964, no more than 20, accounting for over 5 per cent of the total authorized capital and slightly less than 7 per cent of total foreign stake, were in branches other than manufacturing.

TABLE 11

India: Distribution of Foreign Business Investment from Private Sources by Industry, mid-1948 to end of 1961

(Rs crores)

	Mid-1948		End 1961		Percentage Growth 1948–61
	Investment	%	Investment	%	
Plantations (mostly tea)	52·3	20·4	103·8	17·9	198
Mining	11·5	4·5	12·4	2·1	108
Petroleum	22·3	8·7	148·6	25·6	666
Manufacturing	71·0	27·8	219·4	37·8	309
Foods, beverages, etc.	10·1	14·2	36·1	16·0	357
Textile products	28·0	39·4	20·7	9·4	74
Transport equipment	1·0	1·4	13·0	5·9	1,300
Machinery and machine tools	1·2	1·7	11·4	5·2	950
Metals and metal products	8·0	11·3	32·1	14·6	401
Electrical goods and machinery	4·8	6·8	14·7	6·7	306
Chemicals and allied products	8·0	11·3	50·5	23·0	631
Others	9·9	13·9	40·9	18·6	415
Trading	43·1	16·8	29·3	5·1	68
Construction, Utilities, Transport	31·2	12·2	41·3	7·1	132
Financial (excl. banks)	6·8	2·7	6·3	1·1	93
Miscellaneous	17·7	6·9	19·3	3·3	109
Total	**255·9**	**100·0**	**580·4**	**100·0**	**227**

Sources: 1948—RBI, *Survey 1961*, Statement 9, p. 71.
1960—as in Table 4, p. 178 above.

Note: As in Table 4, p. 187 above, it is possible to give a more detailed breakdown for the year ending 31 December, 1960. The changes since mid-1948 for selected industries would read as follows:

[1] ECAFE *Bulletin*, June 1962, p. 7n.　　　　[2] See above, pp. 59 ff.

	Mid-1948 Investment (Rs crores)	%	End 1960 Investment (Rs crores)	%	Percentage growth 1948–60
Within manufacturing:					
Cigarettes and tobacco	6·2	8·7	24·3	13·2	393
Medicines and pharmaceuticals	0·5	0·6	17·0	9·2	3,400
Total (including others)	71·0	27·8	184·3	32·5	260
Other than manufacturing:					
Managing agencies	14·4	5·6	23·3	4·1	162
Total business investment (incl. others)	255·9	100·0	566·3	100·0	221

Sources: 1948—RBI, *Survey 1953*, Table V-3, p. 77; *Bulletin,* May 1961, Statement IV, p. 684; October 1962, Statement IV, p. 1543.
　　1960—RBI *Bulletin*, October 1962, Statement II, p. 1540.

Within manufacturing, the major, at times spectacular, relative advances have been in the technologically-intensive chemicals and allied industries (including drugs and pharmaceuticals) and electrical engineering industries.[1] Again, the table almost certainly understates the technological bias of new investment: the industrial breakdown is crude and, perhaps more important, it makes no allowance for exceptions within an industry. Firms prepared to invest abroad—and permitted entry into India—are likely to be the innovators no matter what the average technological intensity of their industry. Printing, for example, is not technologically intensive as industries go, yet the two foreign investments in the field in the eight and three-quarter years were in the highly-specialized branches of security and high-speed offset printing.

The bias towards technological intensity derives in part from the shift towards manufacturing investments and the typically large size and 'progressiveness' of the investing firm; partly it is a response to official preference for investments embodying new processes or products. The techniques themselves might be genuinely new, or

[1] Chemicals and electrical engineering accounted for three-fifths of total research outlays and research manpower in Britain in 1959–60; man-made fibres, general engineering (including instruments), metal manufacture, and vehicles for another fifth between them; and the rest—another fifth. The aircraft industry is not included in the reckoning. (*Industrial Research in Manufacturing Industry, 1959–60*, p. 12.)

difficult to adopt without years of experience, a developed industrial structure, or massive capital expenditure; they might be unimportant in that they serve to differentiate the maker's brand rather than to satisfy a purchaser's purpose; or a mixture of both. Whatever the case, technological intensity is rapidly becoming a hallmark of new foreign investments. Through the managerial bottlenecks it creates it is a potent factor in limiting the flow of foreign private capital.

(d) *The domestic market*: With manufacturing as its central occupation, the domestic market has naturally shouldered export markets aside as foreign capital's major source of revenue. Data relating directly to this are fragmentary, but two sorts of circumstantial evidence might be adduced in support.

The first relates to India's export trade. Tea and jute, the two major exports for which foreign capital is responsible to a considerable degree, have been stagnant for some time;[1] and the share of foreign capital in these trades has been declining;[2] yet profits accruing to foreign investments have been rising, by about one-fifth during the last decade.[3] The second relates to the changing trade balance of foreign-controlled firms. In 1951 and 1952 their exports exceeded imports by an average of nearly 70 per cent; by 1956–8 they were running an import surplus of 10 per cent on average.[4]

The shift to domestic sales out of local production can be quite dramatic in individual cases. Imperial Chemical Industries, for whom India constitutes the most important single overseas market, have found their turnover from local manufacturing increase from 2 per cent of the total in 1951 to 42 per cent in 1961. In the same year local manufacturing accounted for half the turnover of Associated Electrical Industries (India) Private Ltd., where six years previously it had provided only one-fifth; the firm was expecting to derive four-fifths of its income from local manufacturing by 1966. General Electric Co., of India Private Ltd., originally a purely trading

---

[1] See above, p. 33.   [2] See above, p. 40.   [3] See below, Table 19, p. 308.

[4] From 'Survey of the Distribution of Imports and Exports Between Indian and Non-Indian Firms—1951 and 1952', RBI *Bulletin*, February 1954, Statements 1 and 4, pp. 103 and 105; 'External Transactions of Foreign-Controlled Companies in India—1958', RBI *Bulletin*, January 1960, Tables II and III, pp. 14 and 15.

The swing from an export to an import surplus is exaggerated by the effect of the Korean War-induced export boom. The export surplus in 1952, by which time those effects had considerably abated, was 42 per cent.

concern, also gained half its turnover from locally manufactured products in 1961. And so it is with almost every major company.[1]

II THE INCENTIVE TO INVEST

(a) *Profits at home and abroad:* It is not easy to compare profit rates across frontiers.[2] Accounting conventions and coverage differ; as important, international operation provides firms with opportunities to modify their accounts which few are willing to forego. Such modifications are made to avoid taxation, understate profits in particular areas for political reasons, shunt funds from one currency area to another, and so on. Whatever the reason, they introduce an element of arbitrariness into the comparison that renders the most sophisticated computations suspect.[3] While they do not all deal with the same aspects of profits, or approach the subject in the same way, the few studies published by the Reserve Bank[4] agree that the returns to foreign capital in India have been consistently better than the average at home. The most interesting study, relating to the first half of the fifties, found that American firms were earning an average of 13·5 per cent of net worth in 1953 and 12·8 per cent in 1955 after tax, compared with 10–12 per cent at home in both years, and British firms 11·9 and 9·5 per cent in the two years compared with 8–9 per cent at home.[5] Profits were thus anything between 6 and 35 per cent higher in India than at home for firms, some of which were active in both.[6]

There is ample support in data relating to individual firms. The Tariff Commission dealt with the matter on one occasion. In its *Report on . . . Rubber Tyres and Tubes* it stated that profits to capital employed for Dunlop Rubber Co. (India) Ltd., averaged 26·8 per cent annually between 1947 and 1953, compared with 17·5

[1] Information gained privately.
[2] Profits of foreign and Indian firms in India are compared above, pp. 224 ff.
[3] Examples of adjusting accounts can be found above, pp. 226 ff.
[4] See RBI *Bulletin*, February 1952; January 1956; May 1958.
[5] 'Returns on Foreign Investments in India 1953/1955', RBI *Bulletin*, May 1958, Table 2, pp. 536, 537.
[6] A later study undertaken by the US Department of Commerce shows profits in manufacturing for US firms in India to have been more than one-quarter as much again as in the Philippines in 1961 and 1962, and two-thirds as much again as in Western Europe in the same years. (Cited by R. S. Bhatt, Executive Director, Indian Investment Centre, in the Supplement to *Capital*, 19 December 1963, p. 87.)

per cent for its principal in Britain over the same period—a difference of over 50 per cent.[1] Although this was the only direct comparison drawn, the exceptionally high rate of profit made by Firestone in India—an average of 64 per cent annually between 1946–7 and 1952–3—seems to indicate at least as great a difference.[2] It is possible to make similar comparisons for any number of companies given their Indian and home accounts. The three detailed here are representative of the largest foreign investors; they too appear to have been earning very nearly half as much again from their Indian operations as at home.

TABLE 12

Net Profits as a Proportion of Net Worth; Indian and Parent Companies Compared for Three Major Groups, 1956–61

| | Unilever | | ICI | | Metal Box Co. Ltd. | |
	Home	India	Home	India	Home	India
1956	16·4	15·7	7·2	19·0		
1957	12·7	14·7	8·1	9·2		
1958	13·6	19·0	4·8	3·5	9·3	13·9
1959	15·2	29·7	8·9	10·1	10·5	16·0
1960	12·8	25·6	7·1	23·4	11·2	21·8
1961					8·3	18·3
Average	14·1	20·9	7·2	13·1	9·8	17·5

Source: Annual company reports.

Note: Figures for ICI's Indian profits relate to their largest operation in the country, Alkali and Chemical Corporation of India Ltd., only.

Away from the relative safety of published figures and attributable statements, the economic reporter is likely to come across well-argued and seemingly realistic profit projections in which 80 per cent gross, 25–30 per cent after tax (including Super Profit Tax), are not uncommon—again well above anything that might be advanced for Britain. Naturally, not all branches are equally profitable. But then not all have attracted foreign capital in equal measure since Independence, as a comparison of Tables 7 and 11 on pages 229 and 230 will show.

It is difficult to do more than indicate roughly the reasons for the relatively high level of profits made by foreign capital in India as compared with their performance at home. On the costs side, with

[1] Statements XLIX and L, pp. 100 and 101.
[2] ibid., Statement XLIV, p. 100.

Bank Rate consistently below what it has been in London—at times during the fifties less than half—and the general structure of interest rates skewed sharply in favour of the large, foreign firm,[1] loan finance has been comparatively cheap for those that require it, perhaps 2–3 per cent lower than at home, and capital gearings relatively high in consequence.[2] The cost of new equity finance has also been considerably less on average since the mid-fifties, given the bull market, the frequency of sales at heavy premium,[3] and the consequent low actual yield on representative foreign shares.

Building costs are more difficult to compare, but foreign business seems agreed that lower labour costs, some cheaper materials, and a less exigent climate add up to a saving of perhaps 30–40 per cent on average in standard factory building.[4]

Finally, labour costs. Foreign firms in new manufacturing industries generally pay well above ruling wage rates; yet wages are still very low—one-sixth or one-seventh the British equivalent at the lower end of the manufacturing scale, say at the level of a semi-skilled machine-minder.[5] Owing partly to the practice of granting an annual bonus payment valued at two to four weeks take-home pay,[6] partly to the steeper wage gradient in Indian factories,[7] partly to the

---

[1] See above, pp. 231 f.

[2] British industrial and trading firms at home received 19 per cent of their funds from bank, trade, and other creditors between 1949 and 1953 (Tew and Henderson, *Studies in Company Finance*, Table 1.5, p. 10). British-controlled companies in India averaged 31 and 37 per cent from such sources in 1953 and 1955 respectively. (Based on 'Returns on Foreign Investments in India 1953/1955', RBI *Bulletin*, May 1958, Table 3, p. 536; Statement 2, p. 539.) Foreign branches and subsidiaries in India averaged some 49 per cent in 1958–61 inclusive. ('Finances of Branches of Foreign Companies and Foreign-Controlled Rupee Companies', RBI *Bulletin*, January 1963, Table 4, p. 36; March 1964, Tables 1.3, 2.3, pp. 271, 277. Borrowings by branches were very high—41 per cent.)

[3] See above, p. 232.

[4] Information gained privately.

[5] Rs 0·75–0·80 (1s. 1½d.–1s. 2½d.) an hour (including 'dearness allowance') for that grade of skill was considered princely in the winter of 1962 and scarcely heard of outside the foreign manufacturing sector; it compares with 6s. 10d.–7s. 7d. per hour (including overtime premium) averaged in Britain for the equivalent grade as listed by the Ministry of Labour (*Statistics on Incomes, Prices, Employment etc.*, No. 5, June 1963, Table 3.15, p. 33).

[6] Bonus is computed as so many *months* (perhaps two and a half to three) at the *basic* rate, which, in 1962, was seldom more than one-third the consolidated take-home pay (including 'dearness allowance') and was generally less.

[7] A skilled man might earn three to four times the basic wage of an unskilled worker in the same plant or, after consolidating with the flat-rate 'dearness allowance', one and a half times to twice as much.

larger proportion of office and supervisory staff—including expensive expatriates—to production workers,[1] and partly to a higher rate of absenteeism, a comparison of *total* labour costs shows smaller disparities. In one case studied in some detail, the Indian wage bill amounted to slightly under 55 per cent of the British for a given volume of output.[2]

Productivity is as important as wages in determining labour costs per unit of output, although even more difficult to compare. A safe generalization would be that in India it is in inverse proportion to the labour content of a job as compared with Britain. In highly mechanized factories, output per production worker might be equal to or nearly equal to the British figure; certainly 80 per cent is fairly common.[3] In navvying or clerical work it could be 20 per cent or below.[4] Since new foreign investment is almost entirely in manufacturing and factory plant, and conditions are not too dissimilar to what might be found in the investors' home companies,[5] Indian productivity in the foreign sector compares favourably and does little to offset the differences in wage rates.[6]

There are, of course, elements in the cost structure that do. Indian factories are at the end of a long supply line for imported materials and spares; partly for that reason and partly, as a World Bank Mission pointed out, because of 'a lack of common servicing facilities and ancillary undertakings',[7] they tend to be more self-sufficient than their home equivalents, and to keep outside purchases of

[1] In one important case for which details were made available privately, the proportions of direct labour, indirect labour, and clerical/supervisory staff for a given volume of output were 42:40:18 in India, as against 55:25:20 in Britain.

[2] Information vouchsafed privately.

[3] Information gained privately during interviews in 1961, 1962, and 1965; substantially supported by a World Bank Mission's findings in 1960 'that output a worker engaged in productive operations was at least 75–80 per cent as high, job for job, as in the European countries concerned' (quoted in *Capital*, 8 September 1960, p. 354).

[4] Information gained privately.

[5] Comparison is not always derogatory to India. In a number of plants visited, the British engineers considered layout and physical conditions in the newly-built Indian factories very much superior to anything they had seen at home.

[6] See conclusions and corroborative evidence brought by Eddison, *Industrial Development in the Pulp and Paper Industry*, p. 212; US Department of Commerce, *Investment in India*, p. 4; H. V. R. Iengar, Governor, Reserve Bank of India, speech to the Bureau of Industrial Statistics, RBI *Bulletin*, December 1959, p. 1554; A. K. Bose, 'Labour Productivity Under Indian Conditions', *Productivity*, November–December 1961, p. 44.

[7] Quoted in *Capital*, 8 September 1960, p. 354.

components and parts to a minimum.[1] The result is a generally lower rate of machine utilization—lower by 15–20 per cent in normal times, and perhaps as much again in periods of acute foreign exchange stringency.[2]

Physical depreciation is also generally faster, partly for climatic reasons, partly because of rougher handling during shipment, installation, and use, partly because local raw materials are of uneven quality; notably because of the irregular supply of spares and consequent lower level of maintenance. These factors are compounded by the high cost of processed raw materials, particularly imported ones,[3] and the shorter runs appropriate to Indian market conditions, both of which in turn preclude the use of the most productive techniques and so raise costs.

Without a great deal more research and freer access to data, a final reckoning of the relative levels of production costs in India and at home for those active in both, must remain open. There is, however, nothing like the same difficulty in comparing prices, the other major variable in the profits equation.

In foreign-dominated manufacturing industries, these are almost invariably higher in India than at home. The Tariff Commission has been eloquent on this point. They found that tyre prices were higher, despite the use of locally grown raw rubber, than in either Britain or the United States over a range of products by some 22 and 16 per cent respectively between 1946 and 1954;[4] that Studebaker engines assembled from imported parts were more costly than the imported product;[5] that its foreign collaborators and partners charged Atul

[1] Figures given privately to show differences as large as between 60 per cent internal production in Britain and 98 per cent in India, are backed by published evidence: large American air-conditioning plant manufacturers found that 80 per cent of their components by value had to be made in their own factories, compared with 30 per cent at home (*Capital*, 19 November 1959, p. 683); Standard Batteries 'built machines in its workshop . . . in order to make the factory self-sufficient' (*EW*, 15 December 1962, p. 1925); Tube Investments produce 90–95 per cent of their bicycle components in India (Friedmann and Kalmanoff, *Joint International Business Ventures*, p. 478) compared with 80–85 per cent at home (information supplied privately).

[2] Information supplied in confidence by British managements.

[3] See below, p. 266.

[4] From *Report on . . . Rubber Tyres and Tubes*, Statement LI, p. 103. The situation remained unaltered: in 1962, the Indian price for (basic size) commercial vehicle tyres net of excise duty was 35 per cent higher than the landed cost of its foreign equivalent (B. C. Dutt, 'Automobile Tyres in the Third Plan', *EW*, 24 November 1962, p. 1817).

[5] *Report on the Automobile Industry*, 1956, p. 61.

Products Ltd. higher prices for dyestuffs intermediates than world prices for the finished products, and that the company's prices were exceptionally high in consequence.[1] They found that before the Government intervened in 1953, the Indian Cable Co., Ltd., and the National Insulated Cable Co., Ltd., fixed prices not on the basis of their actual costs, but on the basis of prices quoted by the Export Group, London.[2] The Minister of Finance told the Lok Sabha that ICI were selling soda ash at Rs 250 a ton compared with Rs 130–160 a ton in Britain.[3] The pharmaceuticals industry has been probed more than once. A Russian committee of experts estimated that local chlortetracyclin, if produced to their specifications, could be sold ex-factory at Rs 0·50 per gramme compared with the ruling price of Rs 9·80–10·80; the price of streptomycin could be halved and cuts of a similar nature could be made in other drugs.[4] An American Senate committee was equally emphatic. They showed that the different brands of tetracyclin, whose cost of production they estimated— generously—at 48 cents per sixteen capsules of 250 mg. each, were sold to Indian chemists at $6·52 per sixteen in 1959, as against $5·10 in the United States, and prices—still allowing a small profit—as low as $1·19 in Argentina;[5] that meprobamate, a mild tranquillizer whose retail price in the United States was fifteen times the cost of production, cost Indian chemists half as much again as it did their American counterparts.[6] They concluded that

prices in India for the broad-spectrum antibiotics, Aureomycin and Achromycin, are among the highest in the world. As a matter of fact, in drugs generally, India ranks among the highest priced nations of the world—a case of an inverse relationship between per capita income and the level of drug prices.[7]

Oil, rubber tyre, and soap prices have been commented on in another context; and there are others, from chocolate or bicycles— as any visitor to India might testify—to atomic power stations, as testified by the US Joint-Congressional Atomic Energy Committee.[8]

[1] *Report on the Dyestuffs Industry*, 1955, pp. 30–31.

[2] *Report . . . Power and Distribution Transformer Industry*, 1956, p. 13. National Insulated is an Indian-controlled company.

[3] Debate on the Finance Bill, 1954, *Capital*, 29 April 1954, p. 605.

[4] *Report of the Soviet Experts on the Drug Industry in India*, 1956, excerpts from which were made available privately.

[5] *Kefauver Report*, pp. 25, 40, 43.   [6] ibid., pp. 18, 19.   [7] ibid., p. 112.

[8] The kW cost of construction of the 300 mW nuclear power station at Tarapur was estimated at $300 compared with $132 per kW for the 500 mW station to be built by the same firm—International General Electric—in New Jersey (see *EW*, 14 March 1964, p. 503).

Government action to reduce prices, including price control, has been effective in some cases. Generally, however, it has been applied to industries in which foreign investors have shown little interest, partly because of this intervention;[1] and has been applied leniently, allowing larger, more efficient firms a substantial margin over stated costs.[2] Probably more effective has been the internationalization of the foreign sector and the consequent growth of big-firm competition. But even here more might be read into the measure than is warranted, as the example of the oil industry,[3] the combine of power and distribution transformer manufacturers,[4] or of rubber tyre producers,[5] or the primarily negative collusions of soda ash and aluminium producers might show.[6]

Discussion of the sources of higher profits in India would be incomplete without mention of tax incentives. These cover a 'tax holiday' on the first 6 per cent of profits for the first five years of production; a development rebate which enables investors to deduct 120 per cent of actual expenditure on plant and machinery as depreciation, for income tax purposes; and exemption of dividends from super tax in a score of basic industries.[7] Comparing the actual incidence of taxation in India, Britain, and the United States, the Indian Institute of Public Opinion concluded that at a given level of

[1] Products subject to price regulation in 1962 were coal, electricity, iron and steel, pig iron, cement, sugar, paper, tinplate, caustic soda, soda ash, woollen yarn, automobiles, acetate yarn, rubber tyres and tubes, raw rubber. Only coal, tinplate, tyres and tubes, and raw rubber could be considered foreign-dominated industries, although there was some foreign investment in paper, electricity, automobiles and caustic soda.

[2] See, for example, Rosen, *Industrial Change*, Indian ed., pp. 18, 21. Eddison brings an example from the paper industry: 'The government figure for production costs . . . was based on an analysis of the manufacturing expenses of six "representative" mills. Cost data obtained from these mills were tabulated and then arithmetically averaged, giving equal weight to the costs of units whose annual outputs ranged from 1,200 tons to 20,000 tons. Since four out of the six concerns examined were of small capacity, and since manufacturing expenses in small mills tend to be high, the final figures had a distinct upward bias. Because of this rather generous method of calculating production costs, the more efficient units were able to realise profits of up to Rs 200 per ton on this item alone. . . . The selling and distribution allowance of Rs 169 . . . also allows many firms a comfortable profit cushion. By concentrating their sales in the nearest markets and avoiding long freight hauls, a number of the mills maintain selling costs as much as Rs 100 below the industry-wide mark-up.' (pp. 106–7.)

[3] See above, pp. 166–7.   [4] See above, p. 251.
[5] See above, p. 215 n.   [6] See below, pp. 289–90 f.
[7] *Income Tax Act 1961*, Sections 84, 33, 34, 56A. A more comprehensive list of tax concessions may be found in ECAFE *Bulletin*, June 1962, pp. 11–12.

profits, a rupee company will have brought a return of 145 per cent over a period of fifteen years compared with 114 per cent for a domestic company in the United States and 126 per cent for one in Britain; a foreign subsidiary in India (111 per cent) would do worse than one in Britain (118 per cent) but better than one in the United States (105 per cent).[1] Much has happened since to fault the comparison. In particular, the Finance Act of 1963, passed in the aftermath of the Himalayan War, increased company taxation sharply as part of a general rise in the tax levy. Even then, however, if a company was willing to obey the implicit, if somewhat undynamic, rules laid down by the Indian Finance Minister, and retain a relatively small proportion of gross profits for reinvestment, say 16–25 per cent, it needed to add little to its pre-1963 tax bill,[2] and even less after the concessions made in the 1964 Finance Act.[3]

An additional attraction derives from the many double taxation avoidance agreements concluded between India and capital exporting countries since 1959.[4] Some are particularly encouraging to would-be investors: for example, the 1959 Indo-American accord, unratified as yet, credits US companies not only for taxes paid in India as was previously the case, but also for 'taxes spared' through the special inducements and concessions outlined above.[5] British firms, while not covered by a formal tax treaty, are in practice often credited with taxes paid in India.

(b) *Defence of markets:* Higher than average profits abroad have seldom been sufficient to precipitate a major flow of capital to backward countries without a deeper economic rationale.[6] In imperial

---

[1] IIPO, *Quarterly*, No. 24, April 1960, pp. 36–40.

[2] A private exercise undertaken by a member of the Commonwealth Development and Finance Co. staff shows that an Indian company deriving its income from its own manufacturing activities would need to earn a *taxable* income of some 35 per cent gross on net assets before the effective combined rates of tax (including Super Profits Tax) approached the standard rate on foreign companies in force prior to the Emergency (from information supplied privately).

[3] IIPO, *Monthly*, March 1964, Supplement, p. xiv; *The Economist*, 7 March 1964, p. 918.

[4] See above, p. 159.

[5] As reported in *India News*, 29 April 1961, p. 5; *EW*, 10 October 1959, pp. 1388–9.

[6] This view gains indirect support from detailed investigations of decision-taking in companies: 'the relationship between profits and growth', writes Barna, 'is not a causal one; but rather that both growth and profitability are reflections of the character of the firm' (*Investment and Growth Policies*, p. 20).

times, this was provided by the need to augment supplies of raw materials and food in the developed industrially-specialized countries. Although that need persists today, it has been overlaid and largely supplanted by another—the need to defend markets.

There are two major elements in this shift. One is the emergence of a few manufacturing giants, possessed of technological leadership, at the centre of private international flows.[1] These giants, in the words of a *Times* Special Correspondent, 'know their "foreign" competitors well; they often have close relations with them, they know their relative strengths and costs, and in some trades . . . are inclined to abstain from . . . direct competition on their rival's doorstep.'[2] Whatever the precise phase in the mutual relations of these firms, they are defined in terms of each firm's share of the international market. The second, not unrelated, element is the proliferation of independent states, each reaching out for economic independence and power; each pursuing these goals to some degree through controlling their relations with the world economy. Some of the methods adopted—currency and capital control, protection, and the regulation of international trade—are bound to affect the operations of the giant international firm.

The conflict between these two elements, the growing internationalism of these firms' arena of competition and the sharpening nationalism within it, can be eased in practice only if they undertake manufacturing abroad. There is nothing new here. 'Undoubtedly', writes the chronicler of Unilever, one of the great practitioners of tariff jumping,

foreign tariffs had much to do with the changing character of the British export of capital about 1900. Britain had been exporting capital for the best part of a century. But now British investment in commercial and industrial manufactures abroad began to grow as it had never done before.[3]

Of the firm itself, he writes: 'The story of Lever's European development is largely concerned with attempts to defeat the tariff legislator.'[4]

In India, import restrictions have fathered some of the oldest and most strongly-based industries.[5] Very early in the post-war period they were again singled out as the chief reason for foreign manufacturing

---

[1] See above, p. 31.   [2] *The Times*, 2 March 1960.
[3] C. Wilson, *The History of Unilever*, Vol. I, p. 99.
[4] ibid., p. 192.   [5] For example, matches, see above, p. 215.

investment;[1] and since then, particularly since the exchange crisis of 1957–8, every tightening of import controls has provoked a rush of foreign applications for industrial licences, capital issue consents, and so on. In conversation, foreign managements are invariably eloquent on the dangers of 'unequal competition', that is, competition from *outside* a tariff wall, with a known international rival, and normally see in such dangers the final and compelling reason for investment. Profitability is seldom mentioned.[2]

It is important to stress the connexion between tariff jumping and size and/or technological monopoly in its widest sense. The facts have already been set out.[3] Behind them lies a common-sense reasoning: it is easier to decide on manufacturing abroad if a market has already been built up through exports.[4] And normally it is only the very largest firms that export.[5]

Even in cases where a newcomer might be expected to succeed without great risk, as in the new growth industries, the cards are stacked against the small or medium firm with little experience of foreign operations. It would have to undertake a fundamental reorganization of its business before setting up abroad, the more so if conditions in the foreign market were very different from those it had come to consider normal. As for gaining experience gradually through trade, the few paragraphs on the difficulties of importing

---

[1] See, for example, *American Consulate Survey*, p. 3: 'Perhaps the leading motive of the foreign participator to invest has been the increasing difficulty of exporting his product to India under existing import control regulations. He has decided, therefore, to manufacture it in India.'

[2] As an anonymous American commentator remarked to Sir Norman Kipping, Chairman, Federation of British Industries, 'Anybody who invests in India is a sucker but anybody who does not invest in India is a bigger sucker.' (FBI, *India 1963*, p. 13).

[3] See above, pp. 238 ff.

[4] An unpublished United States Department of Commerce survey of 250 major firms with investments abroad 'supports the conclusion that the majority of our foreign investors have acquired an interest in producing abroad through their activities as exporters or importers, or as a consequence of providing technical services or engaging in other foreign activities such as shipping'. (Mikesell, *United States Private Investments Abroad*, p. 30.)

[5] Even in Britain, an economy exceptionally geared to international trade, twelve companies account for no less than 20 per cent of all manufacturing exports, while the 15–20,000 manufacturing companies employing 10–500 workers each and about one-half of the manufacturing labour force in aggregate, are responsible for no more than 20–25 per cent of such exports (Report of the British Export Trade Research Organization (1952) Ltd., cited by Andrew Shonfield, *Observer*, 24 July 1960).

into India and of importers, even those with long-standing connexions, should suffice to show the odds against succeeding.[1]

Something of the sort can be said about technological leadership. Whether or not it is associated with large size, as is usually the case, its concentration in privately-held industrial firms in the West is a powerful factor in the persistence of technological backwardness elsewhere, and in the near-indispensability of foreign private investment. Given the competition between international firms and the growing freedom in most of the world to choose between them whatever their national origins, the compulsion on the large firm to get behind import bottlenecks is very strong.

Two differences between this sort of incentive to invest and those attached to typical 'imperial' investment are worth noting. In colonial times, a market—in the metropolitan countries—was more or less assured; the problem was one of supply or production. Now a productive apparatus is readily available, and the problem is one of securing markets, production locally being incidental to marketing. Then, local economic development beyond the point at which the economy could be integrated with the world market was irrelevant and, in theory at least, positively harmful; now it has become a desirable background to investment.

The second difference lies in the size of the investing population. Today, the decisions of a handful of foreign firms, a few score men in each creditor country,[2] are vital to the prospects of India and countries similarly placed; in Imperial times, although there was no lack of centralized political control, or of interlocking economic interests, the decision to save and invest abroad was widely dispersed through the home middle class, and potential importers of capital had a wider range of choice in creditors, albeit a narrower one in creditor countries.

(c) *Subsidiary incentives:* The incentive to invest is not exhausted by reference to profits and the defence of markets; there are almost as many as investing firms, although three stand out by the frequency with which they are met.

First in importance, and directly related to what has just been said,

---

[1] See above, pp. 34 f.

[2] Cf. Barna, *Investment and Growth Policies*: 'It seems that even in the giant firms the most important decisions are effectively taken by very small groups, consisting of perhaps four or five people at the most.' (p. 32.)

is the use of investment as a 'sweetener' to the authorities. Development has entailed a sharp increase in India's import bill, in precisely the items—capital goods and industrial raw and intermediate materials—which potential private investors are interested in selling. The firms quoted as having increased the share of local production in their Indian turnover from almost nothing to something like a half in the last decade or so,[1] have managed none the less to sustain and even augment the total volume of Indian purchases from their parent companies abroad. As they admit readily in private, they could hardly have done so in the face of sharpening international competition without the goodwill generated by investment in local industry.[2] The same might be said of technical consultancy, or any of the host of services to the Government that large companies are in a position to provide, which are both profitable in themselves and indirectly in widening the market for home products—local investment is a powerful argument in gaining contracts.[3] A parallel argument works, less frequently and only amongst the largest firms, to prevent disinvestment that might otherwise take place. One giant firm, unwilling to expand in India but anxious to fall in with official wishes that it Indianize its ownership, is effectively prevented from doing so by the Government's known reluctance to allow the repatriation of a large block of capital.

A second type of subsidiary incentive, particularly for smaller firms, revolves around the quick appreciation of capital in India since Independence, and more especially since the late 1950's. Capital gains of over 100 per cent in two or three years are not uncommon.[4] While gains even of this order are unlikely to act independently in promoting capital flows, except, perhaps, in the very special and quantitatively unimportant case of 'venture capital',[5] and must be considered ancillary to arguments on other grounds, they are not a

---

[1] See above, p. 245.

[2] Cf. *The Economist* on the 'growing realization by foreign industry that the only hope of continuing trade with Pakistan lies in making some gesture towards local production, even if the absence of skilled labour means that much of it cannot at first be more than local assembly'. (10 December 1960, p. 1148.)

[3] See above, pp. 222–3.   [4] See above, p. 232.

[5] Venture capital is that which conceives and establishes *new* enterprises abroad without necessarily owning them or controlling them beyond the 'break-in' period (see Dale and Bale, *Private United States Venture Capital*, p. 1), accounting for perhaps 5 per cent of total United States private investment abroad in the 1950's.

negligible consideration, as official representatives know only too well.[1]

Finally, there are a group of incentives relating to a firm's own operations and its relations with other firms in its home market. Among these are the desire to set up a local servicing base once the volume of sales and complexity of product justify it; the desire to provide other firms operating abroad with the same services or products as are provided them at home; or the pressure exerted by such firms on their feeders to do so; a reluctance to disturb the home market through 'aggressive competition' when the alternative of expansion abroad exists; the drive for 'international status' on the part of fast-growing domestic firms; and so on almost *ad infinitum*.

III THE INCENTIVE TO COLLABORATE

(a) *Extent:* Foreign capital was associated with 34 per cent of consents for new capital issues between 1951 and 1963, and with 45 per cent of consents for new issues in the private sector during the period 1957–63 for which separate data are available. Foreign-associated issues accounted for 41 per cent of all authorized capital (1951–63) and for 59 per cent of authorized capital in the private sector (1957–63).[2] Conversely, very few new foreign ventures have been undertaken without Indian participation: of the 324 foreign-associated consents for new issues granted between April 1956 and December 1964, only 15 (under 5 per cent) accounting for 1·2 per cent of total foreign-associated authorized capital envisaged full foreign ownership.[3] At the same time, many wholly-owned foreign companies have taken in Indian capital since the mid-fifties, amongst them giants like Metal Box, Dunlop, Guest, Keen, Williams, Associated Batteries, Goodyear, Indian Aluminium, Union Carbide, Imperial Tobacco, Hindustan Lever, Philips India, English Electric.

---

[1] Calling for joint Indo-American enterprise, an early Indian Ambassador to Washington, B. R. Sen, told the Far East American Council of Commerce and Industry Inc.: 'Americans might start out with say 70 per cent of the corporation common stock and the Indians with 30 per cent, and the proportion might shift, over a ten-year period, to 30 per cent American and 70 per cent Indian, the presumption being that the 30 per cent which the Americans would own ten years later would be worth considerably more than the 70 per cent they started with.' (Speech of 29 January 1952, quoted in Spencer, *India, Mixed Enterprise and Western Business*, p. 81.)

[2] Sources as in Table 13, p. 259.   [3] Sources as on p. 239 n. 5, above.

And this before, perhaps in anticipation of, Government's decision to insist on Indian participation in the *expansion* of wholly-owned foreign subsidiaries.[1]

TABLE 13

India: Consents for New Capital Issues and Amounts Authorized, 1951–63
(Amounts in Rs crores)

Year	Total No.	Consents Amount	Private Sector No.	Amount	Foreign-Associated No.	Amount
1951	46	21·59			15	8·71
1952	23	12·69			6	2·91
1953	31	18·25			7	9·23
1954	74	66·19			18	41·04
1955	76	47·90			10	20·96
1956	79	80·31			15	8·92*
1957	54	43·33	50	36·67*	12	8·61*
1958	38	20·80	33	18·50	18	12·76
1959	51	76·80	47	48·60	25	42·73*
1960	97	99·98	85	50·23	39	29·35
1961	109	77·95	100	72·81	45	33·47
1962	122	73·61	116	66·60	58	46·85
1963	130	126·90	117	84·00	49	50·53
1951/63	930	766·30			317	316·07
1957/63	601	519·37	548	377·41	246	224·30

Source: Ministry of Finance, *Quarterly Statistics on the Workings of the Capital Issues Control.*

Notes: Prior to 1957, Government companies were not marked separately; they accounted for a smaller proportion of consents and authorized capital than subsequently.
  * Approximate figure.

The result has been a significant dilution in the ownership-mix in foreign-controlled investments: in 1955 the average foreign stake in the equity of foreign-controlled rupee companies other than managing agency companies was 82 per cent;[2] in the period April 1956 to December 1964, the average authorized foreign share of foreign-controlled new issues was 56 per cent.[3]

Financial collaboration is not the only, nor perhaps the most important form. While almost all Indo-foreign joint ventures provide for some element of technical collaboration, the vast majority are for technical collaboration only: of the seventy-five agreements finalized

[1] As reported in *Hindu*, 26 March 1961.
[2] RBI, *Survey 1955*, Statement II, p. xv.
[3] From Table 15 below, p. 276. Including the Oil India consent.

between Independence and the end of 1949, forty-one provided for only technical collaboration.[1] More recently, between 1957 and 1963 inclusive, capital issues consent involving new Indo-foreign financial collaboration was granted in 246 cases compared with more than 1,700 involving technical collaboration only—as can be seen from a comparison of Tables 13 and 14. On closer scrutiny, even some of the financial collaborations appear to be no more than technical collaboration agreements with provision for payment or part-payment in shares. Examples are given below. While there is little basis for generalizing here, it does seem likely that most, if not all, of the 104 collaborations in which the foreign financial interest amounted to under 25 per cent between April 1956 and December 1964, were of this type.[2]

TABLE 14

India: Indo-Foreign Technical Collaboration Agreements in the Private Sector: 1957 to mid-1963

	1957	1958	1959	1960	1961	1962	1963	Total 1957–1963
A. Distribution by country:								
Britain	17	34	52	120	126	79	70	498
United States	6	4	10	61	77	57	67	282
West Germany	2	6	13	58	67	42	48	236
Japan	1	3	8	39	30	24	32	137
Switzerland	–	2	1	13	19	19	19	73
France	2	1	2	9	16	14	16	60
Italy	4	4	4	9	13	11	6	51
Holland	1	–	–	6	10	7	4	28
East Germany	–	–	1	5	4	5	10	25
Sweden	1	–	1	13	–	6	1	22
Denmark	–	–	2	6	4	2	3	17
Czechoslovakia	–	–	–	6	5	1	5	17
Austria	–	–	1	3	5	4	2	15
Belgium	–	–	2	4	2	4	3	15
Canada	–	1	–	1	3	6	–	11
Poland	–	–	–	1	6	–	3	10
Hungary	–	–	–	1	2	2	–	5
Yugoslavia	–	–	–	–	1	1	3	5
Finland	–	–	–	2	1	1	–	4
Panama	–	2	1	–	–	–	–	3
Pakistan	–	2	–	–	–	–	–	2
Others	47	44	52	23	12	13	6	197
Total	81	103	150	380	403	298	298	1,713

[1] *American Consulate Survey*, p. 5.   [2] See below, pp. 267 f.

	1957	1958	1959	1960	1961	1962	1963	Total 1957-1963
B. Distribution by industry:								
Plantations	3	6	4	–	–	–	–	13
Sugar	4	2	2	–	–	–	–	9
Cotton textiles	9	4	3	2	–	1	6	25
Jute textiles	1	1	–	1	–	–	–	3
Silk and Wool textiles	–	–	5	2	3	1	–	12
Iron and Steel	2	–	1	1	–	–	12	16
Transport equipment	4	4	11	20	6	9	21	75
Electric machinery	11	11	12	72	73	44	38	261
Machinery, non-electric	8	11	26	107	143	81	55	431
Aluminium	1	1	2	1	1	1	1	8
Basic industrial chemicals	5	–	4	2	3	3	5	22
Medicines and Pharmaceuticals	4	10	9	6	3	9	2	43
Other chemicals	6	9	14	21	29	18	15	112
Cement	3	3	4	3	1	–	6	20
Rubber and manufactures	2	3	3	5	3	–	1	17
Paper and products	2	2	1	9	8	8	3	33
Electric generation and supply	–	–	3	–	–	–	11	14
Trading	4	1	4	2	1	–	2	14
Shipping	–	2	1	–	–	–	–	3
Banks and Insurance	3	4	3	–	–	–	–	10
Others	9	28	38	126	129	123	120	563
Total	81	103	150	380	403	298	298	1,713

Source: Journal of Industry and Trade.

(*b*) *Government policy:* Since the second half of the fifties, particularly after 1957, the Government has insisted on joint collaboration in new ventures. After the Himalayan War it grew to demand that the entire foreign exchange cost of a project be covered by the foreign collaborator.[1] There are a number of strands in this insistence. An important one is that collaboration agreements seem to give painless and immediate relief to the balance of payments by

[1] Chairman's statement, Tata Iron and Steel Co., Ltd., *EW*, 10 August 1963, p. 1377.

providing foreign exchange or its equivalent in imported plant and machinery. Another, and one that limits approval normally to *joint* projects, is the desire to graft foreign managerial and technical skills on to Indian industry. These are well-rehearsed grounds. Probably as important, although difficult to assess, is the attempt to associate Indian capital with the lucrative projects dominated by foreign investors, as well as the desire to avoid charges—from both home and abroad—of bias towards one or other segment of the private sector.

Whatever their precise weight, these and other factors have so affected official thinking that it is now virtually impossible for an Indian firm to start up or expand without presenting a scheme for foreign collaboration. As one journal put it, 'it has become difficult to get a manufacturing licence without prior arrangements for foreign technical collaboration . . . whether [an industry] really needs technical knowhow and foreign capital or not'; and this even in such firmly-based Indian industries as cement, sewing-machines, bicycles, as well as ink, pens, ball-point pens, tooth-brushes, and tooth-paste.[1] Despite the Government having jettisoned the '51 per cent rule' and formal ratios for the ownership-mix, it is almost as difficult for the potential foreign investor to keep out Indian capital. So much is at stake in terms of obtaining the many licences needed, and obtaining them on time, and there are so many other ways in which the 'uncompromisingly foreign' firm can be discriminated against,[2] that it is only under exceptional circumstances, and when it has a very strong bargaining position—a wanted technique and a ready market abroad seem to have stood IBM in good stead at the end of 1961—that a foreign firm will insist on and, more rarely, obtain full ownership.[3] The traffic has in fact been the other way,

---

[1] *EW*, June 1960, p. 829; also 27 May 1961, p. 805.

[2] An early and portentous example of these 'other ways' is contained in the Tariff Board's *Report . . . on the Dry Battery Industry*. After mentioning a request from Estrella Ltd., the major Indian producer, for the Government to purchase Indian batteries only, the Board noted: 'We had some discussion on this subject with Mr. Farrell of National Carbon [the major foreign producer and the largest firm], and he gave us to understand that his company has considered and is still considering a suggestion to throw open a part of their share capital to investors in India, to have Indian Directors on the Board and to train up Indian technical personnel.' (*Report . . . on the Dry Battery Industry*, 1947, p. 17.) National Carbon did nothing, and when the Tariff Board reported again, they were able to state: 'We are satisfied . . . that the present policy of the Industries and Supplies Ministry with regard to stores purchase is reasonable.' (*Report . . . on the Continuance of Protection to . . .*, 1950, p. 18.)

[3] See above, p. 258.

with many of the older, giant firms opening their shareholders' lists to Indians for the first time, and others actively contemplating the step.

(c) *The need for intermediaries:* Government pressure might be less effective were it not that many foreign firms have cogent reasons of their own for seeking local collaboration. Paramount is the growing need for local intermediaries. These are cast in a number of roles, the most important of which, reflecting the expanding area of state economic intervention, is that of coping with officialdom. There is so much to be done on so many levels, from obtaining licences and favourable interpretations of regulations and procedures in New Delhi, to expediting goods through congested ports and getting hold of a couple of railway wagons, that easy access to Governmental authority is itself an important 'factor of production'. All foreign firms require this factor. If they are small, they need it at all levels; if large and well-established, with perhaps one or two ex-ICS men on their Boards, the need might be felt most at the lower levels.[1]

The importance of Indian partners in this role is well recognized. It is written into most of the Collaboration Agreements made available for this study,[2] and is a standard reference in business conversation. It might be illustrated by reference to Atul Products Ltd., a major dyestuffs, chemicals, and pharmaceuticals producer, with Indian, British, American, and Swiss capital involved. The firms' chroniclers write:

The relationship of the Company with both the Government of India and the Government of Bombay State and their agencies, on the whole, has been smooth and cordial. . . . Mr. Kasturbhai [the Indian partner] was encouraged to enter the field because of this favourable attitude. . . . At the inception of the enterprise, the Company needed the government's help in acquiring the extensive site. . . . The legal procedure involved in the acquisition of private land in India is, to say the least, dilatory and complicated. Considering this, the fact that the Company got possession of the land by September 1949 is indeed a significant achievement. The Government of Bombay was extremely helpful to the Company in this respect.

[1] The distinction should not be taken too literally. As the Government grows, and as the ranks of ex-ICS men thin and new generations of officials assume desks in New Delhi, even the aristocrats of the foreign business community are finding it necessary to look for partners with the necessary background of Ministerial connexions, or family and social ties with key men in the Secretariat.

[2] See below, pp. 281 ff.

The factory construction, machinery installation, and commencement of production proceeded without delay due to the promptness with which the Indian Government issued the licences for importation of the requisite machinery and raw materials. The Government showed its goodwill and particular concern towards the company when the Prime Minister performed the inauguration ceremony in March, 1952.[1]

Mediation with the financial institutions which are assuming an increasingly important role in industry can be almost as important, particularly for firms engaged primarily in the sale of knowhow, or which wish to keep their financial stake to a minimum. Again, the Collaboration Agreements testify to this role, many of them specifying the terms and conditions of rupee loans without which the agreement would fall.

Other mediating roles for local partners readily suggest themselves. The supply of local materials is usually best handled by local people; sales and publicity require local knowledge; labour relations equally; and so on. Indeed, the impression gained by almost every observer of Indian business is of a fairly rigid functional specialization in which the Indian partner deals with the items listed, and the foreign side with technical operations, management, foreign supplies, and finance, and, perhaps less frequently, over-all finance. The division is not immutable. It depends to some extent on the proportionate commitment of each side. As a rough approximation, however, it holds.

(d) *Rupee capital:* The high gearing ratios with which foreign capital tends to operate in India[2] are one aspect of a marked reluctance on the part of foreign investors to commit their own resources:

It has been the Government's experience [runs one report on American companies] that many of these [investment] proposals expect the US Export-Import Bank and the Development Loan Fund to lend the bulk of their foreign exchange requirements, and the amounts that the parties are prepared to invest from their own corporate resources are relatively small. Since the resources of these American lending agencies are limited, the desire of many firms to invest in India does not amount to much. . . . The Government's review . . . has also revealed that in a large number of cases the parties rely heavily on the PL 480 counterpart funds to meet practically their entire requirements of rupee resources.[3]

This is not a problem peculiar to India—an American study for

[1] Friedmann and Kalmanoff, *Joint International Business Ventures*, p. 390.
[2] See above, pp. 231, 248.
[3] H. Venkatasubbiah, *Hindu*, 27 December 1961.

1960 shows that the United States Government had to put up between four and five dollars to shift one private investment dollar abroad[1]—nor is it a transient one, since it derives from the somewhat perverse incentives which bring most foreign firms to invest. So long as these hold, rupee risk-capital will offer attractions in its own right, beyond its effect on relations with the Government or with financial institutions, or its role as a catalyst for local intermediaries. The change in the ownership-mix just mentioned tells its own tale,[2] as do the paucity of the flow of fresh capital into India[3] and the expansions undertaken in recent years by the biggest foreign firms, with little or no fresh investment in foreign currency.

(*e*) *Sales outlets:* Reluctance to commit owned funds and limitations on imports combine to favour the use of collaborative ventures to serve as sales outlets for the foreign partner. The pharmaceuticals industry is a notorious example. In its 1954 *Report*, the Pharmaceuticals Enquiry Committee pointed out that for essential drugs the normal course was to pay

huge royalties on finished products imported in bulk and only repacked in this country; . . . where provision for . . . manufacture . . . has been mentioned, the actual manufacturer has stopped at a stage of converting the penultimate product to the final product. . . . In some agreements payment of royalty has been stipulated for the distribution rights in this country of finished products ready-packed for the market. . . .[4]

Two years later a party of Russian experts confirmed:

The pharmaceuticals factories in India are mainly occupied in processing (preparation of mixtures, tablets, injections of solutions, ampoules, etc.) of drugs imported mainly from abroad and almost all the essential drugs . . . are not being produced in the country but imported from outside in 'bulk' form or in the form of completed penultimates from which essential drugs can be produced by methods of simple and easy technological processes.[5]

It was not until the state made moves to enter the field and simultaneously tightened imports of intermediates that local production of some lines was undertaken.[6]

An important condition for this use of collaboration is that the Indian subsidiary or associate be tied to a single source of supply. In the past, this was so general as barely to require substantiation.

[1] Marina von Neumann Whitman, 'US Private Foreign Investment; A Study of the Role of Five Agencies', *EW*, 12 August 1961, pp. 1291–1302.
[2] See above, p. 259.   [3] See below, pp. 309 ff.   [4] loc. cit., pp. 68, 69.
[5] Quoted in Sokhey, *The Indian Drug Industry*, p. 4.   [6] See above, pp. 211 ff.

In the 1946 Agreement between Atul Products Ltd. and the American Cynamid Co. for example, the latter was appointed Atul's purchasing agent in the United States; in its later agreement with CIBA Ltd. Basle, Atul undertook to maintain CIBA's position in the market for Cibazol until its own licensed production attained sufficient volume and quality to be substituted for it; Atul also undertook not to sell its own product to third parties or through distribution facilities of its own without the Swiss partner's consent.[1] Any number of further examples could be adduced.

Sole supplier agreements of this kind have been used—notably in cases where foreign equity is negligible or secondary—to raise prices of the goods and services supplied.[2] 'Exploitation by foreign supplier's was mentioned explicitly in this connexion by the Tariff Commission.[3] They showed that one-quarter of Atul's output was based on raw materials and intermediates imported at anything between the price of the finished product on world markets and twice that price.[4] On another occasion they spoke of 'exorbitant terms' demanded by European firms when approached for technical services and supplies by the only Indian aluminium producer.[5] In one of their reports on the automobile industry, they pointed to the general absence of agreements regarding the cost of individual items in imported knocked-down packs and of provisions whereby their price would diminish *pari passu* with the progressive manufacture of components locally.[6] On yet another occasion they pointed out that 'the handicap of the [para-aminosalicylic acid] industry arises from the high cost of *imported* raw materials which constitutes 90 per cent of the total cost of production'.[7]

Agreements of this type, in which the bulk of final value is imported, are on the way out in most industries. Pressed by a chronic shortage of foreign exchange and encouraged by a growing number of foreign applicants for industrial licences, the Government has been making it increasingly difficult to evade their 'progressive manufacture' requirements. In consequence, the market for foreign firms

---

[1] Friedmann and Kalmanoff, *Joint International Business Ventures*, pp. 381, 383.

[2] Examples of price manipulation to depress profits in controlled foreign firms have been given in a different context (above, pp. 226 ff.). Naturally, there is no hard division between them.

[3] *Report on the Dyestuffs Industry*, 1955, p. 43.   [4] ibid., pp. 30–31.

[5] *Report . . . on . . . the Aluminium Industry*, 1951, p. 94.

[6] *Report on the Automobile Industry*, 1956, pp. 63–64 *passim*.

[7] *Report . . . Para-Aminosalicylic Acid Industry*, 1958, p. 23 (italics in the original).

unwilling to commit themselves fully to manufacturing in India is becoming increasingly one for machinery, equipment, and industrial raw materials.

Here too sales and collaboration intermix. In a substantial number of cases—how many is impossible to know without free access to the Agreements—what appears to be genuine financial involvement on the part of the foreign partner is no more than an allocation of shares in lieu of royalty payments or payment for plant sold to the Indian firm, the latter being a form of delayed and, if all goes well, highly profitable, sales revenue for the foreign partner.[1]

The 1961 agreement to establish Flender Macneill Gears Ltd. seems fairly typical: the German partner's share of equity being made up of Rs 1·88 lakhs in respect of knowhow, and Rs 10·62 lakhs in respect of machinery supplied.[2] In the case of Anand Automobiles Ltd., New Delhi, the American partner received the entire payment for capital equipment supplied—Rs 9 lakhs—in equity.[3] Daimler-Benz *AG* received ordinary shares worth Rs 80 lakhs, two-fifths the issued capital in Tata's automobile division, in consideration of the latter's right to act as sole agents for Daimler-Benz products in the area, to receive technical advice and assistance, to use Daimler-Benz patents, processes, trade-marks, and training facilities—all in addition to royalties, fees for jigs, tools, fixtures, designs etc., and, of course, profits on the assigned shares.[4] Harbanslal Malhotra and Sons Private Ltd., the major producer of steel files, were reported to be setting up a new venture with French participation, in which the foreign partner would receive 30 per cent of the equity in exchange for equipment and knowhow.[5] So important is this market on occasion that one firm wrote a clause into its agreement with an Indian partner allowing a reduction of one-quarter in the price of the machines it was supplying if more than a certain number were ordered within one year of ratification.[6]

These are not isolated examples. In their 1953 *Survey*, the Reserve Bank reported that 'some companies registered in India instead of

[1] These are cases which the Reserve Bank exclude from their definition of foreign-controlled companies even when 'assigned shares' form more than 40 per cent of the total (RBI, *Survey 1953*, p. 12).

[2] Information supplied privately.   [3] Information supplied privately.

[4] Friedmann and Kalmanoff, *Joint International Business Ventures*, pp. 467–8 471.

[5] Tariff Commission, *Report on the . . . Steel Files Industry*, 1960, p. 5.

[6] Information supplied privately.

bringing funds from abroad bring equipment and issue to the foreigners in lieu thereof shares in the companies against the import of goods'.[1] Eight years later, this was shown to be official policy. 'In principle', explained the Indian Information Service, 'the cost of capital equipment to be imported is allowed, as a minimum, to be financed from abroad. This is permitted as equity participation itself or as equity and loans combined'.[2]

Without studying the many private agreements concluded annually no further comment can be made on these sales-for-equity, or on the rate at which equity exchanges for capital goods. However, one thing seems clear from the agreements acessible to this study and from hearsay—that assigning shares in this way is fairly popular. And one suspicion arises from this fact—that much of what appears as 'financial collaboration' is little more than sales of machinery and equipment on (infinitely) deferred-payment terms at a price more likely than not to appreciate with time.

(*f*) *Sales of technique:* Where the foreign investor is a manufacturing concern more or less duplicating its home operations, there is no clear dividing line between collaboration in order to sell machinery and equipment and collaboration in order to sustain a continuing sale of knowhow. The one usually entails the other as a matter of course—special jigs and tools being as necessary to put knowhow to use as is the case in reverse; in both, assigned shares are frequently accepted in payment.

Much of the attraction of technical collaboration agreements lies precisely in the ease with which a firm can find a market for know-how at little extra cost to itself, and in the lucrative nature of this market. Managements are eloquent on the subject and see in the paucity of higher managerial and technical personnel the only real problem. Despite this they have in fact managed to multiply revenue from this source: Indian payments abroad on account of royalties, patent fees, technical and professional services, more than doubled between 1951 and 1960 compared with an increase of one-sixth in total profits accruing to foreign investors during roughly the same period.[3]

---

[1] p. 84.   [2] *India News*, 22 April 1961, p. 5.

[3] See below, Tables 18, 19, pp. 306, 308. The importance of knowhow sales to large companies was underlined when the English Court of Appeal held that payments on this account to Rolls-Royce Ltd. from abroad were to be considered income for tax purposes rather than a sale of capital assets (reported in *Guardian*, 27 April 1961).

The terms on which foreign technical collaboration is accepted are, officially, indeterminate. The Government draws a distinction between royalty payments, payments for 'services rendered', and for 'the continued transmission of knowhow in regard to a licensed product'.[1] While preferring royalties not to exceed 5 per cent, attention has been drawn to the fact that 'there have been practically no instances where negotiations between the two parties have broken down because Government declined to approve a particular rate of royalty as being unduly high'.[2]

At the same time, while only 19 of 376 royalty agreements studied in 1960 and 1961 provided for payment above 5 per cent of turnover, 118 agreements (31 per cent) provided for additional payments of one form or another.[3]

Where substantial equity participation is involved, royalty payments are not normally allowed.[4] However, other payments of a like kind—for drawings, technical assistance in plant layout and installation, purchasing commissions, supply of products, a continuous flow of knowhow and improvements—are even less controlled and, unlike royalties, are tax-free.[5] These accounted for 59 per cent of all payments in the collaboration agreements studied in 1960 and 1961.[6]

The amounts individual firms receive in sales of knowhow in its various forms are sometimes very large indeed, as may be illustrated by reference to a few of the agreements to hand:

1. In the agreement between Steyr-Daimler-Puch *AG* of Austria and Messrs. Birajlal and Co., Lonavla, signed in 1961, the Indian party undertook to pay royalty of £13,000 per annum, subject to Indian taxes, but in no event less than £6,500 per annum, between the fifth and tenth year of the agreement's currency. The Austrian firm would receive, therefore, between

---

[1] US Department of Commerce, *Investment in India*, 1960, p. 157.

[2] The full Press Statement, dated 15 August 1958, reads: 'About royalty itself, Government are not committed to any particular rate though 5 per cent is, in practice, found to be generally the maximum rate—to the extent to which generalization can be made in matters in which the Indian and foreign collaborators themselves agree on. With reference, however, to specific cases where there has been adequate justification, Government have permitted royalties in excess of this percentage. There have been practically no . . .' etc., etc.

[3] Raj. K. Nigam, 'Flow of Foreign Investments', *Company News and Notes*, 1 August 1964, pp. 21–22.

[4] See, however, cases 5 and 6 below, pp. 270–1.

[5] ECAFE, *Bulletin*, June 1962, p. 13.

[6] Raj. K. Nigam, 'Flow of Foreign Investments', op. cit., p. 21.

Rs 432,500 and Rs 865,000 in royalty, besides dividends on its equity of Rs lakhs and interest, at 6 per cent guaranteed by the Reserve Bank, on a 4·5 million schilling loan 'for the purchase of machine tools manufactured and supplied by Steyr'.[1]

2. Two identical agreements concluded between Braithwaite and Co. (India) Ltd. and John Smith and Thomas Smith and Sons (Rodley) of Britain, in 1961, provide for a 5 per cent royalty on the net sales of machines, and one of 7½ per cent on parts. Costs of drawings etc. are extra.[2]

3. An early agreement between Atul Products Ltd. and the American Cynamid Co., signed in 1946, provided for 2½ per cent of net sales for each product in royalty 'whether or not this agreement has expired or been terminated during this period'. In addition there were to be 'such funds as are agreed upon as compensation before the departure' of American technicians on secondment to the Indian firm, and 'all incidental and other expenses including all taxes paid by or on behalf of such persons', 'in addition to the costs of first-class transportation, living accommodation and subsistence for such persons'.[3]

4. Ceat Tyres of India Ltd. undertook, by virtue of its agreement with Ceat Gomma *SpA*, in 1958, to pay a research and technical fee of 3 per cent on net sales on the first 325 tons ouput per month, declining to 2½ per cent on sales of over 600 tons per month; this was in addition to preliminary payments totalling Rs 7·5 lakhs and an oversea purchasing commission of 3 per cent for the machinery required beyond a given output and 1 per cent for raw materials.[4]

5. More recently, in 1960, Synthetics and Chemicals Ltd. undertook payment for technical assistance, knowhow, etc. to its American collaborator, Firestone Tyre and Rubber Co. Ltd., totalling Rs 1·9 crores over a ten-year period. Firestone's investment in the company is no more than Rs 1·5 crores—and earning dividends.[5]

---

[1] From information supplied privately.
[2] From information supplied privately.
[3] Friedmann and Kalmanoff, *Joint International Business Ventures*, pp. 381–2.
[4] *Joint . . . India*, pp. 132–3.
[5] From information supplied privately.

6. A similar agreement is that between the Madras Aluminium Co. Ltd. and Montecatini of Italy. Here too the foreign stake was Rs 1·5 crores and payments for services—Rs 40 lakhs for engineering fees, drawings, and other assistance; Rs 35 lakhs for experts, supervision, and other services; and Rs 45 lakhs for knowhow, totalling Rs 1·2 crores—were substantial. All this in addition to dividend payments.[1]

7. Finally, a case of technical collaboration which, unfortunately, may not be quoted, and in which the partners accept the 'standard' royalty—5 per cent of net sales subject to tax. In addition, they provide for a lump sum of 25,000 Swiss francs in 'consideration to [sic] the capital spent by [the foreign firm] on the development of the contract' and for 'extra payments in future to cover "out of pocket expenses" for some additional fresh designs and other manufacturing details from time to time'.[2]

As is suggested by some of these cases, knowhow imparted through seconding technicians can be very expensive. While evidence from the private sector is not readily available, there is no reason to suppose that the prices vary much from those charged to the Government. These can be exorbitant by Indian standards: an American dam consultant on a ten-year contract was reported to be getting $28,000 a year tax-free (Rs 10,000 a month) over and above his Indian expenses;[3] an American drug firm wanted $100 a day per technician seconded to build the Government penicillin plant at Pimpri;[4] consultants' fees at the three state steel plants were considered unjustifiably high by the Lok Sabha Estimates Committee.[5]

(g) *Acclimatization:* Sales of knowhow are not only lucrative in themselves, they permit foreign firms to acquaint themselves with Indian business conditions and to edge towards full collaboration, equity, and all, with minimum risk. Some agreements for technical collaboration provide for just such a transition. In one already cited, between Steyr-Daimler-Puch *AG* and Birajlal and Co., the Austrian firm reserves the right to convert its loan into equity up to 25 per cent

---

[1] From information supplied privately.   [2] Information supplied privately.
[3] The President of India was then receiving Rs 4,500 a month before tax, super-tax, and a voluntary cut of 15 per cent.
[4] Sokhey, 'Self-Sufficiency in Modern Medicine', *EW*, January 1958, p. 191.
[5] See 'The Construction of Steel Plants', *EW*, June 1960, pp. 941 ff., which gives figures for open and hidden consultancy fees in all three cases.

of the total and—subject to royalty payments being reviewed—even beyond.[1] In another agreement for purely technical collaboration, the foreign party stipulates explicitly that it 'shall have the right to enter into an arrangement with [the Indian party] for financial collaboration or capital participation in any venture which [the Indian party] may undertake for the manufacture or processing of the [named] equipment'.[2]

It is this interest on the part of newcomers coupled with their wariness that probably explains the relative popularity of purely technical collaborations with non-British foreign investors. Given their long association with India, British firms naturally still dominate the foreign private sector, accounting for three-quarters of total net inflow of private capital between 1956 and 1961.[3] But they are party to less than half that proportion of purely technical collaboration agreements—under 30 per cent of the total between 1957 and mid-1963.[4]

An analysis of consents for new capital issues leads to a similar conclusion. Between April 1956 and December 1964, British firms were associated with 109 out of the 324 consents granted with foreign participation (30 per cent). They accounted for only 23 of the 104 issues in which the foreign partner held less than one-quarter of the equity (the minimum required by law to veto decisions) and for only 34 of the 153 issues (one-fifth) in which the foreign partner might still be said not to be in control (i.e., in which under 40 per cent of equity is held abroad). At the other end of the scale, they accounted for 55 per cent of all new consents for foreign-*controlled* firms. With one or two exceptions non-British investors conform to an expected trend of edging towards greater financial involvement even in the short period spanned by Table 16 on p. 286.[5]

(*h*) *Staking a claim:* Possession of an industrial licence, an import permit, capital issues consent, and any of the thousand and one other evidences of official approval confer a substantial measure of monopoly in India's heavily regulated market. By analogy with precautionary patent application many international firms that are not prepared as yet to undertake full-blown production, join with an

---

[1] Information supplied privately.   [2] Information supplied privately.

[3] From RBI, *Survey 1961*, Statements 8, 13, pp. 70, 80–82.

[4] From Table 14, pp. 260–1, above.

[5] See below, pp. 274 ff., for an explanation of the degrees of control differentiated in the text and table.

Indian partner merely to give body to their licences and hedge against the future. Describing the mammoth American firm he was partnering, an Indian businessman put the case succinctly: 'They consider Rs 80 lakhs a small entrance fee to remain in the market until it grows. They don't get very much; they lose nothing. They don't interfere. And they sell us the 15 per cent of components we import at world prices.'

(j) *Politics:* From outside, it is impossible to gauge the influence of non-commercial considerations on business policy. If assertions from all quarters of the political compass are to be believed, it is considerable, particularly among the international giants. Communist Party opinion has it that 'ICI have made a solid insurance against political risks by linking up with Tatas'.[1] Semi-official opinion is no different: thus G. L. Mehta, Chairman, Industrial Credit and Investment Corporation of India Ltd.—'rightly or wrongly, [collaboration] is considered by many to be a sort of security against the vagaries of governmental policy'.[2] The point is that equality of treatment with Indian firms, 'national treatment' as it is known, is as important to foreign capital as is sympathetic treatment for the private sector as a whole. Collaboration secures the former while simultaneously improving the chances for the latter.[3]

Perhaps reflecting these considerations as well as the pull of a booming, more profitable, and less controlled private sector, foreign firms have increasingly shied away from joint projects with the state, in which they were to have put up some equity as well as knowhow. At one time they were happy with this type of collaboration.[4] Now most of those begun have been abandoned in their original form. Among them are Hindustan Machine Tools Ltd., for which Oerlikon Machine Tool Works of Switzerland had put up one-tenth of the initial capital; the Integral Coach Factory at Perambur, Madras, which also started with Swiss financial participation; the Hindustan Housing Factory (Private) Ltd., in which Swedish, then Danish,

---

[1] Bose, *Indo-British Big Business Deals*, p. 35. In the event, the negotiations on which this assertion was based came to nothing.

[2] Quoted in *The Call*, February 1960, p. 16.   [3] See above, pp. 177 ff.

[4] See above, p. 102. As late as 1957, on the eve of the great inflow of foreign private funds, an important daily could still write: '. . . the tendency persists for foreign industrial interests to look more readily to collaboration with state enterprise than with private enterprise in India in their respective expansion plans. . . .' (*Hindu*, 9 March 1957.)

capital was involved in conjunction with Indian private and public money; the Rourkela steel plant in which Krupp-Demag originally held one-fifth of the equity; and a projected Indo-Japanese steel plant which never materialized.[1] In each of these, the initial intention to have foreign private and Indian public capital in harness was recast in favour of full state ownership with foreign technical collaboration.

A few joint ventures of this sort remain, among them Indian Telephone Industries Ltd., in which the Automatic Telephone and Electric Co. Ltd. of Britain has a 10 per cent stake; Indian Explosives Ltd., in which ICI hold four-fifths of the equity (and run as a subsidiary with no more than token Government intervention); Oil India (Private) Ltd., in which Burmah Oil has been relinquishing its holding in recent years and is now equal partner with the Government; or Hindustan Organic Chemicals Ltd., in which the Bayers Consortium hold 42·8 per cent of authorized capital. But these are exceptions in which the Government is either very much a sleeping partner or in the process of replacing the private interest.

IV THE LIMITS TO COLLABORATION

(a) *Extent and growth of control:* Neither increasing collaboration nor the Indianization of foreign investment has resulted in a diminution in foreign control of individual projects. On the contrary, controlled business investment as defined by the Reserve Bank,[2] rose from 79·4 per cent of the total in mid-1948[3] to 99·1 per cent at the end of 1961.[4] Nor has the *desire* to control lessened. Using a far less comprehensive definition of control than the Bank's,[5] and taking no account of prior rejections or amendments by the Capital Issues

[1] Spencer, *India, Mixed Enterprise and Western Business*, pp. 130–3.

[2] That is, companies falling in any of five categories: (1) branches of companies registered abroad; (2) subsidiaries of foreign companies—i.e. companies more than half of whose capital is held by a foreign company; (3) joint-stock companies other than subsidiaries, 40 per cent or more of whose ordinary shares are held in one country abroad unless, in the official view, managerial control rests with the Indian partner, or the shares were 'assigned'; (4) companies managed by a foreign-controlled managing agency in terms of a managing-agency agreement; (5) companies 25 per cent or more of whose ordinary shares are owned by another foreign-controlled company in India (from RBI, *Survey 1953*, p. 12; *Survey 1955*, pp. 10–11).

[3] RBI, *Census*, Table III–27, pp. 85–86.

[4] From RBI, *Survey 1961*, Statement 13, pp. 80–82.

[5] Covering only items 2 and 3 in the Reserve Bank's categories (as listed in footnote 2).

Committee—both of which must result in gross understatement of the results—control was permitted to rest with the foreign collaborator in 169 out of 324 possible cases between April 1956 and December 1964, or 52 per cent of cases accounting for 42 per cent of authorized capital.[1]

This desire bears no relation to the size of operations envisaged at the time of applying for consent. Of the 80 authorized issues of Rs 1 crore and above, only 29 are foreign controlled; the average new controlled issue is four-fifths the average for all new foreign-associated issues (Table 15, p.277, column 10, rows 15, 17) or, if the exceptionally large Oil India issue of 1958–9 be excluded, as it should,[2] under three-quarters (column 10, rows 16, 18). The size of the foreign *stake* is of greater weight. But here too the positive correlation (between the size of the proposed foreign equity and the degree of foreign control) is small, particularly if the Oil India issue is excluded. In the latter case, the average foreign component in foreign-controlled companies is little more than one-fifth larger than the foreign component in all new issues with foreign collaboration (from column 10, rows 30, 32). Nor is there a significant difference in the distribution of investments by size groups as between the three categories of control.

The table indicates a slightly more positive correlation between technological intensity and foreign control: 43 per cent of authorized capital in the industries normally considered to be of high and medium technological intensity was foreign controlled, compared with 42 per cent for all issues and 40 per cent for the rest. But for reasons already stated, the criteria of technological intensity are too crude to be of much value.[3]

Failing an altogether convincing explanation in the nature of the *investment*, reference to the *investor* might be more fruitful. An Indian joint-stock company formed from a branch or set up in conjunction with the foreign parent of a functioning controlled company is more likely to be foreign-controlled than a total newcomer, since the parent will press harder for the continuity of working habits, staff, administrative arrangements, and so on. In the eight and three-

---

[1] The analysis of Capital Issues Consents in this section is based on the sources referred to on p. 239 n. 5.

[2] The Oil India issue was twenty-five times the average issue in size and more than twice the second largest issue, that of the National Organic Chemical Industries Ltd. for Rs 10 crores, in 1964.

[3] See above, p. 244.

TABLE 15. *India: Consents for New Capital Issues with Foreign Participation*

		High Technological Content		
		Chemicals and allied (1)	Electrical Eng. (2)	Sub-total (1)+(2) (3)
1	No. of New Capital Issues Consents (3+5+7)	57	19	76
2	excl. Oil India & Nat. Org. Chems. (4+6+7)	56	19	75
3	Controlled	33	14	47
4	excl. Oil India	33	14	47
5	Indeterminate	11	2	13
6	excl. National Organic Chemicals	10	2	12
7	Uncontrolled	13	3	16
8	Value of authorized issues (10+12+14)	6,827·46	955·80	7,783·26
9	excl. Oil India & Nat. Org. Chems. (11+13+14)	5,827·46	955·80	6,783·26
10	Controlled	2,693·96	615·80	3,309·76
11	excl. Oil India	2,693·96	615·80	3,309·76
12	Indeterminate	2,500·00	135·00	2,635·00
13	excl. National Organic Chemicals	1,500·00	135·00	1,635·00
14	Uncontrolled	1,633·50	205·00	1,838·50
15	Average authorized issue (8÷1)	119·78	50·31	102·41
16	excl. Oil India & Nat. Org. Chems. (9÷2)	104·06	50·31	90·44
17	Controlled (10÷3)	81·64	43·99	70·42
18	excl. Oil India (11÷4)	81·64	43·99	70·42
19	Indeterminate (12÷5)	227·27	67·50	202·69
20	excl. Nat. Org. Chems. (13÷6)	150·00	67·50	136·25
21	Uncontrolled	125·65	68·33	114·90
22	Authorized foreign investment (24+26+28)	2,526·62	382·49	2,909·11
23	excl. Oil India & Nat. Org. Chems. (25+27+29)	2,192·62	382·49	2,575·11
24	Controlled	1,412·59	327·64	1,740·23
25	excl. Oil India	1,412·59	327·64	1,740·23
26	Indeterminate	775·30	35·10	810·40
27	excl. Nat. Org. Chems.	441·30	35·10	476·40
28	Uncontrolled	338·73	19·75	358·48
29	Average authorized foreign investment (22÷1)	44·33	20·13	38·27
30	excl. Oil India & Nat. Org. Chems. (23÷2)	39·15	20·13	34·33
31	Controlled (24÷3)	42·81	23·40	37·03
32	excl. Oil India (25÷4)	42·81	23·40	37·03
33	Indeterminate (26÷5)	10·48	17·55	62·34
34	excl. Nat. Org. Chems. (27÷6)	44·13	17·55	39·70
35	Uncontrolled	26·06	6·58	22·41

Source: as in p. 239 n. 5.

Note: In Indian conditions a shareholding of under 25 per cent is unlikely to carry with it control in new, director-run companies, since it is below the minimum required to block 'special resolutions' (see below, p. 286). Available data

by Degree of Participation and Industry, April 1956 to December 1964

Rs lakhs

| Medium Technological Content | | | | | LowTech.Con. | |
Man-made fibres (4)	Metal mfrs. (5)	Gen. Eng. (6)	Vehicles and parts (7)	Sub-total (4)–(7) (8)	Sub-total (9)	Total all industries (10)
4	26	73	37	140	108	324
4	26	73	37	140	107	322
1	10	41	20	72	50	169
1	10	41	20	72	49	168
—	5	10	8	23	18	54
—	5	10	8	23	18	53
3	11	22	9	45	40	101
1,300·00	2,249·37	3,828·61	2,450·56	9,828·54	9,979·60	27,591·40
1,300·00	2,249·37	3,828·61	2,450·56	9,828·54	7,879·60	24,491·40
250·00	555·00	2,265·11	1,189·87	4,259·98	3,961·24	11,530·98
250·00	555·00	2,265·11	1,189·87	4,259·98	1,861·24	9,430·98
—	535·00	351·00	470·69	1,356·69	1,607·15	5,598·84
—	535·00	351·00	470·69	1,356·69	1,607·15	4,598·84
1,050·00	1,159·37	1,212·50	790·00	4,211·87	4,411·21	10,461·58
425·00	86·51	52·45	66·23	70·20	92·40	85·16
425·00	86·51	52·45	66·23	70·20	73·64	76·06
250·00	55·50	55·25	59·49	59·17	79·22	68·23
250·00	55·50	55·25	59·49	59·17	37·98	56·14
—	107·00	35·10	58·84	58·99	99·29	103·68
—	107·00	35·10	58·84	58·99	99·29	86·77
350·00	105·40	55·11	87·78	93·60	110·28	103·58
303·25	606·40	1,487·31	868·68	3,265·64	3,578·97	9,753·72
303·25	606·40	1,487·31	868·68	3,265·64	2,178·97	8,019·72
150·00	292·51	1,220·99	649·18	2,312·68	2,458·09	6,511·00
150·00	292·51	1,220·99	649·18	2,312·68	1,058·09	5,111·00
—	146·47	110·52	148·84	405·84	517·48	1,733·72
—	146·47	110·52	148·84	405·84	517·48	1,399·72
153·25	167·42	155·80	70·65	547·12	603·40	1,509·00
75·81	23·32	20·37	23·48	23·33	31·39	30·10
75·81	23·32	20·37	23·48	23·33	20·36	24·91
150·00	29·25	29·78	32·46	32·12	49·16	38·53
150·00	29·25	29·78	32·46	32·12	21·59	30·42
—	29·29	11·05	18·61	17·65	28·75	32·11
—	29·29	11·05	18·61	17·65	28·75	26·41
51·08	15·22	7·82	7·85	12·16	15·09	14·94

provide no basis for estimating the number of *controlled* companies within the 25–40 per cent range; that such exist is clear from the foregoing and general considerations. Nor is there any basis for excluding companies from the 'controlled' category, although exceptions must exist.

quarter years covered, there were forty-two identifiable cases of this nature, thirty-two of which resulted in foreign-controlled Indian joint-stock companies. Of these, two remained fully-owned foreign subsidiaries; in eighteen others the foreign holding was more than half.

The size and policy of the Indian partner, if such exists as a single, identifiable person or body, are also significant. A large Indian house is usually able, if it wish, to persuade the licensing authorities of the virtues of economic nationalism; and often able to strengthen its position by spreading its collaborations widely as between foreign firms and countries. Some, like Tata, prefer to be agnostic, and are guided by purely business considerations; others, the Shri Ram group for example, are reputed to adopt a 'nationalist' line. On balance the top houses seem chary of collaborating on a minority basis and appear to have impressed their views on both foreign collaborators and the Government. Data are readily available for only three years, 1959/60–1961/2, and provide little basis for generalization: however, of the 107 new joint ventures in the two years, only seven, accounting for under 3 per cent of all authorized capital, were sponsored by any of the eight largest Indian groups;[1] five of these (four in the Tata group) provided for foreign majority ownership.

Finally, there is the size and international scope of the foreign firm. A big, international company is more likely to demand—and get—control of a new joint venture, than any other. Although the figures for new consents are not altogether unambiguous, they do point in that direction: whereas companies within the top hundred companies at home were associated with under one-fifth of all new Indo-British ventures in the eight and three-quarter years, they accounted for three-quarters of all British-controlled issues; furthermore, in the first five years of the period, except in two cases where financial collaboration was clearly an unimportant by-product of the sale of knowhow (where the foreign shareholding was under 10 per cent), all of the eighteen companies operating in six or more countries were in control of their new joint ventures in India from the start.

(b) *Incentives to control:* The increasing ease and speed with which central control can now be exercised in even the most far-flung international company, gives a sharp edge to many of the arguments for

[1] A representative selection would consist of Tata, Birla, Martin Burn, Dalmia-Jain, Bangur, Thapar, J-K, Shri Ram; together they accounted for 27 per cent of total gross capital stock in the corporate private sector in 1958 (Hazari, *Structure of the Corporate Private Sector*, Table 4.3, pp. 23–25).

it. A strong one rests on the benefits derived by a large firm from the division of labour, or specialization, within it.

In manufacturing, particularly in the technologically-intensive industries where skills and fixed capital rather than raw materials are the key inputs, the large firm generally finds advantage in concentrating production at home, where these inputs are in relatively good supply. In some cases, the advantages of scale point to production in one giant plant; in most, however, and nearly always where assembly is fairly important, the technical and economic case for concentration is less compelling and a firm might find advantage in dispersal while keeping manufacture of some components in one or two plants. The degree of concentration and dispersal are infinitely variable: at one end of the spectrum stands, say, IBM which distributes the manufacture of components between the score or so of countries in which it operates; at the other, ICI perhaps, or Unilever, or Tube Investments, whose manufacturing activities are fairly comprehensive in any one country. Whatever the precise arrangement, advantage normally lies in some degree of concentration and specialization, which management must be in a position to enforce.

Specialization and its corollary, interchangeability of parts, imply strict control over the manufacturing process. But they are not the only reasons. In so far as a firm's market depends on its being able to supply large quantities of even quality, full quality control is essential. In practice, whatever the arrangements for allocating functions between the Indian and foreign partners, whatever the distribution of share capital between them, whether the foreign firm be large or small, with or without a technical division of labour between parent and subsidiary unit—almost invariably, it appears, works management remains in non-Indian hands.

An important form of functional specialization is the concentration of certain general operations in the parent plant, most typically research and development. These have long ceased to be the inspired achievement of individuals; and are the organized, predictable output of teams based on a highly developed educational infrastructure such as is to be found only in the developed world. Here, probably more than anywhere else, concentration of resources and specialization pay off. And naturally it is in research and development that foreign subsidiaries and associates are most dependent on their parent concerns, and least able to undertake fully-independent production over the long term.

A number of non-technical factors reinforce these centripetal tendencies. Some derive from the proliferation of tariff- and quota-protected markets, the very factor which most often precipitates foreign investment. Manufacturing abroad creates a problem of the origin of exports. A large firm normally finds it easier to ship products from its home base: production costs might be, and in the case of technologically-complex products almost certainly will be, lower; exporting knowhow and the necessary contacts are to hand; the parent firm is normally better able than its foreign affiliate to supply credit from its own resources or from the public credit facilities which abound in developed countries.[1] There might be other reasons as well: a firm might prefer to export from a fully-owned subsidiary elsewhere than from a joint venture in India;[2] increasingly, the quota-free export markets are to be found in developed countries in which consumers can be expected to discriminate against the inferior products marketed in backward countries under internationally known brand names; there is often indirect pressure from the Government to 'save sterling' (or whatever the home currency) through exports; and direct pressure from labour to safeguard jobs. For these and other reasons, parent firms have tended to exercise very strict control over the international operations of their associates in India and elsewhere, through formal agreements[3] or informal arrangements.

There are, of course, factors working in the other direction. Some export opportunities arise in India and nowhere else, as when aid funds are allocated for exports to specific countries; or as part of the trading arrangements with Eastern Bloc countries; or when rupee-surplus countries, such as Egypt or Yugoslavia in the early sixties, are willing to buy high-cost Indian products for lack of alternative foreign exchange. The Indian Government is as capable as any other of putting pressure on firms to export, and many firms have seen wisdom in doing so at a discount or at some other inconvenience to themselves, in order to obviate yet greater inconvenience from the Government, or to benefit from more generous treatment. All this said, it remains true generally that the over-all interests of a firm

---

[1] See above, p. 231 n. 3, for examples.

[2] A number of such cases were reported privately to the author, in one of which the preference was so strong that a prospective investment, made conditional on a specific export performance, was not proceeded with.

[3] See below, pp. 281 ff.

manufacturing in a number of countries are strongly opposed to exporting from their local affiliates.

Exports are an aspect of a larger balance-of-payments problem which impinges directly on a firm's freedom to allocate funds—and staff—as it sees fit. So long as the larger problem exists and so long as its effect can be mitigated by adjusting the form of business operation to the precise, and changing, pattern of exchange control—for example, by substituting loans for equity investment; or fees for royalties; or commissions for profits; or by any other method—there is point in exerting the fullest possible control over foreign affiliates. Similar in effect is the wish to keep global tax liabilities to a minimum —in both cases, the foreign investor would wish to be in a position to appoint the 'man who handles the money'.

Control, particularly such as is implicit in the practical division of labour within a firm internationally, is an added form of political insurance. As one student of American management abroad put it, 'especially where United States foreign units are dependent upon parts and materials from the United States, the chances of expropriation are minimised because expropriation would not give the country the most valuable assets of the company'.[1]

There are other factors—one could mention the unease felt by management when working within a diplomatically-charged atmosphere as might exist between equal partners with different traditions,[2] the financial advantage that might accrue to a growing firm from a consolidation of its foreign affiliates' accounts with its own,[3] and so on—but enough has been said to show that the drive to control rests on solid ground both within the firm and in its *milieu*.

(c) *The Collaboration Agreement—instrument of control:*[4] The terms of collaboration between a firm operating in India and its foreign associate are normally set out in an Agreement or series of Agreements between them, governing the scope of local manufacture;

---

[1] Barlow, *Foreign Manufacturing Subsidiaries*, p. 12.

[2] 'The strength of an enterprise lies to a great degree in the unanimity with which it is directed and in which new initiatives are developed.' (Haccoû, *Management of Direct Investments*, p. 73.)

[3] In Britain, this can be done only in the case of subsidiaries or majority-owned companies.

[4] This section is based on twenty-four agreements made available wholly or in part during the course of this study. They relate in the main to the early 1960's. Since they are private documents, mostly shown in confidence, detailed reference is not possible. Other sources are referred to in the normal way.

payment of royalty, fees, etc.; distribution of ownership; allocation of markets; use of trade marks; composition of the board of directors; allocation of administrative and technical functions; provision for arbitration in the event of dispute between the parties, and a host of eventualities that defy classification. While each is a unique document, analysis of the agreements made available for this study reveals certain uniformities, not the least apparent or important amongst which is the dominance of the foreign associate.[1]

Typically, strict control is sought over the use to which the techniques imparted are put. This applies equally to a foreign branch, subsidiary company, or an independent company. The Indian firm is usually enjoined to keep secret, during and even after the currency of the agreement, all information supplied within its terms, by exercising 'due diligence', by not sub-licensing, or by not collaborating with other parties in related fields. In most cases, not all, the use of information received must be discontinued after the agreement lapses, and in a few, the Indian firm must be prepared to return all drawings, specifications, and other data supplied. Moreover, the supplier of the new technique is often protected from imparting a complete technology by clauses which specifically exclude 'fundamental investigation and development', or which permit it not to disclose information 'which it does not have the right to disclose by reason of contractual obligations incurred prior to' the agreement. Finally, while the Indian associate is not always granted exclusive use of the foreign partner's patents in India, it is normally 'not entitled to use any knowledge about inventions of [the foreign firm] for the procurement of own patents'.

Production is almost as tightly controlled. While one agreement permits the Indian partner to develop its own designs, it does so on condition that the foreign partner first be consulted and that 'production does not encroach upon the space needed for manufacture of [the foreign firm's] parts'. In other cases, modifications made abroad must be incorporated into the Indian product whether justified in Indian conditions or not. In one such case, the Indian company

recognises that certain changes in the design of [the foreign] machines may be made by the [foreign company] and that such changes may become mandatory in the design of [the foreign] machines manufactured by [the

[1] Some of the more typical financial provisions have been described elsewhere in this chapter, see pp. 269 ff.

Indian company]. If [the foreign company] makes such a design change mandatory prior to the completion of manufacturing of a [foreign] machine by [the Indian company] the [Indian company] shall bear the cost of any obsolescence which may arise by reason thereof.

Naturally, the foreign firm frequently insists on appointing some of the joint-venture's directors and, almost invariably, some of its key personnel. So crucial is this provision, that one agreement went so far as to insist on an appointment whether or not it was enforceable in law. To quote:

for the period of its participation in the share capital, [the foreign company] reserves itself the right to appoint one Director for the Board of Directors and to delegate a consultative person or adviser of the Managing Director. This right should be laid down in the regulations of the new corporation, provided the Indian Laws permit such procedure; *at any event [the Indian company] has to ensure that [the foreign company's] right for such a delegation is guaranteed.*[1]

The agreements show foreign companies as eager to control the sales side of a joint venture. One of the most frequent provisions—almost universal in Indo-British agreements,[2] and one on which the Tariff Commission has consistently rounded[3]—limits the Indian firm's freedom to sell abroad (although, quite often, the foreign firm is not precluded from continuing to sell in India). In some cases, the right to export is conditional on the use of the foreign firm's sales organization abroad. (There are in fact cases in which production for the *Indian* market is also channelled through a foreign-controlled marketing organization). Where an export territory is permitted, it is usually confined to the narrow, regional markets: Pakistan, Burma, Ceylon, Nepal, Afghanistan. In the few cases in which the export territory is more liberally defined, it is usually in need of development from scratch. This is true, for example, of the permission granted ACC-Vickers-Babcox to sell in South-East Asia, the Middle East, and Africa ('without detriment to the interests of the foreign participating concerns') where, in the words of an appreciative commentator, 'the market would have to be developed over a period

---

[1] Italics added. It is interesting to note that the foreign collaborator held a mere twelfth of the equity in this joint venture. Equally interesting is that the Government of India sanctioned the agreement.

[2] *EW*, 19 July 1958, p. 962.

[3] See, for example, *Report on . . . Rubber Tyres and Tubes*, 1955, pp. 14–15; *Report . . . on . . . the Bicycle Industry*, 1957, p. 33; *Report on . . . the Engineers' Steel Files Industry*, 1960, p. 5.

of time';[1] or of Sen-Raleigh which, following an official request, received permission from its parent body to export to a number of Eastern Bloc countries.[2] Trade marks are not always allowed the Indian company and, finally, a clause stipulating a period of non-competition between the signatories *after* the termination of an agreement is sometimes inserted.

In view of the need to gain official endorsement before they become operative, probably the most surprising aspect of these agreements is the wide scope for extra-territoriality claimed in the interpretation of their provisions. One example—of an appointment which might or might not be legally valid—has been given. It is no exception. Frequently the agreement stipulates that its foreign-language version, not its English translation, is the valid one. Even more frequently, provision is made for arbitration abroad in the event of dispute, or a clause inserted to the effect that 'this agreement shall be construed and enforced according to the laws of Switzerland', or of some other foreign country. In a small number of cases, power to judge the Indian signatory's performance has been vested in the foreign one. In one, the foreign firm reserves the right to terminate the agreement, *inter alia*, 'if [the Indian company] fails to maintain the required level of production, unless such failure is occasioned by circumstances which, *in [the foreign company's] opinion*, are beyond [the Indian company's] control'.[3] Too much can be made of these agreements.[4] In practice, collaboration is more flexible and relations between partners more liberal than would

[1] N. Dandekar, 'Foreign Investment in India', *Hindu*, 12 August 1961.
[2] S. K. Sen, Chairman, the Eighth General Meeting, 27 June 1958, as reported in *EW*, July 1958, p. 952.
[3] Italics added.
[4] Very recently the Government appears to have woken up to the implications of some of the restrictive clauses contained in Collaboration Agreements. If the chemical industry is representative—as officials directly concerned affirm (February 1965)—the most blatantly restrictive clauses are no longer allowed. 'Most of these restrictions', runs an authoritative analysis of the industry, 'no longer appear. . . . In contrast to earlier years, some of the recent agreements not only ensure the freedom to export, but also have a clause which makes the payment of royalty contingent on a *minimum* export performance by the company. Some agreements put the onus of attaining normal production on the collaborator and provide for compensation to the Indian company in the event of failure to rectify defects within a stipulated period. When renewing agreements, the government takes particular care to ensure that restrictive clauses, which virtually force the Indian party into a "non-terminable" agreement, are deleted.' ('Foreign Collaboration in the Chemical Industry', RBI *Bulletin*, November 1964, p. 1386. Italics in original.)

appear from a mere reading of the documents. Where they are not, it is not the formal provisions contained in the agreements that secure compliance by the Indian partner, but the superior strength of the foreign signatory and the measures it adopts to ensure continuing control.

(*d*) *Methods of Control:* Essentially, control rests with the power to initiate and carry through changes in the disposition of a firm's resources, however circumscribed in practice by the Government, labour, shareholders, the state of law or culture, or whatever. It can, and does, take many forms, some of which are sufficiently widespread to be considered standard.[1]

Ownership is the most obvious, and full ownership the most complete. Even today, more than half foreign-controlled investment is in branches which are fully owned by definition, and a further substantial, although indeterminate, proportion in wholly-owned subsidiaries.[2] However, the trend is against; branch organization, which offers considerable advantages in switching funds to and from the parent firm, loses much of its attraction when investments become relatively fixed, as they do in manufacturing enterprises catering for the host market; or when the Government scrutinizes every detail of each transfer. Both have been happening for some time and investment in branches as a proportion of controlled foreign investments has fallen in consequence from 66 per cent in mid-1948 to 47 per cent at the end of 1961.[3] Wholly-owned subsidiaries are also becoming less popular, for reasons already dealt with. Many have Indianized their capital, others are preparing to do so, and new ones are relatively unimportant: the fifteen for which consents were received in the eight and three-quarter years covered by Table 16, facing p. 286, accounted for only 3·1 per cent of the foreign stake and 2·7 per cent of foreign-associated authorized capital.

Nearly as effective in practice are substantial shareholdings short of 100 per cent in Indian joint-stock companies. These are illustrated in the table. A holding of 75 per cent or more ensures passage of the

---

[1] Control through associations and industry-wide organizations has been dealt with in connexion with the old foreign sector. See pp. 8 f., above.

[2] As late as 1951 a well-informed observer could write of foreign branches and 'local and *usually almost wholly-owned* subsidiaries' as 'the sector in which main expansion is taking place'. (Taya Zinkin, *Foreign Capital in India*, p. 46. Italics added.)

[3] RBI, *Survey 1961*, Statement 13, p. 80.

'special resolutions' required by law to change the capital structure of a company, its administration, and much else. Excluding the fifteen wholly-owned companies, there were ten in this category, accounting for 5 per cent of all authorized foreign investment in rupee companies. A further forty (16·5 per cent of investment) were in the less closely-controlled subsidiaries in which foreign capital still held a majority.[1]

The greatest number and amount of investments, one hundred companies and 27·7 per cent of the foreign stake, were in the next category: a minority interest of between 40 and 50 per cent, which the Reserve Bank considers large enough to constitute a controlling one. The increasing popularity of this category is easily explained: it satisfies the '51 per cent rule' which still carries some weight amongst officials and publicists despite its having been formally jettisoned;[2] in a number of cases it masks *de facto* majority ownership through shares held by nominees or Indian employees, which helps to explain the high proportion of holdings in the upper register—no less than sixty out of the hundred being of 49 and 50 per cent of equity; and where the foreign partner is in fact a minority shareholder, it can ensure continuing control by retaining a majority of voting shares[3] or —as is now the only permitted course—by rationing share allotments and so ensuring a wide dispersal of local ownership. Even where the Indian partner is more identifiable than the 'amorphous Indian public' as happens most frequently in the case of new, usually non-British ventures, the large foreign firm seldom links up with its Indian size-equivalent, but looks for the local organization and knowhow amongst smaller fry.[4]

It is unrealistic to suppose that this asymmetry of voting power loses its effectiveness below the Reserve Bank's threshold. The Bank recognizes two per cent shareholding as sufficient to ensure control when backed by a management contract;[5] and even without one, under Indian conditions, where a holding above 25 per cent enables a shareholder to block 'special resolutions' and local ownership is

---

[1] Excluding Oil India.   [2] See above, p. 157.

[3] The Indo-Burma Petroleum Co., Ltd., illustrates the method fairly common until recently: its paid-up capital of Rs 1·5 crores consists of Rs 1 crore in ordinary shares held in the ratio of 60:40 by foreign and domestic interests, and Rs 50 lakhs in preference shares, 98 per cent of which are Indian-owned (*Damle Report*, p. 8). In this way, a minority holding of slightly over two-fifths of paid-up capital is converted into a decisive majority by reservation of voting rights.

[4] See above, p. 275 f.   [5] RBI, *Survey 1955*, p. 15.

often very dispersed, there is a strong presumption that much of the 25–40 per cent category is also foreign-controlled.[1] Below that, although not inconceivable, control is probably the exception, particularly in the lower half of the category—accounting for 46 cases— where share-ownership is probably a by-product of technical collaboration.[2]

While ownership might ensure control it cannot by itself guarantee the smooth running of an enterprise, particularly one producing for the local market. For this, as has been shown, local collaboration is necessary. Even more important, the local partner must feel willing to co-operate over and above his contractual obligations as defined by ownership or any other formal criterion. It is here that the logic of the foreign firm's structure supervenes; its division of labour, administrative integration, technological complexity, and a number of other factors circumscribe the local partner's freedom as surely in practice as majority ownership or its equivalents do in law.

To repeat: if research is to pay off, the research effort must normally be centralized; second, royalties and fees on this account are becoming a factor of growing importance in the type of private investment being undertaken in India today. While there are some firms which find it necessary to adapt their products or methods to local needs, and so undertake a modicum of development research, this is usually done on a modest scale if at all and for strictly limited ends. Fundamental research and major developments in the private sector are, with perhaps the sole exception of Tata, a foreign responsibility.[3]

[1] Cf., for example, H. K. S. Lindsay, Managing Director, The Metal Box Co. of India Ltd.: 'Minority participation does not appear to have prevented the foreign partner exercising a substantial degree of control in technical and operational matters in several important cases. . . . Most of the matters that affect the affairs of the company require a three-fourths majority vote, because of which several foreign investors have found it unnecessary to take more than 26 per cent of the share in the equity.' (*The Role of Foreign Enterprise*, p. 31.) An opposite caveat should be entered here. A foreign company, however powerful, collaborating in a joint venture with a single, influential local concern, might well find its own initiatives stymied and be unable to ward off unwelcome policies.

[2] Firm statements can be dangerous here. In one case—that of Biosynth Ltd.— the Tariff Commission found the company so tied to its foreign associates for raw materials and proprietary processes that no benefits whatever accrued to it, although it was found to be wholly Indian-owned (*Report on . . . the Para-Aminosalicylic Acid Industry*, 1958, pp. 23–24. See below, p. 292).

[3] See, for example, the Tariff Commission on the bicycles industry: 'At present very little research is being done by indigenous manufacturers either on design or for the improvement of quality.' (*Report . . . Bicycle Industry*, 1960, p. 31.)

It would be too much to expect many firms, particularly the international giants, not to take advantage of their technological monopoly. Even if they wished it otherwise, the economics of research would in most cases discourage private capital from undertaking major projects in India until such time as the country, and its educational apparatus, appeared well on the way to maturity. Meanwhile, assuming no violent rupture in economic relations with the West, the technologically-progressive firm would seem securely in control of a joint venture in a technologically-intensive industry whatever its financial stake.

Although not always distinguishable from fundamental research and development, the application of results or operational knowhow is less a natural monopoly. In a sense it can be detached and used independently, either because the basic knowledge is almost entirely embodied in fixed equipment as in some chemical industries,[1] or because it is easily assimilated without expensive apparatus as in advertising, a booming industry peopled almost entirely by ex-employees of foreign agencies. Partly in order to prevent this, partly because technical and managerial skills are real constraints to their expansion, foreign firms have proved reluctant to impart much of their knowhow and skills to local personnel.

Commercial patenting, in force for over a century, has been used to this end. Nearly nine-tenths of the 14,000 registered patents have been granted to foreigners, compared with 13 per cent in the United States between 1930 and 1937, 24 per cent in Japan, and 52 per cent in Britain.[2] Patentees are heavily concentrated amongst the international giants: in 1946, the Controller of Patents received 2,610 applications, of which no more than 266 were from Indians. Of the rest, 223 were made by Standard Telephone and Cable Co., 88 by various divisions of General Electric, 84 by ICI, 60 by DuPont, 33 by Metropolitan-Vickers Electrical, 33 by Société des Usines Chimiques Rhône-Poulenc, 27 by J. R. Geigy *AG*, 25 by Ford Motor Co. of Canada, 24 by N. V. Philips Gloeilampenfabrieken, and so on.[3] It is these concentrations and the fact that one-quarter of patents registered are never exploited[4] that provide the substance of Justice Ayyangar's charge that the system has been used to block industrial

---

[1] See the example of soda ash production, below, p. 289.

[2] *Ayyangar Report*, pp. 13, 306. The few Indian patentees have confined their attention largely to cottage and small-scale industries.

[3] *EE*, 28 November 1947, p. 762.   [4] *EW*, 28 September 1963, p. 1624.

development in the country and for exacting unreasonably high payments from Indian licensees or importers.[1]

Boycotting of local production to conserve scarce skills is also not unknown. Within the industry, there is no mystery surrounding the Government's decision to set up a raw film factory on unfavourable terms with the aid of a relatively unknown French company.[2] One leading firm was offered the entire capital cost of the project and received full assurances about the employment of foreign technicians (forty places were asked for), profit levels, and repatriation of earnings—and still turned it down. Part of the reason undoubtedly lay in the relative narrowness of the Indian market; substantially, it lay in the company's reluctance to impart techniques which are still to some degree an 'art'.[3]

Similar cases are reported from other industries. In its first *Report . . . on the Soda Ash Industry*, 1949, the Tariff Board, as it then was, referred explicitly to the giant foreign producers' technological monopoly and to the difficulties encountered by independent Indian producers, including Tata, a large firm by any standard, in entering the field:

The soda ash industry almost all over the world [they wrote] is operated by a limited number of concerns under strict secrecy of plant design and method of production. The manufacturers in India were, therefore, placed at a disadvantage as they were unable to avail [themselves] of technical advice from manufacturers of equipment or from experts in production methods.[4]

'The chief difficulty', wrote an observer, 'lies in designing plant. Complete soda ash plants are just not available.'[5]

In an early report on the aluminium industry, the Board stated that the only Indian-controlled firm was 'facing considerable difficulty in getting experienced technical personnel and advice'.[6] After describing the unsatisfactory response to a request for technical assistance from European producers who 'demanded exorbitant terms', the Board recommended that 'Government should explore the possibility, under the Point Four Program, of securing the necessary technical advice and assistance . . . from the USA'.[7]

---

[1] *Ayyangar Report*, pp. 49–50, 79 ff.   [2] See above, p. 165.
[3] Information gained privately.   [4] pp. 13–14.
[5] Hitindra Malik, 'India's Heavy Chemical Industry', Supplement to *Capital*, 24 June 1954, p. 43.
[6] *Report . . . on . . . the Aluminium Industry*, 1951, p. 26.
[7] ibid., pp. 94–95.
20

American firms proved as reluctant as their European associates and, in the words of a later *Report*, 'the Aluminium Corporation of India have not been able to secure the necessary technical advice or assistance from [the] USA'.[1] It was not until their 1960 *Report*, more than a decade after the first moves were made, that the Commission was able to announce an agreement for technical collaboration between the Indian firm and a foreign one, Aluminium Industrie *AG* of Switzerland,[2] but by then the Indian company had been reduced to such straits that the expansion envisaged for the industry at the time left it relatively where it was.[3]

In connexion with motor-car production, the Commission drew pointed attention to the absence of any formal commitment on the part of foreign collaborators to make 'provision [for] technical assistance and foreign technical personnel, arrangements for the training of Indian personnel abroad, assistance . . . in securing the necessary collaboration from manufacturers of proprietary components and holders of foreign patents.'[4]

Firms will sometimes be very careful to preserve their know-how. Merck & Co. Inc., the American drug firm, commissioned to develop streptomycin production at Hindustan Antibiotics, Pimpri, is reported to have entered into an agreement with the Ministry of Commerce and Industry whereby information supplied by the company 'will not be communicated to any unauthorised person', and scientists to whom such information is disclosed or who may have access to it are bound by 'security arrangements in a form satisfactory to Merck'.[5] This is the more remarkable since the Government of India had previously undertaken—as a condition for receiving aid for the plant from the World Health Organization and UNICEF—to keep it open to all.

It is possible to go on quoting cases, backing them up with official statements, to the effect that the state oil industry was forced to start from scratch because the foreign companies had failed to train one Indian technologist throughout the sixty-odd years of their operations in the country;[6] that an agreement between Hindustan Motors

---

[1] Tariff Commission, *Report . . . on . . . the Aluminium Industry*, 1955, p. 5.

[2] *Report . . . Aluminium Industry*, 1960, p. 5.   [3] See above, p. 198.

[4] *Report on the Automobile Industry*, 1956, pp. 64–65.

[5] Sokhey, *Indian Drug Industry*, p. 14; 'The Drug Racket', *Science and Culture*, January 1962, p. 11.

[6] K. D. Malaviya, Minister of Mines and Oil, Lok Sabha, quoted in *Hindu*, 16 April 1961.

and the Studebaker-Packard Corporation had had to be abrogated because the Government 'was not satisfied with the technical assistance received';[1] that 'behind the foreign investor or would-be investor . . . there is a hesitation to entrust the Indian concerns with the knowhow for a period of years . . . and very often some of these negotiations with foreign capital break off and end in nothing';[2] that 'in spite of "sweet words" we have not been able to get from the West either the knowhow or the knowledge [for military airplane manufacture]'.[3] The point has been made however: technologically-progressive firms are, in the words of one managing director, 'wary of selling their birthright'.

It has not been lost on politicians, publicists, or competitors. A few days before Krishnamachari rounded on the assembly of foreign businessmen in the terms just quoted, and no doubt contributing to the acerbity of his tone, Khrùshchev had broadcast over All-India Radio:

Your cadres of technical personnel are growing. But to have more such people in your country, we are willing to share our knowledge and experience so that your country may rapidly cross the complicated and difficult way of creating her industry.[4]

While Indian nationalist opinion remains uncontradicted when it concludes: 'It is doubtful whether Indian engineers have acquired the knowledge and experience to build a second DVC or a second Bhakra Nangal [both Western-aided projects]',[5] a pronouncedly pro-Western observer could write: 'what makes [the Russian-built steel plant at] Bhilai specially valuable to India is the training program. Each Russian has at least one Indian understudy, and for three years after Bhilai comes into operation Indians will continue to be trained while working.' She goes on to draw an explicit contrast: 'In the West [Indian trainees] make friends and enjoy cinemas and plays, but they always sense a forbidden technical door. In Russia they get bored and exhausted but are initiated into all trade secrets.'[6]

[1] Manubhai Shah, Minister of State in the Ministry of Commerce and Industry, Lok Sabha, quoted in *NYT*, 30 April 1958.
[2] T. T. Krishnamachari, Minister for Commerce and Industry, at the Annual Meeting of the Associated Chambers of Commerce and Industry, Calcutta, quoted in *EW*, 17 December 1955, p. 1472.
[3] Krishna Menon, Minister of Defence, Lok Sabha, quoted in *Hindu*, 1 June 1962.
[4] Quoted in *EW*, 17 December 1955, p. 1472.   [5] ibid.
[6] Taya Zinkin, *MG*, 15 February 1958.

Withholding techniques is at best a crude defence of technological capital; at worst it is a self-defeating one, particularly in view of the growing internationalization of the Indian economy. Since in many cases it is virtually impossible to enforce secrecy clauses once production has started, a number of foreign firms limit the range of products or processes to be manufactured or used in India. It is difficult to isolate this factor from others that would tend to work in the same direction, such as the cost advantage of producing at home, the paucity of local skills, and so on, but it is clearly one to be considered. Thus, by virtue of an agreement drawn up with Cilag-Hind Private Ltd., a Swiss subsidiary, the wholly-Indian Biochemical and Synthetic Products Ltd. (Biosynth) are precluded 'from manufacturing any products other than those agreed to by Cilag-Hind . . . who decides . . . how the raw materials should be procured'.[1] In another case, 'Auto Accessories (India) Ltd., will not pay any royalty [to the British company with whom an agreement for technical collaboration had been concluded] but buy insulated centres from Smith Motor Accessories Ltd., at a fixed price per insulator and will not be free to manufacture insulated centres without their prior consent.'[2] In another case widely quoted at the end of the war, the decision as to which of the Hindustan 10's components were to be manufactured in India lay entirely with Nuffield which had no capital involved in its production.[3]

Unable to undertake full production, the Indian concern is often effectively prevented from adapting products and processes to local conditions and materials, or from encouraging local ancillary industries, and so becomes even more dependent on imported supplies. The Tariff Commission found considerable evidence of this in their inquiries: for example:

Automobile manufacturers do not appear to be interested in [the lack of Indian standards for piston rings, etc.] as most of the automobile engines assembled or manufactured in India are made in collaboration with overseas manufacturers, and pistons, piston rings, etc. have, therefore, to conform to the design and specifications of the overseas manufacturers of engines and to be approved by them.

Despite their recommendation of three years previously that

[1] Tariff Commission, *Report on . . . the Para-Aminosalicylic Acid Industry*, 1958, p. 6.
[2] Tariff Commission, *Report on the Automobile Sparking Plug Industry*, 1954, p. 6.
[3] *Capital*, 3 January 1946, cited in Bose, *Indo-British Big Business Deals*, p. 32.

indigenous manufacturers of automobiles, motor cycles and scooters, [and] diesel engines, . . . should expedite their negotiations with India Pistons for obtaining their requirements of piston assemblies from the company . . . progress in its implementation has not been satisfactory. . . . it takes time for individual firms to obtain their requirements from India Pistons as it involves in many cases approval of the products by their foreign collaborators. . . . The *ad hoc* Committee on the automobile industry . . . had received complaints that automobile manufacturers were not sympathetic to the ancillary industries and were trying to produce many items which had better be left to the latter . . . even where . . . test facilities are forthcoming and piston assemblies and parts of similar design and quality are known to be used by overseas manufacturers of vehicles, avoidable delay appears to persist on the part of the domestic producers to secure approval. . . .[1]

On another occasion, the Commission found that 'the Indian manufacturers have no option but to adopt . . . the frequent changes in specifications introduced by their foreign associates' at considerable cost to themselves and with little benefit to the consumer. They gave this as a cardinal reason for the delay in implementing the programme for progressive manufacture of automobiles adumbrated three years previously.[2] On yet another, they found that 'some manufacturers still display a marked preference for imported materials even when these are indigenously available at fairly reasonable prices. It would appear therefore that some transformer producers have not taken positive steps to encourage the development of ancillary industries in the country in spite of our observations in . . . our last report.'[3]

The public sector has had its share of difficulties on this score. Although power units for Gnat fighters and Avro 748 transport planes are now being made locally under licence, India is by no means self-sufficient in regard to their manufacture. She is obliged to import the fuel, power control, pressurization, and undercarriage braking systems, as well as radar, communications, and electronic equipment, as 'efforts to manufacture some of these accessories with the assistance of British firms have failed'.[4] Although by no means the only case of imposed dependence on imports, this one

[1] Tariff Commission, *Report on the . . . Piston Assembly . . . Industry*, 1960, pp. 3, 4–5.
[2] *Report on the Automobile Industry*, 1956, p. 47.
[3] *Report on the . . . Power and Distribution Transformer Industry*, 1960, p. 17.
[4] *Guardian*, 6 July 1963.

has been particularly galling to the Indian Government and a source of considerable international friction.[1]

As control is exercised ultimately through people, staffing policy is very important to foreign firms.

The foreign sector as a whole has Indianized its staff quite extensively since Independence. Figures issued by the Ministry of Industry show that the number of Indians employed by foreign-controlled firms at Rs 1,000 a month and above has risen from 504 or 7·9 per cent of the total in 1947, to 12,434, or 77·7 per cent, in 1963.[2] New-type investors have been particularly keen. They find local personnel cheaper by half or more; as efficient as expatriates in comparable jobs after comparable training; better able to interpret and act on local developments, the more so as few expatriates now contemplate an 'Indian career'. They find that control resides as much or more in a firm's internal organization as in the quality or attitudes of individual officers. Finally, Indians in high places makes sense politically.[3]

There are limits, however. As has been mentioned, most foreign firms insist on staffing the major technical posts in any joint venture. Works managers are almost invariably foreign; research departments, in so far as they exist, are normally under foreign direction. In non-technical fields, the foreign collaborator often insists on appointing the general manager and company secretary. Although inadequate in many ways,[4] the Ministry's figures shed some light on these limits: Indianization is still very much confined to the lower salary scales. At the top, say above Rs 3,000 per month, Indians are still a minority, some 31 per cent of the total on 1 January 1963; and at the very top, above Rs 5,000, they are very rare indeed—7·8 per cent on 1 January 1959, when last reported on. Expatriates are tending to concentrate more and more on these higher brackets: the proportion earning Rs 3,000 rising from 22 to 59 per cent between 1954 and 1963.[5]

[1] See Krishna Menon as quoted on p. 291, above; and the issue of arms production generally, above, pp. 117–19.

[2] GOI Press Notes, 8 November 1957, 21 February 1964.

[3] The subject has been treated more fully above, pp. 38–40.

[4] They have been criticized for making no adjustment for inflation; for the fact that replies are voluntary and politically motivated; for being based on a deliberately vague definition of 'salary'; and much else.

[5] From GOI Press Notes, 8 November 1957, 21 February 1964; Answer to Unstarred Question No. 427, Lok Sabha, 24 November 1961, *LS Debates*, 24 November 1961, Appendix I, Annexure No. 44, pp. 71–72.

With the big foreign firms actively pursuing it, and the Associated Chambers of Commerce and Industry willing—since 1960—to press its members to reserve for Indians all posts below Rs 2,000 per month and three-fifths of posts in the Rs 2–3,000 bracket, Indianization is bound to make further headway. Almost as certainly it will stop short of complete staffing by Indians. Even the most enthusiastic of managements with whom the matter was discussed expected to hold out for some expatriate staff for the foreseeable future; as few as three in some cases, as many as fifty in one. The fact is that the very conditions that give rise to pressures for Indianization—the trend towards controlled rupee companies, the growing stringency of foreign exchange control, Government pressure for exports, and so on—are precisely those which make Indianization at the very top embarrassing. It is not surprising, therefore, to find the Chairman of Unilever stressing the selection and remuneration of top management together, as one of the three controls which keep that vast company working coherently;[1] or to find an empirical study of management in backward countries concluding that freedom of choice in staffing key posts is the *sine qua non* of private investment.[2]

There is a second aspect of foreign capital's staffing policy relevant to foreign control. Salaries in well-known foreign firms are adjusted to expatriate levels, and employment in the higher echelons is in practice a considerable privilege. A ubiquitous snobbery—there is no other word for it—reinforces the strong tendency within this group to set itself apart from Indian society, and to identify itself with their firm, at the same time as these firms' constant reiteration of their own 'Indian status' makes identification relatively easy. These are subtle matters which require a subtler analysis than can be attempted here, but even the most insensitive visitor to New Delhi or Calcutta will notice a distinct, 'club' atmosphere amongst the higher Indian personnel of foreign firms, a very strong ingredient of which appears to be their attempt to harmonize at all costs the interests of their country and their employer.[3]

[1] Address to shareholders reported in *The Times*, 3 May 1963. Capital control and each plant's annual operating plan were the other two mentioned.

[2] Haccoû, *Management of Direct Investments*, pp. 47, 51 *passim*.

[3] V. S. Naipaul has caught this atmosphere beautifully in his description of the Calcutta 'box-wallah', the young Indian business executive: 'The Calcutta box-wallah comes of a good family, ICS, Army or big business; he might even have princely connections. He has been educated at an Indian or English public school and at one of the two English universities, whose accent, through all the encircling hazards of Indian intonation, he rigidly maintains. When he joins his firm his

None of the methods of control outlined in this section is fool-proof or continuously employed. Nor can official acquiescence to their use be assumed. On the contrary, the fact that many have been illustrated by reference to official sources shows that the Government of India is alive to their existence and prepared, where necessary in its view, to counter them. That it has been able to do so, has done so, is not disputed. What is surprising is the degree of tolerance it shows.

---

first name is changed. The Indian name of Anand, for example, might become Andy; Dhandeva will become Danny, Firdausi Freddy, Jamshed Jimmy. Where the Indian name cannot be adapted, the box-wallah will most usually be known as Bunty. It is a condition of Bunty's employment that he play golf; and on every golf course he can be seen with an equally unhappy Andy, both enduring the London-prescribed mixture of business and pleasure. Bunty will of course marry well, and he knows it will be counted in his favour if he contracts a mixed marriage, if, say, as a Punjabi Hindu he marries a Bengali Muslim or a Bombay Parsi. Bunty and his wife will live in one of the company's luxury flats; they will be called Daddy and Mummy by their two English-speaking children. Their furnishing will show a happy blend of East and West (Indian ceramics are just coming in). So too will their food (Indian lunch followed by Western-style dinner), their books, their records (difficult classical Indian, European chamber music) and their pictures (North Indian miniatures, Ganymed reproductions of Van Gogh). Freed of one set of caste rules, Bunty and his wife will adopt another. If his office has soft furnishings he will know how to keep his distance from Andy, whose furnishings are hard; and to introduce Andy, who shares an air-conditioned office with Freddy, into the home of Bunty, who has an office to himself, is to commit a blunder. His new caste imposes new rituals on Bunty. Every Friday he will have lunch at Firpo's on Chowringhee, and the afternoon-long jollity will mark the end of the week's work. In the days of the British this Friday lunch at Firpo's celebrated the departure of the mail-boat for England. Such letters as Bunty sends to England go now by air, but Bunty is conscious of tradition.' ('Jamshed into Jimmy', *New Statesman*, 25 January 1963.)

PART IV

CONCLUSIONS

CHAPTER SEVEN

THE COST TO INDIA

I THE FLOW OF PRIVATE CAPITAL

QUANTITATIVELY, foreign private capital has not been very significant since Independence. Between July 1948 and December 1961, some Rs 438 crores of non-banking investments from private sources flowed into India,[1] compared with slightly less than Rs 2,000 crores utilized from public sources,[2] a ratio of 1:4·6.

These are gross flows. Allowing for repatriation of investments and repayments of principal, the net inflow amounted to about Rs 307 crores[3] and Rs 1,800 crores[4] respectively, a ratio of 1:6. The flows are not fully comparable; public funds arise abroad in their entirety; private investments originate partly in India as reinvested profits. About Rs 176 crores, more than two-fifths of the gross private flow took this form, the remainder—the 'fresh capital'—dividing unevenly between investment in kind and in cash in the ratio of 3:1.

As can be expected from its narrow spread[5] the private flow is heavily dependent on the fortunes of two or three industries. The course of petroleum investments alone offers an almost complete explanation of its behaviour, particularly since 1954; while investments in a handful of other industries are enough to fill out the remaining discrepancies. This is shown in Table 17, p. 301.

[1] An estimated Rs 188 crores up to December 1953, made up of Rs 33 crores in cash, Rs 85 crores in kind, and Rs 70 crores in retained earnings (RBI, *Survey 1953*, p. 84; 'Recent Trends in Foreign Investment in India', RBI *Bulletin*, September 1958, Table 2, p. 1010); and Rs 250 crores in 1954–61 inclusive (RBI, *Survey 1961*, Table VII, p. 34). The figures are adjusted 'wherever possible' for valuation changes. The total for 1948–53 is higher by Rs 8–13 crores than the Bank's early estimate (as given in *Survey 1953*, loc. cit.) but is based partly on its own later figures.

[2] RBI, *India's Balance of Payments*, Appendix, Table 35. Figures for public flows relate to financial years ending on 31 March 1962. They include Rs 114 crores invested in the private sector. Public capital *authorized* in the period came to just under Rs 3,425 crores.

[3] RBI, *Survey 1955*, Table 2, p. 28; *Survey 1961*, Table VII, p. 34. Since allowance is made for valuation changes, the total is some Rs 34 crores lower than in the Bank's tables on 'outstanding foreign investments in the private sector'.

[4] See Table 19 below, p. 308.   [5] See above, Table 4, p. 187.

One important result is that the actual flow of fresh investments has consistently confounded projections. The First Plan anticipated a gross fresh inflow of Rs 100 crores as against actual receipts of Rs 42–45 crores;[1] the Rs 100 crore target was kept for the Second Plan and, in the event, doubled.[2] Earlier unofficial forecasts—such as the *Eastern Economist's* for an annual average inflow of Rs 60 crores[3]—proved as wide of the mark.

II EXCESS CAPITAL IMPORTS

(*a*) *Evidence:* Private imports were grossly over-licensed in the initial stages of both the Second and Third Five-Year Plans,[4] and private investments rose well above projected levels.[5] Neither could have occurred had foreign investment always complied with either the Government's own scale of priorities or an efficient allocation of scarce resources and foreign exchange. Needless to say *all* foreign investments add to India's liabilities abroad.

(*b*) *Marginal spheres:* There are a number of obvious sources of excess capital imports. Some projects—in soft drinks, ink, ball-point pens, tooth-paste and -brushes, and razor blades, for example— are marginal by any standards. Other consumer products—from rayon filament to domestic refrigerators—are scarcely less marginal in a development context.

(*c*) *Price mark-up:* Secondly, the value of many investments is inflated by marking up the prices of goods or materials or services supplied as investment in kind.[6] This is done for a number of reasons, two of which are particularly important: a foreign collaborator might wish to bump up the 'necessary' import content of a project in order to

---

[1] PC, *First Plan*, p. 436; PC, *Second Plan*, p. 405.

[2] PC, *Second Plan*, p. 405; PC, *Third Plan*, p. 456. Early in the Second Plan there was little conviction in official circles that the target would be attained; witness the forecast of the Finance Minister, T. T. Krishnamachari, of £40 million (Rs 53 crores), in an interview with a *Times* special correspondent (*The Times*, 16 January 1957).

[3] *EE*, 25 March 1949.   [4] See pp. 125, 127, above.

[5] Net private investment during the Second Plan was Rs 900 crores higher than the Rs 2,400 crore target.

[6] Examples have been cited above, pp. 250–1, 266.

TABLE 17

*India: Net Capital Inflow from Private Sources in Selected Industries, mid-1948
to end-1960*
(Rs crores)

	1948–53 annual average	1954–5 annual average	1956	1957	1958	1959	1960	Mid-1948–60
Net Inflow of which:	25·1	14·9	24·9	17·9	2·4	11·0	53·3	**277·4**ª
petroleum	10·0	13·4	12·3	17·5	–15·6	2·3	29·7	**128·0**
cigarettes and tobacco	3·5	–0·4	0·1	0·2	0·6	–2·0	0·5	**17·7**
medicines and pharmaceuticals	0·9	1·1	0·6	0·9	2·7	2·3	2·9	**16·6**
Other chemicals and allied productsᵇ	2·0	0·1	0·4	0·3	0·4	1·2	1·5	**15·0**
metals and products	0·2	0·4	0·9	0·4	0·3	1·3	4·2	**9·0**
transport equipmentᵈ	0·8	–1·0	0·5	0·3	0·8	0·4	0·7	**5·1**
electrical goods	1·3	1·3	1·2	0·7	0·6	0·6	1·4	**14·3**
construction, utilities, transport	3·5	1·2	6·4	3·1	–3·4	0·4	–0·1	**28·1**
managing agencies	2·1	–0·8	–1·1	–1·0	–0·3	0·9	0·4	**8·9**

Sources: 'Foreign Investments in India', RBI *Bulletin*, September 1958, June
1959, April 1960, May 1961, October 1962.
Notes: ª See note 3, p. 299.
    ᵇ Heavy and light chemicals only until and incl. 1957.
    ᶜ Iron and steel products only up to and incl. 1958.
    ᵈ Automobiles and accessories up to and incl. 1958.
    ᵉ Excluding 'construction' prior to 1959.

establish title to a controlling interest.[1] Alternatively, as has long
been the case in major sectors such as oil, tea, and many manufacturing industries, the foreign investor might wish to mask his real level
of profits by multiplying the forms and adjusting the levels of other
payments.[2]

[1] A number of such cases came to light in private conversation. They rest as
much on the authorities' liberal interpretation of what is 'necessary' as on their
declared policy of allowing foreign ownership to the limit of the foreign-exchange
component of an investment.
[2] See above, pp. 226 ff.

(d) *Technology:* Thirdly, there is the use of unsuitable foreign machinery. While there is an unanswerable case for a backward country to use the most productive techniques available in order to raise its capacity to save and invest, or because they are indispensable in the production of certain important end items or qualities, not all techniques are equally suitable. By importing a technology, lock, stock and barrel, a backward country might easily saddle itself with apparatus that requires too sophisticated a network of servicing and ancillary industries or that cannot be justified in terms of its wage levels. This is particularly wasteful in consumer industries. And so it is in India. In many cases, the paper industry for example, imported Western techniques are inefficiently used;[1] in others, motor vehicles for example, they have imposed a wasteful pattern of fashion-induced changes utterly alien to Indian conditions.[2] Personal observation suggests large areas, particularly in packing and handling, in which machinery has displaced manual labour at great expense.

The foreign investor is clearly not to blame for so widespread a phenomenon. Other factors include the lack of indigenous equipment, the scarcity of managers, the desire to employ the minimum of labour where retrenchment is inhibited, the rise in labour costs and the decline in skill differentials since the war, the overvaluation of the rupee, and the need to compete abroad and at home against units more endowed with capital resources.[3] But the fact that the foreign investor normally has a direct interest in supplying equipment and knowhow; is almost universally in charge of the technical operation of a joint venture; is often chary of imparting skills or development information; is very often ignorant about Indian conditions; and might wish to keep out equipment that can be copied easily—mean that the natural tendency to over-import techniques receives powerful reinforcement.[4]

[1] See above, pp. 23–24.   [2] See above, p. 293.

[3] See, for example, Rosen, *Industrial Change in India*, US ed., pp. 151–5, 173, 181–2, *passim*, which deals extensively with some of these factors as they affect the paper, iron and steel, cement, cotton textile, and sugar industries; 'Capital: Output Ratios in Indian Industry', *IEJ*, Vol. IV, No. 2, October 1956, p. 119; *EW*, 3 March 1956, pp. 279–80; also Little, 'Strategy of Indian Development', NIESR, *Review*, No. 9, May 1960, p. 27.

[4] Commenting on the final withdrawal of the United States from the Bokaro steel project (see above, p. 237), *The Times* correspondent wrote significantly: 'Now that the uncertainty is over, it is expected that reliance on Indian designing and fabricating capacity, which in the steel industry has improved many times over in the past few years, will greatly increase and will help to reduce the cost estimates.' (12 September 1963.)

(e) *Duplication:* Of all reasons to import capital in excess of real needs, the most compelling perhaps is the fact that imported skills do not permeate the economy to any great extent.

There are two factors here: the need to compete in a fundamentally xenophile market, and the reluctance of foreign collaborators to import a complete technology. The second aspect has been dealt with;[1] the first is best illustrated with reference to a concrete example: a well-known Indian firm which favours a more 'nationalist' line than most had very nearly completed arrangements to manufacture ball- and roller-bearings independently of outside help. Machinery had been copied and trials completed. A decision had been taken to start production (but to wait until the product was fully proved before marketing) when the news of the Tata-SKF project—Associated Bearing Co. Ltd.—broke. Knowing how difficult it would be to compete against an internationally-known brand, it felt compelled to enter into an agreement for technical collaboration with another foreign firm—solely to acquire the use of its trade mark.[2] The point of the story is not simply that the Indian firm was forced into purchasing superfluous rights; it lies more significantly in the fact that once imported, a technique is more likely to be duplicated within Indian industry through additional, competitive, and costly purchases abroad than through dissemination by the original importer.

(f) *Government:* The Government is not blameless in this. It has shown great latitude in allowing investments in low priority spheres, or even banned ones, on receipt of promises to export a proportion of the product or to bring in a quantity of foreign exchange. As was admitted during a review of collaboration agreements in 1963, 'the zest for licensing industries and for promoting collaborative ventures has at times resulted in a certain negligence in weighing the economic costs'.[3] Its insistence on collaboration with foreign capital as a normal pre-condition for obtaining an industrial licence; its tolerance of restrictive provisions in the transfer of knowhow; and its policy of

---

[1] See above, pp. 288 ff.   [2] Information supplied privately.
[3] Quoted in *ET*, 27 April 1963. In May a committee of senior officials was set up to find ways of encouraging the flow of foreign capital and knowhow while 'limiting the strain on the balance of payments imposed by excessive payments of royalties by the less essential industries. There seems to be a certain amount of disappointment at the pace of flow of foreign capital to vital industries, and particularly to those significant to defence production.' (*ET*, 21 May 1963.)

encouraging, ostensibly in the interest of industrial democracy and regional development, a number of competing units where one or two will do, have done much to endorse it. The first two have been dealt with.[1] To illustrate the last, it is enough to mention that the Third Plan production targets of 60,000 trucks and 50,000 scooters are distributed between four units in the first case and seven in the second, each with its foreign collaborator and each committed to substantial payments (in foreign exchange) on imported capital and technology.[2] Since high-cost small units ultimately determine prices, over-licensing on these lines adds to the large firms' profits and to their remittances abroad, and so enhances the real value of their investment locally.

Nor is the Government blameless for the other forms of excess imports. Its own plants are normally very capital-intensive throughout and impose a comparable structure on private units in shared industries.[3] Its preparedness to pay high fees seems unlimited.[4] And it is notorious for inviting foreign experts when equally or more suitable local ones are available. In fertilizer plant production, for example, the excess foreign-exchange costs incurred on equipment specified by foreign consultants has been estimated at Rs 500 per ton on nitrogen, i.e., 20 per cent of the total cost, and might well turn out to be more, say Rs 800–900 per ton—altogether some Rs 10 crores a year in foreign exchange. At the same time a proven local design team has been disbanded.[5] In the case of state coal mines, the Lok Sabha's Estimate Committee observed:

The existing practice under which the entire work relating to a project, including the preparation of project reports, working drawings, designs, etc. is done by the foreign collaborators, even though the [National Coal Development] Corporation has the necessary technical knowhow to do it, has many drawbacks.[6]

In the case of steel plant design and construction, the Indian consultants originally assigned the fourth public plant at Bokaro had a

---

[1] See above, pp. 261 ff., 284 ff.　　　　[2] *The Economist*, 6 July 1963, p. 58.

[3] See Rosen, 'Capital: Output Ratios in Indian Industry', *IEJ*, Vol. IV, No. 2, p. 119; 'Capital: Output . . .', *EW*, 3 March 1956, p. 280.

[4] See above, p. 271.

[5] S. K. Mukherjee, head of the Sindri design project group, cited in *EW*, 29 September 1962, p. 1535.

[6] Quoted in A. B. Ghosh, 'The National Coal Development Corporation', *EW*, 21 September 1963, p. 1599.

constant battle to defend their appointment in face of the familiar argument that foreign credits were more or less conditional on foreign design and consultancy.[1]

In other cases foreign consultancy contracts have had to be prematurely terminated; with the French ACL (Ateliers et Chantiers de la Loire) after an Inquiry Committee had held it responsible for defects in ships constructed at Hindustan Shipyards;[2] with the Swiss Oerlikon, technical consultants at Hindustan Machine Tools, where it was found that 'so long as the factory was managed by foreign experts, it did not do anything good. But since the foreigners went away and some of our competent men took charge it is making amazing progress.'[3] And with many others.

III THE COST OF SERVICING

(a) *Quantities:* Foreign private investment is expensive. At the very least profits run at 10 per cent per year after payment of taxes;[4] in all

---

[1] A taste of the struggle, the first phase of which lasted until the United States withdrew from the project in the autumn of 1963, can be savoured from the following report: 'The Bokaro contract with M. N. Dastur and Co. Ltd., Consulting Engineers, was finalised last August; but just before Dastur left for [the] United States, the Secretary of the Steel Ministry asked him to extend his stay in New Delhi by two days for completing the signing of the agreement. Dastur waited but some last minute technicality came in the way and the contract was not "formally" signed. This is purely a matter of formality for in all Government documents, Dastur and Co. are still being referred to officially as the Consultants of Hindustan Steel on Bokaro, and they are continuing the preliminary work. This contract provides specifically that when aid has been negotiated, its terms may be varied—that is, the scope of the work to be done by M. N. Dastur and Co. may be altered—to suit the provisions of the aid agreement. But it has also been made gently known to the visiting AID negotiating team what the contract with the Indian firm of Consultants is, that it was still unsigned and . . . a hint has also been dropped that it will not stand in their way if the Americans do not want it. . . .' (*EW*, 24 March 1962, p. 493.)

Ironically, replacement of United States aid by Russian in 1964 has made M. N. Dastur and Co.'s future as consultants no more secure, since the Russians readily accepted official Indian suggestions that they build Bokaro on a 'turn-key' basis. The suggestions themselves appear to fit into a long-term drift towards building future steel plants in the private sector, or, if in the public sector, as 'turn-key' projects by Western—largely American—companies. 'Dasturism' *v.* 'turnkeyism', still very much in the balance as late as February 1965, is significant to the future of more in India than steel.

[2] *FT*, 30 January 1958; *Hindu*, 23 February, 23 April 1958.

[3] Nehru, at the All-India Congress Committee Session, New Delhi, 11 May 1959 (*Hindu*, 12 May 1959).

[4] See above, pp. 246 ff.

probability they are very much more.[1] To this should be added the high cost of knowhow, licences, and such-like.[2] By comparison, the average rate of between 2 and 3 per cent charged on foreign public capital, including grants, seems modest.

TABLE 18

India: Profits Accruing to Foreign Investors from the Private Sector, 1948–61
(Rs crores)

Year	Retained Earnings	Transfers Abroad[c]	Total	Corrected Total[d]
1948	12·7[a]	30·1	42·8	52·1
1949	12·7[a]	28·6	41·3	50·4
1950	12·7[a]	31·3	44·0	53·7
1951	12·7[a]	28·7	41·4	50·5
1952	12·7[a]	27·4	40·1	48·9
1953	12·7[a]	18·8	31·5	36·5
1954	12·0[b]	24·0	36·0	48·2
1955	12·0[b]	24·3	36·3	41·1
1956	19·5	19·9	39·4	51·8
1957	9·5	24·0	33·5	41·2
1958	9·8	27·1	36·9	42·0
1959	15·3	30·2	45·5	55·5
1960	14·5	33·6	48·1	58·7
1961	15·8	33·0	48·8	59·3

Sources: RBI, *Balance of Payments*; 'India's Investment Income Liabilities Abroad: 1953–58', RBI *Bulletin*, August 1960; 'Foreign Investments in India: 1960 and 1961', RBI *Bulletin*, October 1962, Table 3, p. 1533; RBI, *Survey 1961*, Statement 19, p. 89.

Notes: a Annual average 1948–53.
   b Annual average 1954–5.
   c Financial years. The item consists overwhelmingly of current profits, dividends, and interest, including up to 1952 a small proportion of interest on Government account (averaging Rs 5·4 crores in the three years 1953–5).
   d The figures for 1953–8 inclusive were arrived at independently by the Reserve Bank and found to be consistently higher—by 22 per cent—than could be gauged from published sources. Totals for the remaining years covered by the table have been adjusted accordingly.

[1] See above, pp. 226 ff. Surprisingly, the volume of profits recorded by the Reserve Bank up to 1960 does not reflect either the rates of profit recorded on other occasions or the growth of foreign investments. There seems to be no convincing explanation for the first, although the disparity can be as much as between 10 and 20–25 per cent. The second is probably due to a combination of three factors: fluctuations in the profits of the older, export-orientated foreign sector, particularly tea; the immaturity of most of the post-1958 wave of foreign investments; and the flourishing habit of transmuting profits into other, untaxed, or less highly-taxed forms.

[2] See above, pp. 268 ff.

(*b*) *Effect on the balance of payments:* Foreign investments are expensive in another sense too. In theory, all profits are payable in foreign currency, unlike interest payments on public loans, half of which are made in rupees.[1] The same distinction holds with regard to the repatriation of capital or the amortization of principal. In practice, of course, not all profits are distributed abroad year by year, nor has private capital been repatriated, net, over any length of time. None the less, servicing the two forms of capital flow has put very different strains on India's foreign currency resources, strains out of all proportion to the volume of funds received.

(*c*) *Inflexible foreign exchange cost:* Three characteristics of the payments on private account will be noticed from the Table, p. 308. First, the instability of capital repatriations, due almost entirely to the behaviour of oil investments, as comparison with Table 20, p. 309, will show. Second, the rapid growth in payments for royalties, fees, etc., reflecting the increase in technologically-intensive manufacturing investments and, to an unknown extent, book-keeping transfers into this category. Finally, the relative stability of profits distributed abroad—about Rs 26 crores a year. This last might seem unremarkable; however, if payments are compared with profits earned it becomes apparent that distribution abroad is normally the first charge on profits after tax, and retained earnings are more or less residual subject to most of the fluctuations in over-all earnings.

Plantations are noteworthy in this respect,[2] but they are not alone. Comparison of Tables 17 and 20 shows that in petroleum in two out of the five years for which figures are available—1958 and 1959—retentions out of profits were substantially higher than net investments, the difference presumably going towards retiring the companies' loans from their head offices abroad. In this way, some of the amount which appears as retained profits in Table 20 and repatriation of capital in Table 19, is no different in fact from the rest of profits distributed abroad. Figures for manufacturing are less explicit;

[1] Rs 1,396 crores of the Rs 2,666 crores of loans authorized during the first two Plans were repayable in rupees. About one-third of the remainder—loans from the Eastern Bloc—are in practice rupee loans, although not listed as such by the Reserve Bank.

[2] Tea-planting companies have long been known for their solicitude for shareholders: an analysis of balance sheets for 1939–53 shows that retained profits were inadequate to ensure even the maintenance of fixed capital over the period (*Report of the Plantation Enquiry Commission*, 1956, Part I, pp. 50, 57, 262).

TABLE 19

Foreign-Exchange Cost of India's (non-banking) Liabilities Abroad, 1951–61, calendar or financial years
(Rs crores)

	1951	1952	1953	1954	1955	1956	1957	1958	1959	1960	1961	1951–1961
Private Investments												
Profits[a]	28·7	27·4	18·8	24·0	24·3	19·9	24·0	27·1	30·2	33·6	33·0	**291·0**
Royalties, fees, etc.[b]	9·9	9·2	8·8	9·1	12·5	16·3	16·1	14·9	17·6	23·6	26·8	**164·8**
Capital re-patriations[c]	9·0	9·0	9·0	5·0	5·0	6·3	9·1	24·4	14·8	9·1	13·4	**114·1**
Total private	47·6	45·6	36·6	38·1	41·8	42·5	49·2	66·4	62·6	66·3	73·2	**569·9**
Public loans[d]												
Interest[e]	1·4	2·4	3·6	3·5	3·3	3·4	3·7	7·8	16·3	21·6	27·2	**94·2**
Principal[f]	3·4	4·9	2·9	3·3	3·2	3·2	7·2	7·5	9·5	17·7	65·6	**128·4**
Total public[g]	4·8	7·3	6·5	6·8	6·5	6·6	10·9	15·3	25·8	39·3	92·8	**222·6**

Notes and Sources:

   [a] As in Table 18, p. 306. These figures are grossly understated (loc. cit.).

   [b] Payment for technical and professional services, management fees, office expenses, advertisement charges, royalties, charges for patents, etc. These items do not feature separately in Indian balance of payments statistics but are included under 'Miscellaneous', forming 64 per cent of the total during the years for which separate figures are available 1956/7–1960/1 (RBI, *Balance of Payments*, Table VII, p. 78). For the years prior to 1956–7, three-fifths of the total for 'Miscellaneous' has been used.

   [c] The estimated annual average figure for 1948–53 has been given for the first three columns, and the annual average for 1954–5 in the following two (ibid., Table X, p. 59; RBI, *Survey 1961*, Table VII, p. 34.).

   [d] Excluding loans to state corporations. See p. 122 n. above.

   [e] 1951/2–1956/7: 'Our Public Debt', *Tata Quarterly*, April 1960, Table IV, p. 45; 1957–8 onwards, Ministry of Finance, *Explanatory Memoranda to the Budgets*.

   [f] As in Appendix 4, p. 332.

   [g] The burden of servicing the foreign public debt grew rapidly after 1960. Continuing the table (Rs crores):

	1962–3	1963–4 (*Budget*)
Interest	35·10	42·10
Capital repayments	46·30	61·47
	81·40	103·57

besides, its rapid growth in importance within the foreign sector[1] lends credence to the view that some two-thirds of all real profit retentions should be attributed to it.[2] None the less, as Table 19 suggests, the methods used by plantation and oil companies to transmute profit into capital and 'distribution' into 'repatriation' are open to many international firms and have been used by them.[3]

TABLE 20

India: Profits of Foreign-Controlled Companies by Major Use and Sector, 1956–61
(Rs crores)

	1956			1957			1958		
	Earned	*Distributed*	*Retained*	*Earned*	*Distributed*	*Retained*	*Earned*	*Distributed*	*Retained*
Plantations	10·7	9·0	1·7	5·3	6·8	−1·5	4·9	6·3	−1·4
Petroleum	16·6	6·9	9·7	12·5	7·1	5·4	11·0	5·4	5·6
Manufacturing	12·4	6·8	5·6	10·7	6·9	3·8	12·9	7·8	5·1
Total incl. others	51·8	32·3	19·5	41·2	31·7	9·5	42·0	32·2	9·8

	1959			1960			1961		
	Earned	*Distributed*	*Retained*	*Earned*	*Distributed*	*Retained*	*Earned*	*Distributed*	*Retained*
Plantations	5·7	4·8	0·9	6·7	6·4	0·3	6·7	5·3	1·4
Petroleum	10·8	4·5	6·3	10·0	3·9	6·1	8·0	5·9	2·1
Manufacturing	16·1	9·0	7·1	17·8	11·5	6·3	22·2	13·4	8·8
Total incl. others	55·5	40·2	15·3	58·7	44·2	14·5	59·5	43·7	15·8

Sources: Industry figures from RBI, *Survey 1961*, Statement 19, p. 89. Totals as in Table 18, p. 306.

(*d*) *Paucity of foreign exchange receipts:* While current payments on private account are both growing and relatively inflexible, foreign investments offer little compensation in the way of foreign exchange receipts. Conforming to the almost universal reluctance to place risk capital in India,[4] foreign operations are starved of convertible currencies: Black-Clawson, an American firm, is reported to have set up a Rs 2·5 crore plant without having added one dollar to India's reserves, by using rupee resources for machinery made locally or in

[1] See above, pp. 242 f.   [2] See, for example, ECAFE, *Bulletin*, June 1962, p. 8.
[3] See also above, pp. 227, 265 f.   [4] See above, pp. 264–5, 267–8.

East European countries;[1] a Japanese consortium is said to have contributed their half of Hindustan-Kokoku Wire's Rs 2 crores capital out of 'returned Japanese assets in India'.[2] Needless to say, both suffer no abridgement in their right to receive earnings and repatriated capital in foreign currency at will.

Not all investors are in a position to be as sparing in their use of foreign exchange, yet many run close behind.[3] Given the manufacturing bias and technological intensity of new foreign investment, and the relative abundance of supporting capital, this is not a surprising attitude.[4] It is, of course, immensely significant to India: during the fourteen years for which data exist, in which the foreign investment stake has more than doubled, foreign investors as a whole have taken out of the general currency reserve nearly three times as much as they contributed directly.

TABLE 21

India: Foreign Capital Sector's Balance of External Payments, 1948–61
(Rs crores)

Foreign exchange losses[a]	
Repatriation of capital	141·1
Profits paid abroad	381·0
Royalties, fees, etc.	196·3
	718·4
Foreign exchange gains[b]	
Gross investment in cash	60·2
Gross investment in kind	186·9
	247·1
Debit balance	471·3

Sources: a. As in Table 19, p. 308, notes a–c.
        b. As on p. 299, note 1 above.

Nor is their indirect contribution—through saving imports and adding to exports—any better. On the contrary, the shift from traditional export-earners like tea and jute, to import-users like petroleum and manufacturing that can neither find export markets

---

[1] *Capital*, 28 September 1961, p. 481.   [2] *The Japan Times*, 18 July 1959.
[3] See above, p. 264.
[4] Dale and Bale point out that reinvested profits of subsidiaries accounted for some 70 to 75 per cent of American investment in manufacturing abroad since the war, compared with no more than 40 per cent in any other field of investment (*Private United States Venture Capital*, p. 5).

easily nor are encouraged to do so by their foreign affiliates, has already turned the foreign sector's export surplus into deficit.[1] Despite an increase in outstanding foreign business investments of Rs 325 crores between mid-1948 and the end of 1961, most of which might be attributed to manufacturing (including oil), the increase in new, manufactured exports has been small—from Rs 9 crores in 1950–1 to Rs 25 crores in 1959–60;[2] and of this increase, as much as four-fifths perhaps—metal products, sewing-machines, electric fans —has been the product of purely Indian capital. At the same time, imports of raw and intermediate materials doubled during the decade.

The point is best illustrated with reference to individual industries, rubber tyres, for example. Outlays on imported raw materials ranged between seven and seven and one-quarter crores of rupees a year between 1959–60 and 1961–2,[3] to which should be added an annual remittance out of profits which are now considerably more than the Rs 3·60 crores a year noted by the Tariff Commission in the early 1950's.[4] There is nothing to report on the other side of the industry's payments balance beyond token sales at, presumably, heavy discount, since the Indian ex-factory price of the basic tyre size for commercial vehicles is higher by an eighth than the international export price, c.i.f.[5]

The Government is not unaware of the problem. Tariff Commission reports are studded with recommendations to have the restrictive export provisions of many agreements revoked;[6] the Government has repeatedly made clear its wish for free exports since the 1957–8 exchange crisis. More recently it has been 'tying up, in many cases, new industrial undertakings coming up for industrial Establishment or Capital Goods licences, to an export performance'.[7] But, as the Mudaliar Committee notes: ' "Promises" to export are sometimes lightly given by applicants seeking industrial/import licences; or they may be accepted without detailed scrutiny of the real export potential

[1] See above, p. 245.　　　[2] PC, *Third Plan*, Table 3, p. 135.

[3] B. C. Dutt, 'Automobile Tyres in the Third Plan', *EW*, 24 November 1962, p. 1818. Production of up to 140,000 tyres a year—at which point indigenous raw rubber supplies give out—requires an import content of 54 per cent by value; beyond that number the import content goes up to 81·4 per cent. In 1962, with output at about 200,000 the average import content was 62 per cent (ibid., p. 1817).

[4] From *Report on ... Rubber Tyres and Tubes*, 1955, Statement LIII, pp. 107–10.

[5] B. C. Dutt, op. cit., p. 1817.　　　[6] See above, p. 283.

[7] *Mudaliar Report*, p. 24. A number of foreign firms reported polite official pressure to have them guarantee a certain level of exports.

and prospects of the projects in question or the applicants' program in this behalf.'[1]

In any case, there are limits to what the Government can do. The pull of the domestic market is strong; as well as being hampered by lack of knowledge, the Government lacks the resources to make exporting truly attractive; and foreign firms have the strongest possible incentives not to export.[2] If necessary, they can—and do—replace formal agreements to limit exports with informal, but enforceable ones; sales networks abroad can be denied Indian products; and recalcitrant firms may rest assured in the knowledge that the Government will carry its feud with business or an individual firm well short of the point at which production would have to cease. No wonder that 'quotas have remained conspicuously unfulfilled in ... industries without exposing the units concerned to any penalty'.[3]

IV THE TERMS OF TRADE

The effects of private capital imports go beyond the payments-arithmetic outlined so far. One aspect concerns the terms of trade.

Commodity imports into India tend to be highly priced. There are a number of factors here, only some of which can be influenced by India. An important one is the pricing policy of 'actual user' importers (who account for some 55 per cent of total imports) and their foreign associates.[4] Not unrelated is the Government's weakness *vis-à-vis* suppliers abroad.[5] Together they form nearly one half of the terms of trade equation which moved steadily against India during the first two Plans.[6]

V TECHNOLOGICAL DEPENDENCE

It is frequently argued in support of private capital imports that they graft much needed managerial and technical skills onto Indian industry at little or no extra cost. The evidence, however, points the other way. Research and development are invariably conducted abroad; the fruits of development are imparted, if at all, at very high cost in royalties, fees, and other payments, and then not always in

---

[1] ibid.   [2] See above, pp. 280 f.
[3] 'What Ails Exports', *EW*, 18 May 1963, p. 821.
[4] Examples may be found above, pp. 265 f.
[5] See above, pp. 122 f.   [6] See Appendix 3h, p. 330, below.

their entirety; through their production and staffing policies the major investing firms attempt to systematize a continuing control of knowhow; and much else in the same vein.[1] Since the Indian partner is normally assigned—and readily accepts—a narrowly specialized range of functions, the diffusion of skills that does take place is largely fortuitous. Indeed, since the typical modern investing firm owes its dominance and income largely to its technological monopoly, a different outcome would be surprising.

The consequences are appreciable. Because skills are embodied in machinery as well as in men, technological dependence is a factor in the import dependence dealt with earlier.[2] Together they help sustain the flow of excess capital imports in all its forms, adding to the burden of servicing payments (in foreign currency).[3] In all these ways they are a factor in India's generally adverse terms of trade and, ultimately, in her deteriorating balance of payments.

VI UNEMPLOYMENT

Probably the most portentous aspect of India's technological dependence is the damping effect it has on the creation of new jobs. Foreign investments are themselves capital-intensive. In the competitive Indian *milieu* their effect is amplified through the adoption of similarly capital-intensive investment on the part of indigenous firms, mostly via further foreign collaboration. Since these investments are to a great extent in the consumer goods industries, two contrary processes are set in motion: on the one hand, traditional producers, largely rural, are weakened, resulting in open unemployment in some cases, but more generally in a further narrowing of the range of village occupations; hence in greater underemployment, greater downward pressure on rural wage rates; adding thus to the already massive body of factors preventing a rise in agricultural productivity. On the other hand, technologically-intensive investments in the modern industrial sector tend to push up skilled wage rates and so help generate a secondary round of pressures for capital-intensive, labour-displacing investment. The resulting coincidence of relatively high wages for a small minority, increasing open unemployment in the towns, and unfulfilled expectations amongst the migrants from the country, constitutes a potentially explosive mixture.

[1] See above, pp. 268., 281 f.   [2] Above, pp. 289 ff.   [3] See above, pp. 305 f.

It would be too much to expect of Indian statistics to corroborate this sort of thesis in any detail. But the following facts seem relevant: the first two Plans created 12·5 million jobs directly or, assuming the Planning Commission's estimates for the Second Plan period to hold for both, just under 19 million directly and indirectly.[1] The labour force increased by 47·5 million during the same period[2] with the result that the backlog of unemployed, which planning was meant to eradicate, grew.[3] There is no estimate of job destruction for the period.

VII PLANNING

'By almost any test', wrote J. K. Galbraith midway during the second 'big' Plan, 'the economy of India is less responsive to public guidance and direction than that of the United States. Indeed it is one of the world's least controlled or "planned" economies'.[4] In 1960–1, after a decade of planning, Government revenue at all levels and from all sources constituted about 11 per cent of national income (compared with about 41 per cent in Britain), and state plants accounted for 8·4 per cent of output from organized manufacturing industry.[5] Nor is the picture changing at any speed. While the private sector has consistently over-fulfilled the targets set, public enterprise has lagged as consistently, with consequent changes in some very crucial ratios.[6]

Foreign investments contribute to the weakness of Indian planning in a number of ways, two of which are important. No matter how large the Indian operations of foreign firms—sometimes very large

[1] From PC, *Second Plan*, p. 119; PC, *Third Plan*, pp. 47, 158.

[2] Nasir Ahmed Khan, 'Some Reflections on the Census of 1961—I', *IEJ*, January 1963, p. 231.

[3] Even at its most optimistic, the Planning Commission can see no short-term solution to the problem of unemployment. Its *Third Plan* projects job creation at 14 million and an increase in the labour force of 17 million by 1966 (loc. cit., p. 74). Subsequently, the Government admitted to a 25 per cent shortfall in job creation over the Third Plan period, and a likely backlog of 17 million unemployed—half of them in the towns—compared with an original forecast of 12 million at its close. (Nabagopal Das, reporting a meeting of the Central Committee on Employment held on 31 August 1963, Supplement to *Capital*, 19 December 1963, p. 87.)

[4] 'Rival Economic Theories in India', *Foreign Affairs*, July 1958, p. 589.

[5] From PC, *Third Plan*, pp. 28, 34–35, 97.

[6] Something of the detail as it affects particular industries has been given in Chapter 4. (See above, pp. 141 ff.)

and very important indeed by Indian standards—these seldom form more than a small proportion of their global activities;[1] on the other hand, no matter how small a firm's operations in the country they are part of a single fabric made up of the activities of Government and international agencies as well as private lending, investing, and trade organizations. While each firm might therefore find it relatively easy to withdraw when faced with what it considers an unacceptable demand on the part of the Government—as some indeed have done —India would have to pay a very heavy price for misjudging the threshold of acceptance common to the foreign sector as a whole. It is within this broad immunity that the price and profit adjustments, the erratic investment flows, the restraints on the diffusion of know-how, and the methods of control referred to in this and the preceding chapters flourish.[2]

Even more significant is the way in which foreign investments strengthen the private sector. Much of the dynamism of private industry can be traced directly to the increasing number of collaboration agreements concluded since 1957.[3] These have provided knowhow, finance, foreign exchange, and moral support; they have been used to beat back taxation forays and to annex state projects for the private sector; they have drawn the teeth of the Government's threat to introduce foreign firms to break Indian monopolies. In a word, they have provided Indian industry with a toe-hold of extra-territoriality from which to confound the planners in every aspect of their work.

The distortions go deep. Denied resources, public sector projects are seldom completed on time; private sector demand for their services outruns the levels of supply envisaged in the original Plans, let alone the actual levels attained. Corruption attends the shortages and a lethal drain of materials and men takes place, the latter driven

[1] See above, p. 240.

[2] It is this atmosphere of 'dare' and blackmail which encourages the almost pathological concern with commercial intelligence and security met with amongst foreign firms. One interview in Calcutta, arranged by the London headquarter of one of the largest firms operating in India (and not an oil company at that) went roughly like this: 'Mr. Kidron, I don't know why you're here, and have no comment to make. The firm is in a difficult position with Government and anything I might say would be used in evidence against us. Besides I couldn't say anything without reference to the Managing Director who is away at the moment. Our annual reports give only our public image and a small proportion of our operations. Good-day.'

[3] See above, pp. 258 ff.

as much by the frustrations of working in the public sector as they are lured by the positive attractions of private industry. The state comes to depend more and more on foreign aid for its resources—10 per cent of expenditure during the First Plan, 24 per cent during the Second, and a planned, but grossly underestimated, 29 per cent during the Third.[1] Pressure to permit private industry to break the bottlenecks becomes irresistible and with it the volume of foreign collaborations grows. Out of it all there evolves a foreign exchange fetishism some of whose illogic has to be seen to be believed.[2] The growing dependence on foreign resources and, even more, the growing resignation to such dependence, have affected the whole tenor of the Government's approach to foreign private capital: if in the first decade of Independence the official attitude was governed by considerations of control and economic power, it has since been progressively determined by narrow balance-of-payments considerations with rather self-defeating consequences in further concessions to the private sector, to foreign investors, further dependence on aid, further delays in public sector projects, and so on.

VIII AGRICULTURE

Clearly one of the most ominous results of the decline in state planning and initiative is the failure to jerk rural India into modernity. This is not the place to add to the volume of literature on the subject, but four considerations seem relevant. Unless marketed agricultural output rises more quickly than it seems to have done in recent years,[3] India will become increasingly dependent on imported food merely to keep open famine at arm's length. At 12 per cent of all imports in 1962–3, it represents a dangerous alternative: either continued dependence on American charity or a currently insupportable addition to the country's foreign exchange bill. Second, unless the depressed level of rural incomes is raised through a combination of higher output and a diversion of labour away from agriculture, the

[1] PC, *Third Plan*, pp. 33, 95. From data presented in PC, *Mid-Term Appraisal*, state projects during the Third Plan might depend on foreign aid to the extent of about 32 per cent (see *EW* Annual Number, February 1964, Tables 1 and 3, p. 161).

[2] See above, pp. 261–2.

[3] No one can really claim to know the trends in output with any certainty (see Thorner, *Land and Labour in India*, Chapters X–XV for a critical appraisal of agricultural statistics).

highly productive urban sector will repeat the experience of the textile industry by outgrowing the domestic market. The consequences in aggravated unemployment and further rationalization entailing more unemployment, are obvious. Third, unless far-reaching measures are taken to occupy these unemployed in and beyond the cities, India as a stable society is simply inconceivable. And last, unless the country-side is more closely administered than it is at present—which implies that partial solutions at least are found for the first three problems—the relative immunity of the richer rural population to taxation will remain, and with it the difficulty of finding internal resources for planned development, the centrifugal pull of political power from the Centre to the States, the attendant factionalism and corruption, and much else.

To solve these problems would be difficult enough under any circumstances. For a Government whose initiative is being sapped and whose area of decision narrowed it is virtually impossible.

IX ROLE OF THE STATE

The part played by the state in the economy might well have been even further diminished were it not for its importance as a shield against foreign private capital, its unique ability to balance between the protagonists of the 'old' Cold War, and the disaggregation of Indian economic society into a number of imperfectly co-ordinated, loosely related spheres. Each of these has thrown up an arbitrating function which only the state could perform, and has contributed to the modest but real measure of independence and initiative it has enjoyed during most of the post-Independence period. The subject is too vast to be dealt with here in anything but the broadest outline.

(a) *Shield for Indian capital:* In the mid-fifties, responsible Indian economists expressed some alarm at the growth of the foreign sector; on the evidence then available, it appeared to be outpacing Indian capital.[1] During the Second Plan, however, the relative rates of growth changed: in the six years 1956–61, outstanding foreign-controlled business investments as recorded by the Reserve Bank

[1] See particularly, K. N. Raj, 'Model Making and the Second Plan', *EW*, 26 January 1955, p. 108; 'Profits on Foreign Capital in India', *EW*, 12 February 1955, p. 235.

increased by 37 per cent; total outstanding foreign business investment, including funds from public sources and Indian-controlled
foreign private investment, increased by 54 per cent;[1] at the same
time net assets in the private sector as a whole expanded threefold.[2]
While Indian nationalist opinion might still read an unwelcome
degree of foreign encroachment into the figures, particularly if they
are coupled with some of the methods of control deployed from
quantitatively insignificant bases, it might glean comfort from the
total picture of industrial growth and investment: in approximately
the same period, the state sector accounted for 56 per cent of investment in organized industry and minerals and so did more than
redress the balance.

This goes beyond the interpretation of figures. Even at the height
of the 1957–8 crisis, when the Government was straining every nerve
to attract foreign capital—public and private—there remained
spheres from which foreign private investment was excluded in
practice or subjected to stringent control.[3] Mostly, the state could
count on the support of Indian business. In many cases—rubber
tyres, soap, industrial gases, for example—the latter profited directly
from the curtailment of foreign activities. In others, when Indian
private interests were not directly involved—oil is a notable example
—they preferred a state monopoly to an even more exclusive foreign
one.

Recently, however, this support has shown signs of flagging. By
the sixties, Indian capital had grown in size and confidence; had
become used to collaborating with foreign firms and to calling on
their considerable resources; it was now associated with almost every
important foreign venture in the country, as even the old, wholly-
owned foreign affiliates took in some Indian capital; and it became
aware of some of the new, expansive features of modern manufacturing investments from abroad. It is less dependent on the state sector,
inefficient in any case, slow in delivering the goods, less though not
unamenable to influence, less productive of resources than was
originally foreseen. Disenchantment has already claimed its victims

---

[1] Foreign-controlled business investment increased from Rs 387 crores to
Rs 528 crores; total outstanding foreign business investment—from Rs 460 to
710 crores (RBI, *Survey 1961*, Statement 13, pp. 80–82).

[2] G. D. Birla, *Guardian*, 5 August 1962. See above, pp. 185 f., for a different
computation showing the decline of foreign-controlled assets as a proportion of
the total in the modern sector.

[3] See above, p. 223.

in the leading exponents of state capitalism.[1] How far it will go in reducing further the state's economic initiative depends to some extent on the strength the state can draw from the two other arbitration roles mentioned at the beginning of this section.

(b) *Cold War brokerage:* From mid-1955 until the end of 1961 India received more than one-quarter of the non-military grants and credits committed to countries receiving aid from both the United States and the Russian bloc; she was by far the largest beneficiary of Cold War competition.[2]

Except for a minute proportion, these public transfers have flowed through the Government, bringing it a measure of independence from indigenous resources and indigenous social pressures. The forms they took have been no less significant: if, on the whole and with some major exceptions, Western aid has enabled the state to augment substantially the infrastructure of industrial and social services and, simultaneously, eschew overt compulsion in gathering resources for development, Eastern aid has made it possible to lay the foundations of a relatively independent, public, heavy-industrial sector. It is these Eastern bloc projects in oil, steel, machine building, chemicals, and so on that have proved as invaluable in breaking the foreign hold over key supplies as they have in augmenting Indian production.[3]

Prediction is uncommonly hazardous here. Yet two considerations seem worth mentioning. First, if what has been said about the growing identity in interest and activity between Indian and foreign capital is even remotely true, the importance of non-alignment and with it, of Eastern Bloc aid, would tend to diminish in the eyes of Indian business, particularly as it forms such an obvious buttress to state enterprise. Voices are already being raised against non-alignment; more significant perhaps, Eastern Bloc aid already allocated to specific projects—drugs, heavy electricals, and so on—remains unutilized. Second, if the hesitant mutual accommodation now being sought between the protagonists of the 'old' Cold War becomes more attractive with the rising cost of armaments and China's growing truculence, the advantage to both sides of pouring

[1] See above, p. 152.

[2] *The Times*, 30 August 1962. United States loans and grants to countries in receipt of aid from both sides totalled $9,449 million of which India received $2,726 million; Russian bloc loans and grants were $4,371 of which $963 million went to India.

[3] See above, pp. 166 ff.

aid in its present form into India and countries like her might well recede.[1] If either or both of these eventualities occur, the second prop to independent state initiative will go. For the moment, however, it is still a strong one, and one on which the Government relies for nearly one-third of its current Plan expenditure.

(c) *Domestic brokerage:* The third seems more enduring. India is a congeries of communities rather than a modern nation state. Except within its small, educated, middle class, and not always therein, loyalty to caste, community, linguistic or regional group takes precedence over national consciousness. The business community is no exception and hardly justifies the word 'community': amongst the 'criteria of selection' listed in a recent study of the corporate private sector, two fall strangely on Western ears—caste and provincial origin.[2]

And even as economic development thrusts local business groups on to the All-India economic scene, the codes of family, caste, and community gain added relevance from the diversity of behaviour and standards which is met. Since there has never been a coherent or united labour movement to exploit the situation, business has been able to perpetuate its diversity and prosper at one and the same time. Something has been said of the divorce between Indian and foreign business organizations;[3] it is still possible to point to a similar, if less pronounced, disunity in purely Indian business, with, say, the Birlas dominating the Federation of Indian Chambers of Commerce and Industry, and the Tatas the Employers' Federation of India.

Although not always conducive to easy administration, this is not an entirely unwelcome configuration for the Government. It has enabled the state to expand its economic activity with less opposition from the private sector than might otherwise have been the case. Even here, however, elements of change are discernible. They derive as much from the expansion of the Government as from the growth of Indo-foreign collaboration in the private sector. If the one tends to make business conditions more uniform throughout the country, the other tends to iron out regional and caste differences, making each

[1] It is perhaps in this context that the US Congress's most successful bid as yet to cut foreign aid, winter 1963–4, should be seen.
[2] Hazari, *Structure of the Corporate Private Sector*, p. 26.
[3] See above, pp. 8–10.

unit more representative of the *general* interests of private capital. Both work towards fusing Indian business into a semblance of an All-India class imbued with a self-consciousness that might well weaken the state sector in time, even as it offsets some of the more purely political fissiparous tendencies at work.

APPENDIXES

APPENDIX ONE

BRITISH MANAGING AGENCIES 1938–62

(a) British in 1938 and probably still British-controlled in 1962

Andrew Yule
Balmer Lawrie
Barry & Co.
Binny & Co.
Bird & Co.
Bombay Burmah Trading
    Corporation
Duncan Bros.
Gillanders Arbuthnot
Gladstone Lyall
Gladstone Wylie
Harrison & Crosfield
Heilgers

James Finlay
Kilburn
Mackinnon Mackenzie
Macneill & Co.
Macneill & Barry
Parry & Co.
Planters Stores
Ralli Bros.
Shaw Wallace
Steel Bros.
Turner Morrison
Williamson Magor
Lyall Marshall

(b) British in 1938 and probably Indian-controlled in 1962

Anderson Wright
Angus Co.
Begg Dunlop
Begg Sutherland
Best & Co.
British India Corporation
Burn & Co.
Davenport & Co.
David Sassoon & Co.
E. D. Sassoon
Forbes, Forbes,
    Campbell
George Henderson
Grahams Trading Co.
    (India) Ltd.
Greaves Cotton
Hoare Miller

Howeson Bros.
H. V. Low
Jardine Henderson
Jardine Skinner
Kettlewell Bullen
Killick
Martin & Co.
Martin Burn
McLeod
Octavius Steel
Sassoon J. David
Spencer & Co.
T. Stanes
Thos. Duff
Villiers
W. H. Brady
Volkart Bros.

(c) British in 1938 and inactive, unknown, or unclassifiable in 1962

Eliot & Co.
Henry F. Eliot

Pierce Leslie
James Scott

Note: Companies taken over or lost in amalgamations in the period are treated as independent companies where known; companies that have changed their name are listed under their pre-war name.

Sources: For 1938—Banerji, *India's Balance of Payments*, Appendix C, pp. 224-5.
For 1962—the combined, but not unanimous, judgement of W. D. Bryden, Secretary, Bengal Chamber of Commerce, Calcutta; George Carvelho, formerly of Place, Siddons and Gough, Stockbrokers, Calcutta; James Esplen, Managing Director, Place, Siddons and Gough; Professor R. K. Hazari, Bombay University; Raj. K. Nigam, Senior Research Officer, Research and Statistics Division, Department of Company Law Administration, Ministry of Commerce and Industry; C. S. Pande, Secretary, Indian Chamber of Commerce, Calcutta; E. V. Rajgopal, Paterson & Co., Stockbrokers, Madras.

APPENDIX TWO

INDUSTRIAL DISPUTES 1945–63

Years	No. of Stoppages	Workers involved 000s	Man-days lost 000s
1945	820	748	4,054
1946	1,629	1,962	12,718
1947	1,811	1,841	16,563
1948	1,259	1,059	7,837
1949	920	685	6,601
1950	814	720	12,807
1951	1,071	691	3,819
1952	963	809	3,337
1953	772	467	3,383
1954	840	477	3,373
1955	1,166	528	5,698
1956	1,258	722	7,096
1957	1,630	889	6,429
1958	1,524	929	7,798
1959	1,531	694	5,633
1960	1,583	986	6,537
1961	1,357	512	4,919
1962	1,491	705	6,121
1963 (prov.)	1,394	458	2,902

Sources: 1945–56: *Indian Labour Gazette*, Vol. XIV, No. 3, September 1956, p. 266; No. 9, March 1957, p. 753.

1957–63: *Indian Labour Statistics 1964*, Table 10.1, p. 150.

Note: Coverage expanded after the reorganization of States in 1957. Statistics collected voluntarily by States' Governments.

APPENDIX THREE

ECONOMIC INDICATORS

(a) Index numbers of industrial production 1946–63 (3 series)

1946	100·0		
1947	97·2		
1948	108·4		
1949	105·1		
1950	105·0		
1951	117·2	100·0	
1952	128·9	103·6	
1953	135·3	105·6	
1954	146·4	112·9	
1955		122·4	92·3
1956		132·6	100·0
1957		137·3	104·1
1958		139·7	108·1
1959		151·9	116·9
1960		170·3	129·8
1961			139·3
1962			149·8
1963 (prov.)			164·6

Source: RBI, *Currency and Finance* for these years.

(b) Capital Issues Consents 1950–62 (Rs crores)

Year	Total No.	Total Amount	Initial No.	Initial Amount	Applications No.	Applications Amount	Sum Utilized
1950	263	75·66	47	13·69	320	85·09	
1951	343	59·55	46	21·60	410	68·32	20·22
1952	254	39·79	23	12·69	326	152·35	13·91
1953	232	81·39	31	18·34	272	89·79	40·48
1954	220	110·57	74	57·95	267	116·98	53·90
1955	289	125·39	76	46·90	374	151·42	37·59
1956	281	170·75	61	27·84	362[a]	254·49[a]	59·79
1957	333	135·37	50	36·32	484[a]	182·73[a]	38·41
1958	259	89·45	33	18·50	281	96·93	37·04
1959	242	149·58	47	49·09	264	152·60	33·71[b]
1960	277	150·13	85	50·22	290	151·96	89·74
1961	335	185·06	110	56·43	351	202·06	98·92
1962	397	219·45	115	66·60	410	227·39	105·27

[a] Includes applications from Government companies
[b] Provisional

Sources: 1949–52: RBI *Bulletin*, April 1953, Table 1, p. 341.

      1952–62, cols. 2–7 incl.: RBI, *Currency and Finance.*

      1951–9, col. 8: 'Capital Issues in the Private Sector: 1951–60', RBI *Bulletin*, February 1961.

      1960–2, col. 8: 'Capital Issues in the Private Sector: 1960–63', RBI *Bulletin*, June 1964.

Note: Col. 8: 'Sum utilized' 1951–1959 inclusive refers to the amount paid up other than bonus issues of shares, the amounts shown against the year in which consents were granted. For 1960–2, it refers to capital raised against consents as well as under exemption order; it excludes bonus share issues; and shows the amount against the year in which they were raised irrespective of the date of consent.

(c) *Issue in the Private Sector of Fresh Capital by Public Companies, 1945/6–1963 (Rs crores)*

Year	Initial Issues	Further Issues	Total Issues
1945–46	2·18	35·65	37·83
1946–47	7·99	54·46	62·45
1947–48	6·95	93·06	100·01
1948–49	5·99	60·31	65·80
1951	2·2	5·7	7·9
1952	—	4·7	4·7
1953	—	12·5	12·5
1954	3·5	29·7	33·2
1955	3·0	23·2	26·2
1956	3·5	41·6	45·1
1957	0·4	24·4	24·9
1958	6·1	19·8	25·9
1959	12·5	30·6	43·2
1960	16·8	50·3	67·1
1961	26·6	50·6	77·1
1962	24·9	64·4	89·2
1963	24·2	45·7	70·0

Sources: 1945/6–1948/9: Sur, *The New Issue Market*, pp. 99–100.

      1951–55: Sur, op. cit., p. 103; 'Capital Issues in the Private Sector: 1951–60', RBI *Bulletin*, February 1961, Table 7, p. 179.

      1956–59: 'Capital Issues . . . 1951–60', *loc. cit.*, Table 9, p. 180.

      1960–63: 'Capital Issues . . . 1960–63', RBI *Bulletin*, June 1964, Table 3, p. 742.

Note: Figures do not always add up to totals due to rounding.

(d) *Index Numbers of Variable Dividend Industrial Securities—All-India, 1945/6–1963/4*

	1927–8=100	*1938–9=100*	*1949–50=100*	*1952–3=100*
1945–46	220·8			
1946–47	268·6	252·5		
1947–48	191·9	181·5		
1948–49	162·4	136·5		
1949–50	139·6	115·4		
1950–51		124·2		
1951–52		127·8		
1952–53		107·3	94·0	
1953–54			95·6	
1954–55			112·9	
1955–56			121·6	
1956–57			121·2	
1957–58			100·3	125·4
1958–59				137·3
1959–60				155·3
1960–61				171·7
1961–62				183·7
1962–63				179·5
1963–64				167·1

Source: RBI, *Currency and Finance.*

(e) *Gross Capital Formation in the Private Corporate Sector 1948/9–1960/1 (Rs crores at current prices)*

Year	Fixed capital formation	Change in stocks	Total
1948–49	77	−28	49
1949–50	77	−28	49
1950–51	78	−28	50
1951–52	60	95	155
1952–53	80	−28	52
1953–54	86	−22	64
1954–55	109	16	125
1955–56	135	37	172
1956–57	197	133	330
1957–58	254	73	327
1958–59	221	−1	220
1959–60	167	21	188
1960–61 (prov.)	167	21	188

Source: CSO, *Estimates of Gross Capital Formation in India, 1948/9–1960/1*, Table 5.4, p. 36.

(f) Trade Balance 1948/9 to 1963/4 (Rs crores)

Year	Imports	Exports	Balance
1948–49	557	428	−129
1949–50	609	485	−124
1950–51	567	607	+ 40
1951–52	860	715	−145
1952–53	668	572	− 95
1953–54	567	526	− 41
1954–55	657	588	− 68
1955–56	679	591	− 88
1956–57	849	614	−235
1957–58	1,035	573	−462
1958–59	859	558	−301
1959–60	961	640	−321
1960–61	1,070	643	−427
1961–62	1,090	655	−435
1962–63	1,131	686	−445
1963–64	1,144		

Sources: 1948/9 to 1951/2: *Statistical Abstract* 1951/2.
1952/3 to 1960–61: Ministry of Commerce and Industry, *Report of the Import and Export Policy Committee*, Appendix D, p. 103.
1961/2 to 1963/4: Department of Commercial Intelligence and Statistics, *Monthly Statistics of the Foreign Trade of India*.

(g) Import of Cereals on Government Account 1946–62
(000 metric tons; Rs crores)

Year	Quantity	Value
1946	2,285	76·119
1947	2,371	93·92
1948	2,887	129·7
1949	3,765	144·60
1950	2,159	80·60
1951	4,801	216·79
1952	3,926	209·07
1953	2,035	85·95
1954	843	48·53
1955	711	33·11
1956	1,443	56·34
1957	3,646	162·39
1958	3,224	120·51
1959	3,868	141·41
1960	5,137	192·84
1961	3,495	129·56
1962 (prov.)	3,640	141·09

Source: Ministry of Food and Agriculture, *Bulletin on Food Statistics*, January 1963, Table 8, pp. 58–59.

(h) Net Terms of Trade, 1948/9–1961/2

Year	1948–9 = 100	1952–3 = 100	1958 = 100
1948–49	100		
1949–50	105		
1950–51	122	113	
1951–52	121	141	
1952–53	94[c]	100	
1953–54	91[c]	100	
1954–55		110	
1955–56		103	
1956–57		103	
1957–58		96[c]	
1958–59		101[c]	100[c]
1959–60			107[c]
1960–61			111[c]
1961–62			112[c]

Sources: *India Yearbooks; Statistical Abstracts.*
  Note: [c] = Calendar years.

(i) Foreign Exchange Reserves, 1947/8–1962/3[a] (Rs crores)

As at the end of	Amount[b]	Variation over previous year
1947–48	1,612·0	
1948–49	1,013·5	−598·5
1949–50	1,000·6	− 12·9
1950–51	1,029·2	+ 28·6
1951–52	864·4	−164·8
1952–53	881·1	+ 16·7
1953–54	910·0	+ 28·9
1954–55	891·9	− 18·1
1955–56	902·4	+ 10·5
1956–57	681·1	−221·3
1957–58	421·2	−259·9
1958–59	378·9	− 42·3
1959–60	362·9	− 16·0
1960–61	303·6	− 59·3
1961–62	297·3	− 6·3
1962–63	295·1	− 2·2

Sources: *RBI, Currency and Finance; RBI, Balance of Payments.*
  [a] Includes (i) 7·1 million ounces of gold valued at Rs 62·50 per *tola*; (ii) foreign assets of the Reserve Bank; (iii) Government balances held abroad.

b Includes net borrowing from the IMF of $115 million (Rs 547 crores) during 1956–7; the stand-by credit of $72·5 million (Rs 34·5 crores) during 1957–8, net borrowing from the IMF of $122·5 million (Rs 58·3 crores) during 1961–2; and borrowing of $25 million (Rs 11·9 crores) from the IMF against a stand-by credit of $100 million in 1962–3.

APPENDIX FOUR

BUDGETARY POSITION OF THE GOVERNMENT OF INDIA, 1948/9–1964/5
(Rs crores)

	1948–9	1949–50	1950–1	1951–2	1952–3	1953–4	1954–5
Revenue account:[a]							
Total revenue	371·70	350·39	405·86	515·36	418·28	400·43	441·02
taxes on income, expenditure, and wealth	181·76	161·12	129·51	139·55	130·01	109·35	105·95
taxes on goods and services	176·79	192·56	227·49	320·44	240·22	238·38	278·20
net contribution of public undertakings	9·70	9·38	23·16	20·98	16·61	21·63	26·92
Expenditure	320·86	317·12	346·64	387·27	379·35	391·93	407·51
defence (net)	146·05	148·86	164·13	170·96	179·52	186·30	186·66
Capital account:							
Receipts	317·71	124·14	104·45	53·94	29·00	97·70	177·31
from abroad[b]	not available		7·75	111·95	67·65	18·43	15·55
Disbursements	485·19	203·19	182·59	178·33	124·19	187·20	366·43
discharge of foreign debt	not available		4·11	3·35	4·92	2·88	3·28

Sources: 1948/9–1961/2: RBI, *Currency and Finance*; 1962/3–1964/5: RBI *Bulletin*, March 1964.

1955–6	1956–7	1957–8	1958–9	1959–60	1960–1	1961–2	1962–3	1963–4	1964–5
481·19	563·23	673·38	670·21	778·59	877·46	1036·79	1427·53	1753·28	1970·84
115·78	146·58	157·01	166·09	193·90	205·46	243·05	328·54	407·65	468·15
295·69	347·18	418·32	386·97	448·54	524·68	632·32	732·44	902·41	980·93
28·92	31·81	36·27	35·96	53·89	53·00	65·69	56·07	68·53	66·46
440·74	473·83	631·33	675·46	736·04	826·21	911·94	1314·14	1664·94	1876·76
172·23	192·15	256·72	250·93	230·86	247·55	289·54	425·30	692·55	717·80
280·95	302·75	297·62	590·53	757·92	1127·00	957·34	1204·25	1579·46	1861·95
43·17	41·57	65·30	246·73	266·11	509·64	474·61	543·68	723·09	947·06
470·92	616·78	843·07	813·20	958·24	1000·53	1171·61	1454·38	1825·89	2025·58
3·22	3·21	7·21	7·46	9·48	17·71	65·62	46·30	61·49	67·26

Notes: Accounts 1948/9–1962/3; Revised Budget 1963–4; Budget 1964–5.
   [a] Excludes States' share.
   [b] Loans, US Counterpart Funds, and other special Western aid.

LIST OF REFERENCES

Acharya, T. L. A. (ed.)
Planning for Labour. Indian Labour Forum, New Delhi, 1947.
Agency for International Development.
US Foreign Assistance. Washington DC, 21 March 1962.
A-ICC Economic Review.
All-India Congress Committee Economic Review. New Delhi. Twice monthly.
Aid to Developing Countries.
Cmd. 2147. HMSO, London, September 1963.
A-IMO. *India.*
All-India Manufacturers' Organization. *India and International Economic Policies*, Statement on the Agenda of the International Business Conference at Rye, New York, mid-November 1944. Bombay, 1944.
A-IMO. *Rapid Development.*
All-India Manufacturers' Organization. *Rapid Development of Indian Industries*. Report of the delegation which visited the industrially developed countries of the West (1946–7). Bombay, 1947.
All-India Importers' Association.
Memorandum on Import and Export Policy Committee Questionnaire. n.p. [Bombay], August 1961.
All-India Seminar on Foreign Collaboration, Bombay, 1–3 February 1965, *Factual Background Papers*. (Duplicated)
American Consulate Survey.
US Department of Commerce, Office of International Trade. *Foreign Participation in Indian Industrial Projects since India's Independence*. (Based on a survey made by Paul Geren, Vice-Consul, US Consulate General, Bombay, India; and prepared for release by Rollo P. Stovall, Middle East Branch, Office of International Trade.) 15 March 1950. (Duplicated)
Annual Report . . . Companies Act.
Department of Company Law Administration, GOI. *Annual Report of the Working and Administration of the Companies Act*. New Delhi.
Anstey, Vera.
'Economic Development', in O'Malley (ed.), *Modern India and the West*, q.v.
Anstey, Vera.
The Economic Development of India. 4th ed. Longmans, Green & Co., London, New York, Toronto, 1952.
Arnold, H. J. P.
Aid for Developing Countries. Bodley Head, London, 1962.
Assistance from the United Kingdom for Overseas Development.
Cmd. 974. HMSO, London, March 1960.
Ayyangar, Justice N. Rajagopala.
Report on the Revision of the Patents Law. Government of India. Delhi, 1959.
Background to Burmah-Shell.
Bombay: Burmah-Shell Oil Storage and Distributing Co. of India Ltd., n.d., [1955].
Balakrishna, R.
Measurement of Productivity in Indian Industry. 2nd ed. University of Madras, 1958.

Banerji, Arun Kumar.
India's Balance of Payments. Asia Publishing House, Bombay, etc., 1963.

Barlow, E. R.
Management of Foreign Manufacturing Subsidiaries. Division of Research, Graduate School of Business Administration, Harvard University. Boston, 1953.

Barna, Tibor.
Investment and Growth Policies in British Industrial Firms. National Institute of Economic and Social Research, Occasional Papers XX. Cambridge University Press, 1962.

Basu, S. K.
The Managing Agency System, in Prospect and Retrospect. The World Press Private Ltd., Calcutta, 1958.

BBR
Barclays Bank Review. London. Quarterly.

Berliner, Joseph S.
Soviet Economic Aid. Frederick A. Praeger for Council on Foreign Relations. New York, 1958.

Bettelheim, Charles.
L'Inde indépendante. Armand Colin, Paris, 1962.

Bhagwati, J.
'Indian Balance of Payments Policy and Exchange Auctions.' *Oxford Economic Papers*. February 1962.

Billerbeck, Klaus.
Soviet Bloc Foreign Aid to the Underdeveloped Countries. Hamburg Archives of World Economy. Hamburg, 1960. (Cyclostyled)

Birla, G. D.
The Path to Prosperity, A collection of speeches and writings. Edited by Parasnath Sinha, with a foreword by Sir Geo. Schuster. The Leader Press, Allahabad, 1950.

Black, Eugene R.
The Diplomacy of Economic Development. Harvard University Press, Cambridge, Mass., 1960.

Bombay Investors' Year Book. Bombay. Annual.

Bombay Plan.
A Plan of Economic Development for India, Part I, January 1944; Part II, January 1945. Penguin ed., 1945.

Bose, Arun.
Indo-British Big Business Deals. People's Publishing House, Bombay, 1947.

BOT. *Company Assets . . . 1960.*
UK Board of Trade. *Company Assets, Income and Finance in 1960*. HMSO, London, 1962.

BOT. *India 1949* and *India 1952*.
UK Board of Trade (Commercial Relations & Exports Dept.). *India, Economic and Commercial Conditions in India*, by Rowland Owen, CMG. HMSO, 1949 and 1953.

Brown, Hilton.
Parry's of Madras. A Story of British Enterprise in India. Parry, Madras, 1954.

Brown, W. A., jun.
The United States and the Restoration of World Trade. Brookings Institution, Washington DC, 1950.

Buchanan, Daniel Houston.
The Development of Capitalistic Enterprise in India. The Macmillan Co., New York, 1934.

Bulletin for Industry.
A Monthly Review of the Economic Situation prepared by the Information Division of the Treasury, London.

Burmah-Shell, Survey of Activities 1956.
Bombay: Burmah-Shell Oil Storage and Distribution Co. of India Ltd., 1957.

CA (Legislative) Debates.
Constituent Assembly (Legislative) Debates. New Delhi.

Call, The. Delhi. Monthly.

Capital. Calcutta. Weekly.

Chagla Commission. *Report.*
Report of the Chagla Commission, printed verbatim in *Indian Information,* Vol. I, No. 2., March 1958.

Coale, Ansley J., and Hoover, Edgar K.
Population Growth and Economic Development in Low Income Countries, A Case Study of India's Prospects. Princeton University Press, New Jersey, 1958.

Cohen, Jerome B.
The Role of the Government in Economic Development in India. Centre for International Studies, Massachusetts Institute of Technology. October 1953. (Duplicated)

Commerce. Bombay. Weekly.

Company Law Committee. *Report.*
GOI. *Report of the Company Law Committee 1950–51.* Ministry of Finance, Department of Economic Affairs. New Delhi, 1952.

Company Law Committee. *Written Evidence.*
GOI. *Report of the Company Law Committee 1950–51, Written Evidence.* Vols. I (2 parts) and II. Ministry of Finance, Department of Economic Affairs. New Delhi, 1952.

Company News and Notes.
Research and Statistics Division, Department of Company Law Administration, Ministry of Commerce and Industry. New Delhi. Fortnightly.

Conan, A. R.
Capital Imports into Sterling Countries. Macmillan, London, 1960.

CSM
Christian Science Monitor. Boston. Daily.

CSO. *National Income Statistics.*
GOI. Central Statistical Organization. *National Income Statistics, Estimates of Gross Capital Formation in India for 1948–49 to 1960–61.* n.p. [New Delhi], n.d. (1962). (Duplicated)

Dale, William B., and Bale, Richard N.
Private United States Venture Capital for Investment in Newly Developing Countries. Investment Series 2, International Comparative Studies. International Industrial Development Centre, Stanford Research Institute, California, September 1958.

Damle Report.
GOI. Ministry of Steel, Mines, and Fuel. *Report of the Oil Price Enquiry Committee.* New Delhi, July 1961.

Das, Nabagopal.
Industrial Enterprise in India. 2nd ed. Orient Longman's; Bombay, Calcutta, Madras, 1956.

Department of Commercial Intelligence and Statistics, *Monthly Statistics of the Foreign Trade of India*. Calcutta.

Desai, A. R.
  Recent Trends in Indian Nationalism. Popular Book Depot, Bombay, 1960.

Desai, A. R.
  Social Background of Indian Nationalism. 3rd ed. Popular Book Depot, Bombay, 1959.

Deshmukh, Chintaman.
  Central Banking in India—A Retrospect. Gokhale Institute of Politics and Economics, Poona, 20 March 1948.

DT
  Daily Telegraph. London. Daily.

ECAFE (United Nations Economic Commission for Asia and the Far East) *Bulletin*. Bangkok. Quarterly.

ECAFE. *Survey*.
  United Nations Economic Commission for Asia and the Far East. *Economic Survey of Asia and the Far East*. Bangkok. Annual.

Economia Internazionale. Genoa. Quarterly.

Economic Survey.
  GOI. *Economic Survey*. New Delhi. Annual.

Economica. London. Thrice yearly.

Economist, The. London. Weekly.

Eddison, John C.
  A Case Study in Industrial Development in the Growth of the Pulp and Paper Industry in India. Centre for International Studies, MIT, Cambridge, Mass. February 1955. (Duplicated)

EE
  Eastern Economist. New Delhi. Weekly.

EIU
  Economist Intelligence Unit. *The State Trading Corporation*. Council for Economic Education, Bombay, 1961.

EJ
  Economic Journal. London. Quarterly.

ET
  Economic Times. Bombay. Daily.

EW
  Economic Weekly. Bombay. Weekly.

Export Promotion Committee. *Report*.
  Report of the Export Promotion Committee, 1957. Ministry of Commerce and Industry, Government of India. New Delhi, August 1957.

FBI. *India 1963*.
  Federation of British Industries. *India 1963*. London, February 1963.

Feis, Herbert.
  Europe the World's Banker 1870–1914. Published for the Council on Foreign Relations by Yale University Press, 1931.

fforde, J. S.
  An International Trade in Managerial Skills. Blackwell, Oxford, 1957.

FICCI. *Proceedings*.
  Federation of Indian Chambers of Commerce and Industry. *Proceedings of the 1st [etc.] Annual Meeting*. New Delhi. Annual.

FICCI. *The Third Five-Year Plan*.
  Federation of Indian Chambers of Commerce and Industry. *The Third Five-Year Plan—A Tentative Outline*. New Delhi, 1959.

Fiscal Commission (1921–22). *Report*.
  GOI. *Report of the Indian Fiscal Commission 1921–22*. Simla, 1922.
Fiscal Commission (1949–50). *Report*.
  GOI. Ministry of Commerce and Industry. *Report of the Fiscal Commission 1949–50*. New Delhi, 1950.
Five Glorious Days, July 12–16, 1960.
  Central Government Employees Strike. All-India Trade Union Congress. New Delhi, 1960.
Foreign Affairs. New York. Quarterly.
Foreign Commerce Weekly. Washington DC. Weekly.
'Foreign Investments in India: 1959 and 1960 (Preliminary Trends).'
  RBI *Bulletin*, May 1961.
'Foreign Investments in India: 1960 and 1961 (Preliminary Trends).'
  RBI *Bulletin*, October 1962.
Friedmann, W. G., and Kalmanoff, G. (eds.)
  Joint International Business Ventures. Columbia University Press, New York and London, 1961.
FT
  Financial Times. London. Daily.
Gadgil, D. R.
  Convocation Address at Nagpur University. 20 January 1962. Nagpur University, 1962.
Galenson, Walter.
  Labour and Economic Development. John Wiley & Sons, Inc., New York; Chapman & Hall, Ltd., London; 1959.
Garvin, Stephen.
  India: A Survey for British Industrial Firms. Federation of British Industries, London, 1956.
GATT (General Agreement on Tariffs and Trade).
  Trade of Less-Developed Countries, Special Report of Committee III. Development Plans: Study of the Third Five Year Plan of India. Geneva, 1962.
Gokhale Institute.
  Gokhale Institute of Politics and Economics. *Notes on the Rise of the Business Communities in India*. Institute of Pacific Relations, International Secretariat, New York, 1951. (Duplicated and labelled 'Preliminary Memorandum Not for Publication'.)
Gopal, M. H.
  'Indian Industrial Policy: Its Evolution'. *IEJ*. Vol. IV. No. 4. April 1957.
Gregory, Sir Theodore.
  India on the Eve of the Third Five Year Plan. Associated Chambers of Commerce of India, 1960.
Guardian. London and Manchester. Daily.
Gurtoo, Dukh Haran Nath.
  India's Balance of Payments 1920–1960. S. Chand & Co., Delhi, Jullundur, Lucknow, 1961.
[Haccoû, J. F.]
  Management of Direct Investments in Less Developed Countries. Report submitted to the International Bank for Reconstruction and Development, by the Foundation for Economic Research of the University of Amsterdam. H. E. Stanfert Kroese, Leiden, 1957.
Hall, A. R.
  'A Note on the English Capital Market as a Source of Funds for Home Investment before 1914.' *Economica*. February 1957.

Hanson, A. H.
Public Enterprise and Economic Development. Routledge & Kegan Paul, London, 1959.

Hardinge, Charles.
My Indian Years: 1910–1916; *The Reminiscences of Lord Hardinge of Penshurst*. Murray, London, 1948.

Harrison, Selig S.
India, the Most Dangerous Decades. Princeton and OUP, 1960.

Hazari, R. K.
The Structure of the Corporate Private Sector. Report to the Government of India Research Program Committee, Planning Commission. Bombay, 1963. (Duplicated)

Hindu. Madras. Daily.

Hirachand, Walchand.
'Why Indian Shipping Does not Grow,' *Bombay Investors' Year Book*, 1940.

Hull, Cordell.
The Memoirs of Cordell Hull. 2 vols. Macmillan, New York, 1948.

IA
International Affairs. London. Quarterly.

ICI Handout to Staff. n.p. [Calcutta?], n.d. [1961?] (Duplicated)

IEJ
Indian Economic Journal. Bombay.

IER
Indian Economic Review, The. Delhi School of Economics.

IFNS
International Financial News Service. The International Monetary Fund, Washington. Weekly.

IIPO. *Monthly*.
Indian Institute of Public Opinion. *Monthly Statistical Commentary on Indian Economic Conditions*. New Delhi. Monthly.

IIPO. *Quarterly*.
Indian Institute of Public Opinion. *Quarterly Economic Report*. New Delhi. Quarterly.

IJE
Indian Journal of Economics. Allahabad. Quarterly.

INC. *Resolutions 1924–54* and *Resolutions 1955–56*.
Indian National Congress. *Resolutions on Economic Policy and Programme, 1924–54*, and *1955–56*. All-India Congress Committee, New Delhi, 1954, and 1956.

India.
A Reference Annual. Government of India, Ministry of Information and Broadcasting.

India News.
High Commission of India. London. Weekly.

India Yearbook.
Times of India Directory and Yearbook, Bombay, Calcutta, Delhi. Annual.

Indian Central Banking Enquiry Committee. *Report*. Calcutta, 1931.

Indian Express. Bombay. Daily.

Indian Industrial Commission. *Report*.
Superintendent of Govt. Printing, Calcutta, 1918.

Indian Information.
Ministry of Information and Broadcasting. Delhi. Fortnightly.

Indian Investment Centre.
Investing in India. New Delhi, 1961.
Indian Labour Gazette.
  GOI. Labour Bureau, Ministry of Labour and Employment. *Indian Labour Gazette/Journal.* Delhi. Monthly.
Indian Labour Statistics 1964.
  GOI. Labour Bureau, Ministry of Labour and Employment. *Digest of Indian Labour Statistics 1964.* New Delhi, 1964.
Indian Merchants' Chamber. *Report.* Annual.
Indian Ship.
  Why Shipowners Oppose Indo-Foreign Combine for Shipping. Published by Navin Khandwallah, Deputy Manager, The Scindia Steam Navigation Co. Bombay, n.d. [1958].
Indo-U.S. Technical Co-operation Program. *Report.* Government of India, Ministry of Finance. New Delhi. Annual.
Industrial Research in Manufacturing Industry, 1959–60.
  Federation of British Industries, London, 1961.
Islam, Nurul.
  Foreign Capital and Economic Development: Japan, India, and Canada. Charles E. Tuttle Co., Rutland, Vermont; Tokyo, Japan. Distributed in London by Mark Paterson & Co. Ltd., 1960.
Japan Times. Tokyo. Daily.
Jathar, Ganesh Bharkar, and Jathar, K. G.
  Indian Economics. OUP, Bombay, 1957.
Jenks, Leland H.
  The Migration of British Capital to 1875. Thomas Nelson & Sons Ltd., London, etc., 1963.
JIT
  Journal of Industry and Trade. Directorate of Commercial Publicity. Ministry of Commerce and Industry, New Delhi. Monthly.
Joint . . . India.
  Joint International Business Ventures in India. Country Studies No. 6. Joint International Business Ventures. A Research Project of Columbia University. New York, May 1959. (Duplicated) (Incorporated in part in Friedmann and Kalmanoff, *Joint International Business Ventures.*)
Kaldor, Nicholas.
  Indian Tax Reform, Report of a Survey. GOI. Department of Economic Affairs. Delhi, 1956.
Kannapan, Subbiah, and Burgess, Eugene W.
  Aluminium Limited in India. Eleventh Case Study in an NPA series on Business Performance Abroad. National Planning Association, Washington DC, January 1962.
Karnik, V. B.
  Indian Trade Unions—a Survey. Labour Education Service, Bombay, 1960.
Kefauver Report.
  United States, 87th Congress, Senate Report No. 448. *Administered Prices: Drugs.* Washington DC, 1961.
Khusro, A. M.
  Economic Development with no Population Transfers. Institute of Economic Growth, Occasional Papers No. 4. Asia Publishing House, Delhi, 1962.

Kumarasundaram, S.
 Foreign Collaboration and [the] Indian Balance of Payments. Paper read to the
 All-India Seminar on Foreign Collaboration, Bombay, 1–3 February 1965.
 (Duplicated)
Labour Investigation Committee. *Report.* Delhi, 1946.
Latifi, Daniel.
 India and U.S. Aid. Public Affairs Forum, Bombay, 1960.
Lindsay, H. K. S.
 The Role of Foreign Enterprise in a Developing Economy. The Metal Box Co.
 of India Ltd. n.p. [Calcutta], n.d. [1963 or 1964].
Link. New Delhi. Weekly.
*List of Manufacturing Concerns with U.K. Financial and/or Technical Co-
 operation, as Known to the Trade Commission.* New Delhi, n.d. [October 1959].
 (Duplicated)
Lokanathan, P. S.
 Industrial Organization in India. Allen & Unwin, London, 1935.
Lokanathan, P. S.
 Industrialization. Oxford Pamphlets on Indian Affairs, No. 10. 3rd ed. OUP,
 Bombay, 1946.
LS Debates.
 Lok Sabha. *Debates.* New Delhi.
Malenbaum, Wilfred.
 Prospects for Indian Development. George Allen & Unwin, London, 1962.
Malenbaum, Wilfred.
 'Urban Unemployment in India.' *Pacific Affairs,* June 1957. pp. 138–50.
Mansergh, Nicholas.
 Survey of British Commonwealth Affairs. Vol. IV. *Problems of Wartime
 Co-operation and Post-war Change 1939–1952.* OUP for Royal Institute of
 International Affairs, London, 1958.
Mazumdar, Harendra Kumar.
 Business Saving in India. J. B. Wolters, Groningen; Vora & Co., Bombay, 1959.
MBR
 Midland Bank Review. London. Quarterly.
Mehta, M. M.
 *Combination Movement in Indian Industry, A Study in the concentration of
 ownership, control and management in Indian Industry.* Friends' Book Depot,
 Allahabad, 1952.
Mehta, M. M.
 Structure of the Cotton Mill Industry. Central Book Depot, Allahabad, 1949.
Mehta, M. M.
 Structure of Indian Industries. Popular Book Depot, Bombay, 1955.
MG
 Manchester Guardian. Manchester. Daily. (Now *Guardian.*)
Mikesell, Raymond F.
 Promoting United States Private Investments Abroad. National Planning
 Association. Planning Pamphlet No. 101. Washington DC, 1957.
Ministry of Commerce and Industry. *Foreign Trade Statistics.*
 Government of India. Delhi. Annual.
Ministry of Commerce and Industry. *Information Broadsheet No. 12/1958.*
 Dept. of Company Law Administration, Research and Statistics Division.
 *Information Broadsheet No. 12/1958: Companies Incorporated elsewhere than in
 India and having their Branches in this Country, 1957–8.* Duplicated ('For
 Departmental Use Only'), n.d. [1958].

Ministry of Commerce and Industry. *Information Broadsheet No. 1/1960.*
Dept. of Company Law Administration, Research and Statistics Division. *Information Broadsheet No. 1/1960: Subsidiary Companies in India as on 31st March, 1958.* Duplicated ('For Departmental Use Only'), n.d. [1960].

Ministry of Commerce and Industry. *Report.* New Delhi. Annual.

Ministry of Finance. *Budget Papers.*
GOI. Ministry of Finance. *Budget.* New Delhi. Annual.

Ministry of Finance. *Explanatory Memoranda.*
GOI. Ministry of Finance. *Explanatory Memoranda to the Budgets.* New Delhi. Annual.

Ministry of Finance. *External Assistance.*
GOI. Ministry of Finance, Dept. of Economic Affairs. *External Assistance.* New Delhi. Annual.

Ministry of Finance. *Quarterly Statistics on the Workings of the Capital Issues Control.*
GOI. Ministry of Finance, Dept. of Economic Affairs, Office of the Controller of Capital Issues. New Delhi. Quarterly.

Ministry of Food and Agriculture. *Area, Production and Yield per Acre, Forecast Crops 1949–50 to 1959–60.* New Delhi, December 1960.

Ministry of Food and Agriculture. *Bulletin on Food Statistics.* Delhi. Annual.

Ministry of Food and Agriculture. *Food Situation in India 1939–53.* Delhi, 1954.

Ministry of Food and Agriculture. *Indian Agriculture in Brief.* 6th ed. New Delhi, 1963.

Ministry of Labour. *Report . . . [on] Organized Workers in India,* 1948.
GOI. Ministry of Labour. *Report Relating to the Enquiries whether the All-India Trade Union Congress or the Indian National Trade Union Congress is the most Representative Organization of Organized Workers in India.* Simla, 1948.

Ministry of Labour. *Statistics on Incomes, Prices, Employment and Production.* HMSO, London. Quarterly.

Ministry of Production. *Establishment of Oil Refineries. Texts of Agreements with the Oil Companies.* New Delhi, 15 September 1953.

Misra, B. B.
The Indian Middle Classes. Their Growth in Modern Times. OUP for the Royal Institute of International Affairs, London etc., 1961.

Mitchell, K. L.
Industrialization of the Western Pacific. Institute of Pacific Relations, New York, 1942.

Mohnot, S. R.
Concentration of Economic Power in India. Chaitanya Publishing House, Allahabad, for Bureau of Economic Studies, Calcutta, 1962.

Monthly Statistics.
GOI. Department of Statistics, Central Statistical Organization. *Monthly Statistics of the Production of Selected Industries of India.* Calcutta. Monthly.

MSA (Mutual Security Agency).
MSA Mission to the United Kingdom. *Economic Development in the United Kingdom, 1850–1950.* n.d., n.p. (Duplicated)

Mudaliar Report.
Ministry of Commerce and Industry. *Report of the Import and Export Policy Committee.* New Delhi, 1962.

Myers, Charles A.
Labour Problems in the Industrialization of India. Harvard University Press, Cambridge, Mass., 1958.

Myers, Charles A.
'India', in Galenson, *Labour and Economic Development*, q.v.
Natarajan, L.
American Shadow over India. 1st ed. 1952; 2nd ed. 1956. People's Publishing House Ltd., Bombay.
NCAER. *Managing Agency*.
National Council of Applied Economic Research. *The Managing Agency System*. Asia Publishing House; Bombay, Calcutta, New Delhi, Madras, London, New York, 1959.
NCAER. *Taxation and Foreign Investment*.
National Council of Applied Economic Research. *Taxation and Foreign Investment. A Study of Taxation Laws in India in Relation to Foreign Investment*. 2nd rev. ed. Asia Publishing House; Bombay, Calcutta, New Delhi, Madras, 1958.
Nehru, Jawaharlal.
An Autobiography. Bodley Head, London, 1936.
Nehru, Jawaharlal.
The Discovery of India. 4th ed. Meridian Press Ltd., London, 1956.
Nehru, Jawaharlal. *Independence and After. A Collection of Speeches 1946–1949*. John Day & Co., New York, 1950.
New Commonwealth. London. Monthly.
New Statesman. London. Weekly.
NIESR. *Review*.
The Economic Review. London, National Institute of Economic and Social Research. Bi-monthly.
Nigam, Raj. K.
Managing Agencies in India (First Round: Basic Facts). GOI. Ministry of Commerce and Industry, Dept. of Company Law Administration, Research and Statistics Division. n.p. [New Delhi], n.d. [1958].
Nigam, Raj. K., and Chaudhuri, N. C.
The Corporate Sector in India. GOI. Ministry of Commerce and Industry, Dept. of Company Law Administration, Research and Statistics Division. New Delhi, 1960.
NPC. *Chemical Industries*.
National Planning Committee. *Chemical Industries*. Report of the Sub-Committee. Vora & Co., Bombay, 1947.
Nurkse, Ragnar.
Patterns of Trade and Development. Basil Blackwell, Oxford, 1961.
NYHT
New York Herald Tribune. European ed. Paris. Daily.
NYT
New York Times. New York. Daily.
NZZ
Neue Zürcher Zeitung. Zürich. Daily.
Observer. London. Weekly.
OEP
Oxford Economic Papers. Oxford. Thrice-yearly.
O'Malley, Lewes Sydney Steward. (ed.)
Modern India and the West, a Study of the Interaction of their Civilizations. Oxford University Press, London, 1941.
PA
Pacific Affairs. New York. Quarterly.

Palande, M. R.
  Introduction to Indian Administration. 5th ed. Oxford University Press, Bombay, 1951.
Pardiwalla, J. J.
  Exchange Banks in India. Ph.D. thesis submitted to the University of Bombay, 1950. (Typescript)
Park, Richard Leonard, and Tinker, Irene.
  Leadership and Political Institutions in India. Princeton University Press, Princeton, New Jersey, 1959.
Patel, Surendra J.
  'Export Prospects and Economic Growth: India.' *EJ*, September 1959.
PC. *Appraisal and Prospects.*
  GOI. Planning Commission. *Appraisal and Prospects of the Second Five Year Plan.* May 1958. n.p. [New Delhi].
PC. *Draft Third Plan.*
  GOI. Planning Commission. *Third Five Year Plan. A Draft Outline.* n.p. [New Delhi], 1960.
PC. *First Plan.*
  GOI. Planning Commission. *The First Five Year Plan.* New Delhi, December, 1952.
PC. *Mid-Term Appraisal.*
  GOI. Planning Commission. *The Third Plan Mid-Term Appraisal.* New Delhi, November 1963.
PC. Panel of Economists. *Papers.*
  GOI. Planning Commission. Panel of Economists. *Papers Relating to the Formulation of the Second Five Year Plan.* New Delhi, 1955.
PC. *Planning in the Public and Private Sectors.*
  GOI. Planning Commission. *Planning in the Public and Private Sectors—Scope and Method.* New Delhi, 1950.
PC. *Review First Plan.*
  GOI. Planning Commission. *Review of the First Five Year Plan.* New Delhi, May 1957.
PC. *Second Plan.*
  GOI. Planning Commission. *The Second Five Year Plan.* n.p. [New Delhi], 1956.
PC. *Third Plan.*
  GOI. Planning Commission. *The Third Five Year Plan.* n.p. [New Delhi], n.d. [1961].
PEP. *Management.*
  Political and Economic Planning. *Management and Underdeveloped Countries.* 1 June 1959.
Pharmaceuticals Enquiry Committee. *Report.*
  GOI. Ministry of Commerce and Industry. *Report of the Pharmaceuticals Enquiry Committee.* New Delhi, 1954.
Plantation Enquiry Commission. *Report.*
  GOI. *Report of the Plantation Enquiry Commission.* Part I—'Tea'; Part II—'Coffee'; Part III—'Rubber'; 3 vols. New Delhi, 1956.
Powell, J. Enoch.
  Saving in a Free Society. Published for the Institute of Economic Affairs by Hutchinson, London, 1960.
PPS
  Petroleum Press Service. London. Monthly.

Prasad, Parmanand.
Some Economic Problems of Public Enterprises in India. H. E. Stenfert Kroese, NV, Leiden, 1957.
Problems of International Investment. Royal Institute of International Affairs. London, 1938.
Productivity.
Journal of the National Productivity Council. New Delhi. Monthly.
Radcliffe. *Memoranda, Minutes.*
UK Committee on the Working of the Monetary System. *Principal Memoranda of Evidence.* 3 vols. *Minutes of Evidence.* HMSO, London, 1960.
Radcliffe Report.
UK Committee on the Working of the Monetary System. *Report.* HMSO, London, 1959 (Cmd. 827).
Raj, K. N.
The Monetary Policy of the Reserve Bank of India. Ph.D. thesis, London, 1947. (Typescript)
Rangnekar, D. K.
Poverty and Capital Development in India. OUP for the Royal Institute of International Affairs. London, 1958.
RBI. *Balance of Payments.*
India's Balance of Payments 1948–49 to 1961–62. Reserve Bank of India, Bombay, 1963.
RBI. *Bulletin.*
Reserve Bank of India *Bulletin.* Bombay. Monthly.
RBI. *Census.*
Reserve Bank of India. *Census of India's Foreign Liabilities and Assets.* Bombay, 1950.
RBI. *Currency and Finance.*
Reserve Bank of India. *Report on Currency and Finance.* Annual.
RBI. *Survey 1953.*
Reserve Bank of India. *Survey of India's Foreign Liabilities and Assets.* Bombay, 1955.
RBI. *Survey 1955.*
Reserve Bank of India. *Survey of India's Foreign Liabilities and Assets.* Bombay, 1957.
RBI. *Survey 1961.*
Reserve Bank of India. *India's Foreign Liabilities and Assets 1961—Survey Report.* Bombay, 1964.
Readers' Digest. New York, etc. Monthly.
Report of the Bankers' Mission.
Abs, Hermann J., Franks, Sir Oliver, and Sproul, Allan. *Report of the Bankers' Mission to India and Pakistan.* International Bank for Reconstruction and Development, Washington DC, 1960.
Report of the Soviet Experts on the Drug Industry in India. 1956. (Typed extracts.)
Rosen, George.
Some Aspects of Industrial Finance in India. Asia Publishing House, 1962.
Rosen, George.
Industrial Change in India. Free Press, Glencoe, Illinois, 1958, for MIT Centre for International Studies; Asia Publishing House, Bombay, 1959.
Rosinger, Lawrence K.
India and the United States. The Macmillan Co., New York, 1950.
Sarma, S.
Foreign Investments in India. Paramita Prakasani Ltd., Calcutta, 1951.

2222

Schwartzberg, Joseph Emmanuel.
Occupational Structure and Level of Economic Development in India. A Regional Analysis. Ph.D. thesis submitted to the Graduate School of the University of Wisconsin, 1960. (Duplicated)

Science and Culture. Calcutta. Monthly.

Searchlight, The. Patna. Daily.

Seventeenth Tripartite.
All-India Trade Union Congress. New Delhi, 1959.

Shelvankar, K. S.
The Problem of India. Penguin Special, 1940.

Shonfield, Andrew.
The Attack on World Poverty. Chatto & Windus, London, 1960.

Simha, S. L. N.
The Capital Market of India. Vora & Co., Bombay, 1960.

Simon Report.
Report of the Indian Statutory Commission. 2 vols. Cmds. 3568–9. HMSO, London, 1930.

Sokhey, Major-General S. S.
The Indian Drug Industry and its Future. Published by the author, 1959.

Sousa, J. P. de.
History of the Chemical Industry in India. Technical Press Publications, Bombay, 1961.

Sovani, N. V., and Dandekar, V. M.
Changing India, Essays in Honour of Professor D. R. Gadgil. Asia Publishing House, London, 1961.

Spencer, Daniel L.
India, Mixed Enterprise and Western Business. Martinus Nijhoff, The Hague, 1959.

Statist, The. London. Weekly.

Statistical Abstract.
GOI. Central Statistical Organization. Annual.

Statistical Outline of India.
Tata Industries Private Ltd., Bombay. Annual.

Strachey, John.
The End of Empire. Gollancz, London, 1959.

Sur, A. K.
The New Issue Market and the Stock Exchange. Indian Institute of Social Welfare and Business Management, Calcutta, 1961.

Swarajya. Madras. Weekly.

TC. *Report . . . on . . . Abrasives.*
GOI. Tariff Commission. *Report on the Continuance of Protection to the Coated Abrasives Industry.* 1955.

TC. *Report . . . on the Aluminium Industry.*
GOI. Tariff Board. *Report of the Tariff Board on the Aluminium Industry.* 1947.
GOI. Tariff Board. *Report . . . on the Continuance of Protection to. . . .* 1951.
GOI. Tariff Commission. *Report of the Tariff Commission on the Continuance of Protection to. . . .* 1955.
GOI. Tariff Commission. *Report . . . on the Continuance of Protection to. . . .* 1958.
GOI. Tariff Commission. *Report . . . on the Continuance of Protection to. . . .* 1960.

TC. *Report on the Automobile Industry.*
　　GOI. Tariff Commission. *Report on the Automobile Industry.* 1956.
TC. *Report on the Ball Bearings . . . Industry.*
　　GOI. Tariff Commission. *Report on the Ball Bearings and Steel Balls Industry.* 1952.
　　GOI. Tariff Commission. *Report on the Continuance of Protection. . . .* 1956.
　　GOI. Tariff Commission. *Report on the Continuance of Protection. . . .* 1960
　　GOI. Tariff Commission. *Report on the Continuance of Protection. . . .* 1962
TC. *Report on . . . Bare Copper Conductors.*
　　GOI. Tariff Commission. *Report on the Continuance of Protection to the Bare Copper Conductors and A.C.S.R. (Aluminium Conductors Steel Reinforced) Industry.* 1957.
TC. *Report . . . on the Bicycles Industry.*
　　GOI. Tariff Board. *Report of the Tariff Board on the Bicycles Industry.* 1946.
　　GOI. Tariff Board. *Report . . . on the Continuance of Protection to the Bicycle Industry.* 1949.
　　GOI. Tariff Commission. *Report of the Tariff Commission on the Continuance of Protection to the Bicycle Industry.* 1954.
　　GOI. Tariff Commission. *Report . . . on the Continuance of Protection to the Bicycle Industry.* 1957.
　　GOI. Tariff Commission. *Report . . . on the Continuance of Protection to the Bicycle Industry.* 1960.
TC. *Report . . . on the Cotton Textile Machinery Industry.*
　　GOI. Tariff Board. *Report of the Tariff Board on the Cotton Textile Machinery Industry.* 1949.
TC. *Report on the . . . Diesel Fuel Injection Equipment Industry.*
　　GOI. Tariff Commission. *Report on the Continuance of Protection to the Diesel Fuel Injection Equipment Industry.* 1957.
TC. *Report . . . on the Dry Battery Industry.*
　　GOI. Tariff Board. *Report . . . on the Dry Battery Industry.* 1947.
　　GOI. Tariff Board. *Report . . . on the Continuance of Protection to the Dry Battery Industry.* 1950.
TC. *Report on the Dyestuffs Industry.*
　　GOI. Tariff Commission. *Report on the Dyestuffs Industry.* 1955.
TC. *Report on the Electric Motor Industry.*
　　GOI. Tariff Board. *Report on the Electric Motor Industry.* 1949.
　　GOI. Tariff Commission. *Report on the Continuance of Protection to the Electric Motor Industry.* 1955.
TC. *Report on the . . . Fountain Pen Ink Industry.*
　　GOI. Tariff Commission. *Report on the Continuance of Protection to the Fountain Pen Ink Industry.* 1953.
TC. *Report . . . on the Motor Vehicle Battery Industry.*
　　GOI. Tariff Board. *Report . . . on the Motor Vehicle Battery Industry.* 1948.
　　GOI. Tariff Commission. *Report . . . on the Continuance of Protection to the Motor Vehicle Battery Industry.* 1952.
TC. *Report on . . . Paper and Paper Boards.*
　　GOI. Tariff Commission. *Report on the Fair Ex-Works and Fair Selling Prices of Paper and Paper Boards.* 1959.
TC. *Report on . . . the Para-Aminosalicylic Acid Industry.*
　　GOI. Tariff Commission. *Report on the Grant of Protection and/or Assistance to the Para-Aminosalicylic Acid Industry.* 1958.

TC. *Report on the Piston Assembly . . . Industry.*
    GOI. Tariff Commission. *Report on the Piston Assembly (Piston, Piston Rings and Gudgeon Pins) Industry.* 1955.
    GOI. Tariff Commission. *Report on the Continuance of Protection to the. . . .* 1957.
    GOI. Tariff Commission. *Report on the Continuance of Protection to the. . . .* 1960.
TC. *Report on the Power and Distribution Transformer Industry.*
    GOI. Tariff Commission. *Report on the Power and Distribution Transformer Industry.* 1952.
    GOI. Tariff Commission. *Report on the Continuance of Protection to the. . . .* 1956.
    GOI. Tariff Commission. *Report on the Continuance of Protection to the. . . .* 1960.
TC. *Report on . . . the Preserved Fruits Industry.*
    GOI. Tariff Commission. *Report on the Continuance of Protection to the Preserved Fruits Industry.* 1957.
TC. *Report . . . on . . . the Rubber Plantation Industry.*
    GOI. Tariff Board. *Report . . . on the Prices for Raw Rubber and Protection and Assistance to the Rubber Plantation Industry.* 1951.
TC. *Report on . . . Rubber Tyres and Tubes.*
    GOI. Tariff Commission. *Report on the Fair Prices of Rubber Tyres and Tubes.* 1955.
TC. *Report on . . . the Sewing Machine Industry.*
    GOI. Tariff Board. *Report . . . Sewing Machine Industry.* 1949.
    GOI. Tariff Commission. *Report on the Continuance of Protection to the Sewing Machine Industry.* 1954.
TC. *Report . . . on the Soda Ash Industry.*
    GOI. Tariff Board. *Report . . . on the Soda Ash Industry.* 1949.
    GOI. Tariff Board. *Report . . . on the Review of Protection Granted to the Soda Ash Industry.* 1951.
    GOI. Tariff Commission. *Report . . . on the Continuance of. . . .* 1958.
TC. *Report . . . Sodium Thiosulphate.*
    GOI. Tariff Board. *Report . . . on the Sodium Thiosulphate, Sodium Sulphite and Sodium Bisulphite Industries.* 1949.
TC. *Report on the . . . Sparking Plug Industry.*
    GOI. Tariff Commission. *Report on the Automobile Sparking Plug Industry.* 1954.
    GOI. Tariff Commission. *Report on the Continuance of Protection to the. . . .* 1957.
    GOI. Tariff Commission. *Report on the Continuance of Protection to the. . . .* 1960.
TC. *Report on the . . . Steel Files Industry.*
    GOI. Tariff Commission. *Report on the Engineers' Steel Files Industry.* 1955.
    GOI. Tariff Commission. *Report on the Review of. . . .* 1958.
    GOI. Tariff Commission. *Report on the Continuance of Protection to the. . . .* 1960.
TC. *Report on . . . Tinplate.*
    GOI. Tariff Commission. *Report on the Review of the Retention Prices of Tinplate, Produced by the Tinplate Company of India Private Ltd.* 1958.
TC. *Report on . . . the Titanium Dioxide Industry.*
    GOI. Tariff Commission. *Report on the Continuance of Protection to the Titanium Dioxide Industry.* 1961.

348   LIST OF REFERENCES

TC. *Report on the . . . Wood Screws Industry.*
    GOI. Tariff Commission. *Report on the Continuance of Protection to the Wood Screws Industry.* 1960.
Tata Quarterly. Bombay.
Tew, Brian, and Henderson, R. F. (eds.)
    Studies in Company Finance. National Institute of Economic and Social Research. Economic and Social Studies XVII. Cambridge University Press, 1959.
Thorner, Daniel.
    Investment in Empire, British Railway and Steam Shipping Enterprise in India 1825–1849. University of Pennsylvania Press, Philadelphia, 1950.
Thorner, Daniel and Alice.
    Land and Labour in India. Asia Publishing House, 1962.
Times, The. London. Daily.
TOI
    Times of India. Bombay. Daily.
Transport. Bombay. Monthly.
Tyson, Geoffrey.
    Managing Agency, A System of Business Organization. n.p. [Calcutta], n.d. [1960].
UN. *Private Capital 1956–1958.*
    United Nations. *The International Flow of Private Capital 1956–1958.* New York, 1959.
UN. *Study of Trade.*
    United Nations. *A Study of Trade between Asia and Europe.* Geneva, 1953.
US Department of Commerce. *Investment in India.*
    US Department of Commerce, Office of International Trade. *Investment in India, Conditions and Outlook for U.S. Investors.* Washington DC, 1st ed. 1953, 2nd ed. 1961.
US Department of Commerce. *Raw Materials in the United States Economy.*
    US Department of Commerce, Bureau of the Census. *Raw Materials in the United States Economy.* Working Paper No. 1. Washington DC, 1954.
US Department of Defence.
    US Department of Defence. *Military Assistance Facts.* Washington DC, 1 March 1962.
US Department of State. *Foreign Relations of the United States, Conferences at Cairo and Teheran.* Washington DC, 1960.
USIS. *The Threat of Soviet Economic Policy.*
    United States Information Service, n.p. [London], n.d. [1962?].
Vakil, C. N.
    Economic Consequences of Divided India. Vora & Co., Bombay, 1950.
Venkatasubbiah, H.
    Indian Economy Since Independence. 2nd rev. ed. Asia Publishing House, London, 1961.
Vivian Bose Report.
    GOI. *Report of the Commission of Inquiry on the Administration of Dalmia-Jain Companies.* Ministry of Commerce and Industry, Dept. of Company Law Administration. Delhi, 1963.
Wadia, P. A., and Merchant, K. T.
    Our Economic Problem. 5th ed. Vora & Co., Bombay, 1957.
Wiggins, Guy A.
    Private Foreign Investment in the Development of India. Unpublished M.Sc. thesis, London School of Economics. July 1956. (Typescript)

Wilson, Charles.
  The History of Unilever. 2 vols. Cassell & Co., London, 1954.
Zinkin, Taya.
  Foreign Capital in India. Eastern Economist. Pamphlet No. 11. New Delhi, n.d. [1951].

INDEX

AB Separators, 206n
Abrasives
— foreign capital in, 207
ACC-Vickers-Babcox (see A-V-B)
Acrow India Private, 199
ACSR cable
— foreign capital in, 142
Agricultural machinery
— foreign capital in, 189–90
Aid (see also 'Aid India Club',
  Balance of Payments, Eastern Bloc,
  individual countries), 113ff
— utilization, 99, 122
— and Cold War, 99, 119, 121, 163ff
— and Plans, 123
— cost of, 122, 306
'Aid India Club'
— formation, 120
— membership, 120n
— extent of aid, 120–2
— and India's oil policy, 172–3
Air Conditioning and Refrigeration
  Private, 205n
Alfa Laval India (Private), 206n
Alkali and Chemical Corporation of
  India, 196, 213, 214, 235, 240
Alkalis
— Development Council for, 235
All-India Cycle Manufacturers'
  Association, 8
All-India Manufacturers'
  Association (A-IMO), 67
— and planning, 73
— and nationalization, 87
— and foreign capital, 105, 107, 110
All-India Trade Union Congress
  (AITUC), 75, 82
Allen, George V., 112
Aluminium
— Hungarian aid, 116
— shift to private sector, 144
— foreign capital in, 197–9
— plans, 198
— withholding of knowhow, 289–
  290
Aluminium cable
— Hungarian aid, 115
Aluminium Co., 198n
Aluminium Co. of Canada, 197, 241n

Aluminium Corporation of India, 198,
  199, 290
Aluminium foil
— foreign capital in, 199
Aluminium-Industrie, 198n, 290
Amalgamations (Private), 189n
Amar Dye-Chem, 210, 211
American Cynamid, 209, 210, 212, 213,
  266, 270
American Refrigerator Co. Private,
  205n
Amritlal Co., 210–11
Anand Automobiles, 267
Andrew Yule, 6, 8, 57, 59n, 60, 190, 235
Anglo-Indian Jute Mills, 196
Antibiotics (see also Drugs), 211–12
Antony Gibbs and Sons, 203
APV Engineering Co. Private, 206n
Arms Budget (see also Budget), 125,
  126
Arms supplies
— East–West competition in, 117–19
— 'reserved', 143
— private sector in, 151
Asaf Ali, 97
Ashok-Leyland, 200, 235
Asian Cable Corporation, 203
Assam Oil (see also Burmah-Shell, Oil
  companies), 167, 169, 192
Assam Silliminite, 190
Associated Battery Makers (Eastern),
  201, 235, 258
Associated Bearing Co., 207, 303
Associated British Machine Tool
  Makers (India), 235
Associated Chambers of Commerce
  and Industry (ACCI), 9, 59, 234,
  295
Associated Electrical Industries (AEI),
  188n, 202n, 203, 204n, 205, 223,
  235, 245
Association of Indian Industries, 66n,
  67, 68
Ateliers et Chantiers de la Loire, 305
Atic Industries (Private), 210
Atul Products, 210, 213, 250-1, 263,
  266, 270
Austria
— in aid consortium, 120n

351

DATE DUE

OC 12 '67			
DEC 2 1 1972			
GAYLORD			PRINTED IN U.S.A.